THE SHARED WITNESS OF
C. S. LEWIS AND AUSTIN FARRER

THE
SHARED WITNESS
OF
C. S. LEWIS
AND
AUSTIN FARRER

· + ✦ + ·

Friendship, Influence, and
an Anglican Worldview

· + ✦ + ·

PHILIP IRVING MITCHELL

The Kent State University Press ▣ KENT, OHIO

Chapter 5 includes material from a previously published article wih *Mythlore*. "'Written by the
Finger of God': C. S. Lewis and Historical Judgment," *Mythlore* 38, no. 2 (2020): 5–23.

CONTENTS

List of Abbreviations   vii

Acknowledgments   ix

Introduction   xi

1 Modernity   1

2 Myth   30

3 Analogy   66

4 Virtue   94

5 History   130

6 Theodicy   170

7 Apocalypse   207

Coda   239

Notes   251

Works Cited   264

Index   280

ABBREVIATIONS

AUSTIN FARRER

BM	*The Brink of Mystery*
CF	*A Celebration of Faith*
CY	*The Crown of the Year*
EM	*The End of Man*
FI	*Finite and Infinite*
FO	*A Faith of Our Own*
FOW	*The Freedom of the Will*
FS	*Faith and Speculation*
GND	*God Is Not Dead*
GV	*The Glass of Vision*
IB	*Interpretation and Belief*
LA	*Love Almighty and Ills Unlimited*
LIB	*Lord I Believe,* 2nd ed.
Light	"The Christian Apologist"
RF	*Reflective Faith*
RI	*A Rebirth of Images*
RJD	*The Revelation of St John the Divine*
SB	*Saving Belief*
SMSM	*St Mathew and St Mark,* 2nd ed.
SSM	*A Study in St Mark*
TV	*The Triple Victory*
WL	*Words of Life*

C. S. LEWIS

AL	*The Allegory of Love*
AM	*The Abolition of Man*
CR	*Christian Reflections*
DI	*The Discarded Image*
EC	*An Experiment in Criticism*
ELSC	*English Literature in the Sixteenth Century, Excluding Drama*
4L	*The Four Loves*
GD	*God in the Dock*
GO	*A Grief Observed*
HB	*The Horse and His Boy*
LB	*The Last Battle*
Letters	*Collected Letters*, 3 vols.
LM	*Letters to Malcolm (Chiefly on Prayer)*
LWWR	*The Lion, the Witch, and the Wardrobe*
MN	*The Magician's Nephew*
MX	*Mere Christianity*
OS	*On Stories and Other Essays on Literature*
OSP	*Out of the Silent Planet*
PC	*Prince Caspian*
PP	*The Problem of Pain*
PPL	*Preface to Paradise Lost*
PR	*The Pilgrim's Regress*
RP	*Reflections on the Psalms*
SBJ	*Surprised by Joy*
SC	*The Silver Chair*
SIW	*Studies in Words*, 2nd ed.
SL	*The Screwtape Letters*
SLE	*Selected Literary Essays*
SMRL	*Studies in Medieval and Renaissance Literature*
THS	*That Hideous Strength*
TWHF	*Till We Have Faces*
VDT	*The Voyage of the Dawn Treader*
WG	*The Weight of Glory*
WLN	*The World's Last Night, and Other Essays*

ACKNOWLEDGMENTS

Early versions of this book were presented in the Friday Symposium at Dallas Baptist University. I am grateful to audience interest, patience, and pointed questions, especially those from Karen Alexander and Michael E. Williams. I am also grateful to Robert McSwain and Curtis Gruenler for their reading of the manuscript and many helpful suggestions for improving it, as well as to Anna Shearn, Anna-Marie Wells, and Jenderia Santos, all who played a role in proofing and preparing the chapters.

My family has continued to offer me encouragement and love through every step of the process. I'm deeply blessed to have Noelle and Grace as my daughters, but above all Kristin, my companion and friend for over twenty-five years. Words pale before how much I owe her.

INTRODUCTION

In 1965, Reverend Austin Farrer wrote in "The Christian Apologist" that C. S. Lewis "was a bonny fighter," and insisted that, as far as intellectual debate went, the late scholar and popular writer had the virtue of being both theologically orthodox and imaginatively engaging. "You cannot read Lewis and tell yourself that Christianity has no important moral bearings, that it gives no coherence to the whole picture of existence," that it has no ethical or aesthetic or metaphysical implications (*Light*, 25–27). A few years earlier, Lewis, in his own preface to the American edition of Farrer's sermon collection, *Said or Sung*, had observed of his friend's work that "because he writes with authority, he has no need to shout." Perhaps this was a nod to Farrer's quiet, quirky, and intense personality. Lewis noted that Farrer's sermons were clear and precise and ones that any reader could approach easily. The irony was that they were by "not only one of the most learned theologians alive but by the theologian whose critics most often accuse him of excessive subtlety" (*FO*, 8, 9–10). Farrer's humility, Lewis wrote, was priestly in that, being self-effacing, he exalted Christ and drew others to God, "but this is one of heaven's jokes—nothing makes a man so noticeable as vanishing" (*FO*, 10).

Lewis and Farrer spent their adult lives voicing, publishing, and debating ideas, and each carried out his various intellectual roles—the one as apologist, literary historian, and popular novelist; the other as philosophical theologian, exegete, and priest—within contexts that were contested. Lewis (1898–1963) needs little introduction. He is best known for his children's series, *The Chronicles of Narnia*, and by many for his work as a Christian apologist, which included not only nonfiction books like *Mere Christianity* or *The Abolition of Man*, but also fictional ones, such as *The Screwtape Letters*. In turn, Lewis's friend, priest, and sometimes confessor is far less known, yet he, too, is of no mean reputation. Farrer (1904–68), often called the greatest mind of twentieth-century Anglicanism, published works of philosophical theology, scriptural interpretation, and spiritual formation, as well as wrote and delivered numerous sermons, these judged (not by Lewis alone) as works of wit, clarity, and authority. Theologian J. I. Packer, for example, described Farrer as "an independent, lucid, agile, argumentative and articulate mind, fastidiously whimsical, witty in the manner of a metaphysical poet, Newmanesque in sensitivity, incantatory in expression, and committed to a rational creedal orthodoxy" (1988, 253).

Despite their differences in calling and personality, Farrer and Lewis shared a number of things in common. Both were converts—Farrer from Baptist to Anglican; Lewis from atheist to theist to Anglican, and both stood against theological modernism. Farrer was decidedly more Anglo-Catholic than Lewis, though Lewis's devotional practice was open to sacramentalism and purgatory. Educated respectively at University College, Oxford, and at the prestigious Balliol College, Oxford, Lewis and Farrer were trained under tutors who had been shaped by Philosophical Idealism;[1] and in such environments, both encountered the argument that myth became history in Christ.

Both men taught at Oxford for much of their careers. Farrer, after four years at modest St. Edmund's Hall, served as tutor and chaplain at Trinity College for fifteen years, while Lewis was a fellow of Magdalen College for almost twenty, and each participated regularly in the intellectual discussion groups that marked university life. The Inklings now form an important aspect of Lewis's mythos. Farrer, likewise, participated in the theological discussion group called the Metaphysicals, which included such luminaries as Eric Mascall, Basil Mitchell, Iris Murdoch, and Helen Oppenheimer. But Lewis and Farrer were not limited to these. Lewis's Oxford Socratic Club became a shared venture for the two, and many thought Farrer might assume its leadership after Lewis (Ward 2014).

Lewis and Farrer were both known as demanding tutors who, nevertheless, bolstered the courage of many a student. Lewis was remembered for "his magnanimity, his generous acceptance of variety and difference" (Brewer 2005, 125), while one student recalled Farrer as having a "keen and penetrating mind" and an approach to others "informed by holy wisdom" (Curtis 1985, 84). Each man, too, after suffering disappointment, in his last decade made an academic transition—Farrer, after being passed over for the Regius Professorship of Divinity, became warden of Keble College, while Lewis, unable to obtain a professorship at Oxford, accepted an appointment as chair of Medieval and Renaissance literature at Magdalene College, Cambridge. As public writers and apologists, each achieved a measure of popular success in Britain and later in the United States. Each man also had family members who suffered from alcoholism (Lewis's brother, Warnie, and Farrer's wife, Katherine), and each experienced the death of loved ones and the emotional struggle that accompanies it.

Surprisingly, not much has been written of their shared witness. Partly this is because the paper trail is a thin one. There are few letters, for instance. When Lewis and Farrer spoke of each other in print, it was either to praise each other, or in the case of their work in theodicy, Farrer chose to politely critique Lewis. But they certainly read each other. For example, in 1957, Farrer drew the attention of the congregation gathered at Westminster Abbey to Lewis's recent autobiography *Surprised by Joy* and offered it as an example of an atheist coming to faith (*EM*, 30), while Lewis read Farrer's Bampton Lectures, *The Glass of Vision,* and recommended them highly (*Letters*, 2.961). This was also the case with at least one manuscript, possibly more. Farrer critiqued drafts of Lewis's *Reflections on the Psalms,* and Lewis, in turn, dedicated the volume to Austin and his wife (Sayer 1994, 390–91).[2]

While their mutual influence goes back to the 1940s, biographers, in speaking of their friendship, have tended to focus on the role Farrer played in Lewis's later years. The Farrers were close to Lewis and to Joy Davidman, once she entered Lewis's life, and some think it was Joy's friendship in particular with the Farrers that strengthened Lewis and Austin's (Wolfe 2020, 72). The priest was a witness at the civil marriage of Lewis and Joy, administrated Absolution to her on her deathbed, presided at her funeral, attended on Lewis in his dying days, read the lesson at Lewis's own funeral, and delivered his memorial address at Oxford (see Jacobs 2005, 290; W. Griffin 1986, 439–49).[3] This personal component was certainly important; still, their common commitment to their faith also formed an essential element in their involvement with one another. This is not surprising, given that the two shared attitudes, not only toward the Bible and the church, but also toward the role of the imagination in theological understanding and liturgical formation. They also shared similar assumptions about myth, about theological analogy, and about hermeneutics. Of course, they had some important intellectual differences. Along with their measured disagreement regarding the problem of evil, they also had practical differences in the manner in which they approached questions of history and ethics, though even here they held much in common.[4]

In the second of Farrer's Bampton Lectures, "The Supernatural and the Weird," he used the term "luminous apex" to describe how in the hierarchy of human understanding the mind transcends its "shadowy" components, in particular how rational consciousness draws from the preternatural even as it is also open to the supernatural (*GV*, 29, 32). Throughout this book, I will be contending that a sense of an illuminating hierarchy is essential to understanding both Lewis and Farrer. They each assumed and insisted upon a world informed by the transcendent and the teleological. Admittedly, some twenty-first-century readers may question why reading either is a worthwhile endeavor. As Wesley Kort has acknowledged, Lewis was not addressing contemporary concerns with gender, sexuality, or even race, and to read him well asks of such readers a measure of goodwill (2016, 16–17, 98). The same can be said of Farrer. Both were men of their times with its particular limitations and insights. At the same time, a dehistoricized reading of either writer has its dangers. It is important to remember that their common witness is one they shared not only with each other, but also with conservative Anglican Christianity, and with Christian theism in general. My goal is to give readers a larger sense of Lewis and Farrer's intellectual worlds in hopes that their continued applicability may be understood without unintentionally distorting what they actually said and why. For Farrer, this requires a farther-ranging study than has yet been offered of him. To my knowledge, no work involving Farrer has yet sought to study in-depth his views on the meaning of history or to bring his concerns with ethics and myth into conversation with his writings on religious analogy or apocalypse. While much more has been written on Lewis, I would contend this approach likewise offers new insights into what motivated him. In particular, Lewis's views of history and apocalypse deserve further study. By placing him in juxtaposition with Farrer, we are able to see Lewis as a conservative Anglican of his time and place. They were each writing as moderns who were self-consciously aware of their opposition to desacralizing cultural trends. This, then, requires a study about more than just Lewis and Farrer. It also examines their other interlocutors, Christian and otherwise.

THE METHOD OF INTELLECTUAL HISTORY AND FORECASTING THE BOOK

As will become clear, a history of Austin Farrer and C. S. Lewis as moderns and countermoderns assumes that conceptual history is conflicted; that the personal and the social are often at odds; and that a biographical and/or personal context can shade an ideational picture. Such a history also assumes that a narrative of tradition is necessary to understand their ecclesial responses and contexts; and that the larger cultural debates, while they need not always have traceable personal connections to Lewis and Farrer, help unpack the questions they were facing. I judge this as important because often we cannot understand well why Lewis and Farrer reached similar conclusions without seeing how they learned from and argued with other thinkers. This, in short, requires a history of ideas.

The twentieth-century debate over what was once called "the history of ideas" and is now often referred to as "intellectual history," has brought with it three chief insights. First, *ideas or concepts cannot be isolated entirely from their cultural contexts.* A belief about the meaning of freedom or evil takes on particular meanings in different times and places. R. G. Collingwood, for instance, pointed out that just polity differs whether one has a small ancient Greek polis in view or an early modern nation state (2013, 60–65). The same can be said about the manner in which Lewis and Farrer engaged the meaning of history and apocalypse. Second, *ideas and concepts rarely ever achieve complete consensus among their users.* Sometimes they have highly contested meanings, such as John Locke versus Jean-Jacques Rousseau on freedom. Other times, they are simply multifaceted, even approaching fluidity. In this way, they are open for prescriptive definition, expansion, and contraction. We understand Lewis and Farrer's views about analogy or virtue ethics if we can keep before us their intellectual teachers and opponents. What Farrer gained from theologian Erich Przywara or how Lewis refined his views alongside Christopher Dawson tells us in part how they came to terms with their world in general. Third, *some ideas or concepts deeply matter to their cultures and communities.* This naturally follows from the first two points, but it bears further emphasis. Even ideas, such as the meaning of theological analogy, which may not seem to us as debatable, could be sources of intense disagreement in the past and thus carry significant weight as to what people believed and how they behaved.

Throughout *The Shared Witness of C. S. Lewis and Austin Farrer* I will focus on a different topic in each chapter. I will explore the related thought of Lewis and Farrer, tracing their often parallel concerns and solutions in an intertextual fashion. At times, this will call for a close study of how Farrer and Lewis were interacting with one another's thought, such as regarding myth and theodicy, and as often, how they were responding with similar concerns to related cultural matters, such as that of analogical language about God or the meaning of the apocalypse. At other times, this will call for a parallel study in areas such as that of virtue ethics and historical practices, where they had differing focuses yet shared concerns. In these latter cases, what they had to say to their fellow academics, be they Christian or otherwise, is as important as their shared positions. While, with the exception of the Coda, the chapters can be read separately and in any order, there is a logic to their organization. The chapter on myth raises questions about the meaning of religious imagery and language, which the one on analogy answers by exploring the likeness and unlikeness in all analogy; the chapter on analogy sets up better the tension between the natural and supernatural, which matters of ethics and of history live within. In these, Lewis and Farrer sought to relate sacred revelation with natural law and sacred purpose in time with the temporal practice of historical judgment, and such topics in turn raise questions more thoroughly explored in the chapters on theodicy and apocalypse. One cannot examine the shape of human action and history without asking questions about evil and teleology. The closing coda, however, does depend upon some knowledge of the chapters since it examines the potential reception of Lewis and Farrer within the academic study of a pluralistic postsecularism.

Chapter 1, "Modernity," begins by examining the roles they played in each other's personal and academic lives. Because of World War II, but also because of their early adult conversions and late life academic appointments, Lewis and Farrer's lives have similar shapes. Each was to become an influential author, though Lewis's notoriety was far greater. What they shared was a strong commitment to the Christian faith and argued for its rational and imaginative power, and they shared this commitment during a period when the Anglican faith was embattled, even waning. Both men addressed what role Christianity had played or should play in England and Europe, and each examined what faith meant in university life, and all of this during a period that many judged as one of cultural, even civilizational crisis. Though this was a period of increased ecumenical cooperation, both men had not only to position themselves against wider secular opponents, but also within their particular Christian confessions. While Lewis was inclined to appeal to "mere Christianity" and Farrer was a committed Anglo-Catholic, each distanced himself at times from the Roman Catholic and evangelical influences of the day. Likewise, Lewis and Farrer critiqued theological modernism as often as modernism in general.

Chapter 2, "Myth," explores how both men addressed myth and its relationship to religion. To do this, Farrer and Lewis navigated a variety of theories about the origin, meaning, and social role of myth, and these debates had embedded in them assumptions about modernity in general. Both men argued that myths pointed to the numinous, and, while each was willing to concede ground to psychoanalytic, anthropological, and existential theories of myth, each also sought a higher meaning and purpose for it. Myth clearly explored issues of social anthropology, ritual, science, and the ethical, yet for

Lewis the key concerns were aesthetic and theological—specifically, that of the mythopoeic. Farrer addressed the question, too, though in order to defend the rationality of the biblical canon. Both men defended human imagination. This latter concern was particularly true in how both Farrer and Lewis sought to understand the Christian scriptures, especially in opposition to the demythologization of Rudolf Bultmann.

How myth can do justice to noumenal experience and its place in Christian revelation points to the nature of religious language itself. Chapter 3, "Analogy," examines how Farrer and Lewis engaged a philosophical and theological debate about language used about God. The *analogia entis,* the analogy of being, raised questions about what (if anything) natural philosophical language could say about the divine. Their position required them to account for both dialectical theology and Neo-Scholastic views of language. Analogy has to do with the intelligibility of communication and truth, especially in a world calling it into question. Both men were defending the rationality of the transcendent and embraced analogy because it recognized the infinite difference of God and yet spoke of divine being in a manner recognizable to human desire and ethics. In turn, Lewis and Farrer recognized that the metaphoric nature of language pointed to the limits of human understanding and to the call to prayer inspired by this.

Virtue has to do with the practice and possibilities of ethical habits, behavior, and its rationality, for free will is real and human flourishing happens in a particular environment. Chapter 4, "Virtue," traces in parallel fashion how Farrer and Lewis defended natural law. Both men argued for virtue ethics as the best way to understand human action and the desire for the good, and each looked to tradition and moral education as keys to cultivating virtue in human beings. Both defended their position against various Kantian, utilitarian, and behaviorist theories of ethics. Farrer focused more upon a defense of free will and rational judgment, while Lewis was more concerned with the shared natural law (or Tao) and how it was cultivated in each generation. Each writer was convinced that free will and salvation said something about an actual judgment—that is, a real heavenly telos, for, even given its pictorial and analogical language, the orientation and end of the ethical is real. And thus, Lewis, but also Farrer, looked to the formative power of narrative and put hope in the Christian understanding of the eternal, divinized, or exalted state.

Both Farrer and Lewis, as I show in chapter 5, "History," were concerned with the scope and veracity of history, yet they primarily addressed the issue in separate fields—Farrer that of biblical history and Lewis that of literary history. This also meant they engaged different writers on these matters. Lewis explored history in regard to larger questions of human culture and heritage, seeking to build readers' sympathy with historical characterization, analogy, and the use of historical periods. For Farrer, the nature of history was first and foremost a concern with the interpretation of the Gospels. He insisted that the ancient audience would not have separated theology and history, so the search for an "historical Jesus" behind the texts was a vain one. Both men were opposed to a metahistory that would reduce human freedom to determinist, axiomatic predictions, and both also placed a high premium upon the personal, humanistic reading of the past.

Such a reading of history, however, did not deny the immense suffering that humanity has experienced, both from natural causes and from human actions. Chapter 6, "Theodicy," examines how Lewis and Farrer each addressed the problem of evil, and Farrer quite likely with Lewis's own work in mind. While they shared a number of basic Christian assumptions about salvation and the afterlife, they also disagreed upon the meaning of Adam and Eve, Satan, and the purpose of animal pain. Both men had to struggle with how to account for evolutionary history, and how to integrate human beginnings with the presence of evil. Each man also considered the actual experience of evil and suffering at an existential level, and they shared an expectation of *theosis,* the final framework against which human suffering could take on redemptive value. This common expectation, I will argue, outweighed their often significant differences, for it held that the problem of evil was one framed by Christian hope, and, indeed, answered fully by that hope.

In chapter 7, "Apocalypse," I trace how Lewis and Farrer were drawn to the apocalyptic as a way of taking seriously an eternal, vertical world that the modern secular world suppressed for a horizontal and temporal one. Apocalypse connects to both theodicy and history in that the eschatological is an answer to the meaning of history, as the apocalyptic is also an answer to evil. While Lewis's apocalyptic works were primarily fiction and Farrer's were commentaries, both also wrote essays and sermons that explored the matter. Each stressed that the apocalyptic should be taken seriously as a judgment upon the moral failings of persons and civilizations, and each writer employed yet mitigated the violence inherent in the genre. Both stressed moral consequences, noted or employed the use of parody, and recognized that the apocalyptic was a call to attentive repentance. Lewis and Farrer grounded all this in a Christian hope, which was *already-and-not yet* in its expectations, and that this knowledge is received in liturgical settings also shaped Lewis's notion of sacramental transposition, as well as Farrer's theology. Each saw in this hope a sense of the endless offer of an ever-improving eternal existence.

Finally, in the coda, I explore how Lewis and Farrer's positions on these matters might be received in our twenty-first-century pluralist context, specifically in a postsecular academy. There I argue that the immanent approaches of postsecular theorists can be brought into a hospitable and fruitful conversation with Farrer and Lewis. My hope is to conclude with showing that both writers are still relevant today because they take seriously the transcendent and teleological as real, objective realities and yet ones that speak into our personal, corporate experiences.

MODERNITY

We no longer force you into a common pattern of churchmanship by religious test or by compulsory worship. We leave it to you to see that no one in the College is left out, or made to feel inferior.... We leave it to you to make such a use of the Chapel, that the ideal of a common churchmanship on the part of all churchmen receives genuine and visible expression.

—Austin Farrer, "Keble and His College" in *The End of Man*

A minimal religion compounded of spirit messages and bare Theism has no power to touch any of the deepest chords in our nature, or to evoke any response which will raise us even to a higher secular level—let alone to the spiritual life. The god of whom no dogmas are believed is a mere shadow. He will not produce that fear of the Lord in which wisdom begins, and, therefore, will not produce that love in which it is consummated.

—C. S. Lewis, "Religion without Dogma?" in *God in the Dock*

In 1941, C. S. Lewis began his great war sermon "The Weight of Glory" with a meditation upon an historical shift in ideas. He observed that, if asked to identify the most important virtue, his contemporaries would answer "Unselfishness," while for centuries Christians would have replied that it was "Love" (*WG*, 25). Lewis noted that this shift was more than a difference in terms. The modern assumption in unselfishness, he suggested, is that self-denial has its own intrinsic value, while Christian caritas saw as its final reward "infinite joy." This difference was not only a matter of intrinsic and extrinsic motivation, it was also a question of cosmology. Modern people have no need for the heavenly since the next life seems to preclude the goodness of this world. But Lewis insisted this was a failure of imagination: What is being offered by

Gay has characterized this rejection of the Christian past as the "lure of heresy" along with "a commitment to a prolonged self-scrutiny" (2008, 3–5), and yet, this struggle of the new with the old was hardly unilateral or unidirectional but was a series of shifting loyalties and truces (P. Gay 2008, 15). The rejection of tradition, of the authoring father(s), played an important role in the rise of the individual self. Something similar could be said of the high modernist search for a mythic order or controlling symbol.[1] Arguably, the ideological rejections of modernity were sustained by the nascent rejection of the transcendent that was (and continues to be) embodied in the political, social, and economic structures of the contemporary world (C. M. Gay 1998, 13–16). Craig M. Gay has noted how the secularity of modern institutions have built into them "a tacit repudiation of divine authority" (1998, 238), and Rémi Brague also observes that a humanism came of age in the nineteenth and twentieth centuries and came to reject any recognition of God, both on the grounds of God as a divine oppressor and as a failed master (2018, 128–30). Taken together, a once widespread assumption of theistic religion had to give way as new definitions of a desacralized world took on greater credibility.

At the same time, this rejection could take on diverse forms and intensities, and often while accompanied by religious influence, even periodic religious renewal. Resistance to modernity, such as that of Lewis and Farrer's, was often found in defending a version of the older world, though one that sought to speak a mediating language to the flatter, secularized world. The older sacred world that they each invoked is imaginatively thicker and speaks of movement between the natural and supernatural, so that in invoking it, both men were reintroducing not only that which is above, but also that which is beyond. The shape of the *luminous apex* that both men desired (as did millions of other believers) was one looking to the absolute realm beyond the temporal world and to the promise of perfection that lay beyond history. As I will argue throughout this work, it was precisely the intertwining dance of natural and supernatural that made their response to secularizing modernity possible rather than, as Berger once charged, a division that made secularization inevitable.

Modernity was not only a period of rupture and change, it was also one in which vestigial, and often very active, elements remained into the present, even as these were accompanied by conflicting elements and creative adaptations. Both men were very much a part of the modern world, and their work is unimaginable without that conflict. To understand Lewis and Farrer's resistance better, they must be seen as part of debates that have their basis in the history of ideas, for the modern self and society were deeply sedimented and built upon centuries of historical change and conflict. The mechanistic world picture of the Enlightenment, the organic picture of Romanticism, and the shifting anthropology of Evolutionary Naturalism all continued into the present and could be adopted by the same person at differing times, or even at the same time. As Alasdair MacIntyre has pointed out, one person could employ the vestiges of natural law, duty, and emotivism in piecemeal fashion, though the original context that made each rational was long gone (2007, 6–13). The same conflict can be seen in the developmentalism of Enlightenment Progress or Social Darwinism or the cultural relativism of Historicism. The three great powers of Marxism, Fascism, and Enlightenment Progress have their origins in Judaism and Christianity, but not as religion's inevitable replacement. The Edenic impulses of these large world-pictures have theistic echoes, and each takes its eschatological and utopian aspirations from its transcendent predecessors and with great loss flattens them into historical, material, and biological factors, even as older religious counterparts still had energy to offer a compelling countermodernity.

To understand the roles that Farrer and Lewis played in such a world of rupture and renewal, this chapter will first conduct a brief overview of their parallel lives as shaped by the academy, by the church, by the public, and by world war with all its accompanying questions. Then I will explore a period that involved (1) the waning of Christian influence in Britain but also a period of renewal in certain quarters; (2) an academic world in which Christianity continued to play an institutional role, though a diminished one, and in which various Christian groups sought to renew its influence; (3) an Anglicanism that was itself divided among varying responses to modernity, even as it positioned itself alongside Roman Catholicism and various evangelical associations; and (4) varying apologetic contexts across a diversity of counter-Christian visions and post-Christian projects. Each of these shaped the ideological and creative debate that helped generate both Farrer and Lewis's work.

MODERN LIVES

While it may seem artificial, Austin Farrer and C. S. Lewis's lives can be justifiably divided into four periods. In part, this is because of the widespread disruption caused by World War II, as well as the late career move of each man. Likewise, in the period between the two world wars, each man experienced his religious conversion. Yet Lewis and Farrer's career divisions are also such because the key emphases in their intellectual work fall out in this manner. Both men had their formative years in the period between the wars, a period though he hardly retreated as a Christian in the public eye. After all, in 1952, Lewis's broadcast talks were combined in a single volume, *Mere Christianity,* perhaps his most influential apologetic work, and he continued to engage in published debate on issues of ethical and religious importance. Nevertheless, his fiction increasingly took pride of place. Lewis published his seven Narnia books and what some consider his greatest novel, *Till We Have Faces* (1956), as well as his autobiography of his childhood and youth, *Surprised by Joy* (1955). This was also the period when, after Janie Moore's death in 1951, Lewis's friendship with Joy Davidman grew and led initially to a civil marriage of convenience, as well as when he would move from Oxford to Cambridge. His collection *Transposition and Other Addresses* was released in 1949, and he finally brought to press his magnum opus of literary history, *English Literature in the Sixteenth Century, Excluding Drama* (1954), as part of the Oxford History of English Literature series.

If Lewis in these years underwent both literary, scholarly, and domestic transformations, Farrer entered an entirely new period of his career. In 1948 Farrer delivered to large audiences the prestigious Bampton Lectures, which were later published that same year as *The Glass of Vision.*[4] *The Glass of Vision,* Farrer's own magnum opus, represents the beginning of the period of his focus upon typological biblical interpretation, as well as a transition from the austere neo-Thomism of *Finite and Infinite.* During the years 1946 to 1956, he published three important, if, for many, puzzling works of biblical criticism: *A Rebirth of Images: The Making of St. John's Apocalypse* (1949), *A Study in St Mark* (1951), and *St Matthew and St Mark* (1954), as well as his own answer to the Synoptic problem, "On Dispensing with Q" (1955). He also published in 1952 a series of meditations called *The Crown of the Year;* that same year an important response to Rudolf Bultmann's *Kergyma and Myth;* a meditation on the creed, *Lord I Believe* (1955, 1958); and a compendium of the most important passages of scripture in 1956, entitled *A Short Bible* (*Core of the Bible* in the United States). This last work Lewis highly prized for its ability to speak clearly to general audiences (*Letters,* 3.754). Yet Farrer continued in this period to speak on philosophical topics at the Oxford Society, read papers to the Metaphysicals, and wrote the entry on "Analogy" for the *Twentieth-Century Encyclopedia of Religious Knowledge.* He also delivered BBC addresses for the school program in 1952 (a series of six addresses entitled "Religion and Philosophy") and in 1956 on the topic of Faith and Knowledge (Curtis 1985, 142).

The final period of Lewis's career, 1957 to 1964, would be marked by Joy's cancer, their ecclesial marriage, her remission, then eventual death in 1960, as well as his own failing health and death on November 22, 1963, the same day as the death of Aldous Huxley and the assassination of President John F. Kennedy. Significantly, the only fiction Lewis would publish in these years was the short piece, *Screwtape Proposes a Toast* (1961), for *Harper Magazine*. On the other hand, he would publish three works of devotional writing: *Reflections on the Psalms* (1958), *The Four Loves* (1960), and posthumously, *Letters to Malcolm, Chiefly on Prayer* (1964), as well as a pseudonymous reflection on Joy's death, *A Grief Observed* (1961). It was also a period devoted to a renewed attention to academic publication. He released two further collections of essays, *The World's Last Night* (1960) and *They Asked for a Paper* (1962), as well as three important academic books for Cambridge: the first edition of *Studies in Words* (1960), *Experiment in Criticism* (1961), and the also posthumous *The Discarded Image* (1964). A number of other essays and lectures were also composed and later published after his death.

Farrer would outlive Lewis by four years. The years 1957–67 saw the public return of Farrer's work as a philosophical theologian. His delivery of the 1957 Gifford Lectures, published in 1958 as *Freedom of the Will*, marked the beginning of his most productive period of publication. He contributed two important essays to Basil Mitchell's collection of philosophy of religion, *Faith and Logic* (1957). He was also appointed warden of Keble College in 1960. During this period, Farrer moved to a more voluntarist stress on God's agency and a clearer emphasis upon Christian belief as fundamental for philosophy. He lectured in the United States several times, notably delivering lectures at Yale University in 1961 and the 1964 Deems Lectures in New York. Along with *Freedom of the Will*, Farrer published four important volumes—his theodicy, *Love Almighty and Ills Unlimited* (1962)—a work that Lewis read and disagreed with in part (*Letters*, 3.1308)[5]; *Saving Belief* (1964), a brief systematic theology; *A Science of God?* (*God Is Not Dead* in the United States) (1964), a sequel of sorts to *Love Almighty*; and the published version of the Deems Lectures, *Faith and Speculation* (1967). In addition to the sermons in *Said or Sung* (*A Faith of Our Own* in the United States) (1960), he released a revised commentary, *The Revelation of St. John the Divine* (1964), and a Lenten book on the temptation of Jesus, *The Triple Victory* (1965). On August 8, 1967, Farrer delivered a BBC talk on "Transcendence and 'Radical Theology'" and would the next year, in fading health, preach his last sermon, "The Ultimate Hope" on December 22, 1968, then pass away on the twenty-ninth. A number of his sermons and essays would be published posthumously.

Thus, while each man had differing, even greatly differing roles, as academics and published authors, they shared a commitment to Christian truth and to defending that truth in an increasingly post-Christian world, and they prized one another for this mutual work. Lewis, in his blurb for Farrer's *Saving Belief,* wrote that Farrer's clear prose was pregnant with meaning: "Almost every answer says more than we realize at first glance," and, rather than thin and trendy theology, Farrer's orthodox insights "open new horizons to us on every other page." Even if one admits this statement to be promotional material, it nonetheless says much about how Lewis understood Farrer's published work. He valued Farrer as a priest under authority, as one who refused to go beyond the received truth into futile speculation, and yet recognized that his theological work was hardly simple. Lewis said as much, too, of his sermons: "They lead us through a structure of thoughts so delicately balanced that a false word, even a false tone, might land us in disaster" (*FO,* 9), and Lewis prized in Farrer's writing the ability to seemingly effortlessly instruct audiences, and said as much in a private correspondence. *Love Almighty,* he told Farrer, "is full of felicities that sound as unsought as wildflowers" (*Letters,* 3.1308). Of course, these were ideals to which Lewis himself aspired.

If Lewis saw in Farrer an ideal, Farrer, in turn, extolled in Lewis what the theologian himself most valued. Farrer praised Lewis for presenting ethical concerns with "sharp lucidity" and for connecting them to "the divine will," two areas that Farrer wrote on extensively. He prized Lewis for "feeling intellect," his ability to hold in balance the rational and the propositional with the imaginative and aesthetic: "But his real power was not proof, it was depiction" (*BM,* 46). And Farrer saw in Lewis a writer who valued his audience, sought to meet them halfway, whether in print or in correspondence, and who openly and without apology displayed his own literary debt to other thinkers, living and dead (*BM,* 47).

Each man understood that there were distinct differences between their methods and concerns. Lewis's summative analysis of Farrer as a priestly writer says as much. Farrer made a distinction between the theologian, whose task is to articulate clearly and precisely the dogma of the faith, and the true apologist, who is responding to attacks on the faith in the moment, as it were. Farrer saw Lewis as doing the latter, and while rational argument does not engender faith, it does preserve it against assault: "What seems to be proved may not be embraced; but what no one shows the ability to defend is quickly abandoned" (*Light,* 23–24, 26). Yet this, too, sounds like something of a rationale for not only Lewis's canon, but also Farrer's own philosophical theology. Taken together, both writers understood that a Christian apologetic required of them philosophical exactitude, rhetorical persuasiveness, and seductive imagery. And they undertook these responsibilities in a period in England in which the Christian faith was on most fronts embattled and failing.[6]

A REVIVAL OF RELIGION?

Between 1920 and 1960, England on many fronts ceased to be even superficially Christian, and this in spite of its Christian monarch and its official support for Anglicanism. This was much remarked upon, and more than one study was done to try and address its causes. While it is true that during the late 1940s and early 1950s, there was a rally in general Sunday School enrollment, Anglican baptism, and an overall increase in Protestant church membership, the height of Christian affiliations had been much earlier, in 1905, and with the exception of Roman Catholicism, general attendance in all denominations had been trending down until 1939, and would do so again in the late 1950s, 1960s, and afterwards. Anglican Easter Day communicants, for example, from 1920 to 1960 fell from 3,537,020 to 2,861,887, while membership in other Protestant groups fell as significantly (S. J. D. Green 2011, 31–32, 60–62, 70). Even after 1962, Catholic gains would begin to reverse themselves, in part through increasing mixed marriages (Hastings 1987, 561–63).

The general numeric decline is certainly not the whole story. Cultural influence continued to manifest itself. Senior clergy in general were taken seriously by public leaders (Grimley 2004, 10). The 1920s had seen the impact of F. D. Maurice's Christian Socialism and of ecumenical movements, such as the Birmingham Conference on Politics, Economics, and Citizenship (1924) and the Universal Christian Conference of Life and Work, Stockholm (1925) (Neill 1977, 253). Likewise, in the 1920s, Evelyn Underhill was highly regarded and introduced many to Christian mysticism. In the 1930s, there was a revival of Anglican intellectual authority, inspired in some quarters by the leadership of William Temple, and in others by high-brow converts, such as T. S. Eliot (Hastings 1987, 254–56), and this would continue into the 1950s with Lewis's own popularity, as well as that of fellow Anglican, Dorothy Sayers.

And this was equally true of some English Non-Conformists. After World War II, historian Herbert Butterfield, a Methodist, enjoyed great success with his lectures on Christianity and history. His six BBC radio lectures made him a celebrity, becoming some of the most listened to broadcasts in BBC history (McIntire 2004, 176–77).[7] English Catholicism also experienced a cultural renaissance. Evelyn Waugh and Graham Greene would define twentieth-century English fiction as much as would C. P. Snow or Anthony Powell. Historian Christopher Dawson would become an influential outsider and deliver the Gifford Lectures in 1947 and 1948, and the translation of French Catholic thinkers, such as Jacques Maritain, Gabriel Marcel, and Étienne Gilson, and of French novelists Georges Bernanos and François Mauriac, assured that they would also that sometimes the most taxing challenge to one's faith came after one had bested a rival in debate, not when suffering defeat: "No doctrine is, for the moment, dimmer to the eye of faith than that which a man has just successfully defended." Yet even given this, a debate "has a life of its own," and "no man can tell where it will go" (*GD*, 128).[9]

To follow the argument to its end is a basic academic commitment, but also a basic Christian one. The origins of the medieval university were that of Catholic Christianity and built upon a combative pedagogy. One can also make the case that the twentieth-century university continued to be a place socially structured to make knowledge most valuable when it is most debated. Yet this tension also had professional ramifications. The likely reason that Lewis was passed over for a full professorship at Oxford, despite his academic standing, was because many resented his popular apologetics. When Lewis began his professorship at Magdalene, Cambridge, it was with wry awareness that he offered himself as the Christian who might give to his students the rare insights of one who actually still believed much of what their Medieval and Renaissance authors confessed: "Where I fail as a critic, I may yet be useful as a specimen" (*SLE*, 9, 12, 14).

An Anglican official in a mostly secular setting, Farrer's experience at Keble College was similar. Keble's historic relationship to the Oxford Movement had meant that ties to the Church of England were slow to dissolve. Only in 1930 did undergraduates at Keble no longer have to be Anglican; only by 1952, with the full incorporation of the college into the life of Oxford, were fellows no longer required, but even then the obligation for the warden to be Anglican clergy was not dropped until 1969 after Farrer's death. Farrer found himself the official spokesperson for orthodoxy among a mostly non-Christian faculty and student body (Curtis 1985, 150–54; Horan 2000, 230; Archer 2020, 32–33). Yet under Farrer, chapel attendance increased, and this despite Keble finally discontinuing compulsory expectations (V. H. H. Green 1964, 366). Against this background, Farrer's late sermon, "Keble and His College," takes on apologetic resonances. Farrer held up the Tractarian theologian for whom the college was named as being motivated by "a truth-seeking mind," as one who "looked at conscience within, at the situation without, at history and scripture lying behind, with selfless candour, and opened his mind to the teaching of God: for he loved him" (*EM*, 156). This amounted to a defense not only of Keble, both the individual and the college named after him, but also of the continued compatibility of Christianity and the intellectual life.

Nevertheless, the tension between Christians and their non-Christian counterparts is not the entire story either. The ideological pressure between

Christianity and various modern oppositions was bound to also manifest itself within the faith, and this tension was apparent in the Church of England. Its own divisions were a sign of the ideological strain that has characterized modernity. This tension, too, was part of Lewis and Farrer's embattled contexts.

EMBATTLED ANGLICANISM

It is a common story to tell of a Church of England divided into three camps: the broad, liberal center; the high and dry Anglo-Catholic ritualists; and the hot gospeler Evangelicals. Each could claim a long history, and these have not always fitted their stereotypes. While the Anglo-Evangelicals had their origins in the Awakening under John and Charles Wesley and expanded their social influence with the Clapham Sect of William Wilberforce and Hannah More, the Anglo-Catholic party had nineteenth-century origins in the Tractarianism of Edward Pusey, John Keble, and John Henry Newman. The broad center, in turn, could trace its origins to the seventeenth century of Cambridge Platonism and Sir Thomas Browne. William Wolf has suggested that Anglican theology is based on "the group approach," in which parties of the like-minded gather together in movements that are both theological and political because they have institutional investments (1979, 138–39). Twentieth-century Anglicanism, rather than being reduced to just three movements, had at least five movements interacting with one another: to be sure, broad latitudinarianism, Evangelicalism, and Anglo-Catholicism, but also *Lux Mundi*–style Liberal Catholicism and Theological Modernism. And Anglicans were also interacting with Non-Conformists, Neo-Barthians, Neo-Scholastics, and the general ecumenical movement, all of which shaped their theology, worship, and social activism.

In practice, this meant that what a theological party made of Christ also shaped what they made of salvation and perhaps also of the Church. In 1959, Archbishop Michael Ramsey could reflect common wisdom and speak of the *Lux Mundi* writers as having been an important voice from 1889 until 1939, or perhaps until the death of Temple in 1944. Their strong stress on Christ's Incarnation and upon all of humanity being subsumed into divinity also meant a parallel stress upon social ministry and political involvement, yet Ramsey could rightly charge them with a dangerous de-emphasis upon the Atonement, which seemed to fold the divine into all persons without need of any redemption (A. M. Ramsey 1960, vii–viii, 4–9). That the *Lux Mundi* school, which itself had seemed a threat to many traditionalists, could feel threatened in turn by the Modernists says much about the shifting debate in the twentieth

He, likewise, had a well-known distaste for most English hymns, which the early "low" service enabled him to avoid. Early after his conversion, he settled upon receiving communion once a month as a sort of compromise position, though George Sayer believes Lewis was partaking weekly by the 1950s (1994, 227). At the same time, Lewis was clearly a sacramentalist in his view of communion. He practiced confession, had some room for prayers for the dead, and would come to hold a non-Romanist position upon purgatory. And he was a committed churchman in other ways. The last four years of his life, Lewis served on the Committee to Revise the Psalter, alongside T. S. Eliot. Those who knew only Lewis and Eliot's literary reputations might have been surprised by their positions on modern language in biblical translation, but not those who also knew their religious persuasions. The Anglo-Catholic Eliot was far more likely to try and preserve older, aesthetically pleasing language, while Lewis tended to side with modernization of the text (Warner 2011, 55). Lewis's position on female priests, on the other hand, was far more conservative, and not only because he was concerned that a woman would confuse how a priest, "wearing the masculine uniform . . . provisionally, and till the *Parousia*," represents Christ in the liturgy (*GD*, 237–39). He was also concerned the shift would create additional barriers between Anglicanism and global Christianity.

We should not forget that neither Lewis nor Farrer was restricted in his work to academic audiences. Both spoke as educated persons to general audiences. Farrer's first parish was in working-class surroundings, and he never forgot the need to meet others at their point of need. His Lent book and his other devotional books, such as *Lord I Believe*, were written for more general, if pious, audiences. Both men spoke over BBC radio, and during World War II, Lewis gave numerous talks to RAF audiences. This latter task he undertook because he saw it not only as "War work," but also as evangelism (Sayer 1994, 281–83). Given Lewis's commitment to "mere Christianity," it is not surprising that evangelical and Catholic alike claimed him. For the broadcast talks that made up "What Christians Believe," he carefully chose not only an Anglican priest to check them before broadcast, but also a Roman Catholic, Dom Bede Griffiths; a Methodist preacher with the RAF, Joseph Dowell; and a Presbyterian, Eric Fenn, who was working for the BBC. Lewis's strong ecumenical position during World War II may have had about it something like the rallying of the pan-Christian troops against the quasi-religious Nazi threat (McGrath 2014, 148).[11] Yet more than one critic has pointed out, and Lewis knew himself, that even his definition of a Church and his metaphor of various rooms of a connecting hallway were hardly models that could reach

complete consensus among Christians. Lewis avoided one of the most controversial—the doctrine of Mary—which he omitted from *Mere Christianity*
because one side sees her with "chivalrous sensibility that a man feels when
the honour of his mother or his beloved is a stake," while the other side fears
"that Polytheism is risen again" (*MX*, 7). It is also interesting to note that
Lewis did something similar in his *Discarded Image*. As Peter Milward points
out, Mary is passed over there as well, which is fairly shocking considering
the central role she plays in medieval life and thought (1995, 61–63).

Lewis's relationship with both British and American Evangelicalism was
equally complex. Adrian Hastings suggests that the general flow of the Christian intellectual culture of the period was, on one side, from liberalism to the
neo-orthodoxy of Niebuhr, Brunner, and Barth and, on the other, from Protestantism toward Catholicism (1987, 289). This was likewise the case within
Anglicanism itself. Significantly, when the Commission on Christian Doctrine
appointed by the Archbishops of Canterbury and York issued its *Doctrine in
the Church of England* in 1938, Temple admitted that if they could do it over,
they would focus on a theology of redemption rather than incarnation, for
Barth's influence had brought the Krisis theology to center stage (Butler 2004,
44). Arguably, Anglican Evangelicalism's lack of philosophies of history and
of religion had rendered the movement vulnerable to the nineteenth century's shifts in science and higher criticism,[12] though Barth's thought revitalized
them in other ways (Nichols 1993, 105, 107–8).

The same could be said of Non-Conformist Christianity in general in England. The very successful evangelistic crusades of Billy Graham in 1954 and 1955
altered for a season the public face of Evangelicalism in Britain. Over two million attended Graham's 1954 crusade in London with over thirty-eight thousand recorded decisions. Similar numbers attended the Glasgow crusade with
over fifty-two thousand decisions. Unlike Farrer who, having been raised a
Baptist, had a more skeptical position as to Graham (Curtis 1985, 142), Lewis
was supportive of Graham, remembering him as "a very modest and a very sensible man" (*GD*, 265). Graham had asked Lewis about how best to approach
evangelism at Cambridge in 1955 (Marsden 2016, 101–2). Not surprisingly,
Lewis became linked by some with the evangelist, yet he was reluctant to be
associated too closely with his organization and turned down Graham's new
journal, *Christianity Today*, when asked to be a contributor (Marsden 2016,
105; Gehring 2017, 198).

Lewis had similar cautions about Roman Catholicism. J. R. R. Tolkien famously accused Lewis of having too much of the Ulster Protestant in him, and
Lewis could admit as much (*SBJ*, 31).[13] This distrust, which he had had as a

child, continued after his return to Anglicanism. When Dent & Sons Limited, his publisher for *The Pilgrim's Regress,* gave Catholic publisher Sheed and Ward rights to a second run, Lewis was troubled by it being released by a "Papist" press, though he amicably consented when Sheed and Ward asked to reissue the modern allegory in 1944. More than one reader had interpreted the figure of Mother Kirk in *The Pilgrim's Regress* as the Catholic Church, perhaps because there were other characters who represented aspects of Anglicanism— Mr. Broad (the Broad Church) and Mr. Neo-Angular (the Anglo-Catholic). Nevertheless, the real issues for Lewis were not ones of childhood prejudice as much as ones of adult conviction. Lewis simply was never convinced either of the authority of the papacy or of the acceptability of Marian devotion (Pearce 2003, xxii). He did confess the Real Presence within communion and received last rites from Farrer upon his deathbed, but he was finally distrustful that a developing doctrine within Catholicism left it open to great abuse. In a 1944 draft of an unpublished address, "Christian Reunion: An Anglican Speaks to Roman Catholics," Lewis outlined for himself the difference between Anglican and Roman Catholic:

> To you the real vice of Protestantism is the formless drift which seems unable to retain the Catholic truths, which loses them one by one and ends in a 'modernism' which cannot be classified as Christian by any tolerable stretch of the word. To us the terrible thing about Rome is the recklessness (as we hold) with which she had added to the *depositum fidei*—the tropical fertility, the proliferation, of *credenda*. You see in Protestantism the Faith dying out in a desert: we see in Rome the faith smothered in a jungle.
>
> I know no way of bridging this gulf. . . .
>
> I have, however, a strong premonition as to the way in which reunion will *not* come. It will not come at the edges. 'Liberal' Romans and 'high' Anglicans will not be the ones who meet first. For the odd thing is that the nearer you get to the heart of each communion, the less you notice its difference from the other. (Lewis 1990, 17–19)

This is a revealing passage for a number of reasons. Lewis was clearly aware that for many a Roman Catholic, Anglicanism seemed to finally end only in a vague, mushy Modernism. Meanwhile, for an Anglican such as himself (and Farrer, too), Catholicism seemed equally open to another kind of muddy compromise. But even here, Lewis's instinct was to a mere Christian core and not to the parties of Anglo-Catholicism or Modernist Catholicism. Late in life, he would write Jesuit Father Peter Milward, "We can do much more to heal the schism by our prayers than by controversy. It is a daily subject of mine" (*Letters*, 3.1426). He joked as well to Sister Penelope upon the invitation to lecture in the Catholic Gate House: "I accept gratefully, though the Protestant in me has just a little suspicion of an oubliette or a chained skeleton—the doors do open outwards as well, I trust" (*Letters*, 2.479).[14]

It was, then, Theological Modernism that Lewis and Farrer most strongly opposed. "It is no use trying to preserve the Church as John Betjeman and his friends aim to preserve a fragment of Victorian Oxford. We shall merely wake up to find ourselves a museum article; or rather, we shan't wake up; for museum articles don't. They are dead and stuffed and pickled in preservative" (*EM*, 103). Farrer wrote this in 1967 near the end of his life. Without a constant witness in word and sacrament, he insisted, there would be nothing even in form to hold on to. This form signifying nothing had late in Lewis and Farrer's life infamously found its voice with the new Cambridge theology. In some ways its modernist questioning was nothing novel. *Essays and Reviews* (1860), the notorious Victorian collection of Anglican essays that had legitimated higher critical readings of scripture, was over a hundred years old, and a line could be traced between these nineteenth-century modernist positions and that of Cambridge theology in the early 1960s. In 1962 a public debate had broken out over the Cambridge essay collection, *Soundings*, and over Alec Vidler's subsequent November 4 appearance on BBC television. Each seemed to throw the doors open to both the sexual revolution and to godless Christianity (Clements 1998, 155–67). Farrer would mock their positions the next year in a published poem:

> The phrases of the Common Prayer
> Are steps in hell's descending stair.
> The bars and brothels of Tangier
> Make the inward vision clear. (qtd. Clements 1998, 173)

Later that year, this critique was only more justified with the publication of Bishop John A. T. Robinson's *Honest to God* (1963), a work that was as influential in the 1960s as Lewis had been in the 1940s and 1950s (Hastings 1987, 536–38). Almost a million people bought a copy of the March 17, 1963, *Observer* to read Robinson's essay "Our Image of God Must Go," and the book sold thirty-five thousand copies and was translated into six languages within the first year of its release (Clements 1998, 179). It created perhaps the loudest, ugliest debate over English religion in the twentieth century; that it had the power to do so says much about residual power of the Christian past even in a post-Christian culture. A young Alasdair MacIntyre would famously quip of Robinson, "The creed of the English is that there is no God and that it is wise to pray to him from time to time" (Clements 1998, 205). This was perhaps not entirely fair, but still rather to the point. Robinson's book was simply a synthesis of the work of Paul Tillich and Rudolf Bultmann with some of the more gnomic statements of Dietrich Bonhoeffer in his *Letters from Prison,* yet it seemed to portend the end of traditional theism, of the divinity of Christ, and that of traditional morality. And it likely did, at least if carried out consistently, though Robinson was hardly ever consistent.

Lewis, in 1963 when Robinson's book was released, turned down the opportunity to write a one-thousand-word public rebuttal of the doubting bishop, though Lewis suggested that passages in *Letters to Malcolm* would answer him implicitly (*Letters,* 3.1422, 3.1424–25). Lewis was likely in too poor health to do more. Farrer, nevertheless, saw Lewis as Robinson's direct opposite, and said so in print: "It sounds well to say that the true prophet is a revolutionary, going further and faster than the forward movement of the age; but the dictum bears little relation to experience. The prophets have resisted the current of their times," and Lewis had been a prophet, calling his age back to orthodoxy and away from the Zeitgeist (*Light,* 30). Farrer acknowledged that Robinson's appeal was to those who desired no "iron curtain between the official Church and the contemporary mind," but such was a desire for a Christianity without "any strict coherence of ideas." Farrer insisted that Lewis offered instead "delight in a world of clarity" (*Light,* 29).

TWO SNAKES

From beginning to end, then, Austin Farrer and C. S. Lewis spent their careers defending a conservative version of Anglican faith. But more than that, they defended a comprehensive Christian imaginary in a world that countered it on numerous fronts. To do so was to take a wide field of ideas and their histories seriously. At one level, Farrer and Lewis were simply functioning as academics and educated Christians, and by appealing to the history of the ideas in question, they were suggesting that certain differences could be understood, perhaps even advanced, by a knowledge of the past. Yet, at another level, they were also trying to out-narrate their opponents, helping others to imagine a different and richer universe. The conditions of modernity made these historical differences only too apparent. Lewis argued that all models of the universe are replaced because each age is driven by certain concerns, and its models flow out of those perceived needs. A culture has a particular "taste in universes," and will focus on phenomena that support that epistemic, aesthetic desire (*DI*, 216–23). At the same time, the revelation of God in Christ is given through an incarnate Church transcending history.

Lewis wrote in "Dogma and the Universe" that he was sure that it was "not Christianity which need fear the giant universe," but the creative evolutionist, such as Henri Bergson or G. B. Shaw (*GD*, 44). Christian tradition can adapt because it remains anchored to divine reality, a reality experienced in prayer and sacrament: "Like mathematics, religion can grow from within, or decay. The Jew knows more than the Pagan, the Christian more than the Jew, the modern vaguely religious man less than any of the three" (*GD*, 46–47). To lose the orthodox faith was to lose important categories about the world. Farrer observed, too, that in every era Christianity was charged with being an authentic witness to and against its age: "Christianity has constantly been digesting new historical situations; . . . The two snakes, Christianity and modernity, are out to see which can swallow which. Faced by such an issue, we are driven back to a scrutiny of our origin in Christ and in the Apostolic faith" (*CF*, 125–26). Farrer's chosen imagery echoes both Moses's battle with Pharaoh's magicians and the ancient ouroboros. But while the second might suggest an inescapable circularity, the first is a reminder of a power encounter between two rival systems. Whoever survives does so by digesting, on its own terms, the other. Historian Rémi Brague has argued that both Europe as a cultural tradition, and the Christian church as an interpretive endeavor, owe their longevity to the cultural practices of "secondarity," or to what might be called "a relationship of conservation." Rather than absorbing past cultures, secondarity seeks to interpret and pass along what has been received in a continual gesture of *ressourcement* (*Eccentric Culture*, 93, 102–3, 114–16, 122). Lewis and Farrer had this understanding in mind. Christianity is able to adapt to the challenges of each age because it can, at the same time, return to its foundational roots; it can discover anew what else is implied in the tradition, and it is only under those conditions that anything like appropriation of another's insights can authentically take place. The faith is always about the work of secondarity.

Lewis's early allegory, *The Pilgrim's Regress,* was his first spiritual autobiography, and in many ways, it dated itself almost immediately, yet its story is one of modernity in general. It is an account of what answers the Church offered in the face of a swamp of other options. The allegory's intellectual portrait was one of the 1920s and 1930s, a world in which Enlightenment rationalism, Freudian psychoanalysis, and modernist Dadaism competed with Anglo-Catholicism, Philosophical Idealism, and Secular Humanism, as well as with Fascism, Marxism, and Nietzschean will-worship. And all about them were the seductions of materialism, pragmatism, self-satisfied stoicism, and sexual excess. Yet with the exception perhaps of Idealism, almost all had parallels throughout the remainder of the century, and still do.

The hermit, History, is one of the central characters that makes it possible for the protagonist, John, to finally give in and trust Mother Kirk. History, who dwells significantly in a chapel, teaches John the genius of each people, unpacking for him the truths and half-truths that each practices. He is able to do this because he can trace the changes that the various lands (i.e., the allegorical ideologies) have gone through. The hermit cites the Stoics, Manichees, and solider cults of ancient paganism as examples (*PR*, 150). History is also able to give John a better narrative than he has so far received, one that explains how the Shepherd People (i.e., the Jews), who have been given the revealed rules of the Landlord, and the Pagans, who have been given the pictures that create transcendent longing, were meant for one another. "The pictures alone are dangerous, and the Rules alone are dangerous. That is why the best thing of all is to find Mother Kirk at the very beginning," and only then to partake of the Eucharist and forgiveness, for these transcend both rules and pictures (*PR*, 153–54). History also reveals to John that the distorted pictures he has encountered along his journey are the vestiges of previous counterattacks that the Landlord had used to try and break through to past cultures in their ignorance. Thus, the study of and engagement with non-Christian philosophies, histories, and cultures is still affirmed as a valuable project, but with a specific salvific end in mind. For Lewis, the past is best explained through Christian eyes.

Farrer also understood historical reasoning. For example, when he addressed the Voltaire Society on the topic of "Causes," he chose to engage R. G. Collingwood's *An Essay on Metaphysics* in order to affirm one of its central truths and to deny several others. Collingwood understood that scientists in any era have certain models that go unquestioned; indeed, research cannot go forward if they are, yet the historian can look back and observe that these do indeed change over time: "I shall observe such facts if I go round the place primed with the Freudian mythology and ready to plant on my human environment the questions it suggests" (*RF*, 203). So far so good, yet Collingwood's point raises an additional problem: after all, we now claim to know what motivated the Freudian. We, too, are members of a culture and time and shaped toward particular questions and outcomes, so we, too, have less than objective methods and motives. Yet, Farrer insisted, Collingwood's idealism should not end in subjectivism: "Nothing of the sort; his story shows the progressive attempt to interpret environment through the model of one's own environmental factor" and in such a way that one alters one's actions in particular circumstances and environments (*RF*, 204).

Farrer went on to suggest that such a model should cause us to go back and examine again the jettisoning of final causes that took place in the Renaissance and that continued into the seventeenth and eighteenth centuries. While descriptions of human action continued in post-Renaissance approaches, they were increasingly reduced to reflex responses:

> Hence the glorious scientific revolution of the late Renaissance—to make physics exact, and bring it all under mathematical discipline, it was found convenient to ignore what natural agents are apt to do, and concentrate on how they mutually condition one another.... Their action is, in fact, a mere passivity. Hence the universe of Descartes and Newton. It was jolly for science; what was awkward was, you couldn't fit in agents who really do act or react, and not merely suffer displacements, e.g. you and me and the cat. And that, of course, was Descartes's headache. (*RF*, 206)

This shift has been labeled in a number of ways by intellectual historians. Louis Dupré has described it as a series of cognitive and imaginative shifts: from artist to engineer (1993, 66); from participation to representation (86); and from an open system to one that is instrumental, quantifiable, and closed, and without contemplation (68–69, 75): "Method turns into a screen imposed upon the subject matter that restricts the investigation to what will most effectively and most speedily yield reliable results" (Dupré 1993, 73). Paul Griffiths, likewise, has designated this change as a restriction to that of *mathesis*, a limitation to efficient causes and simple nature. Such a change had a corresponding trust in the efficaciousness of a perfect method, an algorithm that provides exhaustive predictions, and as a result, it also had a preference for textual tables and subheadings that aspire to making matters discrete, passive, and transparent (Griffiths 2009, 145–51). What Farrer did was to argue that this fundamental historical shift, even while it may have gained certain scientific rigor, lost as much in its inability to describe how agents actually act in the world. The methods of quantification and exhaustive prediction could not faithfully model what happens when humans (or even higher mammals) act in intentional ways in the manipulatable world. A historically explainable loss had occurred.

Yet this was not the only historical loss that Farrer wished to question, and his skeptical audience in inviting him had expected it. They expected him to defend God. And he did, though in a rather muted manner. Collingwood's history, Farrer argued, raised the question of what "we *cannot but believe*," which was a strange question given the historical embeddedness of thought that Collingwood espoused. Collingwood's approach seemed to reduce the divine to an aesthetic, in which "the world-picture of the time looks better with a deity in the top right-hand corner," yet which, given time and change, there could be no guarantee that "the little baroque heaven at the top right-hand corner will retain its position" (RF, 209–10). Farrer realized that the analytical philosophers of his own day would entirely reject even the validity of this historical examination, and he suggested that Voltaire's deism and his own Christianity were each subject to such scrutiny. One must, in short, also defend the efficacy of human action and investigation, and for this Farrer suggested the metaphysical need for a "privileged graded model" of action, simply because without it, one cannot do justice to the actual manner in which humans intentionally engage the world. And because one cannot, there is still room for "the Creator, the supreme archetype of his own efficacity . . . in whose likeness he has himself been made." Farrer insisted that this understanding was more natural to us "when we see how man has thought, does think, and must think about natural causes" (RF, 212–17).

Lewis and Farrer were hardly alone in arguing that something had gone wrong with the modern world. They shared with numerous others—Eliot, G. K. Chesterton, Dawson, and Jacques Maritain, to name only a few—the narrative that essential aspects of the West and of global culture in general were abandoned with the rise of the modern world. In the twentieth century, in particular, resistance to modernity has often been expressed by defending a version of the premodern sacred world, one thicker and more porous, both transcendent and teleological. Charles Taylor has examined how the modern world in certain quarters has lost its sense of the sacred and why that loss is not only unintelligible to most, but also unthinkable to many as anything but the only rational option. Taylor discusses how the modern world is a closed, horizontal universe and how the modern self is a "buffered self," one protected from the supernatural, even to some extent from the truly interpersonal. In such a narrative, both universe and self greatly contrast with the older open, vertical cosmos of the ancient and medieval worlds and with their conception of a more porous personhood shaped directly by magical and transcendent powers (Taylor 2007, 7–14). The premodern, porous self did not have clear divisions between the bodily, mental, or moral—each could influence the other, while the Cartesian self could even be said to be "super-buffered" (Taylor 2007, 136). This was a distinction that Lewis and Farrer understood only too well. Farrer in *The Glass of Vision* described humans as hierarchical, being made up of preternatural, natural, and supernatural aspects. "Self-knowledge has a hierarchical structure: it is the knowledge of the luminous apex of consciousness, taken as supported by such a psychic base as it may be found to have" (GV, 29). The apex is illumined because its tier dwells in realms not generated solely by the self. Humans are open to more and beyond themselves.

Likewise, Lewis and Farrer each appealed to a thick, hierarchical universe. Christianity, Lewis argued, has both elements of a world-denying religion like Buddhism, and a world-affirming one, such as Confucianism. This is so because its dual character embraces both nature and supernature. Christians "live in a graded or hierarchical universe where there is a place for everything and everything should be kept in its right place" (*GD*, 148). The celebration and mortification of existence follows for the Christian because one believes in both the Creation and the Fall. Farrer, in similar fashion, could insist that our created world, even one with numerous emergent levels and systems, at every level is radiated with the being of God in a deeply personal manner: "The inescapable sovereignty of God is a distinct attention of personal will bestowed upon every creature" (*SB*, 44). God can give every manifestation at every level, as it were, undivided and continuous attention. Indeed, there one finds a continuous unity and interaction of all creatures over which God is ever and always creatively involved (*SB*, 53–54). In such a world, the possibilities of joy, humility, and reverence remain, and this makes it very different in character from the flatter world that modernity proposed. *World* as a common term for both the premodern cosmos and the modern universe is misleading; they share little in common. Not only because the old sublunar and lunar distinction is lost, but also because the modern approach to modeling the universe with a developing and progressing theory is vastly different than a conception of an eternal cosmology (Brague 2003, 186–89).

Part of what attracted Lewis to the medieval cosmos was not, as he openly acknowledged in his *The Discarded Image,* that it could stand the ultimate test of empirical examination, but that it gestured toward an experience of the world that we do have—one more humble, reverent, joyous, and mysterious, and such a world is by nature thicker, more open to what is beyond the natural world. The medieval older world is closer to the paradigm of existence that we should be seeking to construct. Farrer defended Lewis's *Discarded Image* by insisting that Lewis was not trying to disappear into the medieval worldview as a way of being Christian, but rather as a way of illustrating what a Christian mind might look like and that in order that one could now seek an analogous vision (*Light*, 27–29). Both Lewis and Farrer thought that there were better ways to imagine the universe and all life within it and that the modern world was in need of help, indeed correction, from older understandings. It was to this work that both their lives would be committed, and they argued for it as committed and orthodox Anglican thinkers.

·✦2✦·

MYTH

Myth is the mountain whence all the different streams arise which become truths down here in the valley; *in hac valle abstractionis*. Or, if you prefer, myth is the isthmus which connects the peninsular world of thought with that vast continent we really belong to. It is not, like truth, abstract; nor is it, like direct experience, bound to the particular.

— C. S. Lewis, "Myth Became Fact" in *God in the Dock*

The mythic story no longer guarantees the general truths, as it did to the simpler age; on the contrary, the general truths must now be proved in their own right, and the validity of the myth depends on them. . . . The Christian story of redemption looked outwardly like a myth; it was born in the very age which was dissolving myths in allegory, yet it resisted such treatment and claimed for itself to be the only myth that is hard historical fact.

— Austin Farrer, "Can Myth Be Fact?" in *Interpretation and Belief*

The twentieth-century debate over myth arose within modernity, both as a critique and defense of it. That there was broad interest in the topic, much less a live debate, might seem surprising in light of secularism's desacralizing, closed cosmos, but, if anything, myth became a marker of human culture-making and a judgment of its capacities. For some, too, it was a reminder of an older, wider cosmos. At the heart of twentieth-century treatments of myth was the assumption that human thought becomes self-aware of its capacity for symbolism, even as it must use symbols to rise above the representations themselves. "The genesis of symbolic forms—," wrote Ernst Cassirer, "verbal, religious, artistic, mathematical, or whatever modes of expression there be—is the odyssey of the mind" (1946, ix). Or at least that was one way of putting it. While there was a wide consensus that myths dealt with questions of origins, cosmology, the transcendent, and that of human aspiration, there was also deep disagreement over whether myths were positive and/or negative aspects of life, as well as whether they were in any sense adequate to reality. Were they primitive vestigials that humanity has evolved beyond, or were they still essential to the most basic of engagements with the world?

C. S. Lewis and Austin Farrer both held that myth was a human narrative activity yet insisted it had bridges to the supernatural. They were not alone in this, though they were hardly in the majority. At the same time, Lewis and Farrer did seek to accommodate other approaches. They agreed that, while myth was not reducible to the psychoanalytic, it did draw from the products of human psychology, and that while myth was existential, it was not self-generated, but a noetic creation that responded to a real transcendent beyond. These beliefs also shaped why each writer allowed for the category of myth within the Christian faith, even within the Christian scriptures. For both of them, myth became a means of testing and preparing for a deeper sense of wonder and glory. Some myths, they insisted, were God-ordained.

In order to better understand why these themes were important to each writer, I will explore in this chapter Lewis and Farrer's need to navigate, accommodate, and at times refute rival understandings of myth. This background will help frame how Lewis and Farrer answered rival views by absorbing them into a wider vision of reality. That debate was important not only to how they handled mythic images and narrative, but also how they answered theological positions they judged as substandard, such as that of Rudolf Bultmann's program of demythologization. In the last analysis, both Farrer and Lewis's ultimate foundation was one based in the Incarnation, in Christ as True Myth, and such a position had radically personal, as well as public, ramifications.

ACCOUNTING FOR MYTH IN THE MODERN WORLD

In C. S. Lewis's late work, *An Experiment in Criticism* (1961), he proposed six general characteristics for myths: (1) mythic experience is not dependent upon the strictly literary; (2) myth possesses a structure for contemplation; (3) its characters are not ones we necessarily identify with, though they have "a profound relevance" to our lives; (4) myth's subject is the fantastic; (5) it has a quality of joy rather than comedy, and of gravity rather than absurdity; and (6) myth can result in numinous awe, and thus resists reduction to allegory (*EC*, 43–44). Such a list staked its claims in a highly contested arena, as

Lewis was well aware. And in 1961, he was afforded something of hindsight, so he was careful to distinguish his position from theories of the subconscious or the prehistoric, as well as from anthropological ritual. He clearly felt myth still mattered, was even essential, in developing a taste for universes, but he was careful to distinguish myth from the purely aesthetic or linguistic. Its qualities of joy, the fantastic, and the numinous were not reducible to psyche or symbol. What myth did offer, he insisted, was a window into something more profound than a mundane, flat modern world.

Each of these possibilities—the primitive, the psychological, the anthropological, or the conceptual—was a theory with particular claims about natural science, human cognition, and human society. Lewis's choice to defend the aesthetic and imaginative relevance of myths placed him on one side of a divisive issue. He insisted, "To inquire how they arise—whether they are primitive science or the fossil remains of rituals, or the fabrications of medicine men, or outcroppings from the individual or collective unconscious— is quite outside my purpose" (EC, 44–45). This concession was an academic one. Lewis argued that his analysis of myth was in no way dependent upon an origins account or even upon one that considered social function. Nevertheless, even as his worldview allowed for a cosmic framework that could accommodate other natural and human elements, he was also staking claims about why myth really mattered, and what was ultimately its transcendent aspirations. As Matthew Sterenberg points out, for figures like Lewis, myth was a way not of countering the authority of natural science, so much as arguing for its limitations (2013, 89–91).

Austin Farrer's own explorations of myth were within a more limited set of questions, specifically the role of images, the imagination, and archetypes in scriptural revelation. But even this restricted concern had to assume a universe close to the one Lewis was advocating. Farrer, too, could make the academic concession. For example, he could admit that behind the narrative of Balaam and the ass, there might be "an older Balaam, a figure of pure fairy tale" upon which the divine account in Numbers builds its deeper explorations. "I hope it will cause no scandal," mused Farrer, "if I simply confess that the theologizing of the magical represents the historical beginning of the supernatural" (GV, 23). Such a viewpoint included claims about human history, including symbolic history. Yet such a concession did not surrender the belief that imagery and fantastic narratives had to be the product of conscious imagination, for they were connected, not just to the preconscious, but also to the greater world beyond the conscious. Human aspects of the creative process were subsumed by supernatural action for God's own purposes. The fairy tale as a product of imagination was preparatory and in no way contradictory to the divine surplus making use of it: "We reach the end of fairyland and pass the boundary-stone . . . only through the supernaturalising of natural agents by God" (*GV*, 23).

Farrer was thus willing to concede that psychological and anthropological origins might play determinative roles in myth, yet the scriptural narrative could not be reduced to them, as if these origins were reductively predictive. In the same way, diminished explanations for human creativity, such as the materialist ones of Marxism, did not quite account for everything human, especially for "human inventiveness which works out the solutions," and moreover, for "whatever imaginative overplus there is in divine revelation" (*IB*, 43). Not unlike Ernst Cassirer, Farrer was willing to accept that myths may even have their origins in prehistoric, primitive literalism, yet such myths remain because they "seem to obey in their style and formation certain profound laws of the human imagination" (*IB*, 165). Myths, whatever their historical origins, exist for some greater, more universal and continuing purpose, and any good account of them has to allow for forces below and above the human, even while not overlooking how persons actually employ concepts and images.

Positions that affirmed both the human and the transcendent meant that Lewis and Farrer were knowingly staking locations in a centuries-old conflict of ideas. In the late nineteenth and twentieth centuries, theories about myth (and the varying points of divergence among theorists) were as much about chosen fields of specialization as their particular explanations. Sociologists, psychologists, anthropologists, and scholars of comparative religion had positions to take on myth, as did philosophers, theologians, linguists, and literary critics. Yet all modern accounts of myth were evolutionary or developmental in their basic models, even as they differed on most other fundamentals. This meant that a theory of myth was often built upon a narrative of origins, upon the resulting social purposes of myth and religion, and as to whether myths themselves were something history had transcended. Lewis, operating primarily as a literary historian and critic (though also as a novelist), and Farrer, operating as a philosophical theologian and biblical exegete, had to navigate these cultural debates, ones that were part of modernity's increasingly fragmented approach to persons, the world, and religion. Indeed, theories about myth were very often attempts to validate modernity itself.[1]

How turbulent, then, were the ideological waters that Lewis and Farrer had to navigate? Any account of Western theorization about myth includes a story built around tensions between the trust and distrust of faith, as well as the mystery that myth seems to invoke and the mundanity with which it can be

nature and, therefore, a kind of early philosophy of science. Myths are about the external, natural world and society, but they are understandable to moderns only in terms of a downward reduction.

Alongside these "outside down" accounts were "inside down" accounts that saw myths as products of the subconsciousness, yet these accounts were divided in the trust level they assigned to myth (Scarborough 1994, 24–26). Some thinkers, following Sigmund Freud, would dismiss myths as neurotic, while others, following Carl Jung, would praise them as archetypes. Especially in Freud's middle and late periods, myths are projections of instinctive drives and traumas, which we rid ourselves of, at least partially, once we can interpret their true significance. For the Freudians, too, myths are vestiges of unconscious, suppressed desires and dreams of primitive peoples, as well as tribal memories of actual events in the primitive past. On the other hand, for Jung, archetypal symbols form the collective or transpersonal unconsciousness, and myths transform lower instincts into higher ones, becoming a code for understanding the world with some measure of psychic enlightenment and personal integration.

If early primitivist models treated myths as vestigial holdovers, while psychoanalytic models looked to the subconscious as the source of mythic structures, there were "inside up" theories (Scarborough 1994, 20), such as that of the neo-Romanticism of Cassirer, or of quasi-Idealists, such as R. G. Collingwood. Given evolutionary models of mythology, a related dispute arose as to whether the self-reflexivity of mythology took place only in the prehistoric past or whether myth-building happens continually within all image-making in all eras. Cassirer posited that myth is a continuing aspect of human cognition, different than discursive reason or investigative science, and perhaps always preparatory in some measure, yet myths, though they once provided liberating power, also create oppressive custom.[3] Collingwood, in similar fashion, argued that a proper approach to myths and fairy tales must remove contempt from our descriptions of their belief systems. Instead of treating them as theology, we should discover how they work as imaginative reenactments of the world. Collingwood insisted that "the savage is not outside us; he is inside us." Civilized beliefs of the West are no different; each structures understanding, emotion, and ritual action (Collingwood 2005, 115–20, 129–30, 182, 206–8).

This stress on symbolic engagement ran parallel with yet a fourth approach, "inside middle" theories, in which myths arise from the inner world of human selfhood and provide existential realization (Scarborough 1994, 23–24). Here myths are in conflict with modern scientific understanding, but they can be demythologized. The theologian Paul Tillich could argue that myth (like science and religion) is a cultural endeavor that seeks to intuit the character of reality, "a whole set of symbols, expressing man's relation to that which concerns him ultimately" (Tillich 1949, 306). As symbols (mythic or religious or imaginative), they participate in the reality that they seek to describe and experience, and thus cannot be disturbed and yet maintain their psychic power.

Viewed together, these four approaches—the primitivist, the psychoanalytic, the symbolic, and the existential—had in common an assumption that myths represent some cognitive explanation: mistaken in its approach to the outer world; seductive in its repressed inner world; or essential to make meaning in both worlds. A fifth set of approaches to myths looked at the social side, priding itself on actual field study. Theories that draw from anthropology argued that myths serve the daily needs of a people. Scarborough positions these as "outside middle" accounts. For such, myth was a very present phenomenon and one explained in functional social-scientific terms, such as those of Émile Durkheim or Bronislaw Malinowski. Myth, while still cognitive, had purposes for managing the actions and interactions of groups. Embodied in rituals, myths function as the "collective representations" of a society's beliefs and practices, and gave a shared sense of exaltation, group transcendence, and collective effervescence. They are about the outside of social organization and cohesion, and the day-to-day of human (i.e., middle) existence (Scarborough 1994, 17–18).

Finally, for some, such as Rudolf Otto or Mircea Eliade, myth as a religious phenomenon points to something sacred outside itself, and this need neither be feared nor escaped. These "outside up" approaches treat myths as poetic and imaginative responses to the outer world, which have their own valuable literary and artistic flavors (Scarborough 1994, 18–19). They require phenomenological descriptions that can also be historical. Myth responds to feelings and intimations of the sacred world that arise when contemplating certain objects, places, and persons, even if evolutionary in origin. Eliade, for example, based his understanding of myth upon "the repetition and imitation of divine models" that allow people to "remain in the sacred" and "sanctify the world" (1957, 99). Myths model a basic *hierophany*, an inbreaking of the sacred into human experience, because all persons, in primitive terror before a dangerous world, desire to dwell in a meaningful center, the *axis mundi*. These outside-up approaches, then, could all be said to be theological in some sense.

Such a wide range of disciplinary entry points into mythology were expressions of varying embodied *Weltanschauungen*, of encultured worldviews. So even when they reductively tried to focus on a certain aspect of human life as the key to unpack mythologies, they could not avoid their counterparts.

Primitive vestigial accounts had to also explain why myth has its counterpart in the modern world, just as psychoanalytical accounts tended to repersonify forces such as Freud's Eros, Thantos, and Science in *The Future of an Illusion,* or the Collective Consciousness of a *Spiritus Mundi* in Jung. These points of historical tension also remind us that the middle level of the socio-personal, whether existential or anthropological, was even less firm than the others, for existential accounts or anthropological descriptions could be drawn upward into the mythopoeic and the supernatural or downward into the semiotic use of the psycho-material and preternatural. And even upward accounts, which began with the symbolic, the noumenal, or with cosmic time, also could be put to hermeneutical and scientific questions.[4]

ENGAGING CONTESTED MYTH

Austin Farrer and C. S. Lewis's own transcendent, upward approaches to mythology owed much to the Romantic, even while they, too, sought to accommodate the evolutionary, and this double debt meant that they also had to answer the twentieth-century spectrum of mythic theories. Both drew from Romantic emphases on the imagination and on poetic inspiration, and these they judged as reflective of the human side of myth creation. If, at points, they could tease out the differences between the poetic and the mythic, they often treated them as overlapping. Lewis and Farrer also took into consideration an evolutionary basis for some aspects of the imagination. This was possible because the transcendent account of their Christian theism posited a thick, hierarchical universe in which the temporal, even the unconscious, could play a component role. This hierarchical world also meant that human imagination might stand midway between the sub- and supraconscious. Such a hierarchy made it possible for both writers to accommodate the range of the debate, including the psychological, anthropological, existential, and symbolic. Lewis, for example, did not discount that myth could have evolved or had psychologically shared aspects. "The desire to investigate the parts below has genuinely scientific justification," he conceded (*EC*, 45), yet his approach was one that valued myth for a certain kind of experience. Lewis prized "myths contemplated, but not believed, dissociated from ritual, held up before the fully waking imagination of a logical mind" (*EC*, 45).

Farrer, as well, could argue that the human imagination might experience poetic inspirations as if from below or beyond, "but they would not have occurred but for previous intellectual labour," nor would such moments be understood as pregnant with meaning if "they had not been seized and elaborated by the same intellectual power which had been their remoter cause" (GV, 30). Farrer described creativity as parallel to Aristotelian-style virtue. The poet is one who makes artistic decisions, interacting with the made work, and during the process, the making of the poem will involve intentional action, unintentional or more tacit composition, and the testing of the text in process: "Invention makes up, however, in sheer innovation what it lacks in control . . . decision and invention are equally required, to give it substance" (FOW, 294). Much of Farrer's biblical criticism would grow out of this single insight.

Farrer and Lewis's approaches obligated them as well to say something about the nineteenth-century school of Max Müller, Edward Taylor, and James Frazer. The vestigial, outward-down approach treated not just myth, but also religion in general as primitive science living past its evolutionary usefulness. To answer such a charge, Farrer and Lewis each argued that the vestigial account overlooked even the wider intimations of unbelievers. In Lewis's novel, *Till We Have Faces,* the young priest Arnom interprets the meaning of the goddess Ungit for the queen Oral. His interpretation is very much that of nineteenth-century vestigial reduction. According to Arnom, Ungit is symbolical shorthand for Earth, which is "the womb and mother of all living things," while the god of the Mountain is air and sky, which are better understood as evaporation and cloud formation. That the sky god is also the husband of the earth goddess is a way of explaining how rain makes Earth fertile (TWHF, 270–71). By many lights, the young priest's explanations should be more up-to-date, more civilized. After all, Arnom has installed a beautiful, more Greek-like statue of Ungit, but Orual realizes something is amiss in these explanations and in his aesthetics of beauty. They cannot explain the comfort the older Ungit gives to a weeping peasant, nor the joy of true belief when the people, at the emergence of the priest in the rite of the Year's birth, shout together, "He is born! He is born!" (TWHF, 272–73).

Farrer, too, understood this pagan intimation. In one of his last sermons, "Fathers' Sons," he contrasted the myth of Phaethon with the Gospel of John. Farrer had schools of comparative mythology in the background, and he opened his sermon describing the apocalyptic landscape that Phaethon, the child of the Sun-god, had created: "Everything burns: the mountain forests blaze like torches, the lakes and seas dry and the fishes die gasping: all the sonorous names on the ancient world map spring out of the poet's page in letters of flame as the irresistible terror sweeps from east to west" (CF, 166). Phaeton brought about such destruction because he asked to drive the solar chariot for a day. According to Farrer, the account in John is similar: the child of the

God of Light comes to do his father's will, and he suffers a great tragedy. But there the similarities end: the Incarnate Logos desires a new beginning for all humanity, not for himself alone as did Phaethon. Phaethon needed a miraculous proof that the Sun-god is his father, while Jesus told us simply that it is his very life to do the Father's bidding.

One might question whether Farrer's use of the classical myth was simply illustrative, a startling image to keep his collegiate, half-believing audience's attention. Yet his choice, especially his impassioned description, suggests more. Behind the comparison was the long-standing practice of Frazer, which Farrer was accepting and yet subtly critiquing. Frazer's "law of similarity" asserted that if separate peoples share similar rituals, their motives and reasoning are similar (2009, 26–27). In such a reading, Jesus was simply one more dying-god myth. Farrer could assume his collegiate audience had at least a murky sense of such claims. And, in a sermon, he could assert what he might otherwise argue for, but he did so by practicing his own comparative analysis. Phaethon's death serves as a predecessor to Christ's, but Christ's death transcends the Greek myth. While both stories make a moving imaginative claim on an audience, the narrative in John is also history. Farrer felt no need to deny the imaginative power of the Phaethon account; his own recounting affirms its power; however, he also invited his hearers into yet greater emotional and mental engagement with the Christian texts. Rather than treat the gospel as one among many prescientific systems, as vestigials of the primitive mind, Farrer treated John's account as existentially present precisely because it referenced a transcendent reality beyond human subjective constructions. Imagination played an important role because it responded to an actual power outside the self.

In this case, Farrer employed the myth and its comparison to John's account to teach his hearers about silence and Christian prayer, specifically to recommend the Ignatian exercise of meditating upon scenes in the Gospels, and in doing so Farrer was offering a way to approach image in a more profound and thorough experience:

> Take any such scene, with the written word to help you—and—this is the great point—do not begin preaching yourself a sermon on your duty as resulting from what you read but do your best to go into the mind and heart of Jesus as he is presented, and there occupied. See what his attitude is, what is the set of his will and the movement of his love towards his Father or his fellow men: and identify yourself, let yourself go with it. (CF, 169)

Rather than using the scriptural narrative for ethical instruction—something Farrer did regularly and without apology—here the potential contemplative is instructed to employ imagination to imitate Christ. Impression requires repeated, sensory meditation. Such contemplative prayer, widely practiced, would bring a better fire to the land than Phaethon's (*CF*, 167–70). There is, then, a general principle for the hearer. Awe before the numinous engages the person at levels other than the simply rational, but not all such awe is exactly the same. Farrer invoked the capacity to use images to gain a sense of divine truth, and this required of him a sense of the psychological impact of the archetypal. He also sought to teach Keble College congregants to employ their imaginative faculties in spiritual formation. As Farrer testified, "We identify ourselves with what we adore" (*CF*, 169).

Lewis knew this truth about adoration very well. For example, his appeal to the "argument from desire" was able to acknowledge the horizontal, human components of myth while still suggesting that they pointed to a vertical, transcendent order. He had experienced this before he came to mature Christian conviction. In his 1955 autobiography, *Surprised by Joy*, Lewis recounted his childhood and school involvements with Norse myth as early experiences of *Sehnsucht*, that is of longing for the ideal, or what he simply titled "Joy" (*SBJ*, 7, 17–18).[5] One of his earliest was upon reading, in a translation of *Tegner's Drapa*, the words: "I heard a voice that cried, / Balder the beautiful / Is dead, is dead—" Even without knowing the myth, Lewis found himself longing for something not easily describable (*SBJ*, 17). Years later, he would encounter this longing again with *Siegfried and the Twilight of the Gods*, and only then would he know it as distant country for which he was heartsick (*SBJ*, 73), nor would this kind of experience be the sole way that Lewis would encounter or employ myth. In retrospect, he realized that Norse myth in his school days also gave him a "new appreciation of external nature," and it taught him "some capacity for worship against the day when the true God should recall me to Himself" (*SBJ*, 77).[6]

In *Till We Have Faces*, Lewis finds this same pre-Christian desire in the Cupid and Psyche myth. In Lewis's retelling, Psyche understands that the philosopher Fox does not have a complete picture of truth or of reality; indeed, there are portions of it that he knows but will not admit to loving, such as the sweet lies of the poets. Likewise, there is much neither the old priest nor the Fox can explain, such as "how little difference there is between dying and being married" (*TWHF*, 73). Psyche has longed for death all her life, and in expectation of being given to the Shadowbrute, she excitedly wonders, "How if I am indeed to wed a god?" (*TWHF*, 71). With the skeptical Orual, Psyche lapses into fear at the horrible possibility that she will be left to wild animals or worse, but she fears only for so long; she knows more deeply that something beautiful is coming. And if we are to believe it, in Orual's later vision in the valley of the god, the god indeed has a face of angelic beauty, though for much of the novel, the reader is left wondering if all this can be explained by purely psychological means.

Lewis's mature approach allowed him to still see the value in psychological and anthropological approaches to myth because they could be better explained by a more noumenal theory. As a literary critic, Lewis thought that psychoanalytic theories, both the Freudian and the Jungian, had the positive effect of reopening the mystery of the world, and this in spite of much that he either dismissed or mocked in their approaches: "Psycho-analysis heals some of the wounds made by materialism. For the general effect of materialism is to give you, where you expected an indefinite depth of reality, a flat wall only a few inches away. Psycho-analysis offers you some kind of depth back again—lots of things hidden behind the wall" (*SLE*, 299). This is at first glance a profound concession, especially given that Lewis had crafted an entirely opposite symbol in his *Pilgrim's Regress* nine years earlier. There, John is jailed by Sigismund Enlightenment, whose giant Despair forces his prisoners to see in X-ray fashion the inner organs of creatures, as if this were their true selves, and then are forced to recite in catechism the reductions of Freudian theory (*PR*, 49–54). But in his 1942 essay, Lewis was not so much interested in those who parrot materialism as he was in the manner in which master symbols "exhibited" rather than "concealed" that which was higher (*SLE*, 295). As in *Pilgrim's Regress*, Lewis still rejected the Freudian reduction of joy and beauty to being "really" about sexual repressions and neuroses. At the same time, he held that imagination had both free (i.e., mythic or fantastic) forms that one could create with and servile (i.e., repressive) forms that one sought to escape (*SLE*, 290). *Sehnsucht* explained the attraction of psychoanalysis rather than the reverse. While Lewis thought the Jungian collective unconscious a more "humane interpretation of myth and imagery," he concluded so because he judged the associations of Jung to be examples of the mythopoetic rather than explanations for them (*SLE*, 296, 300).

Lewis, in similar fashion, could question anthropological criticism in literary studies because it reverses the source of attraction. Here, too, he placed a position on myth within a hierarchical conception. Anthropological approaches, like others, overlooked the supernatural order to which they pointed. The reduction of the "Maiden in the mor lay" to an image of Jungian collective unconsciousness, to esoteric wisdom, or to anthropological ritual misses why all three are attractive: because all tap into the transcendent: "the last surviving trace, the tantalizing glimpse, the veiled presence, of something else," of an origin story, which if a ritual, need not be legitimated by field description (*SLE*, 308–9). Lewis's complaint was not that anthropological study might establish functional, ritual origins for some stories, but that one would ever need anthropology to justify feeling something deeply mysterious (*SLE*, 310). What anthropology (or better, historical study of ritual and belief) does offer is contextual insight.

Lewis did understand that human rituals have legitimate social and psychological components. In *Till We Have Faces*, the weeping of the King at the sacrifice of Psyche is not exactly hypocritical. "He believed it while he did it," observes the Fox, "His tears are no falser-or truer-than Redival's" (*TWHF*, 84). Yet Orual's own accusation before the gods and before the dead has a very different character. It, too, is a kind of ritual, a summary judgment, and she also is both true and false to herself. However, unlike the King's only psychological relief, Orual comes face to face with the divine, and in the end divine beauty. This is what it means that "the god is coming into his house" (*TWHF*, 287–89, 307–8).

In several of Lewis's other novels anthropological rites also become markers of this higher meaning, but as often these take place in uncorrupted worlds where the distance between their mortal meaning and their supernatural purpose has not been introduced. In *Out of the Silent Planet*, the passing of the Oyarsa of Malcandra through his subjects is formal and ritualistic, but also natural and without artifice:

> Every visible creature in the grove had risen to its feet and was standing, more hushed than ever, with its head bowed; and Ransom saw (if it could called seeing) that Oyarsa was coming up between the long lines of sculptured stones. Partly he knew this from the faces of the Malacandrians as their lord passed them; partly he saw—he could not deny that he saw—Oyarsa himself. He could never say what it was like. (*OSP*, 118)

The scene is complicated by Ransom's near incapacity until this moment to see the angelic *eldila*. How the Malcandrians respond is altogether fitting. How else should one see the embodiment, albeit stellar, of authority or royalty? That Weston and Devine are unable to see the Oyarsa shows that Thulcandrian brokenness renders this natural response opaque. That the *pietas* and *gravitas* of the Martian creatures is a given assists Ransom not to understand as if he were an anthropologist engaged in thick description, but as a devout person, as a creature who experiences right piety. Ransom recalls something similar at seeing a *hrossa* funeral. The *hrossa* go singing down to the lake with three gray-muzzled elders, who are departing in a boat to die. It is solemn yet without grief, for these older ones depart with those of their generation, and without fear or regret (*OSP*, 156–57).

In *A Preface to* Paradise Lost, Lewis described Milton's poetic decorum as possessing the quality of *solempne*, a Middle English concept that, while comparable to the Modern English "solemn," is not marked by "gloom, oppression, or austerity," but instead, ritual pomp and stately pleasure. *Solempne* is serious yet joyful, full of expected actions, and ones fitting to the occasion (*PPL*, 16–17). Arguably, this quality is present in both Malacandrian rituals. It is also present in *Perelandra,* though in its most natural, unfallen, and artful form. There, the Oyarsa of Perelandra and Tor greet one another formally. The former greets Tor and Tinidril, the Adam and Eve of Venus, with a legal and celebratory oration, transferring to them dominion of the planet, while in turn Tor bids the Perelandrian Oyarsa to stay and be their counselor, which she formally accepts (Lewis 1944, 177–78). It is not likely that either has been taught this manner of exchange; it is simply who they are. Anything else would be unfitting and signal a disconnect between body, mind, and occasion. These are fully integrated beings. A similar formality occurs as Tor names places and as the *eldila* repeat their chosen names. His is performative language: the great sea forest's name is Lur, as the place of judgment and royal rule is named Tai Harendrimar. The *eldila*'s repetition of these names is both an act of confirmation and celebration. One does not need to parse out whether this is psychologically beneficial, socially advantageous, or semiotically meaningful. It is simply all of these and without difficulty.

In "The Supernatural and the Weird," Farrer's second Bampton lecture, he, too, held that creativity and inspiration are shaped by both the supernatural, that which is above human ability, and the preternatural, that which operates in realms which no one can speak of with confidence. To hold on to three levels meant opposing those who conflated even the seemingly miraculous to abnormal natural causes, and this meant also that Farrer must insist on a hierarchical universe, which, as human involvement, is bodily experienced (*GV*, 25–28). The human mind is not just its "luminous apex," its connection to the higher supernatural, or its "shadowy base," its cellar of the pre- and subconscious, but the energetic movement between these (*GV*, 29). And yet the movement is not a two-way street of equal forces. Farrer insisted that human inspiration owes a debt to both, yet these should not be promiscuously mixed; they are different phenomena. The sublime moments of inspiration in the epistemic summit are intertwined with the clear and rational work of the mind—"inspired wit is a normal part of the life of the mind's conscious apex," while the image from the "weird abnormal consciousness" must be reworked as best one can within reason's craft (GV, 30). For Farrer, the luminous and the weird arrive as moments that seem to overwhelm our conscious control, yet they cooperate differently with the moment of inspiration. Only the "luminous apex" can do any significant work with the day-to-day data of experience; the "psychically weird" is too muddy for clear creation (GV, 32).

Given such a threefold hierarchy of the inner world, how did Farrer hold cognizance together with the outer worlds of the anthropological? Though his chief focus was inspired by scripture and apostolic tradition, he sought here, too, to account for the purpose of the mythic element. In field observations, the tribal use of myth could be understood as social cohesion and pragmatism, even as ideology and cognitive reductionism, and, in turn, myth can be read as an upward movement of ritual validation that appeals as much to sacred time and sacred origins as to the purely ethical. In addressing the matter, Farrer drew from the anthropology of myth. The enacted event is always lived within a framing parable or set of symbols: "Certainly the events without the images would be no revelation at all, and the images without the events would remain shadows on the clouds" (GV, 42). For Farrer, events do not appear phenomenologically without a frame (Slocum 2007, 54–55). The historical event by itself is not revelatory per se; the event needs the divinely superintended images that awaken and enliven its meaning.

At the same time, Farrer believed that God superintended not only the events to be mythic, but also the mythic frames to be present in history for others to understand the events. It was their interchange that cooperated with revelation (Hefling 1979, 68). In lecture six of his Bamptons, Farrer recognized that pagan images are part of the larger historical picture. Here, he had anthropological and other developmental models of mythology in mind, especially the notion of the divine father and divine king. In holding such a view, he was certainly not unique. Farrer shared with Owen Barfield a belief that because "the human king and his divine archetype arise at once, they are inseparable: each makes the other" (GV, 85).[7] Farrer understood that the outside middle of anthropological practice could have a part in the inside-up symbolism of the supernatural hero account, which in turn could have a place within the outside up of the scriptural narrative. However, it was the latter that shaped the divine meaning of the rest.

MYTH AND NATURAL IMAGERY

So, C. S. Lewis and Austin Farrer accommodated the mythic positions of others and still held to a transcendent realm that could be said to actually exist. Given that both writers shared a hierarchical model of human understanding, imaginative creation held an important place, and they could see the value of poetic imagery and acknowledge its very human contexts. At the same time, this allowed them to stress that the image could signal a natural awe before intimations of the numinous, itself a power that is also active and at work.

In *Surprised by Joy*, Lewis recognized that myths are natural conceptions with highly personal elements, but to reduce them to the natural alone was always far from his intent. Myths are evidence of a larger, more vertical world because they are a bridge to the transcendent, and yet they are not transcendent themselves. They are expressed with human words and in human images. Lewis was staking a claim that drew from mythic theory, even as he explored the fantastic more specifically. Myth as noumenal in its aspirations was a particular kind of inner-upward symbol system. Myths were aesthetic— they lingered in the imagination in a way that reading for information does not—but they could be mixed with and, therefore, also possess what Lewis called a "realism of presentation" (*EC*, 57), that is, they provided details that reflected the believability of the supernatural in the general world. It is fair to argue, as does Matthew Sterenberg, that Lewis owed part of his emphasis on the transnarrative quality of mythology to Samuel Alexander, for whom the concrete can be the only abstraction that humans may experience (2013, 87). For Lewis, myth does have an historical aspect, yet this human and material quality of phenomenal solidity is what helps prepare for other higher meanings. Milton Scarborough's schematic treats views such as Lewis's as outside and up because they function as typology; the poetry and fiction of myth act as preparations for Jesus Christ, the true myth. In this matter, pagan myth served for Lewis as more than foreshadowing in history; it also functioned in forming a natural ability upon which the supernatural might settle. It led up to the reality of Christianity in cognitive and emotive ways, something one could only understand in retrospect (*EC*, 235). To be typological entailed something very this worldly with which to begin.

Lewis embodied these understandings of the natural and transcendent in his own fiction. For example, the latter chapters of *The Voyage of the Dawn Treader* use natural imagery to increasingly invoke supernatural wonder. Within the world of Narnia, this is manifested through the literary trope of magic, yet the concrete, material descriptions also invoke a world of richness not only beyond the mundane, but also beyond human technique to create. Aslan's Table is, at first, bountiful and uncanny. It is set in a ceremonial space, pillared without a roof, and the long table's stones chairs are "richly carved and with silken cushions upon the seats." The banquet itself is splendid, and Lewis's description appeals to the senses with a catalog of delights:

> There were turkeys and geese and peacocks, there were boar's heads and sides of venison, there were pies shaped like ships under full sail or like dragons and elephants, there were ice puddings and bright lobsters and gleaming salmon, there were nuts and grapes, pineapples and peaches, pomegranates and melons and tomatoes. There were flagons of gold and silver and curiously wrought glass; and the smell of the fruit and the wine blew towards them like a promise of all happiness. (*VDT*, 165–66)

On one level, this pledge of gastronomic goodness is thoroughly of this world, yet on the other hand it also acts as a sign of something greater—of someone's, that is Aslan's, grace. It appears without the normal effort and work that accompanies eating in the novel. It is miracle. But this offer of joy is also complicated by the three sleepers, who are covered in hair and seem to be something inhuman. Naturally, the crew is afraid of a curse. As the story unfolds, however, and the table's identity is made known, joy and bounty return in a greater manner. The "star at rest" Ramandu and his daughter sing a song that eclipses description. Out of the rising sun, thousands of white birds arrive, one carrying for Ramandu what could be "like a little fruit, unless it was a little live coal" (*VDT*, 178), and the snow-like flock settles upon the remaining feast and eats. Yet it is the rising of the sun itself upon the table that Edmund recalls as the most exciting moment of their journey. Within the text, none of this is entirely explained. We do learn that the three sleepers are the last three Narnian lords who quarreled with the sacred stone knife and that Ramandu's taking of the fireberry is reversing his age, yet these explanations hardly reduce the mythic events to existential symbols. As myths, they cannot be epistemically reduced to something entirely comprehensible. They invoke a richness beyond their descriptions.

There is a "semiology of inexpressibility" in Lewis (McGrath 2014, 114). Repeatedly in *Voyage of the Dawn Treader*, characters have experiences that transcend their ability to describe them, even to remember them. Eustace struggles to express the fear he felt as a dragon when Aslan first approaches him; the experience at Deathwater cannot quite be recalled by those involved; Lucy cannot remember the story "for the refreshment of the spirit," though

Aslan assures her he will tell it to her all her life; the joy of the dazzling sea near the World's End is so exciting that the crew speaks less and less as they sail into it; the lilies give such richness that Lucy and Caspian agree that "I can't stand much more of this, yet I don't want it to stop"; and the smell and sound of the breeze from Aslan's Country "would break your heart," yet it is not at all sad (*VDT*, 88, 108, 133, 136, 204, 207, 212).

For Lewis, myths are neither equivocal fictions without connections to the truth nor are they believed as univocal studies of the real. Instead, they are analogies between the natural and supernatural. Lewis shared this understanding with others who were at least sympathetic to theological mysteries. Myths were, thus, similar to Alexander's point about the conceptual taking a form that bridges the general and the particular. To provide this bridge, fairy tales seek to make the unfamiliar more familiar: "The strange events are not clothed with hypothetical probability in order to increase our knowledge of real life by showing how it would react to this improbable test. It is the other way around. The hypothetical probability is brought in to make the strange events more fully imaginable" (*EC*, 66). In one sense, Reepicheep's impossible last journey up the standing wave of the Last Sea at the End of the World is rendered as straightforward narrative. His sword, cast away, stands up right in the sea of lilies. His coracle ascends the wave and he is gone. The strange is made natural by its simple description. Yet, in another sense, the tale escapes our ability to explain it easily. It can be recounted, but the power of a journey into that which is beyond this world creates a longing for truth rather than its strict analysis. Lewis recognized that myth has a narrative structure, yet he insisted not only that it is a simple one, but that it is transferrable across various versions. "The man who first learns what is to him a great myth through a verbal account which is badly [. . .] or cacophonously written, discounts and ignores the bad writing" because the myth itself is something other than the words themselves (*EC*, 46). It is inviting something that is, strictly speaking, beyond its material form. It points to the numinous, or rather, it receives it. Phenomenologically, the myth is a reception point for an experience that gives itself to the audience rather than solely being an act of psychological transference or ritual enactment.

Farrer shared with Lewis this trust that the mythic image is a bridge between imagination and that which actively transcends human explanation. The main thrust for the analysis in *The Glass of Vision* is not the shape of the image-rich event itself, but its direction within the canonical revelation, yet Farrer also understood this vital aspect. God uses the natural unfolding aspects of culture and anthropology to prepare for and enliven the divine images of Christ. The received myths present themselves in an inspired manner to the prophet or other biblical writer. As such, the generative patterns that a seer might adopt—for example, the sevenfold patterns that the Apocalypse unfolds—are comparable to the meters and forms that a poet adopts, yet this tells us nothing about the divine superintendence of the scriptures themselves (*IB*, 51–53).

Admittedly, for the skeptic this is not entirely convincing. Just as a critic of Lewis's might seek to reduce the vertical presence of the transcendent in *Voyage* to only the horizon of the psyche or the social rite, so might one be suspicious of Farrer's confession of divine inspiration of the biblical authors and redactors. For example, H. D. Lewis's criticism of Farrer arguably misses one of the latter's key concerns: the meaning of the divine images itself is an act of revelation, and to attempt to explain them and to create a method by which to test their fittingness is to already cross the line between finite creature and Infinite God (Eaton 1980, 145–47). Admittedly, this puts back one step the interpretation of the images to apostolic and theological authority (Dalferth 2013, 149–55). Farrer's approach can be read as "not principles of literary but of *theological* hermeneutics" (Dalferth 2013, 151). Such a model raises questions about not only divine revelation, but also the way the historical context of anthropological symbols arises in cultures and yet is superintended by God. David Brown, too, has argued that Farrer could be faulted for not offering a clearer discussion of the actual mechanism of symbolic revelation. Yet Brown admits that, viewed in terms of nature and the unconscious, approaches that stress heavily the social and psychological could end up rendering revelation as entirely immanent in history (2013, 139–46).[8]

Farrer was fully aware that some images in scripture are more fecund, of greater depth, and thus more resonant across the centuries. Farrer included in these the master images of the throne of God, the True Adam, the representative of Israel, the blood atonement, the Divine Son, the Redemptive Sufferer, the Wisdom and Word of God, and the Supper/Marriage Feast. In the latter, he observed, Christ "displayed, in the action of the supper, the infinitely complex and fertile image of sacrifice and communion, of expiation and covenant" (*GV*, 42). What these images reveal is that salvation history does not require writers to create new master-images. Rather the master-images branch out in new secondary meanings because divine seminal possibilities are already present. That they derive from psychologically and anthropologically occurring myths should not shock for the myths were designed by Providence with openness all along: "The stuff of inspiration is living images" (*GV*, 43). Farrer in particular saw the apostolic writers as sharing in the mind of

Christ because Christ took to himself the master-images of the Hebrew scriptures: "These tremendous images, and others like them, are not the whole of
Christ's teaching, but they set forth the supernatural mystery which is the
heart of his teaching. Without them, the teaching would not be supernatural
revelation, but instruction in piety and morals" (*GV*, 42). Rather than being
doctrinal propositions or theological analysis, or even liturgical formulas or
religious experience, the master-images, though they participate in all these
things, are poetic associations that expand in relationship to divine actions
in history. Revelation is both image and event together, and in Christ, image
becomes event (*GV*, 44–47).

Just as Lewis noticed that myths escape our entire understanding, so Farrer noticed that scriptural images allow for imaginative immersion. They ask
of the reader more than simple and reductive comprehension. A text, such as
God "sent forth his Son, born of a woman . . . that we might receive the adoption of sons," reminds the Christian of Christ's entrance into the believing
heart in order to confirm his (or her) own sacred adoption. Such results in
the reader's gratitude, awareness of identity, and radical reaffirmation of the
world as a place of darkness that veils the light. Awareness of one's own failure, however, is not a pledge to morally trying harder:

> He throws himself on the love of the Trinity, more patient with him than he
> is with himself, and silently operative to produce in him even such penitence
> and vision as now he has. All these motions of the soul take place within the
> field of the image: they do not pass out of it into the thin upper air of defini-
> tion and speculation, nor down into the flat ground of mere penitence and
> self-management. (*GV*, 50)

The image is a microcosm of the drama of human capacity and divine edifi-
cation. Such is not simply psychological, existential, or symbolical, even if all
are present. It is an actual divine encounter and is not reducible to horizontal
and evolved epistemic abilities.

Lewis's argument from *Sehnsucht* shared with Farrer's recommendation of
lectio divina a recognition that there is a power at work within experience that
is more than literary or preternatural. For Farrer, some sense of the natural
means of myth and symbol was preparatory for their divine employment, even
for their development in the scriptural canon, and this was all the way from
the most literal to the most spiritual (Slocum 2007, 58–59). That myths have
noumenal possibilities is the natural shape of human meaning-making, and
one divinely intended all along for the specificity of the Jewish and Christian

messages. Just as Lewis saw pagan myths as preparatory for Christian ones, so Farrer saw human images as able to function as instruments of divine revelation, and as Judith Wolfe points out, Farrer's emphasis helped address "*which myths carry the relevant meaning*" in preparation for the Incarnation (2020, 81). Indeed, for Farrer, such images were created as such all along. This, then, raises questions about the nature and purpose of the Christian scriptures themselves, and to this concern, Farrer and Lewis shared much in common.

MYTH AND BIBLICAL HISTORY

If C. S. Lewis responded to myth primarily as a literary theorist and novelist, he nonetheless shared with Austin Farrer a concern with myth's place in sacred history, especially in regard to Jesus Christ. As an Anglican, when it came to the Christian scriptures, Lewis operated in a theological space between fundamentalism and modernism that was neither neoorthodox nor evangelical (Vanhoozer 2010, 80–82). The same could be said of Farrer's Anglo-Catholicism. Each of them practiced a combination of literary sensitivity and spiritual reading that accepted ahistorical (i.e., mythic) readings of many biblical narratives, yet at the same time insisted upon their event-status as more than simple allegory. Unlike its larger cultural counterpart, the twentieth-century theological discussion about myth and scripture was a debate in which no one was using "myth" to simply mean a lie, but by it they might mean anything from (1) language that seeks ineffectively to describe God's actions in the world; to (2) fictions about God that describe our personal experiences projected onto the past; to (3) events that have happened but that cannot be accounted for by critical documentary history (Fiddes 1992, 134). Lewis and Farrer charted a middle course between a full-scale existentialist (i.e., outward-middle style) demythologization of scripture and a fundamentalist practice that, by their lights, ignored the very human element in the scriptures. Their shared approach included an appeal to the aesthetic imagination as cognitively basic and to a strong stress on the Incarnation of Christ as the event that holds history and myth together, and it is that emphasis that allowed both to acknowledge the insights of theorists of myth without necessarily denying the reality of the supernatural.

   In Lewis and Farrer's complementary essays, "Myth Became Fact" (Lewis 1944) and "Can Myth Be Fact?" (Farrer 1945), the two sought to address those who discounted the symbolic in the Christian faith as archaic, embarrassing, and worth jettisoning. Their essays shared a general typological language, while (not surprisingly) approaching the mythic and historical nature of the Incarnation from opposing directions: Lewis was more concerned with those who reject Christianity as primitive, vestigial myth, while Farrer was more focused on the development of the typological symbolism of the Old Testament by New Testament writers. Because both men shared a view of symbol's imaginative sustenance and history's providential superintendence, they were willing to countenance some scale of judgment as to a biblical event's historicity. Some events, each would claim, are described in ways that are more or less historically referential by modern standards, while others are better described as fiction or myth. Both Lewis and Farrer assumed that the events in Genesis 1–11 are mythic instead of strictly literal; they nonetheless felt that its narratives pointed to some actual change in the past. They also held that God superintended divine history so that it fulfills the imaginative expectations of the older myths. Such a position raised two questions: What is the truth content of the biblical myths? And why hold on to the myths themselves if they are not historical records in the sense that a critical historian could accept as factual?

Alister McGrath has observed that for Lewis, "myth interprets both our external and internal worlds," and does so by giving them a clear structure and set of implications within "the distinct rationality affirmed by the Christian myth" (2014, 72). Myths are saying something about the wideness of the universe, as well as inner, more existential encounters, and Christian myth sorts out what is truly real in the aspirations of those myths. Because myths are symbols and images with a narrative structure, while not strictly historical, they do make reference to things in the world, past, present, and future, so they cannot be jettisoned as primitive holdovers from the past, and this includes elements that might be considered mythic in the Christian faith. Moreover, the myth still provides a personal connection to the God of traditional Christian theism.

In "Myth Became Fact," Lewis held that myth is "the vital and nourishing element in the whole concern," and this is why most practicing Christians are loath to let go of the stories (GD, 64). As supernatural fabulae they engage reality in a way that logic or experiment cannot. "Nourishment" for Lewis is experiential and lived, tasted rather than abstracted, and therefore, myth is closer to the center of human imagination—it foregoes abstractions for concrete, storied experiences; at the same time, myth cannot be delimited to fiction. It is as often intertwined with real history and can even be a matter of recordable event. Lewis thought that trying to demythologize biblical myth only led to weaker, less enriching remythologization (Sellars 2011, 163). In his experience, Christian faith called for more than rational ascent; it demanded imaginative betrothal. Following Samuel Alexander's insight, Lewis could argue, "It is only while receiving the myth as a story that you experience the principle concretely.... It is not, like truth, abstract; nor is it, like direct experience, bound to the particular" (GD, 66). We experience what engages us empathically. At the same time, the historicity of Jesus is nourishing because it also engages us *mythopathically* (to use Lewis's coinage), and furthermore, it transcends myth in a manner similar to how myth transcends abstraction. The life of Jesus was a real event in history. If myth mediates the archetypal vastness of symbol to the smaller, distanced world of abstraction, then Christ's incarnation mediates myth and history, "claiming not only our love and obedience, but also our wonder and delight" (GD, 67). In Lewis's judgment, myth is a fundamental form of human understanding, and it stands in some lesser or greater measure to the specifics of the world, culminating in the particularity of Jesus.

Farrer's essay, "Can Myth Be Fact?" was published one year after Lewis's, and his tack on these questions anticipated the theory of his Bampton Lectures. Mythology, according to Farrer, in human history was first believed, eventually universalized, then generalized, and so by becoming allegorized, the principles were separated out from the stories. Yet these mythic stories still tap into certain shared impulses for imagination and narrative (IB, 166). In such claims he is not unlike Owen Barfield—the hierarchical structure of human knowing is also mirrored in symbolic language's historical development. Farrer, in *The Glass of Vision*, asserted that there was no other way to think about the supernatural: "Man cannot conceive it except in images: and these images must be divinely given to him, if he is to know a supernatural divine act.... Faith discerns not the images, but what the images signify: and yet we cannot discern it except *through* the images" (GV, 92–93). Because they began as cognitively whole engagements with the world, they cannot be simply discarded.

In this kind of developmental model, Farrer offered an account of the history of mythology and language that he held with Lewis and Barfield, as well as their fellow Inkling, J. R. R. Tolkien.[9] Barfield had argued that in early human cognition, there was no real distinction between the literal and metaphoric (1973, 80–92). The mythic was not an alien or mistaken way of dealing with the world; rather, it was abstraction that was a rather late development: "Mythology is the ghost of concrete meaning. Connections between discrete phenomena, connections which are now apprehended as metaphor, were once perceived as immediate realities" (Barfield 1973, 92). With a like mind, Farrer traced the secularization of poetry in the West, arguing that in the beginning no culture would offer "a great and deep poetry" that was not also religious in nature. Only gradually did the myths become allegorized, generalized, and humanized, then finally bereft of even that, "undergoing poetical death, their last dissolution" (*GV*, 98). But in accepting this, Farrer did not conclude that myth could simply be laid aside as developmentally primitive.

Farrer also shared with Barfield, Lewis, and Tolkien, as well as others, such as G. K. Chesterton, Christopher Dawson, and David Jones, the notion that the pagan myths prepared the way for the true myth of Christ: "Men may construct a myth expressive of divine truths as they conceive them, and the stuff of the myth will be words. God has constructed a myth expressive of the divine truths he intends to convey, and the stuff of the myth is facts. And this can very well be, because God's control of facts is infinitely more complete than our control of words" (*IB*, 167). It is a matter of Providence that the historical is also mythic. Just as the fitting poem creates the "uniquely appropriate symbol," so God in confirming the prophets "seems to fulfil, and more than fulfil, all the figures of myth" (*IB*, 168–69). Here again, Farrer approached the question, not as Lewis from the question of pagan mythology, but from that of biblical imagery. The fullness of the symbols and their associations between each other—Adam to Daniel's "Son of Man" to Christ the new Adam—were not solely the product of human imagination. Farrer offered a reading of the Testaments that, in being typological and recapitulative, did not wish to entirely remove Genesis 1–3 from the actual past, even if what they recounted were not historically critical documents. The Adamic account though mythic, held Farrer, cannot be dissolved into the ahistorical: "It does not illustrate a principle, it expresses the whole fact of man's existence, created and fallen. . . . Something happened (so the myth is telling us) in the relations between man and his creator" (*IB*, 170). The myth, then, was not disposable because its truths cannot be surgically abstracted and removed. Even if there was no literal Adam, neither was the account removed to the purely existential.

Lewis concurred up to a point. In his *Miracles,* for example, Lewis treated Genesis chapter 1 as "poetry," and insisted that he was following the patristic example of Jerome. The account being poetic, in Lewis's mind, did not render it less worthy of dogma or understanding; indeed, it is better than many scientific pictures. The story was "told in the form of a folk tale," yet in comparison to stories involving the dissection of giant bodies or pre-Creation floods that needed evaporation before Earth's actual creation, the Genesis poet had a "depth and originality" that outshone the other myths. "The idea of *creation* in the rigorous sense of the word is there fully grasped" (Lewis 1960b, 33). Lewis's supposition raised a larger set of reductive issues surrounding myth and human depth–psychology. By treating myths as worthwhile cognitive acts that engage the actual world, Lewis and Farrer both assigned to them some measure of critical realism. Myths speak to reality, and they offer insights into actuality that science or logic cannot. But here they offer something other than critical history.

Given our proclivity for self-deception and projection, how trustworthy can our myths be? Are they anything more than our desires, consciously or unconsciously projected upon existence's brute physicality? Farrer understood that there is a space between myths and that which they reference. For Farrer, images could be alive in a sense not unlike Lewis's defense of their nourishment, yet that nourishment was not guaranteed. The problem, as Farrer saw it, was that systems of theology, as generalizations, could make the same false moves that any other system of inquiry could make; they can try to force the picture into being the reality, rather than standing for it:

> In ages for which religion and poetry were a common possession, the basic images lived in the conscious mind; men saw their place and destiny, their worth and guilt, and the process of their existence, in terms of them. Being externalized, the images taken for the reality of the divine became idolatry, and taken for the reality of false science. The rejection of idolatry meant not the destruction but the liberation of images. Nowhere are the images in more vigour than in the Old Testament, where they speak of God, but are not he. (*RI*, 13–14)

As a result, Farrer placed a stronger stress on the difference between a literal and mythic meaning, and even acknowledged something comparable to nineteenth-century models of myth, yet even here the myth within the canon itself is not replaceable.

So, Lewis and Farrer shared a trust that myth and history were distinguishable yet intertwined. Lewis, in responding to the charge that the Bible should be rewritten with the primitive "fabulous" parts removed, dismissed the claim that earlier cultures were less intelligent than those of modernity. Critics dare not tamper with the fabulous too much. In particular, he appealed to a developmental model of Hebrew history not unlike the one Farrer was assuming: "As to the fabulous element in the Old Testament, I very much doubt if you would be wise to chuck it out. What you get is something *coming gradually into focus.*" While Jonah and Noah are fictions, the court history of David was as much a reliable document as was a history of Louis XIV's court. But taken together, the fable and the history were preparing for the historical arrival of Christ the true myth, and thus, "if we *could* sort out all the fabulous elements ... I think we might lose an essential part of the whole process" (*GD*, 57–58).

Kevin Vanhoozer points out that Lewis's intuitive claim was that as a critic, as someone trained to read literary texts, he had a sense of what was meant to be myth or legend or fiction and what was meant to be history, even documentary history. Similar to Farrer's method, in Lewis's open-ended approach, the mythology of scripture was "chosen by God to be the vehicle of the earliest sacred truth" (Vanhoozer 2010, 80). The Spirit of God meant certain quasi- or nonhistorical narratives to have imaginative and spiritual authority in the Church's life and practice. There are parallels to be drawn as well between Farrer's approach and his influence upon Lewis's *Reflections on the Psalms* (1958), which Lewis dedicated to Austin and Katherine Farrer, and which Austin helped critique and edit for Lewis. Lewis's informal introduction to the Psalter models in practical ways the developmental approach that their Anglican position required. Lewis's book also modeled how Farrer and Lewis could accept much of the current historical criticism of Old Testament texts. Rather than adopting the patristic practice of allegory to smooth out troubling passages in the scriptures, both men were willing to simply treat them as bound by the limitations of their culture. For example, Lewis identified what could be abused or is abusive in the psalms themselves, or at least how they embodied stubborn pride, priggishness, and judgmentalism, and yet insisted they still offer repeated lessons in moral self-examination.

At the heart of this approach was the typological assumption he shared with Farrer—that the texts of the Old Testament are leading to the life in Christ, that even if they are human texts, they still have a divine purpose that is typological and liturgical. Lewis, for example, saw the ancient Jewish picture of judgment (i.e., God's vindication of his falsely accused people) as complementing the Christian picture of judgment (i.e., God's verdict on general wrongdoing). The older one is good for Christian readers because it steels them to hold a high standard of justice in the world and not to pass too quickly over the wrongs done to others. At the same time, prayers for punishment of one's enemies run the risk of self-righteousness, and Christian teaching warn us against assuming we are without sin. Lewis could, therefore, be initially distrustful of the imprecatory psalms: "The hatred is there—festering, gloating, undisguised—and also we should be wicked if we in any way condoned or approved it" (*RP*, 22), yet they too must have something to teach Lewis's Anglican readers. Their fury and indignation revealed a purer moral sense in the ancient Jewish culture that other contemporary cultures lacked—the higher the moral standard, the greater the potential outrage.

This was a very Anglican way of preserving dogmatic fidelity. Lewis wrote to Clyde Kilby that the question of historicity of a narrative like Ruth was beside the point when it came to spiritual reading. For some matters, such as Christ's Resurrection, history was very important, but for others, such as the fate of Lot's wife, not terribly significant: "And the ones whose historicity matters are, as God's will, those where it is plain" (Kilby 1964, 153). But, of course, this is precisely what was not plain to everyone. Supposedly one could tell the difference, and Lewis appealed to genre clues as helping make the distinction. Legend and fiction have intentionality to them; such accounts were not meant to be taken as historical records. Lewis admitted to Kilby, "The very kind of truth we are often demanding was ... never even envisaged by the ancients" (Kilby 1964, 154). Yet a critic could respond that presumably the myth in question was believed by those who recited, enacted, or recorded it; it functioned at a metaphysical level for them; and modern analysis now downgrades it to linguistic pictures or *mythoi*. Does this not, then, leave open the danger of treating myth as a human construct that can be desacralized? Lewis sought to avoid this danger by insisting that the myths in question are "God's myths," that is, the ones that God chose and therefore still have value. Nonetheless, a potential fissure, one that both Farrer and Lewis sought to bridge, remained in such a confession. As Brevard Childs has pointed out, "the supernatural elements of the myth do not stand isolated; they are intimately connected with a total understanding of reality" (1962, 14). Once we open up a space between the narrative and the reality, under what conditions, and by what means, do we distinguish the difference? Even a revealed myth runs the risk of being demythologized.

ANSWERING THE DEMYTHOLOGIZATION
OF SCRIPTURE

C. S. Lewis, in a May 11, 1959, address to Westcott House at Cambridge, complained strongly about the tendency of liberal theologians to deny the historicity of the Gospels. He had in mind Anglican theologian Alec Vidler's late-career claim that the miracle at Cana was simply literary embellishment. Vidler at that time was dean of the Chapel, King's College, Cambridge. King's College was a center of antireligious sentiment, though not one entirely opposed to religion, as the Chapel's presence indicated. Three years later, Vidler would himself organize the modernist theological collection, *Soundings* (1962). In the address, however, Lewis chose as his chief target New Testament critic Rudolf Bultmann, though he also briefly critiqued turn-of-the-century Catholic modernist George Tyrell. There were many in Lewis's audience that morning— faculty and graduate students—who espoused the positions that Lewis chose to confront (Heck 2014, 6–11). Bultmann is a revealing choice, for his *New*

Testament and Mythology (1941) created something of a firestorm in the post–World War II period. Lewis's objections included the assertions that Bultmann missed the overarching (and obvious) impact of the biblical texts as a whole; that his was a spurious historical practice, out of balance because it assumed that those living in the period could completely misunderstand someone, while modern interpreters like Bultmann could know the real truth of Jesus's teachings; and that Bultmann was making an un-Christian assumption that the miraculous cannot happen.

In particular, what Lewis objected to was Bultmann's practice of criticism that sought to identify when an idea in the text was too developed for its time period and, therefore, must have been redacted from a later one. Lewis complained that an evolutionary set of assumptions treated ideas in the New Testament as from a less developed (i.e., less evolved) period. A critic might respond that what Lewis willingly accepted in the Old Testament, he was not willing to extend to the New Testament. This was not, however, capricious on Lewis's part. What he found objectionable was not the presence of myth, even in the New Testament, but any approach that made the gospel portraits of Christ something projected on to Jesus, rather than their being a true revelation of himself within history. Bultmann had, as far as Lewis was concerned, argued that the Gospels were entirely a later generational development.

Lewis had problems with the quest for the historical Jesus, and saw in it a project that undercut the Gospels and the unique nature of the Incarnate God-Man. In his *The Screwtape Letters,* Lewis chose to have its senior devil extol the quest's usefulness to the demonic mission. There, Uncle Screwtape echoes the critique that Albert Schweitzer had brought against nineteenth-century lives of Jesus. By claiming to be able to separate out the Jesus of history from the Gospels themselves, the critics end up with a Jesus who mirrors their own sociopolitical agendas: in the last generation, one along "liberal and humanitarian lines," and in the current one, "on Marxian, catastrophic, and revolutionary lines" (*SL,* 124). While Screwtape's counsel always has to be read on the slant, in this case he is giving voice to Lewis's mistrust of the whole source critical project. The tempter's analysis of the approach shows how readings of the past are shaped by current desires and prejudices. On the one hand, Screwtape notes, the critics tend to have a strong distrust of later Christianity; they are in search of an original purity, yet they also, by way of their political theories, have forgotten what draws converts to the faith, which is the proclamation of the actual Resurrection of Christ, and thus their "recovery" of the primitive Jesus is nothing more than what they most prize in their current context.

Like Austin Farrer, Lewis saw in the quest a false approach to history in general, and in particular to the Gospels' revelatory form. The belief that the original purity of primitive Christianity was lost within a generation arose out of a radical Protestant distrust of later Church tradition. Even given Lewis's mere Christian sympathies, his traditional Anglicanism was bound to be resistant to this. At the same time, a stress on the original kerygma balanced this insight in Lewis. Converts have come to the faith because they believed in the Christ, and his salvific promise has answered "a sense of sin they already had" (*SL*, 126). The Gospels were written to confirm believers in the faith rather than to bring them to initial belief. Understood this way, the Gospels assume communities of the faithful gathered around the kerygma; they were written to confirm what Christians already believed. Screwtape insists that no modern life of Jesus, be it that of nineteenth-century liberalism, or of more recent radical versions, can produce Christian devotion, nor can it build up a strong sense of natural ethics, which, for the demon, is all the better for the destruction of human souls.

It is important, however, to keep in mind that Bultmann cannot be conflated completely with liberal Christianity. Bultmann saw himself as an ally of the neoorthodoxy of Karl Barth and Emil Brunner, though both theologians rejected his approach as being back on the road to the presumptuous criticism of Adolf von Harnack and Albrecht Ritschl. Bultmann discarded the quest for a historical Jesus who could be extracted from either inside or behind the New Testament texts. He too felt that the nineteenth-century quest for the life of Jesus was impossible and always led to a Jesus of critics' own making, typically a hero for their own agendas. The Christ of faith found in the preaching of the Church was all that mattered, he insisted, and even more importantly, the Christ of faith received in that existential moment in which he was encountered. But this move is what separated him from Lewis and Farrer.

By myth, Bultmann meant any world-picture that, because of modern science, would be regarded with contempt and therefore stand in the way of the existential confrontation with the Christ that the modern person needs. In this, Bultmann was clearly part of Scarborough's inward-middle position regarding myth: "The real purpose of myth is not to present an objective picture of the world as it is, but to express man's understanding of himself in the world in which he lives" (Bultmann et al. 1961, 10). Bultmann held that myths, as past world-pictures, were believed as literal statements about the actual world, and thus myths themselves were in conflict with modern scientific understanding, and yet they were products of the inner world of human selfhood. They now provided possibilities for existential realization. Myths could indeed be demythologized in order to be asked existential questions of human importance. Bultmann's project was intended to make the text of the New Testament relevant to modern readers by bringing out its key life content (Dorrien 1997, 101–3; Grenz and Olson 1992, 86–99). But this was a position that Lewis and Farrer were bound to reject. It gave up too much on rather arrogant grounds.

In 1953, Farrer had responded to a collection that included the English translation of Bultmann's *New Testament and Mythology* and four German criticisms of it, along with Bultmann's own rejoinders. Farrer's "An English Appreciation" became the fifth critical engagement in the SPCK volume. And his objections shared much with Lewis's later ones. Farrer held that at the center of the debate was the modern refusal to value myth, which he divided into four types: (1) a "necessary" refusal following from established standards for history and science; (2) an "accidental" refusal that came from not understanding ancient principles for a thing; (3) a "lamentable" refusal that lacked the faculty for appreciation (such as those who find poetry difficult); and (4) a "factitious" refusal by those whose ideology (e.g., materialism or Marxism) committed them to not finding any value in myth. Farrer held that accidental and lamentable refusals were ones that could be reversed with the right training or information. In our post–Kuhnian age, that Farrer divided the necessary and factitious refusals may strike some as suspicious, but actually his point was as simple as, on the one hand, received and public procedures, and on the other, the ideological commitment to deny counterevidence. In the case of training or information, the required approach was not "demythicization" but "remythicization," while factitious refusals as to what can constitute either history or even meaningful symbol were where the real debate began (Farrer 1961a, 214–15).

Farrer focused on two refusals that, rather than being necessary, he treated as factitious: first, the refusal to believe in miracles, and secondly, the difficulty as to how symbols actually refer, especially to the transcendent. To the first, Farrer responded rather tersely, "[Bultmann] writes as though he knew that God never bends physical fact into special conformity with divine intention.... but I am not convinced that I know it." If God so wishes to take something we know as symbol and make it physical fact, that is the divine prerogative. Farrer's discussion of transcendent symbols, on the other hand, was more in-depth, for he pinpointed a key weakness in Bultmann's existentialism. Existentialism too easily surrendered whatever constitutes the natural world for a restricted experience of the personal. There can be history that, though it does not follow the procedures of historical evidence and criticism, can be believed because it comes from a trustworthy source: "What Christians find in Christ through faith inclines them at certain points to accept with regard to him testimony about matter of fact which would be inconclusive if offered with regard to any other man" (Farrer 1961a, 216, 220). Received and believed history was not automatically subject to historical critical doubt and skeptical questioning, though it was not closed to their methods. Just because an event took on symbolical resonances, even though its facticity also echoed the stuff of legend, did not automatically render it a thing outside time. There was more than one use for history and for myth.

Admittedly, Bultmann himself did not hold that one could jettison the myths themselves, but rather they had to be interpreted for modern times in terms of existential crisis. He felt that one could not simply abstract out the key eternal truths; rather, one had to come with certain questions, and he felt that existentialism asked the correct questions for modern readers. In this way, he did not think that existentialism was an alien mythology imposed on the New Testament, but an appropriate beginning place (i.e. an inward middle position of the existential) for moderns to actually listen to the apostolic kerygma: "I *am* trying to substitute anthropology for theology, for I am interpreting theological affirmations as assertions about human life" (Bultmann et al. 1961, 107).

Yet, arguably, Bultmann's program in doing this nevertheless emptied biblical symbols of anything but personal, nonreferential meaning. Paul Ricoeur has asserted that Bultmann's project was better labeled as *demystification*. To "demythologize," according to Ricoeur, was to abstract, to allegorize, or to moralize in some fashion the literal myths, that is, to interpret them for their meaning and value in regard to self-understanding (1974, 389–92). This is simply the stuff of generalization. To interpret a myth is to already conceptualize it because we assume there are some truths that can be extracted from the myth, or rather all interpretation carries some measure of universalizing. To this, Farrer would hardly object; he rather thought it necessary, and perhaps gave more credence than Lewis to the need for such demythologizing, at least in uncovering what is polyvalent and symbolic (Sellars 2011, 159–60). Bultmann, on the other hand, demystified that which should remain mystical—at least, this was Farrer's charge.

Now this concern would seem to be true, especially if one confirms the necessity of not jettisoning the mythic narrative itself and of recognizing the myth as "God's ordained myth." One might argue that a myth always has certain mytheopathic reader responses that are divinely intended. If these truths and responses are true, then they must also speak at some level to the actual order of the cosmos, God, human anthropology, and so on. Their history may be prehistory in the sense of human documentation—the outward down of nineteenth-century myth theory—yet they must be making real claims about cosmological, geological, biological, and anthropological history, at least in certain broad affirmations. Lewis and Farrer thought this to be the case. As Farrer pointed out, event and image cannot be forced apart (Slocum 2007, 54). Lewis said something very similar in critiquing Max Müller's attempt to reduce all mythology to linguistic metaphor. Pure subjectivity of experience was not enough without reference to a real world of desired wonders: "The Subject is as empty as the Object. . . . The patient has the experience of being nobody in a world of nobodies and nothings" (1986, 83–84). For Lewis, "transcendence reinvigorates the immanent by placing it in a context of participatory ontology" (Sellars 2011, 167). This raises, then, another set of concerns: on what grounds did the imaginative encounter with myth, especially revealed myth, amount to more than simply a personal (i.e., existential) meaning? When and how did it name, even if only by evoking, the world as it is?

ENCOUNTERING JESUS

Austin Farrer and C. S. Lewis were themselves very concerned with reading as encounter—as Farrer's instruction in Ignatian reading of the Gospels reveals. In this, too, they were comparable with Rudolf Bultmann. He had argued that the transcendence of God could only be met in a personal I-Thou moment that has authority for the individual. Lewis charged Bultmann with reintroducing another myth in place of what he rejected, and finally with being inconsistent. Lewis insisted that the universal ideals cannot be removed from their mythic narratives, a position he shared with others as diverse as Gustaf Aulén and Karl Jaspers.[10] Lewis felt that in doing so, Bultmann accomplished the very opposite of what he had intended. He argued that Bultmann's project robbed readers of the nearness of Jesus's personality in the Gospels: "What is gained by trying to evade or dissipate this shattering immediacy of personal contact by talk about 'that significance which the early church found that it was impelled to attribute to the Master'?" (CR, 157). Lewis charged that the encounter, in becoming purely existential, lost its necessary *mysterium tremendum*. What distinguished Lewis and Farrer from Bultmann, then, was not personal encounter, but the manner in which that encounter happened and the historicity upon which that encounter was grounded. Bultmann's approach reduced Jesus to a mythic Phaethon. Both Lewis and Farrer insisted that Christians, when reading the New Testament with faith, met Jesus there, which was not to deny that the worldview and conception of the authors stand between the reader and the Christ therein revealed.

Certainly, Farrer understood the justice of the point that the gospel authors also had their own perspectives. "As a student of Christian origins I do not touch Christ, though as a Christian who receives the sacraments, I may. As a student, I touch Paul, Mark, and John," Farrer conceded. "When I have learnt to know them, I may hope to perceive what, in them, is reaction to Christ and to his saving acts; and so I may come to perceive what manner of Christ it is, to whom they react" (Curtis 1985, 234). But Farrer did not stop there, for to apprehend Jesus in the biblical authors, one must come with "a personal understanding of Christ," for the history of the God-Man is like no other human history: "No rules, forms, or principles of historical procedure can see us through such a task . . . independently of our estimate of what we can see Jesus of Nazareth to do" (Curtis 1985, 237). Just as any historical act of understanding required some attempt at imaginative sympathy with past persons, so the unique God-Man cannot be understood apart from the sympathy given only by the Holy Spirit: "We cannot know Christ in the history about him, except by the Holy Ghost. . . . There is therefore no neutral history of Christ common to unbelievers and believers" (Curtis 1985, 238).

The mythic language that appears to surround Jesus is at once the human attempt to speak of the divine action and the Divine Actor's choice to take such language and transform it. Bultmann's existentialism put an unnecessary layer of subjective reduction between the modern reader and the gospel story. Farrer pointed out that the development of the Old Testament images could as easily have been done by Christ himself as by his disciples, and Farrer rejected as unhistorical the nineteenth-century liberal argument that Jesus began with an ethical distillation of Jewish religion that was then encrusted again with myth by his followers (*RI*, 14–15). Christ wanted those who encountered the gospel to know him by these images. Fundamental to Farrer and Lewis's bridging of myth and history was the particularity and actuality of the Incarnation of Jesus: The affirmation of the actuality of this event, as True Myth, was central to what Lewis and Farrer held. They could allow for some measure of mythic material because those myths were always anchored by the concrete Christ, who is acting to draw humans to himself. Neither Lewis nor Farrer insisted on belief without reason or evidence, nor on revelation without some measure of natural theology. What each maintained, however, was that there was more than one perspective involved in viewing the evidence.

As R. J. Reilly points out, Lewis did not conceive of Christianity as the final myth remaining only metaphorical. Myth and fact are merged (1971, 114–15).

Lewis's famous toolshed analogy speaks to this point. To look along the beam of light entering the shed is not the same as looking at the light. In the latter case, one is reductively examining the parts that make it up, be they psychological, sociological, or biological. In the former, one is experiencing the light. The emergent aspects of life cannot be understood by dissecting them into their parts alone. "We must, on pain of idiocy, deny from the very outset the idea that looking *at* is, by its own nature, intrinsically truer or better than looking *along*. One must look both *along* and *at* everything" (*GD*, 215). The transcendent realities are always experienced via mediation. We are embodied creatures. How we experience does not tell us what we experience or why. The truth may be constructed of things that we can experience aesthetically as myth, but the truth is not reducible to our mythic consciousness.

Farrer, too, insisted that grace does not employ a method counter to human receptivity: "the supernatural enhances and intensifies, but does not remove nature" (*GV*, 39). The infinite and the finite meet together in mystery, for the material mediates the supernatural. The two—myth and history, image and subject—were always in tandem, always received together; this was the mystery of the Incarnation. In Farrer's analysis, nature and grace are a double action with a single end. God's divine control of history does not violate the freedom of his creation: "Grace is the action of the Creator in the creature. He acts in the creature everywhere; when he acts in the rational creature he is pleased to act in that creature's mental and voluntary life, bringing them into his own" (*FS*, 67). Divine action is not violating human cognitive capacities in images, myths, and symbols when God chooses to use them for his purposes. It was essential to an approach like Farrer and Lewis's not to let divine action become a myth that we tell ourselves, as if it were only a human wish projection or social tool. God has spoken; God is acting; God has taken on flesh and dwelt among us. Brian Hebblethwaite points out that in Farrer's essay "Revelation," he established the Incarnation not as a symbol of abstraction but as the action about which symbol is now understood (2007, 105). As Farrer put it, "The self-enacted parable of Godhead is parable relatively to the divine Being, but it is the very stuff of ours. . . . Christ does not save us by acting a parable of divine love; he acts the parable of divine love by saving us. That is the Christian faith" (1958b, 99).

Farrer and Lewis would concur that images are the heart of revelation; they are what God has chosen to engage the reader/hearer spiritually. Images, like myths, cannot be removed from the content nor can the principles be entirely extracted. Farrer allowed that some "legendary embellishments" were possible, yet we "go too far if we assume that everything supernatural is legendary." Even miracles are not a violation of the natural order, but an enhancement or extension of God's creation (*SB*, 81–82). Farrer sniffed at the attempts of modern scientism or deism to reduce divine action "to a soulless physicalism, a contempt for individuality and a denial of providence" (*GV*, 87). He likewise insisted that it was a mistake to reduce archetypes to some kind of general law: "A man cannot apprehend anything without an act of imaginative creation" (*GV*, 96). God is particular and personal in every repeated act. We must avoid a view in which God is only a principle underneath the father and king. At the same time, we must avoid a picture of the divine will that is only metaphorical (*GV*, 88). God took a third way—the Incarnation of Christ, which transcended the archetypes by taking them to himself, "for God to supernaturalise his instrument is incarnation" (*GV*, 91). Providence came forth and myth became reality; the archetypes, being incarnated in Christ, now acted in history.

The historicity of Christ was essential to their position because it is his divine action that holds together their trust that myth leads to history. For Farrer and Lewis, true myth had both pagan and Old Testament predecessors that functioned typologically as anticipations and preparations of the complete truth. The Old Testament myth was especially ordained by God; it could not be peeled away from its meaningful core nor be univocally identified with its subject. God's divine reality transcends all attempts to describe him. Nevertheless, myth was an essential aspect of human cognition, with certain rewards and temptations, and God has willingly used it. Indeed, myth was part of God's providential and revelatory plan in Christ and provided Christians with spiritual and liturgical nourishment. As a result, the totality of any biblical myth must be a part of our spiritual and liturgical formation, for we dare not assume we can know with absolute assurance what is not important, and we must be suspicious of our own propensity to demythologize as if we were lords of history and gnosis.

·✦3✦·

ANALOGY

May we not, by a reasonable analogy, suppose likewise that there is no experience of the spirit so transcendent and supernatural, no vision of Deity Himself so close and so far beyond all images and emotions, that to it also there cannot be an appropriate correspondence on the sensory level? Not by a new sense but by the incredible flooding of those very sensations we now have with a meaning, a transvaluation, of which we have here no faintest guess?
—C. S. Lewis, "Transposition" in *The Weight of Glory*

There is a superstition among revelationists, that by declaring themselves independent of any proof of God by analogy from the finite world, they have escaped the necessity of considering the analogy or relation of the finite to the infinite altogether. They are completely mistaken; for all their statements about God must be expressed and plainly are expressed in language drawn from the finite world.
—Austin Farrer, *Finite and Infinite*

On February 18, 1940, C. S. Lewis complained to his brother, Warnie, that even among Christians at Oxford, he was not able to escape "the horrible ferocity and grimness of modern thought," though of a sort for which he had been unprepared: "They've all been reading a dreadful man called Karl Barth, who seems the right opposite number to Karl Marx. . . . They don't think human reason or human conscience of any value at all," and worse, the young Barthians dismiss any understandable connection between God's goodness and human understanding: "There's no reason why God's dealings should appear just (let alone, merciful) to us" (*Letters*, 2.350–51). Lewis thought Barth part of an "abominable" tradition of Protestant theology that bifurcated the natural and supernatural to such a degree as to make them incomparable (*Letters*, 2.165n38). While the school of Barth might pull the liberal theologian up on his petards for questioning dogmatic orthodoxy, Lewis worried that their position amounted to a God entirely alien to human sensibilities. Such a God offered no recognizable ideal to which a Christian might even conform.[1]

In 1931, Austin Farrer had traveled to Bonn to study under Barth, but after two lectures, he had been unimpressed. He thought the Swiss theologian came across as an academic posing as a prophet (Curtis 1985, 97). Farrer's initial interest was understandable. Barth himself, in the 1932 preface to the English translation of his famous *The Epistle to the Romans* (1918), took the trouble to ask English readers who "have some notion or other of what is often called 'Dialectical Theology', or the 'Theology of Krisis', or 'Barthianism', or the like" to make an effort to approach the book without those preconceptions (vii). That Barth requested this says much about how widespread his influence had become in the 1930s, as well as that of other neoorthodox thinkers such as Emil Brunner, and likewise how formed was a certain conception of dialectical theology in the reading public. John Baillie could note that "nobody seems to talk theology these days without mentioning him" (qtd. Domestico 2017, 44). Even though Barth himself was evolving to a more restrained, even patristic approach, this did not alter how the strong *either-or* of his method shaped the theology of others.[2]

Be that as it may, by Farrer's 1948 Bampton Lectures, the Anglican priest was still expressing difficulty with theologians of Barth's stripe.[3] Essentially, as he pointed out, their position denied any possibility of human relation to God being investigated philosophically—to attempt this, for the Barthian, would be idolatry.[4] All communication about God is special communication from God and if so, then "they are no longer talking about the way in which God reveals himself to the philosopher, they are talking about the response which the revelation evokes" (*GV*, 20). But Farrer, like Lewis, insisted that this was a failure of nerve, "for if our cravenheartedness surrenders the ground of metaphysics, it will have surrendered the bridgehead which the supernatural liberator might land upon" (*GV*, 68). Farrer held that to capitulate the possibility of natural, philosophical language about God was finally to give up the truthfulness of the revealed language of scripture. The existential moment of proclamation would, by implication, be all that mattered, and it need have no relation to scripture's own logic, if indeed scripture would be allowed to possess any.

The history of Christian revelation is dependent upon visual, aural, and oral sign-making, but this, Farrer and Lewis held, does not render such language rationally empty or simply wish fulfillment. In particular, the controversial *analogia entis,* the analogy of being that draws comparisons and contrasts between creature and Creator,[5] informed both Farrer and Lewis's language about God, as well as their endeavor to understand the relationship between the Creator and creature. The questions surrounding the *analogia entis* were driven by three concerns regarding God, language, and human understanding.

Firstly, these were matters of language and rationality. The distance between God and ourselves makes difficult the discourse we use about God, and yet it is necessary for the believer to explain that difficulty's purpose. As Farrer put it, "You can no more catch God's infinity in a net of words, than . . . you can fish out of the sea the glories of the dying day" (*RF,* 47). When we say that God is all powerful, all knowing, and present everywhere, we are affirming the limits of what is imaginable, rather than what is conceivable. Each of the classic terms—omnipotence, omniscience, omnipresence—is a recognition of what we are not, a telling of the truth by extrapolation from our finitude to the eternal. Farrer understood that "all our thinking about God is infinitely short of his real nature" (*RF,* 45). We know that we do not know what the truly infinite would be like, yet we intuit something when we reflect upon it, even from our own limited power, knowledge, and presence. Thus, analogical thinking is neither irrational nor presumptuous.

Secondly, when God reveals himself to humans through means of symbol and language, what are we to conclude about God as such from images as diverse as fire and wind to rocks and lions to kings and lovers? If they cannot be said to directly describe the Infinite Being (or Being beyond being), what do they do, and under what circumstances? Lewis could point out that God is "the opaque centre of all existences," for in being the upholder of all things, his Being outstrips any comparison: "The positive quality in Him which repels these limitations is their only ground for all the negatives" (1960b, 88–89). Farrer, too, stressed that we may not discover God by virtue of our reason, and yet we must use our reason to approach what God reveals when he does so (*GV,* 15). That God addresses us at all in symbolic ways tells us that he too is a symbol-making being, and the *analogia* is by divine initiative.

Thirdly, if all language is a chain of symbolic references, is language meaningful, and given that it is, why? Why are we dependent upon the symbolic and metaphoric to say almost anything? And how do we continually say such things when we only know darkly? Does our language apprehend something of reality or only our ideals about it, and what does this reveal about cognition? Farrer would assert that the nature of thought itself is dialogical, imagistic, and analogical. We can only speak of a thing-in-itself by analogy (*RF,* 88). It is not theology alone that possesses the curious matter of speaking, as it were, over a mystery; "thought about things-in-themselves and selves has the same oddity, and the same curious combination of expressiveness and sterility" (*RF*, 90). Yet though one cannot establish by reason alone "the existence of the perfect knower," human rationality mimics and aspires to "'participation in the form' of perfect knowledge" (*FI*, 292). Even if language is analogical, it desires what is real.

Farrer and Lewis were not troubled that God uses our imaginations—such as that found in myths, images, analogies, and metaphors—to divulge himself to us, nor were they worried that such analogical language was always enacting a dance about deity. God's very nature could not be exhaustively or even adequately described, even while God uses language by which we may draw nearer to him. But Farrer and Lewis were concerned that the demise of natural theology spelled the demise of any meaningful language about God, or even from God. To defend analogic language, they had to keep in mind not only the objection from Barthianism that philosophical theology was guilty of "not allowing the self-revealing God to be his own interpreter," but also the objections from logical positivists that religious language was conceptually empty and from psychoanalytic critics that such language was only wish fulfillment or the collective unconscious (*RF*, 68). This threefold threat meant that the strong *either-or* of dialectic theology seemed to provide nontheistic critics with the evidence they needed that religious language was irrational and possibly neurotic.

THE DEBATE OVER ANALOGIES FOR GOD
AND NATURAL REASON

The twentieth-century debate about divine disclosure was concerned with not only the character of God, but also the natural ability of his creatures. Karl Barth infamously compared the *analogia entis* to the "invention of Antichrist," though this comment was often distorted outside its original context. Barth, in particular, was concerned about a misguided road back into the nineteenth-century Protestant theology that he had rejected. His radical rediscovery of the otherness of God had allowed him to short-circuit both a liberal theology that offered an entirely human Jesus and a modernist Christian ethic that seemed to always reflect the spirit of the age. Barth worried that the high trust of Vatican I in natural theology offered no safer ground, certainly no safer ground for a Protestant because I can see no third possibility between play with the *analogia entis*, legitimate only on Roman Catholic ground, between the greatness and the misery of a so-called natural knowledge of God in the sense of the *Vaticanum*, and a Protestant theology self-nourished at its own source, standing upon its own feet, and finally liberated from such secular misery, I can therefore only say No here. I regard the *analogia entis* as the invention of Antichrist, and think that because of it one can not become Catholic. Whereupon I at the same time allow myself to regard all other possible reasons for not becoming Catholic, as shortsighted and lacking in seriousness. (Barth [1936] 1963, I/1 x)

Barth was insistent that he was in no way disregarding the patristic teaching of the Church in matters such as the Trinity and the Virgin Birth. That many Protestants had rejected these key doctrines was only symptomatic of the anemic state of Protestant theology in general. "Secular misery" was emblematic of Christianity's inability to protect itself against the empty categories of modernity, and he thought Vatican I's stance would not stand the test of modernity either. He insisted that the *analogia entis* would lead to "the circumvention and neutralisation of the decisive character of revelation and faith" (Barth [1936] 1963, I/1 44).

Barth's early dialectical theology may have studied but did not easily trust human philosophy. Indeed, his Jerusalem was overtly hostile to an Athens of natural rationality. Only grace makes any knowledge of God possible, and only by the analogy of faith found in Jesus Christ may one know of God, much less know God experientially. For Barth, there was no natural disposition toward receiving divine revelation, no potential for obedience. Revelation's character is such that it is wholly other than any human capacity. It is entirely a divine inbreaking. To speak of any similarity between the Creator and the creature is to risk introducing "equality in the inequality" and to begin to erase the line between God and creation (Barth [1936] 1963, I/1 274). The oft-cited maxim of Thomas Aquinas, "grace does not destroy nature but perfects it," was at odds with Barth's Reformation position that grace must abolish nature. For Barth, there could be no compatibility between divine disclosure and human ability, the latter entirely corrupted by sin. This is not to say that Barth had no place for philosophical language and history, but it was to be carefully circumscribed (Guarino 2005, 293–95). He held that "analogy is another example of fallen nature seeking to compromise and minimize the gratuitous gifts of God" (Guarino 2005, 221), but was that actually the case?

Barth's most famous opponent in the debate, Erich Przywara, argued that the *analogia entis* was more than a logical form; it was the shape of our own creatureliness.[6] That which is finite and temporal is grounded upon the infinite and eternal Creator. Language about God is analogical, not comprehensive. Przywara shared with Barth a concern that the difference between the transcendent God and dependent creation always be kept inviolable. Only in God are existence and essence in complete unity. As a Roman Catholic theologian, Przywara appealed to the Fourth Lateran Council's formula: "For between creator and creature there can be noted no similarity so great that a greater dissimilarity cannot be seen between them" (Fourth Lateran Council, article 2). Przywara argued that the *analogia entis* made it possible to acknowledge both the transcendence and immanence of God without vainly claiming to comprehend the divine nature. Analogical language, instead, was an example of how any attempt at describing God would fall short, yet of necessity must be made, and its limitation was itself part of its truth.

The *analogia,* in turn, provided a way for Przywara to describe the human condition as "essence in-and-beyond existence" or as "open upwards" (2014, 189–91; 1935, 29–34). Humans are a "suspended middle," yet not a self-stabilizing one. Such a cosmological anthropology means that God has perfect freedom toward his creation, and the creation only bears his image because God freely makes it so. Creatures, by definition, *receive.* Yet in being the similitude of God, persons also hunger for something more than themselves. To be temporal is to be moving in time, not yet complete in essence—a becoming. This means that just as language about God must always be holding in paradoxical mystery the transcendence and immanence of God, so the human condition reflects our limitations and aspirations.

Analogical language realizes that what can be said of God always reveals an aspiration toward God, as well as the limitation of any words to do justice to him. The same is true of the human experience of the truth. The creature's temporal oscillation among the finite and infinite never resolves yet ever forces us onward to the perfected end. Such is why all persons implicitly desire truth and excellence. We are living analogies: "It is endless striving towards God as endless experience of His (absolute) Infinity in the creation; endless striving in the presence of God and endless adoration of His absolute Infinity above all creation . . . seen in the rhythmic movement between the intimacy of love and aloofness of reverence" (Przywara 1935, 62). According to Przywara, the history of philosophy is emblematic of the human condition. As persons, we fluctuate between the general and particulars of our existence, as well as the subjective a priori and objective a posteriori of knowledge, and this movement reveals much about the aspirations and failures of our worldviews (Przywara 2014, 307–14).

Both Barth and Przywara understood that in the modern age, language about God was confrontational, and they both held that any language about God was a condescension to our creaturehood. Yet each was also concerned that the other's position seemed to erase the proper distance between Creator and creature. For Barth, the *analogia entis* was an attempt to replace grace with a preexistent obligation of God to humanity and, therefore, another species of failed natural theology. He particularly distrusted Przywara's language of "open upwards" as assigning too great an innate capacity to the creature. Given that the human being "is to be strictly understood as a reality willed and placed by God . . . alongside God's reality," then "this continuity cannot belong to the creature itself but only to the Creator *in his* relation to the creature" (qtd. McCormack 2011, 103). The relationship of salvation must be a unilateral one, offered and completed by God's action.

In contrast, Przywara objected that Barth's system could not adequately account for the relationship of the Creator with his creation. He charged Barth with a denial of human freedom and with a cosmology in which God is the only significant actor (2014, i349). If Barth was trying to navigate a middle course between liberal Protestantism and Roman Catholicism, Przywara was trying to find a path between the extremes of pantheism and "theopanism," the latter a term he coined. Pantheism, Przywara charged, could be the end result of any philosophical system that accorded human beings mastery over their destinies because "God" within such systems was reduced to the evolutionary ideal. Theopanism, on the other hand, was any system that made the creation a practical illusion, a shadow play that God carries out without any human action (Przywara 2014, 165–67). It was not the analogy of being that would lead to modernist theological compromise, Przywara insisted, but a failure to explain why such movements were temptations to begin with. He appealed to the Incarnation as holding together Creator and creature in what could only be intuited in a rhythm of mysticism, and he worried that the radical distrust of the creature as found in Reformation thought led to a hatred of creation, and finally to antimaterialism and/or atheism.

This debate within modernity about the place of analogy and creatureliness shaped Austin Farrer's thought directly and, perhaps more indirectly, C. S. Lewis's. Its general concern was part of their common project to recover a thick, sacred cosmos. Just as both men in their treatment of myth held to a personhood that straddles the subconscious and the supernatural, so they both saw in analogy an understanding of the place that reason and faith share. Human illumination reaches above and beyond the primeval because it is oriented to the transcendent. Farrer and Lewis held that human knowing points to an Infinite Knower, and that this "joint" is real and not psychoanalytic projection, and yet by its very nature it is ontologically unspecifiable, not a "something" in the world in quite the same way as any other creaturely thing (Morris 1994). For both men, it was not an idolatrous question to consider how God had made rational and bodily persons for himself; it was one that was near the heart of their longings. The bridge between human consciousness and divine disclosure was real yet hidden, ever both an invitation to and an awareness of our limitations, and by this pendulum, persons learn much about God, but even more about themselves. There is simply no other way to be a creature than this.

THEOLOGICAL ANALOGY AND DISCLOSURE IN FARRER'S THOUGHT

It is perhaps not surprising that C. S. Lewis would label Karl Barth a modern, even if at the opposite end of the spectrum from Marx. Austin Farrer and Lewis were both attempting to stand with the older classic tradition of metaphysics, and Barth's heavy break between grace and nature must have struck Lewis in 1940 as another degradation of creation, not unlike materialism or positivism. Naturally, Farrer as a philosophical theologian engaged the question of religious language in a more detailed way than Lewis. Farrer sought to work out the relationship of faith and reason over the course of his career, and his own position was bound to be compared to other popular ones. To some it seemed as if traditionalists like Farrer would have been allies with the existential theologians or perhaps with the Neo-Scholastics. In the 1930s and 1940s, the broad Anglican establishment had to negotiate between the new movements of Reformed neoorthodoxy and continental Neo-Scholasticism. Both movements shared an opposition to theological liberalism, and some felt they could be fellow conservative travelers. This left more than one option for a thinker like Farrer. Julian Hartt would recall that at the time of Farrer's *The Glass of Vision*, it was not entirely clear whether the Anglican priest was mapping out a different course than a Thomist such as Jacques Maritain,[7] for Farrer was clearly siding with natural proposition over fideist experience (Hartt 1983, 12–14). But even this was not evident to everyone; some saw Farrer as a potential synthesizer of Barth and Scholasticism (Kerr 2002, 23).[8]

Farrer, fairly early in his career, was drawn to the dynamic aspect of Erich Przywara's thought. In his review of *Polarity*, A. C. Bouquet's 1935 translation of Przywara's *Religionphilosophie katholischer Theologie*, Farrer saw in the

German theologian a shift of accent from that of typical Second Scholasticism. Farrer supposed that while Przywara likely agreed with the traditional Thomistic notions of casualty, his emphasis was upon the *analogia* as a structure that holds together human attempts at understanding with the relationship between these and God. Farrer insisted that the danger was in how often philosophers isolated one facet of existence or knowledge and made it a key to a philosophical distortion. They build a system upon the immanent sense of self-constraint, the transcendent sense of the above and beyond, or the temporal trajectory of time and its obligation to become more. The actual key is to know that this is divinely given, and Farrer thought that Przywara's "rhythm of alteration" and its necessity of a "dialectical oscillation" was an inspired response: "The tension, accepted as inevitable, remains none the less actual: the religious mind experiences both a necessity and an inability to grasp the reality of God and creature together, and falls into a rhythm of alternation between the two. . . . the subjective unity of the whole religious consciousness and the reality of natural revelation, and yet the absolute uniqueness of the supernatural revelation in Christ" (Farrer 1935, 362–63). Analogy offered a means of framing the complexity of human and divine differences. Farrer noted that, for Przywara, the human mind is "dynamically conceived" even as it seeks a unity of rationality and experience. The relationship between the Infinite God and the world is one source of perpetual tension and sought resolution, while the impulse to grasp such a Being and the inevitable failure to do so is another.

Farrer was especially drawn to how Przywara mapped the structure of such an interplay, employing the *analogia entis* because humans are "unconscious analogiasts" (Farrer 1935, 362). The success of this approach was to recognize that the classic tensions in modern philosophy can be explained by the analogical nature of human attempts at truth. Przywara's model offered a trifold shape for analogy—the epistemology of deduction and induction; the ontology of the eternal and the material; and the axiological of the potential and the actual. This tridirectional experience helped prepare for action and prayer, volitionally and not just apprehensionally. Przywara's discussion, Farrer noted, was more than just a rational theological solution; it was also a pattern of contemplation and worship. Przywara described this movement as "a twofold unity: (i) Experience of the infinity of God *in* the endless rhythm of life, and (ii) Adoration of the same infinity *above* the endless rhythm of life" (1935, 62). And because such a creaturely rhythm is in response to the Creator, the elements of action, contemplation, experience, and comprehension, even if parseable as separable movements, "have a factual interconnecxion"

(Przywara 1935, 47). A rightly ordered person, then, is a better answer to philosophy's modernistic conflicts than a more airtight system of ideas.

Whatever attraction Farrer may have felt for Barth in 1931, here he concluded that Przywara had the better of the argument. Farrer insisted that Przywara had addressed the theologically strong objection from the Barthian *either-or* in two important ways: (1) with Barth, Przywara agreed: the liberal dialectic of history is not enough, one needs the unique revelation of God in Jesus Christ; and yet (2) against Barth, the *analogia* itself points to "the supernatural relation of man to God" by crossing through the shifting oscillation of the self and its attempts at truth. Philosophical history's numerous schools of thought are all partial answers to the creaturely analogical condition of existence and essence. The inability to resolve questions, such as transcendence and immanence, subjectivity and objectivity, the a priori and a posteriori, the ideal and the real, or the infinite and the finite, was itself a sign that our essence is both *in-and-beyond* our existence. Humans are not able to statically insist on one or the other, and when they do, various philosophical heresies arise. Farrer's excitement at this model was rather palpable: "May we not find in this doctrine what we want—the subjective unity of the whole religious consciousness of man and the reality of natural revelation"? Even granting that consciousness of Being (in purely natural terms) still has a divine purpose in its variety of approaches, the revelation of God in Christ can be recognized as superior in what it communicates because creatures in the suspended middle have a direction forward in time—a divine destiny as to what they are becoming (Farrer 1935, 363).[9] Thus, Christ revealed by his Incarnation for what end the human potential for obedience had always been intended.

As his philosophical theology developed, Farrer assessed this radical dependence as a measure of that which is beyond us. The finite is how we begin to know of the infinite, and yet the infinite is the condition of finite being itself. Knowledge of the higher depends upon our knowledge of the lower, and yet the higher is not measured in any way by the lower (RF, 51, 53). The radical dependence on the creature, as well as the aseity (i.e., the absolute difference) of God, preserves the creature's individual existence. We are not God; neither are we independent from God. The immanence and transcendence of human consciousness each assume and depend upon the other, and are each finally dependent upon God rather than us. As Eric Mascall observed, in Farrer's thought, natural and revealed theology were contrasted by being both the "natural and supernatural self-communication of God" (1956, 39). They operate together because of the creaturely nature of language and understanding. We are always close to and distant from God, and yet the nature of human becoming is only understood by the knowledge that we were created for the supernatural end. And if we grasp this, we will avoid positing a world that is pantheistic, as well as a world that is theopanist (Przywara 2014, 165).

In Farrer's first and most Scholastic volume, *Finite and Infinite*, he passed over the more traditional Thomist scales of nature for a simpler internal scale of desired perfection (Eaton 1980, 9–10). It is our own inclination toward our better selves and yet our deep awareness of this impossibility that help us to apprehend that there is One Who Is Perfect. In turn, what we do apprehend of God via that of nonhuman creaturely activity we nonetheless know by virtue of our own action and apperception (*FI*, 41–48).[10] Both human understanding and will suggest by their limitations that there is a Perfection beyond them. Thus, our aspirations bespeak of God but cannot prove the divine existence, including "*delight* in their fulfillment, *goodness* in their realisation of their own principles, *love* in their pure interest in and fostering of their objects, and the enjoyment of *beauty* in the contemplation and creation of the forms of things" (*FI*, 52).

The Anglican priest summed up the fundamentals of *Finite and Infinite* in his 1947 paper "Does God Exist?" for Lewis's Socratic Club at Oxford. Farrer stressed that "we never know the unique by mere inference from other things nor God by mere inference from the world," and yet we come to see that "a Godless account of things is incomplete." Farrer was making "an argument through which the dependence of the world on God may make itself felt by our minds" (*RF*, 39). Human existence is of a special sort in that we experience it as self-determined and yet as becoming something more than we are now. Our very open-endedness point to a God. Dynamic beings as we are suggest that there must be one who "has caught up with his own perfection, who is all the good he sees, and sees all the good he is" (*RF*, 44). This possibility intuits that there may be one (i.e., God) beyond the desired perfection by whom it is measured. We desire perfection; there is likely one who is just that.

As Farrer pointed out, none of this can actually grasp the Infinite God, but it does gesture toward him. It is the unlimitedness of God that teaches us our limitations by drawing us upward to the apex of apprehension, and that apex (however loosely located) is a sign both of our limitations and of God's limitlessness. Our finitude of desire and becoming suggests one who transcends it, yet this, too, is not a proof of God's existence, as if we had the means to provide one. "If God might be comprehended, he would not be God" (*RF*, 46).[11] Apprehending God (always a gift of grace in the last analysis) was not the same as a more extensive comprehension.

For Farrer, it was such a middle place between "adequacy and complete frustration" that analogical language sought to occupy (*RF*, 45). How to go about analyzing this analogy? The two kinds of analogies discussed by Thomas Aquinas—the analogy of attribution and the analogy of proportionality—are logical descriptions with epistemic and metaphysical implications. In the analogy of attribution, the two parts for comparison share a common quality.[12] Yet, as Aquinas stressed, such a triangulated analogy will not do when we seek to compare God and human. God—who is Being himself or even beyond Being—is the ground of the finite being of all created things. The Creator and his creatures do not share existence as if it were a third independent quality. The same is true for any quality by which we speak of God—his truth, goodness, beauty, wisdom, and so forth. Perhaps this was why Farrer in his discussion of analogy quickly turned to the analogy of proportionality, a comparison of four parts:

> When we are talking about God's wisdom we are talking about something which we do not directly or properly know, and of which we are forced to judge from our knowledge of our own. So to say that God is wise is to say that something stands to God's being as our wisdom stands to our being. It would mean nothing to say this, unless we had some understanding (however formal) of the relation or 'proportion' between our being and God's. (*RF*, 66–67)

To assert that (*human wisdom* is to *humanity* as *divine wisdom* is to *God*) is to offer that the relation on each side of the analogy can be meaningfully compared. It does not, however, mean that human or divine wisdom partakes of an independent wisdom (apart from God) by which either can be judged. We are instead to try to understand God's wisdom from the finite place of our own. Farrer insists that this is not a simple comparison of two relations. Instead, there are actually four proportions involved because how divine wisdom relates to God is different than how human wisdom relates to ourselves. We cannot know what the fourth part, the mode of divine wisdom (viz., the divine *esse*), is; only God can know this, and yet this difference does not consign us to an equivocal distance without meaning. God's wisdom can be apprehended even at the moment that we realize it is beyond us.

Instead of being a poor phenomenon that we can exhaustively master, the analogy offers us the rich shape of a mystery, which is that of an intuited gesture toward and away from the divine nature (*FI*, 51–59). We cannot really know what it is for God to be without accidents, nontemporal, or self-sufficient; we can only draw analogies from our limited existence, and yet these limitations open us to the creaturely energy in the act of thinking (circuitously) about God: "In this act there is no rest . . . we have never arrived; as we seem on the point to do so, our thought evaporates in the emptiness of mathematical unity, or . . . passes into an ecstasy and ceases to be thinking" (*FI*, 60). Exploring analogies is a move toward identity, and yet analogies work by negation—they are as much about how the analogues differ as how they supposedly concur (Eaton 1980, 136–37). But since we are dealing with the absoluteness of God, we draw near only to discover the incredible differences. As Farrer adds," If we wish to think on, we must return humbly to the bottom of the ladder, and climb again" (*FI*, 60).

Farrer insisted that our epistemic inquiry, our own finite knowing and naming, only make sense against the background of an Infinite Creator. As Jeffrey C. Eaton has noted, in Farrer's early thought, the three analogies of divine essence, creativity, and independence are drawn from our finite existence, and yet by their finiteness they speak of an Infinite One. At the same time, they cannot contain or explain God without compromising themselves as finite things (Eaton 1980, 5–6). God's creation must be made by him, yet his creation must not be reduced to him, nor be a necessary act that God has not freely (and lovingly) chosen.[13]

Admittedly, Farrer's position on reason and faith would also be complicated by his own evolving understanding. Scholars of Farrer all agree that over a thirty-year career, development took place in the Anglican priest's thought: he moved from a quasi-Thomist position to a stronger stress on biblical typology, to more voluntarist views of God's agency and the will.[14] The very "suspended" nature of rational analogy meant that Farrer need not, indeed, could not have taken a hard-and-fast position on the matter. Analogy could commit neither to a purely natural set of claims nor to a fideism of utter equivocation. Even if analogy was ostensibly an aspect of the natural reason of human creatures, it already contained an instability that could draw the believer in both directions at various times and for various reasons.

In the 1958 preface to the second edition of *Finite and Infinite,* Farrer came to understand that he "could not [any longer] be content to derive the structure of being from the grammar of description" (*FI*, ix). "Every grammar is a grammar of speech, but speech is human being, and uniquely revelatory of the rest of it" (*FI*, ix–x). And yet he still held that the only way to think of anything else, including the Infinite Creator, is "through an extension of our self-understanding" (*FI*, x). If anything, Farrer would come to understand that all thought is analogical, not just the *analogia entis*. As J. N. Morris points out, Farrer was already in *Finite and Infinite* bridging the distinction between rational and revealed theology: "The personal character of the cosmologi-cal relation could only be grasped by analogy" (Morris 1994, 578). He would move from a stress on the *analogia entis* to an *analogia opeantis* (Eaton 1980, 54), but never away from analogy itself.[15]

Such a constant, career-long stress enabled Farrer to hold a nuanced un-derstanding of nature and grace, and it is this framework that held together all stages of Farrer's philosophical theology and exegetical exploration. The *analogia entis* has often been referred to as the analogy from creation. Grace is neither deserved nor achieved, yet the condition of creatureliness does still tell of a Creator. The "nature" of something, as understood in Christian terms, is always based in that of creation, and therefore as the creature of God, one's nature is made with a potential and orientation toward grace. Such an analogy is not a product of human reason alone, for it acknowledges a grace prevenient within God's good world. This recognition of God's gifting his creatures with a certain orientation is never the same as their possessing an obligation from their being created or as being a category of equal and independent standing with God.[16] Like Przywara, Farrer came to conceive of humans as oscillating in their creational existence while the infinite, perfect God condescended to them even as they aspired toward the divine. Analogical language is true yet always manifests inherent creaturely limitations. We know and experience God in this world truly and yet mysteriously because he has first given of himself.

THE BODY AND ANALOGY IN LEWIS

C. S. Lewis understood these truths and explored them in key moments in his career. He, for example, pointed out the nonparallelism of God and lan-guage in one of his last works, *Letters to Malcolm*. Lewis clearly shared much with Austin Farrer with regard to the *analogia entis* and recognized the truth of the analogy of proportionality. God's being is not "somehow parallel to my own. . . . He is always both within us and over against us. Our reality is so much from His reality as He, moment by moment, projects into us," so that deeper grace comes to us the more it becomes our own (LM, 68–69). And Lewis, too, understood some of the basic concerns that Farrer shared with Przywara. It is only in the balance of the analogy, in the suspended middle of creatureliness, that the worshipper can avoid either pole's temptation—de-ception by equating God with his creation or despair by giving up any cre-ational language by which to approach him. Both images and abstractions are, in one sense, not the "real" thing: "Both are equally concessions; each singly misleading, and the two together mutually corrective" (*LM*, 21). Yet they are a necessity. By no other normal means can temporal creatures approach the infinite Creator. Lewis, following Owen Barfield, put it this way: "On the one hand, the man who does not regard God as other than himself cannot be said to have a religion at all. On the other hand, if I think God other than myself in the same way in which my fellow men, and objects in general, are other than myself, I am beginning to make Him an idol" (*LM*, 68). The oscillation of the suspended middle is the very stuff of devotion. Divine transcendence and divine immanence are both necessary elements of how we contemplate God and his creation. As Lewis observed, borrowing a phrase from Charles Williams, "Therefore of each creature we can say, 'This also is Thou: neither is this Thou'" (*LM*, 74).

These were not just conclusions Lewis reached at the end of his life. They were also something he explored earlier in his fiction. In *Till We Have Faces*, the old priest of Ungit insists that Greek philosophy's attempt to explain the gods clearly keeps rationalists from really understanding them. "I know that they dazzle our eyes and flow in and out of one another like eddies on a river," and this amorphous character means that no analogy is truly successful in summing up divine action. "Why should the Accursed not be both the best and the worst?" (*TWHF*, 50). The Fox in the world of the dead reaches similar conclusions. Ungit has a thousand faces, he concedes, and "the real gods [are] more alive," for they are not "mere thought or words" (*TWHF*, 295). But this is not just true of pagan, pre-Christian intimations; in various places throughout the Chronicles of Narnia, Aslan takes on multiple forms to express aspects of himself. When the crew of the *Dawn Treader* is trapped in the waters of Dark Island, Aslan arrives as an albatross full of light to lead them to safety (*VDT*, 159–60). He is not only the various lions that force Shasta and Bree and Aravis and Hwin together and forward on their journey, he is also the comforting cat who stays by Shasta's side among the tombs (*HB*, 82, 85–86). In Aslan's Country, Aslan meets Edmund, Lucy, and Eustace as a lamb who offers them a breakfast of fish. "I am the great Bridge Builder," he tells them, and they learn they were brought to Narnia so they might know him better by another name in England (*VDT*, 214–16). By such examples, Lewis took advantage of traditional Christian imagery to bring out aspects of Christ's character, yet he also implied the distance between any picture and who God is.

Lewis, in his Pentecost sermon, "Transposition" (May 22, 1944), went about this proximity and distance in a different way, and here, too, he shared with Farrer the realization that the bridge to God is a graced one. Indeed, our creation itself is a gift from the Creator. This tie can be thought, but human names for it are only

analogies from human experience. Lewis knew this notion played into the hands
of critics, both those who saw language of the spiritual as nonsense and those
who saw it as reducible to psychoanalytic projection. They could charge that
mystics use erotic metaphors only because they are really verbalizing displaced
sexual urges, or that a "revelation from beyond Nature" suspiciously employs
"nothing more than selections from terrestrial experience" (WG, 94). Lewis's
strategy was to point out that we have aesthetic experiences of many types for
which we must, as a means of description, fall back upon physical sensations, and
the sensations judged as sensations can tell us little about their higher meaning.
Many, such as a flutter in the diaphragm, are transferrable across a spectrum of
different feelings. Neural responses, likewise, reveal no real difference between
a report of a tragedy and a response to a comic opera. "If the richer system is to
be represented in the poorer at all, this can only be by giving each element in
the poorer system more than one meaning" (WG, 99). The analogy of musical
transposition suggests both connection and distance.

Lewis widened his sense of analogical understanding to include not only
language, but also bodily experiences. He suggested that the rapture of the
mystic may physically manifest itself like that of a romantic lover, but the actual occurrence is hardly the same. The one who has had only erotic moments
may be tempted to doubt the more spiritual relations of the mystic, but that
hardly renders such skepticism assured. The same can be said for even those
experiences that we aspire to and yet of which we have only some hint: "At the
worst, we know enough of the spiritual to know that we have fallen short of
it, as if the [two-dimensional] picture knew enough of the three-dimensional
world to be aware that it was flat" (WG, 106). The Christian's hope for the
Beatific Vision, in this world, is going to be based upon weak temporal existence, fluctuating moments that will one day be swallowed up by a far greater
glory. For now, we can only intuit it in our imaginations and in our "nerves
and muscles" (WG, 108).[17]

In The Lion, the Witch, and the Wardrobe, the very mention of Aslan's name
has an imaginative and therefore bodily impact on the four children, even before they meet him. The meaning is dreamlike, "either a terrifying one which
turns the whole dream into a nightmare or else a lovely meaning too lovely
to put into words." Edmund responds with horror; Peter with courage; Susan
senses beauty; and Lucy knows she is at the beginning of summer or a holiday
(LWWR, 64–65). Each experience can be judged as sensations responding to
repressed impulses, or they can be understood as superlative impulses that
the mind and body prepare for and ennoble. Thus, the four children bodily
transpose imaginative responses into a higher register.

Lewis learned something of analogical understanding and bodily experience from Edwyn Bevan's 1934/35 Gifford Lectures, *Symbolism and Belief*.[18] Bevan was particularly good at tracing how the bodily phenomena of height, time, light, and breath manifest themselves in religious language, and he mustered much anthropological research. Bevan weighed in against reductive theories of "anthropological intimidation" that tried to treat bodily analogies as vestigial holdovers from "primitive delusion" (Bevan 1938, 51), and because of this, he felt it was just about impossible to describe transcendence without the bodily consciousness of spatial metaphors, of weight, height, and depth (Bevan 1938, 68).[19] Likewise, Lewis could observe that someone who says "God out there" does not mean "spatially external to the universe" but that space and time are not limitations to God, and thus in no way exhaust his Being. We can speak not only of God above us but also below us in the sense of ground or of holding us while also above us (*GD*, 184).

It is fitting, for example, that as Lucy matures, so Aslan grows larger (*PC*, 148). At times, she cannot quite pin down his size. Perhaps he was comparable to a cart horse or to an elephant (*VDT*, 107–8). Lewis also insisted that this is true of anything noncorporeal. There is no way to speak of that which is beyond our senses except as if it were comprehendible by our senses: "All speech about supersensibles is, and must be, metaphorical in the highest degree" (Lewis 1960b, 73). Lewis admitted that the symbol does not always address the physical experience of the sacramental moment. A sacrament—for example, such as the Eucharist—is a sign beyond a sign, and there the bodily and psychological sensation "digests, transforms, transubstantiates" the sacred meaning, so that it becomes part of us physiologically (WG, 102–3). But even in the more general sense, the bodily and the metaphorical are not that far removed from one another.

None of this, however, was meant to in any way downgrade the Incarnation of Christ. Lewis certainly understood and believed the classic patristic doctrine that Christ is both fully God and fully human. Bree the horse's docetic belief in *The Horse and His Boy* must be corrected by Aslan. Bree cannot believe that Aslan could really be a lion, that he is one of the creatures that Bree has been afraid of all his life, and Bree insists that the analogical language only means "he's as strong as a lion" or "as fierce as a lion," and not "a Beast just like the rest of us," But when Aslan manifests himself, the doubting Thomas must touch and smell Aslan: "I am a true Beast" (HB, 191–93). Here, the analogical and the bodily meet, not only doctrinally but mystically. For the Christian reader in particular, the difference between this account of Aslan and that of the Incarnate and resurrected Christ is still very present, and yet the tale makes manifest a real claim on the imagination and upon the bodily sensations, for we too may respond to the possibility of Aslan's paws and whiskers.

Nor does this bodily experience imply that in this world analogies have no limitations. Eschatologically speaking, how can the gods "meet us face to face till we have faces?" (*TWHF*, 294). Lewis learned firsthand with the cancer and death of his wife Joy Davidman that the experience of loss and anguish could also be a trans-substantative and analogous encounter, though one by way of negation. His pseudonymously published journal, *A Grief Observed*, narrates a process in which not only do his illusions about his real wife suffer a "knocking down of the house of cards," but suffering does the necessary damage to his idols of God. God is "the great iconoclast." Indeed, "all reality is iconoclastic," for in the end we need actuality rather than our self-created, comforting falsities (*GO*, 66–68). Lewis's journal was a struggle among analogies. In his grief, he wondered if God is a Cosmic Sadist and Vivisectionist (*GO*, 30, 38) or a Great Surgeon with painful healing tools (*GO*, 40–42, 64–65). It was his loss of Joy ("H.") that taught him of his need for the actual God. Just as marriage taught him that a real woman was more complexly rich than any fantasy, so her loss reminded him that God is more than wishful reductions of him: "I need Christ, not something that resembles Him. I want H., not something that is like her. . . . Yes, and also not my idea of my neighbour, but my neighbour" (*GO*, 65, 67).

Both Lewis and Farrer saw in the *analogia entis* a way to speak about the rationality of God language, and they each learned that such language shows us to be limited and aspiring creatures. As temporal, bodily beings, we think, act, and yearn in ways that give evidence for our finitude and our being drawn toward Infinity. If analogical language about God speaks a true word to our imaginations, such language also reminds us that we are temporal and driven by broken and fallible desires. Lewis and Farrer found it necessary, therefore, to reply to those who would reduce these desires for the Infinite to psychoanalytic wish fulfillment. They did this by acknowledging some insight in such theories in regard to our consciousness, even as they also found ways to argue for that which transcends the psychological.

CONSCIOUSNESS AND ARCHETYPES

Sigmund Freud's claim that the Heavenly Father is only wish fulfillment, a neurotic compensation for disappointment with an earthly father, was one example of the analogy of proportion turned in upon itself. While C. S. Lewis and Austin Farrer answered psychoanalysis from their differing fields—Lewis as a literary historian and critic; Farrer as a philosophical theologian and scriptural exegete—they both agreed that psychoanalytic criticism was too reductive, especially regarding the aesthetic and descriptive value of metaphoric language. The examination of consciousness with its "luminous apex" of rationality, as Farrer had labeled it in his Bampton Lectures, need not ignore its psychological and/or uncanny depths, but then neither should it reduce higher intuitions to a flat realm of evolved and sublimated survival instincts. Instead, the suspended middle of human existence takes on a bodily, epistemic layering. Farrer posited a "doctrine of the cone" (GV, 30), a model of cognition in which even if intelligence draws off the subconscious, it reworks the material not for regression or transference but for the incandescent possibility of beauty and truth. "Two bundles of mysterious phenomena," that of top-level inspiration and that of bottom-level uncanniness, he noted, may both play a role in that of poetic images, yet trying to trace powerful symbols back to their origins is mostly a nil-sum game (GV, 31).

Farrer's Glass of Vision was certainly not closed to theories that posit the historical evolution of the mind, which with its development has learned to place and control the experimenta vaga of earlier human consciousness (GV, 32), yet Farrer distrusted psychoanalysts "with their investigations into the plumbing and the cellarage of our volitional life," which to him owed much to "rhetoric" and "not to science" (GV, 28). He also distanced himself more particularly from a Freudianism (perhaps Otto Rank's theory of birth trauma), which claimed we may have some vague memory of our births. We have no such memory of our conception or our creation, Farrer insisted. "I am not aware of God's creative act unmediated. I am only aware of it, in so far as it is mediated to me by my own created existence, or by some other created existence" (GV, 75). Farrer understood that the psychoanalyst would likely not take much of his exploration of human image and divine inspiration seriously, but he argued that even considered from a natural perspective, neither Shakespeare nor Jeremiah was explainable in reductive terms.[20] Psyches have sources that are unconscious in nature, but also a "greatness" in their construction and artistry (GV, 106). Farrer held that the mind is recognized "by the highest principle in its hierarchic constitution, not by the indefinite multitude of subsidiary elements" (GV, 29). Mind is consciousness and rationality, not the obscure aspects that may at some unrecognized level help feed its creative expression. The hierarchical shape of consciousness is itself a kind of analogy of our attempts to know and name God. Just as our own apex draws our instincts upward, so the brilliant beauty of God draws us upward to luminosity even as it dazzles and overwhelms us.

For both Lewis and Farrer, Freud's methods lost the pleasure of diversity and complexity. Reduction does not explain well why there should be such diversity to begin with or why it brings us joy that is richer than the need for a stoic tragedy. According to Peter Gay, Freud's tendency toward reductionism was a need for simplicity of explanation—his wanting a single key (2008, 91). Freud always took the rich and saturated and sought to break it as poor phenomena. The beloved always became a disease.[21] Farrer thought that if psychoanalysis were seen for what it actually asserted, it was simply not serious enough. Religious consciousness obviously fulfilled "some pretty widely needed function," but the reductive nature of psychoanalytic analysis failed due to its lack of scope—it actually explained too little. Farrer insisted that "a view that can anchor religion in a function essential to our very existence is the most plausible of all." Analogical understanding was indeed more plausible because it treated seriously "the positive testimony of the devout about the objective character of what they experience" (RF, 16).

Lewis famously pushed back against this kind of reductionism in his Narnian tale The Silver Chair. The wicked Queen of Underland attempts to convince the Marsh-wiggle Puddleglum, Prince Rilian, and the children Eustace and Jill that Narnia is only a trick of their imaginations. They have created a thing called "the sun" based on the lamp in the room and projected a dream of the lion Aslan on the basis of cats. The witch queen charges them with analogical bad faith: "You see? When you try to think out clearly what this sun must be, you cannot tell me. You can only tell me it is like the lamp" (SC, 155). She insists to them that their "make believe" world is only made of versions of the "real world, this world of mine, which is the only world" (SC, 157). And yet, of course, she is lying. She knows there is no other way to refer to an unknown than by a known.[22]

Lewis held that the philosophical views of both Freud and Jung were at odds with Christian morality, mostly given the grounds upon which they based the origins of right and wrong, yet he did not think that psychoanalysis as a diagnosis of neurotic behavior was itself off limits. Pathological behavior was a disease to be cured, not a sin in need of repentance (MX, 84–85). Lewis held a similar mixed view about Freudian readings of literature. He was willing to concede that there could be a servile (i.e., neurotic), as well as free (i.e., creative) artistic impulse. Yet he was insistent that Freud's theory of singular bound symbols, while it might have therapeutic purpose, had no bearing on aesthetics, and what Farrer had argued about religious consciousness, Lewis said was true of aesthetic experience: "If we are disappointed at finding only sex where we looked for something more, then surely the something more had value for us?" (SLE, 291–92, 295).

Lewis's last novel *Till We Have Faces* (1956) was a more complex exploration of this matter. He fashioned a novel of historical realism that offered the supposed real events behind the classic myth of Cupid and Psyche. Set in the third century BC during the Hellenistic period before the rise of Rome as a Mediterranean power, the story takes place in the fictional kingdom of Glome, somewhere in "barbarian" Scythia, either in South Russia or near the Danube and the Balkans (Myers 2018, 163–67). Lewis expected his readers to read according to the genre of the historical novel. Unlike his Narnian fantasy, where magic is real, or his science fiction books, where the generic friction between the mythic and that of the interplanetary is collapsed, fantastic events in *Till We Have Faces* always leave open the possibility of a naturalistic explanation. The reader must decide how much trust to extend to the first-person narrator Orual.

At the same time, the book practices another kind of historical correlation. It employs a typological structure in which Greco-Pagan religion and Greek Stoic philosophy echo the concerns of the Jewish and Christian faiths. The dreams of Orual can be read as psychoanalytic expressions of her lifelong pride, envy, and resentment, and they do allow her to express these, yet they also transcend themselves as analogies of greater supernatural possibilities. A reader may choose to treat everything as a projection of the narrator's anxieties and repressions, but something more wondrous is lost: "What other answer would suffice? Only words, words; to be led out to battle against other words. Long did I hate you, long did I fear you" (*TWHF*, 308). Here, Lewis brings together the typology of his myth theory with the suspended middle of his analogical experience with God, and yet the matter is left with the reader to believe or deny.

A similar quandary faced the scriptural exegete. Farrer treated archetypes as a special category of metaphor, as divinely revealed and yet historically contingent (*GV*, 86). He held that the prophetic created a sense of history that is not progressive in the modernist sense. "The reason why archetypes become dangerous is that they favour dogmatisms," and yet this is one of their necessary functions (*GV*, 87). Certain scriptural archetypes within a historical context are chosen by God to reveal himself, so we cannot reduce them to simple human attempts at the divine nor can we decide just any archetype equally able to disclose the divine: "Faith discerns not the images, but what the images signify: and yet we cannot discern it except *through* the images" (*GV*, 93). Farrer was not particularly bothered that human consciousness played a significant role in this: "The First Cause [can find] his second or instrumental cause in some working of my natural phantasy. If . . . the voice is a voice by metaphor only, and more properly a movement of thought, then the second cause which God employs is some part of my mental activity; and he employs it to address in his name another stream of my thinking, which is at the moment arrogating to itself the name of *me*" (*GV*, 18). Lewis held a comparable position about scripture. The exegete should "never take the scriptural images literally" and the emotional "purport" of the images should always be trusted. Abstractions, based on the logic of analogy, are no more real than the images. They are "a continual modelling of spiritual reality in legal or chemical or mechanical terms." The revealed archetypes call forth our emotional and bodily obedience; it should not surprise us that they are imaginative and personal phenomena as well (*LM*, 52). For both Lewis and Farrer, the psychological side of our desires for the Infinite God did not undercut them; instead, such desires only further reinforced the transcendence of one who would deign to create us for himself, then come to us in a manner that drew upon our abilities, even as it revealed our finitude.

POETIC METAPHOR, POSITIVISM, AND PRAYER

For both C. S. Lewis and Austin Farrer, then, the transcendence of God is necessary for our own true transposition, drawing us upward and saving us from the idolatrous impulse to bring God down. Our minds may speak of God after the event of his disclosure, and to know God is to speak to him even as part of our mental existence, yet, even there, only by the gift that he so chooses to give. The gift of God's self, which is received in salvation, is first intuited in creation. Both are divinely enacted gifts. As Farrer put it, "The vast shadow of my Creator himself might fall over my shoulder into the field of finite things before my eyes" (*GV*, 75–76). We can speak of God because we become aware of an analogy between the finite thing and the infinite God (*GV*, 81), yet this awareness arrives fait accompli as a gift, a gift that by its very proximity and distance invites us to participate in its dynamic fluctuation, a double agency of meaning that both encourages and humbles.

This dynamic view of language as a gift had something to say about the shortcoming of another of Lewis and Farrer's opponents, that of logical positivism. For the positivists, religious language had no empirical content and, therefore, was really vapid nonsense. Yet this claim was famously shortsighted. Logical positivism sought, by a verification principle, to discount all statements that are not empirically verifiable or logically necessary, but the principle is itself neither verifiable nor necessary. In Lewis and Farrer's early careers, the position of A. J. Ayer and Bertrand Russell loomed as dark storm clouds on the intellectual horizon. Yet Basil Mitchell could point out by 1957 that doctrinaire logical positivism was already a minority position; the more exacting challenge was the positivist rejection of ethics and religion in general (1957, 4–5). Still, for a short period its charges were serious indeed.[23] "The problem of theological analogy remains," warned Farrer in 1955, "and the critique exercised by modern linguistic philosophy upon the very meaningfulness of theological statements forces it upon our attention" (*RF*, 68).

What Lewis and Farrer each sought to show was that real, everyday language was wider than positivist constraints implied. The conditions of analogy are the conditions of speech itself. Lewis argued at one point—the essay, "The Language of Religion" was not published in his lifetime—that there is a difference between scientific and poetic language. Scientific language is an unusual form of ordinary language concerned with making accurate predictions on which to base actions (*CR*, 130–32). Lewis thought that general religious language was no unique kind of language, while theological (i.e., dogmatic or creedal) language was more akin to scientific language in its proclivity for exactness (*CR*, 135–36). It was poetic language, Lewis insisted, that was the more common form of speech, for it encompassed far more of the phenomenal realities of human existence: "To be incommunicable by Scientific language is, so far as I can judge, the normal state of experience" (*CR*, 138).

Poetry, Farrer also stressed, is more than emotion; it is a form of normative descriptive language (*RF*, 29). It is "time-conditioned" (*GV*, 96), and resists theological precision, yet it is also intended to "arouse all possible echoes" (*GV*, 99). He could insist to a collegiate audience of students, "Please don't think that I am going to tell you that theology is just figurative poetry: that is a very wicked thing to say, though some people have not shrunk from it. The relation between poetry and theology is not so simple as that" (*RF*, 24). Instead, Christian reflection should be iconic—the image is the meeting place of human conception and divine descent. The violent pictures of God as bloody warrior, angry husband, and raging father reveal God, but they are not God himself in his essence. "All the statements we make about God are similitudes. ... All words about God pose a riddle" (*RF*, 35). Nevertheless, the images of salvation history have a particularity safeguarded by God; they cannot be simply set aside since God has a purpose in revealing himself within them.

This had wider implications. Language itself is neither capable of univocal, absolute naming of the world nor guilty of an equivocal structuralism that has no actual relationship to reality. It instead bears an analogy to the *analogia entis*. Lyle H. Smith Jr. has proposed that Lewis's approach anticipated Paul

Ricoeur's tensional model of metaphors; particularly that Lewis understood that metaphor must be placed within the narrative level of discourse, and likewise, that Lewis's model of transposition recognized in such discourse the *is not within that which is* (Smith 1991, 22–27). This rhythm of discourse shares much with the analogical models that Przywara and Farrer advocated. The tensional truth of the metaphor is parallel with the mutable suspension of human being itself. For Farrer, the image is typical speech because the suspended middle is the actual condition of human being. All imagery makes a pledge of, and a limit to, more meaning. The imagery we use about the world is parallel with the virtuous person who sizes up the situation and what it requires. "Reasoning is not a source of knowledge but an instrument to clarify apprehension," offered Farrer, following a fairly straightforward Thomist account, and by this "what we apprehend we accept in the last resort in the evidence of its self-presentation" (*RF,* 50). We use analogy to clarify existence and thereby how best to act within it. In a sense, all metaphoric tension is cognitive action; for we are dynamic beings receiving the world and coming to terms with it (Henderson 2004, 173–74).

Psyche's desire for death in *Till We Have Faces* has this kind of suspended middle, which achieves understanding and action. She clarifies her apprehension through the images her culture has given her. Her longing for the Grey Mountain and her desire for something that death seems to hide point to that which is not fearful but beautiful. "Everything seemed to be saying, Psyche come!" (*TWHF,* 74). Her longing is further clarified by the analogies of home and country, "the place where I ought to have been born," and who exactly is awaiting her with joy and happiness (*TWHF,* 75–76). All this is typical human experience and yet is not contained in this world, for every analogy offers reality yet withholds its complete essence and manifestation. Psyche is justified here because her heavily metaphoric language better suits the situation than would abstractions or ethical maxims.

Farrer also appealed to the lover's language as a way of understanding the fecundity of committed metaphor. Love does not blind the lover but enables him or her to comprehend more. "It takes the violent passion of love to break down the dull custom of incomprehension ... My mind is a vessel, having a certain capacity of vision, and just now it is filled to overflowing with the contemplated being of the women that I love and I am only sorry that I have not room to contain more" (*RF,* 31). Love needs many names, and that no name exhausts (or comprehends) the beloved is no slight on love. Or like that of the lover, we can accept that metaphoric language employs language to speak of the beloved, falters because such language cannot do him or her justice, and yet praises once again because love cannot be silent in the beloved's presence. The same can be said of a passionate engagement with God or with God's creation.

Farrer more specifically used this triadic form to describe "real metaphors," that is, analogies. Here again, Farrer recognized the devotional implications of Przywara's formulation. According to Farrer, metaphors have explanatory power because they have an *is* of "family resemblance" and an *is not* of "unlikeness." This is why the metaphoric is often described as inspired: "There is no technique for finding out the analogy of scarlet to the trumpet-note: it has just to be seen or not seen" (*RF*, 32–33). Yet conceived in this manner, the condition of gratitude is also always upon the horizon of dependence. "God does not limit us by being limited; he only limits us by being true" (*SB*, 34). We always encounter the *is/is not* as creatures and respond with either an idolatry tending toward one or the other or (if being redeemed) with a doxology of gratitude and address to our Creator.[24]

This experience of language also parallels with the various approaches of Christian mysticism. The positive way affirms how the creation bears the Creator's image, while the negative way realizes that no created thing can fully reflect the Creator. Yet this is a pattern that never ends, the negative purifies the positive that it may overflow yet even more. "There is a huge overplus of sheer promise in what the figures express" (*GV*, 58). We continually encounter God's transcendence and nearness within our own finite, dependent, and mutable becoming. The "world-environed self" and divine Godhead are two active centers, and thus the way of worship is a dynamic way, neither static nor wayward. According to Farrer, "My knowledge is the knowledge of my own active existence. Yet the limitation of my knowledge to the field of my own finitude does not involve me in the supreme lie about it, the supposition that it is *uncaused*"; instead, the mind has a sense of its dependence upon God, even if that is "the bare form of an absolute act" (*GV*, 33). If there is "no rest" within the suspended middle of apprehension, for Farrer there is still "rest for the spirit, which through the act of discourse maintains contact with that which alters not, and acquiesces in it. . . . Only thus is God known, but to know Him is not to know the terms" (*FI*, 60–61). Open upwardness (following Przywara) is not just an apprehension of one's condition but a call to live it out doxologically.

Along similar lines, Sharon Jebb calls attention to the balancing of *via positiva* and *via negativa* within Lewis's thought and spirituality. Jebb perhaps overreads Lewis somewhat: in arguing that he distrusted the apophatic tradition, she cites as her evidence Lewis's approval of the very Thomist dictum that grace does not destroy nature. At the same time, she is spot on in her recognition in Lewis of the need for the "blinding darkness" of the dark night (Jebb 2011, 210–12). Certainly, Lewis tended toward the positive way of images. His rich portrait of Aslan is but one example. But Lewis understood that the positive way did not speak univocally. In *Perelandra,* Tor wears the face of Christ, "that face which no man can say he does not know." Yet Ransom insists that in looking upon it, idolatry is impossible. He realizes that such a living image can be both near and yet still unlike: "Where likeness was greatest, mistake was least possible." Such could "never be taken for more than an image" (Lewis 1944, 176–77). Even in paradise, the perfect icon will not erase the difference between image and original. The *analogia entis* by its very form taught Lewis the necessary balance: God is both Iconodule and Iconoclast. Lewis speaks of the "real self" that is "far from being rock-bottom realities," and thus must face its own humiliation in prayer (*LM,* 81). The shape of our creaturely analogy of proportionality, suspended between *via positiva* and *via negativa,* is not far removed from the open-ended shape of general metaphor. Just as we cannot know the fourth part of the analogy (i.e., God's own being), neither can we know with certainty our temporal mutability, at least in any static manner.

Viewed linguistically, analogy is a species of metaphor, that is, a more exacting form of four parts. Viewed ontologically, metaphor is only one expression of our creaturely existence, suspended between the timeless and temporal, for we are finite beings made for beholding the Eternal God, a Being beyond being whose infinite nature we may not know except as he reveals himself in analogies to us, and yet these analogies are also meant to loosen our grip on the images so that God may call us to himself through them and yet beyond them (Betz 2014, 49). For example, a logic like Przywara's unfolds Shasta's meeting with Aslan in Lewis's *The Horse and His Boy.* Shasta had been taught among the Calormenes that Aslan was a great demon sorcerer in Narnia. As they cross a treacherous path in the mountains through a dense cloudbank, he learns along his journey that Aslan had been both the lions and the cat, yet who Aslan *is* remains a profound mystery. "Myself," the Voice says three times in the darkness, accompanied by, in turn, emotions of power, gaiety, and gentleness (*HB,* 159). And when Shasta finally beholds Aslan, it is nether in the realm of positive analogy nor in the cloud of unknowing, but with a profound and overwhelming silence. Shasta falls at the feet of one surpassing terror and beauty (*HB,* 160).

Strangely, it may be the language of address in prayer, as Lewis noted, that best offers a model for this creaturely analogy of dependence in general. "The world was made partly that there might be prayer," he observed, for "all it does and is, down to the curve of every wave and the flight of every insect"

(*LM*, 56). Lewis recognized that this language of bodily being and analogy in prayer is manifest in a manner that practices both:

> This talk of "meeting" is, no doubt, anthropomorphic; as if God and I could be face to face, like two fellow-creatures, when in reality He is above me and within me and below me and all about me. That is why it must be balanced by all manner of metaphysical and theological abstractions. But never, here or anywhere else, let us think that while anthropomorphic images are a concession to our weakness, the abstractions are the literal truth. Both are equally concessions; each singly misleading, and the two together mutually corrective. (*LM*, 21)

If the language of analogy keeps us from treating imagery of the divine in a way that insults the *aseity* of God, so the concrete images themselves keep us far from a deity that we could never approach.[25] What remains, then, is the actual practice of prayer. Like Shasta, we adore.

Here again, we come to one of the conditions of language itself, which in turn suggest the metaphysics and ontology of our creaturehood. For Farrer, we are always referring to things via other things. All epistemic events engulf our apprehension at some level, and our apprehension occurs before our analogies attempt to unpack what we are beholding (*RF*, 75–81). It is practice in prayer that forces us to keep revising our image of God by operating within the images as a conduit of our address: "I may pray for God to act in me by shaping his idea in me, but he, the living God in me, is not the idea but the power who shapes it. When I speak to God I fix my eyes on my idea of God and do not, in practice, distinguish it from him. Yet I cannot always shut out the truth—no idea of God is God." We yield, Farrer observed, learning that God is invisible to our conceptions, and we surrender to be refashioned as he sees fit (*LIB*, 14).

What Lewis and Farrer both understood is that analogy is a natural condition with a supernatural orientation, and God created such a condition with a final, teleological end always in mind. There is no other way to be a creature or to reason as one. The triadic and tensional nature of metaphor, the circuitous nature of symbol, the multirelational nature of analogy, all are naturally preparatory not only for the mutable nature of human apprehension, but also for understanding the analogy of nature and supernature. As Przywara helped Farrer to understand, and as Farrer influenced Lewis, the condition of creaturehood makes language possible, yet the nature of language is prepared for the transpositional gesture to the higher. "Cleverness," wrote Farrer, "will not take us to the knowledge of God, but wisdom will, and wisdom is a rarer gift"

(*RF*, 44). Our humanity cannot be reduced to simple instinct or to fantasies of transference. What if "God Himself, alive, pulling at the other end of the cord, perhaps approaching at an infinite speed, the hunter, king, husband" came to us?" Lewis asked (1960b, 94). And for Lewis and Farrer, of course, he indeed has.

·✦4✦·

VIRTUE

Even on the biological level life is not like a river but like a tree. It does not move towards unity but away from it and the creatures grow further apart as they increase in perfection. Good, as it ripens, becomes continually more different not only from evil but from other good.

—C. S. Lewis, *The Great Divorce*

His disciples, in virtue of the same renunciation, are fit partakers of his royalty—for when the poor are promised the kingdom, they are made princes, not subjects. By unity of heart with the royal will, they share the sovereignty of heaven over earth.

—Austin Farrer, *The Triple Victory*

Both C. S. Lewis and Austin Farrer believed in an integrated purpose for the natural and the supernatural worlds, that of eternity with God, which each confessed had a vertical and a horizontal component to it, for not only did they believe in a hierarchy in which the eternal enters the temporal, they also believed humans have a final purpose that gives shape to their lives. Not surprisingly, the ethics of each man shared concerns with his positions on myth and analogy. Both defended myth as a bridge to the transcendent, which could accommodate aspects of psychology, anthropology, and literary symbolism, just as scripture's divine purpose could include myth's imaginative power. In similar fashion, they turned to the logic of analogy to hold together the finite and infinite, while acknowledging the vast distance between the temporal and eternal. The *analogia entis* helped them recognize humans as living within a "suspended middle." Thus, analogy, too, employed both hierarchy and telos.

Parsing out the supernatural and the natural meant taking seriously that human capacities are not alien to the work of grace, and that in turn neither is grace so radical that it violates the normal categories of reason, ability, and goodness. Farrer wrote, "The gifts of grace recover to us the pattern of true nature and enable us to develop its capacity beyond what nature can.... If we hold that grace restores and perfects nature, we must also hold that Christ restores and perfects natural moral 'sense' or 'reason'" (IB, 178). With this *potentia obedientialis*, Lewis concurred. Writing to the archetypal Malcolm, he noted, "If grace perfects nature it must expand all our natures into the full richness of the diversity which God intended when He made them, and Heaven will display far more variety than Hell" (*LM*, 10). Lewis and Farrer each focused upon the transfiguration of the human person—a process that ends in divine divinization or theosis. For both men, the Beatific Vision and theosis were tied together. These are the telos, the final end or purpose, in which moral excellence is a good of beholding and becoming. Thus, each wrote on matters of the natural law, even as they also held to a larger Christian hope. To the question *Does the supernatural nature of the Christian gospel and the seemingly natural observations of virtue ethics go hand in hand?* Lewis and Farrer would answer with a qualified affirmative. Just as with myth, the two answered secular and religious alternatives, and just as with analogy, they navigated theological and linguistic assumptions. With ethics, each writer sought to explore both the theology of nature and grace, as well as the applicability of virtue ethics to contemporary secular concerns.

FARRER AND THE UNDERSTANDING OF HUMAN ENDS

To understand how humans are designed for the reception of grace, Austin Farrer and C. S. Lewis looked to a description of moral purpose that accounts for character formation, and they did this because their Christian anthropology held that humans are created with a divine end in mind. How exactly does the infusion of supernatural strength combine with moral decision-making and personal ethical action? Both writers answered this question by arguing that natural ethical reasoning and decision-making are the faculties that grace matures and perfects. H. Richard Niebuhr has described this position as "Christ above Culture." The order of grace is a higher one than the natural order, yet grace is constantly entering into nature to assist it and bring it along (Niebuhr 1975, 130–41). Farrer and Lewis, not surprisingly in theological publications, addressed the relationship of dual means (that is, nature and grace) and of a single end for ethical action. In the middle 1930s to early 1940s, Farrer worked out his own stance in both Anglican and ecumenical venues. Lewis in the early 1940s did so in the Anglican journal, *Theology*, as well as in popular publications.

Like his work with religious analogy, Farrer, as a philosophical theologian, had to answer objections from *Krisis* thinkers, such as Emil Brunner or Karl Barth, who rejected any remaining capacity for natural law. One of Farrer's most important essays was his contribution to *The Christian Understanding of Man* (1938), part of a series of books that followed the 1937 Oxford Conference on Church, Community, and State. The July conference was one of the foundational events of the twentieth-century ecumenical movement, and a good example of the kinds of theological conversation that Farrer had been involved in since the late 1920s and early 1930s. By most accounts, the conference events were considered successful.[1] Seven volumes on its political and social topics were commissioned, with contributors representing a wide variety of Christian traditions and nationalities (including Roman Catholic thinkers who had not been present at the conference), and essayists in each volume had a chance to read the other selections and revise theirs if they wished.

Farrer's contribution was the assigned title, "The Christian Doctrine of Man." One reviewer thought it offered a clear contrast between its British milieu and a Continental one, such as that of Brunner's companion piece in the same volume (Garvie 1938, 360). While Farrer did not mention Brunner (or Barth) by name, he was clearly playing the continuity of nature and grace off the *either-or* of "dialectical theologians." Neoorthodox ethics rejected any nod to natural ethics, and in turn stressed the inability of humans to reason and act ethically without renewal in Christ. Farrer's essay explored not only what distinguished a Christian ethic and conscience, but also what each shared with non-Christian formulations, and in his argument he set out classic distinctions between the natural and supernatural realms in a form comparable to the Thomism he had been studying. His chosen concerns for the essay, then, were understandable, for they were some of the key topics of variance at both the conference and in the companion volumes.

This variety was not surprising. While the conference talks were ecumenical in spirit and purpose, they hardly avoided disagreement. Even if the Roman Church had not sent delegates, Catholic thought was in evidence, particularly due to the influence on attendees of historian and social critic Christopher Dawson and of neo-Thomist philosopher Jacques Maritain. Protestant neoorthodox thought, likewise, formed a substantial presence. J. H. Oldham had used the system of "co-opted delegates" to insure that *Krisis* or dialectical theologians made up a large contingency of those in attendance, and they emphasized political realism and a deep distrust of the natural self. In light of the growing threat from Nazism, Fascism, and the rising Communist governments, old-style postmillennial optimism was hardly in favor (Thompson 2015, 125–27).

Brunner, for example, had argued at the conference that a creation-based natural ethics was not the primary responsibility of the Church; rather, the need of the hour was a more singular focus on proclaiming the gospel of salvation and its transformative power (Oldham 1937, 28–29). This did not mean that Brunner rejected any discussion of culture and polity. In his essay for *The Christian Understanding of Man*, Brunner summarized ideas that he had first argued for in his book *The Divine Imperative*. Brunner owned that the Bible does not deny humanity's natural conception of itself, and he accepted that every culture has an understanding of justice, economics, psychology, and so on. Brunner argued, "There is no special science of Christian anatomy," or of psychology and so forth, "but there is a special Christian doctrine of freedom . . . of the destiny and personal existence of man." While Christians and non-Christians could share a common natural science, non-Christian and Christian views of philosophy made a decisive break with one another (Brunner 1938, 142–46). Yet even this emphasis made him a mediating figure between Barth and someone like Farrer.[2]

In 1934, Brunner and Barth had had their legendary debate over nature and grace, and Barth had infamously misunderstood the former's position, in part because Barth in the 1930s was looking on in horror as German Christians were being seduced by the "natural" immanent claims of the Nazi *Volk*.[3] Until the debate, the two men had been considered of the same theological perspective. Yet their divergence was one that Farrer had already foreseen. In 1931, the year that he had heard Barth in Bonn, Farrer read Brunner's *The Mediator* with great profit, and opined to his father that Brunner was "Barth with the rhetoric pulled out and thought inserted in its place." Brunner convinced Farrer that there was a breach between God and humanity and not a continuous gradation (Curtis 1985, 78–80). The next year, Farrer studied under Brunner in Zurich and came to believe Brunner closer to the "Catholics" than to Barth's "Dialectical School." Farrer continued to find Brunner attractive except for his use of antithesis (Curtis 1985, 96–100). By 1938, then, Farrer had a clear sense of what he was agreeing with and what he was opposing.

Farrer purposefully considered both creation and redemption. A relationship with God is twofold: first, that of a creature with a telos intended by the Creator, and secondly, failure in pursuing that end, which needs the "gracious intervention of God" to help restore the creature (*IB*, 74–75). Farrer also set out a definition of depravity that a dialectical theologian was sure to reject. Depravity, rather than being a complete inability of the human creature to do any good, is a disorientation with an eschatological outcome: "If a creature is so behaving as to lead to its becoming a final and total loss, then there is good sense in saying that it is totally off the right line," but not in claiming that it is incapable of any virtue whatsoever: "There is only one thing that is definitely and simply 'lost'—a sure, true and objective vision of God" (*IB*, 77). Instead of speaking of having solidly lost the image of God, one must speak of losing that image over time (*IB*, 91–92). Some natural rationality can still be trusted by the ethical actor because the long arc of a culture is not the same as its various deposits of truth. Good remains, however soiled.

Farrer's stress that a natural moral condition prepares for a supernatural perfection did have implications for natural ethics. Believers understand that religious practices and habits of self-discipline help create "the state of life conducive to the contemplation of God" (*IB*, 85). Farrer treated contemplation as an ethical element, not unlike law and duty, consequentialism, or moral creativity (*FI*, 154). He argued that practical reason was analogous to contemplative reason, that just as contemplation is oriented to a higher reality so moral decision-making responds to Being (*FI*, 101). Therefore, contemplation is not only the province of the mystic. Even the highest aspiration of Christian ethics—that of the Beatific Vision—has its foundations in natural considerations and capacities. Farrer pointed out that humans can have a confused sense of moral purpose and yet have an "actual aspiration towards the divinely appointed end," even if distorted by sin (*IB*, 78). Humans achieve an inconsistent patchwork of moral principles, regardless of whether they possess any sense of divine caritas or hold a place in their reasoning for the first principle of the love of God. This intermediate patchwork does not preclude the end for which humans are made. Even the natural virtues practiced by the Christian need a supernatural end if they are to achieve their integrated purpose (*IB*, 79–83).

A twofold analysis of nature and grace does not conclude, then, that there are two separate ends for humanity, as some neo-Thomist thinkers in the tradition of Second Scholasticism had judged to be the case. Adrian Hastings has pointed out that the Roman Catholic books that debated this question in the 1940s and 1950s were not widely read in England, though some were being translated, and their basic concerns were under discussion in educated circles, both Roman and Anglo-Catholic (486).[4] The division in thought was in part concerned with how best to picture the "natural" state, especially that of pre- and non-Christian cultures. All Thomist thinkers understood that humans make ethical and practical choices based on the means to desired ends. But this point raised a question about fallen people who had yet to be renewed by grace: Were all humans created with the one end of divinization in God? Or did they possess two differing ends with two resulting sets of purposes, the first that of natural happiness and justice; the second that of eternal happiness with God? Those who stressed that there were two ends, such as Jacques Maritain or Réginald Garrigou-Lagrange, did so because they held that saying that humans were created with the Beatific End in mind made it sound as if they were owed it, rather than it being a gift of grace. And they thought that a purely natural end helped make sense of why non-Christians could be capable of great good. Those who held to a singular position, such as Joseph Maréchall or Pierre Rouselot, as well as Henri de Lubac and Henri Bouillard, stressed repeatedly that an orientation toward the one end in God could only be activated by divine power, in creation, yes, but more so in the work of saving grace. To say that humans were made for life in God was not to undercut the gratuity and freedom of divine action and choice. Still, both positions understood that humans were in need of grace if they were to receive the paradise, for nature was not an airtight category in actual salvific history.[5]

The center of the debate was how best to account for the supernatural in relation to the natural. De Lubac, in his infamous 1946 *Surnaturel,* had argued against "pure nature," a supposition of those who stressed a double end for nature and grace. Pure nature was a theoretical category only, but it posited that God could have created a perfect natural Adam without any benefit of sanctifying grace, and that in theory he could have died unfallen and not achieved divine beatitude. Even though de Lubac was willing to concede such a view as a way to safeguard God's gratuity in granting salvation, he thought the idea tempted Christian thinkers toward a functional secularism by creating a category of existence to which the supernatural need not be considered (Boersma 2009, 91–96).

This particular issue had been discussed in English circles in the 1930s. Even those who allowed for the two-end position, such as English Jesuit Martin D'Arcy, had to admit that "Man with nothing but his natural endowments is an abstraction; he has never existed" (1964, 160). C. C. Martindale could counter that "Adam was created in Grace" (1936, 10). Farrer, too, by 1948 set forth an answer by stressing the "double personal agency" of finite humans and an infinite God (*GV,* 36). He wryly noted that the hypothetical natural "unfallen" Adam could have Aristotle's intellect, Paul's religious zeal, and Francis's humility, and yet, strictly speaking, nothing would be supernatural per se. Farrer stressed that such a person, rather than not being in need of grace, would be, despite its glories, still too limited and unable to ascend to its divine destiny. But then nature never existed without grace: "If a child cannot walk unsupported, that is not to say that he is simply dragged, and does not walk at all." The believer who walks in grace is not a superhero with extraordinary abilities: "There is nothing non-human in what we are thus enabled to do: it is not the act of some other creature tacked on to us" (*GV*, 33–36). Farrer responded that we were always intended for the society of heaven and for the divine dance. Nature can never be conceived as a freestanding entity, independent from God's creative sustaining consent. While one may speak in theoretical terms of nature and supernature, there is no "pure case of a natural mind," for the distinction was never meant to imply that "the mind unaided by grace will be able to arrive at an adequate rational theology." Likewise, human reason "unaided is also unredeemed and so its natural forces are to some extent weakened or depraved" (*RF*, 63).

Arguably, a two-level cosmos in which nature and grace exist in completely separate realms not only undercuts nature, it also compromises grace. This was why both Farrer and Lewis affirmed the *analogia entis* not only for purposes of speaking of God, but also for getting a description of human anthropology correct. As Aquinas put it, "grace requires nature as its presupposition" (Kerr 2002, 146). The natural creation of the human being has, as its final end, renewal in Christ. Farrer shared the neoorthodox point about divine regeneration: the perversion of the human faculties place them in a need for grace, yet he did so by affirming one of the basic claims of Catholic theologians—that the good faculties given at our creation cannot in and of themselves save: "Their freedom before grace need be only such that they *exist*, not such that they are capable of response to God apart from God's enabling action" (*IB*, 90).

Any account of natural morality, then, has to include that of divine intention. In 1957, Farrer employed the same pattern of creation and redemption he had used in 1937:

> On the one hand the action of God is creation; through all the processes of events contributory to the formation of our neighbour, God has shaped and is shaping an unique creature, and is to be reverenced in his handiwork, in the very man as he is. On the other hand, God's action is redemption. Patient of the man's imperfections, God forgives but does not tolerate. For, by a costly and incessant action bearing on the man's free will, he persuades him towards his everlasting good. (*RF*, 124)

Farrer balanced these two aspects of Christian theology in moral anthropology. The end of the human creature is not recognized in the natural capacity for moral value and decision-making, but only in retrospect by the fuller teaching of theosis. Thus, one could reasonably speak of natural ethical concerns without forgetting that a larger telos was at stake. Farrer imagined the philosophical skeptic treating God as a token prop only—a way to uphold the source of an otherwise natural set of injunctions and prohibitions—and Farrer insisted that no believer would be satisfied with this approach since one's relationship with God is primary and personal. And this is so even though Farrer understood that we meet creation in the "only possible phenomenon, the creature" and redemption in the "forgiveness, the persuasion and the calling" that make up "actual character or situation" (RF, 126, 127).

For Farrer, it is this purpose that gives Christians a special sympathy with the plight of their non-Christian neighbors. Non-Christians, too, understand that one should strive toward the desired good, and one's creaturely success is a matter of "the clarity, force, and unity with which the object of aspiration" manifests itself to understanding, as well as the "concentrating attention and activity" given to accomplishing it (IB, 89). In taking such a position, Farrer was employing the Christian doctrine of the *imago dei*, as well as its subsidiary assertion that human beings by their very existence impact us with their essence. The conditions of a social ethic are, at bottom, creational. He had made similar appeals in his later *Freedom of the Will*, stressing the responsibility to human dignity and essence, which must be treated as sacred: "What I do with my life, what I do to my neighbours," is something that cannot be violated, "even if I am free to damn myself, I am not free to betray or outrage them" (FOW, 308).

Furthermore, Farrer argued that there are existential claims made upon us by others' reality that are comparable to physical aspects like gravity and material hardness. To comprehend their claim upon us is to already be in the process of acknowledging it and acting upon it (RF, 132–33). In a late work, the 1960 sermon "In the Conscience of Man," Farrer made this insight even more explicitly Christian. The mysterious aspect of human being commands our conscience and yet that command arises from "the man God is making; as it were the Christ in the man, struggling to be born" (IB, 35). Is there, then, natural justice apart from revelation? In the last analysis, no. The single end for all natural goods is that they become transmuted into supernatural ones: "For the Christian there can be no mere morality. His moral judgements may agree with other men's but his obedience to them is obedience to God" and thus, they are a means toward that final end, which is a greater good than ethical happiness in this world (*IB*, 88). The final human condition may stretch our conceptions of the natural to the breaking point, but theosis, the final glorified state, need not be an alien imposition. As Farrer declares, "There is a point beyond which infinite God could not divinize his creature without removing its distinct creaturely nature." To do anything more would be the "equivalent to its annihilation" (*GV*, 36).[6]

CULTURE AND THE TRANSTEMPORAL IN LEWIS

In 1940, C. S. Lewis was also struggling to sort out these various layers of human and divine action. In his essay "Christianity and Culture" for the Anglican journal *Theology* (as well as in a follow-up letter and a tertiary response to criticism), he explored whether culture was at odds with the final goal of human existence (*CR*, 12). He sought to avoid the conclusion that the aesthetic has parity with the ethical, that one's taste is somehow saintly or sinful. Lewis was responding to George Every's support of aesthetic education for theologians, which Every, a lay brother of an Anglican order, had advocated in an earlier issue of the journal.[7] Every's assertion had set the terms of their discussion; "culture" referred to high culture, or at least fine culture—poetry, literature, music, and so on. Lewis thought that Every's position implied theologians were lacking something essential to their vocation, and he worried that this conflated "*psyche* and *pneuma*," that is, "nature and supernature," a temptation for which he blamed the Victorian cultural critic Matthew Arnold, among others (*CR*, 13). This was not to say that a lecturer in literature such as Lewis discounted the aesthetic experience, but he did see a difference. Moral qualities in literature are experienced at times through aesthetic and critical perspectives.

Lewis went so far as to list six literary values that would not be of supreme importance to salvation in Christ and to the glorification of God: honor, sexual love, wealth, pantheistic contemplation, *Sehnsucht*, and "liberation of impulses," the last presumably dealing with modernist theories of psychoanalytic and sexual freedom (*CR*, 21–22). His penultimate example of *Sehnsucht*, that is, the longing for a still awaited joy, is a surprising one, given Lewis's strong experiences of it and its role in his own desire for God, but Lewis also understood that in its Romantic forms, it could end in the fruitless pursuit of eroticism or the diabolic (*CR*, 22). The other values he listed, while obviously not divorced from a Christian ethic, as literary explorations were more aesthetics than soteriology.

This separation of literary values and Christian virtues might seem an odd way to parse faith and literature, even in the light of Every's concern or of Arnold's pseudoreligion of culture. Yet Lewis's distinctions did bear the shape of the theological debate concerning nature and grace, though he was less directly influenced by it than was Farrer. At first blush, one might conclude that Lewis was promoting something more like the dualism of the two-end model, and while this was not the case, he was certainly concerned with the issues it raised. Here, too, Lewis sought to distance himself from the Barthians, and he admitted later to Every in correspondence that he had tackled the issue of nature and grace to mostly get it out of the way. Lewis thought that it was dividing Every and himself since the lay brother had mistakenly thought Lewis a Calvinist. Lewis affirmed to Every, "I certainly think with you that the natural virtues are sustained, even in unbelievers, by Divine aid" (*Letters*, 2.448). To address the issue, then, Lewis assumed that there were matters that were natural and preparatory for the supernatural, and he classified separately the concerns of the temporal world and those of the eternal one. But by arguing that the literary critic and the Christian priest had two different fields of concern, he was not denying they were each concerned with ethics. Lewis concurred "that culture is a storehouse of the best (sub-Christian) values" (*CR*, 23). Secular literature does have moral content; its characters and plots portray lives that we emulate or spurn, and as Lewis admitted, they can assist the virtues because they teach stock responses and thus reinforce a habitus of reactions. However, as aesthetic matters they will not save us, though they echo in their natural qualities the greater supernatural concerns. For that reason, if no other, a priest in training does not need good literary taste, and the aesthetic canon need not be part of his textual study and mastery.

Arguably, Lewis's list of literary values was not unlike classical Christian thinking about the cardinal and theological virtues. The temporal virtues of prudence, temperance, fortitude, and justice serve here in between times (in the *saeculum*), but they are not of much benefit beyond in eternal destiny. For Lewis, some good and evil in literature was of a lower class than that of the chief mortal sins, even if the literary could be symptomatic of the higher class of vices and virtues (*CR*, 35). "Though not the true end of man (the fruition of God)," such values possess "some degree of similarity to it, and are not so grossly inadequate to the nature of man as, say, physical pleasure, or money" (*CR*, 26). The moral faculties can be shaped by aesthetic texts, but the aesthetic sense necessary to appreciate them was itself not required by even most plain persons on the road to God. This did not, however, render them without purpose or help, nor confine them to some space without need of grace. As Lewis insisted, there is no neutral ground. All is claimed by God or Satan (*CR*, 33), and yet not all is claimed in quite the same manner and for the same reasons. While one might be able to distinguish the natural and supernatural, in the end the natural ethics of humanity has a supernatural destination, whether it is apprehended or denied.

Lewis, like Farrer, understood that the natural human virtues have their place within the Christian discourse of salvation, and Lewis expounded upon this conviction in other places. Christianity, he wrote, is "addressed only to penitents, only to those who admit their disobedience to the known moral law. It offers forgiveness for having broken, and supernatural help towards keeping, that law, and by doing so re-affirms it" (*CR*, 46–47). We are in the process of being saved from or damned by our vices. In *The Great Divorce*, Lewis addressed some aspects of his ethics, and as eschatological pictures, the fictional scenarios inevitably did so. Lewis insisted that "the transmortal conditions" of his theological fantasy were "solely an imaginative supposal: . . . not even a guess or a speculation at what may actually await us" (1946, x). They were fiction, even if moral fiction, and were neither dogma nor canon law. At the same time, as analogies or fables, they were reflective of Lewis's religious hopes and fears. In the book, the character of George MacDonald, playing Virgil to Lewis's own Dante, puts forth a notion of good and evil that is retrospective: the end will turn out to be what the pursuit was about, not just in terms of the practice of the thing, but in terms of character (1946, 68–70).

Lewis's fictional method also assumes his view of anthropology. His episodic tale is built around life narratives that allow the reader to imaginatively engage typical, concrete particulars, including delusion and irrationality, which will not receive an offer of goodness. The ghosts in *The Great Divorce* are set in their moral character, and as a result, most cannot respond to the offer of bliss except out of (or perhaps *as*) their particular vice. Each vice has extinguished its personality, even its individuality. There is one exception in the text, possibly two others who may yet repent, and still other penitents that MacDonald describes as having already done so. The sacred and redeemed spirits, on the other hand, are individuals; each has become more and more his or her true self. They are varied in their beauty since grace has perfected nature. From out of their joy, they offer help and counsel to the visiting ghosts, and they name the sin at hand with candor, and yet with the promise of release, though only on God's conditions.

In such a context, free will is never self-sufficient. Lewis allows that some natural desires are higher than others, yet their potential for greater good also renders them more sinister when corrupted. In *The Great Divorce*, he employs several ghosts to illustrate this pattern. The once great artist has forgotten that light itself was once his joy and not the internecine conflict of painterly movements. He is unable to die to all that surrounds his old loyalties, and precisely because they seemed hardly sinful, even admirable (1946, 82–87). All the more reason why a figure, such as the mother in bondage to her obsessive love for her son, must be helped to make even the most basic turn from her dominating vice (1946, 103–4). She can claim her love to be highest and holiest, and with a modicum of believability, but according to Lewis, such natural love must be buried before it is resurrected, perfected, and rendered unfallen: "Every natural love will rise again and live forever in this country: but none will rise again until it has been buried" (1946, 105). The gift of that death is seen with the ghost subject to lust who is delivered, though through intense pain. The damned ghosts can hardly do anything to effect a change, though by the influence of another's sanctifying love, they may grow into something solid. All beasts become themselves in the saintly Sarah Smith's love, as do all persons who beheld her (1946, 119–21). Lewis affirmed that we do not have the natural without its source in supernature. The highest conditions, the transcendentals, "each has come into Nature from Supernature; each has its taproot" in the eternal God, and each is an "incursion of that Supernatural reality into Nature" (1960b, 28).[8] We were created for glory all along, as the lasting nature of the true, good, and beautiful imply.

Lewis elaborated upon this understanding in *The Four Loves*. There, affection, friendship, and romance are conceived as "proximities of likeness" to the divine love (1960a, 20–21). The natural loves are preparatory for the love of God, and they have long-lasting meaning only if they are corrected by and built upon the disinterested agape of Christian charity (4L, 37, 61, 76). Affection can turn sinister, all the while pretending to be unselfish in its slavish manipulation of the one supposedly loved. Friendship can as easily be a school of vice as of virtue, while the god Eros becomes a demon if he is not ruled by God himself; indeed, all the loves cannot fulfill their potential without grace (4L, 115, 160, 166, 174). Lewis is careful to insist that the natural loves exist for divine charity and not the reverse. Grace is not an added stopgap to help along the broken machinery of nature; natural love all along was meant as a theater for true agape to manifest itself and its pure gift-nature: "Natural loves can hope for eternity only in so far as they have allowed themselves to be taken into the eternity of Charity; have at least allowed the process to begin here on earth.... And the process will always involve a kind of death" (4L, 187–88). For Lewis, then, the single end of the natural virtues was always to be taken up into an eschatological bliss that shines in grace. Creaturely existence, as gift, was always preparatory for theotic gift. This is what the future orientation of a creature was from the prelapsarian beginning.

POSITIONING VIRTUE ETHICS AND HUMAN FREEDOM

A narrative of divine grace and human ability is, therefore, compatible with C. S. Lewis and Austin Farrer's shared stress on lifelong sanctification because it assumes that ethical success and failure are the scaffolding upon which Christian salvation builds. Farrer and Lewis could also write on ethical rationality and defend it. Humans are moral and habitual beings with a history and a future, so we can narrate what we have done, why we have done it, what it has made of us, and, as a result, what we are in the process of becoming. Understandably, Farrer and Lewis were also defending why Christians should be involved in the cultural conversation about ethics, policies, and laws. Each man was concerned that modern (a)moral accounts of ethics had sinister possibilities, and while Lewis and Farrer's audiences were different, their basic concerns were similar. Both Anglicans sought to take seriously ethical decisions, situations, and habits within an account of character, and if they were also to speak to how grace perfects conscience and effort, they sought to engage the typical concerns of Western ethics as well.

Academic discussions predictably shaped both Farrer and Lewis's ethics. The early twentieth-century debate in British ethics was organized around the objective states of duty and utility, as well as the subjective faculties of intuition and emotion. This difference owed much to a renewed interest in Immanuel Kant and the continuing influence of utilitarianism. Kant's categorical imperative stressed that doing one's duty was to rise above self-interest, natural inclination, or circumstantial caveats. An imperative to be obeyed had to be what one could will for any other person regardless of culture or class and with indifference to its likely outcome. At the other end of the objective scale, the utilitarian theory of J. S. Mill made the pursuit of pleasure central, though pleasure was to be organized upon a scale of low to high values. The external standard was as to whether an action maximized the pleasure (and reduced the suffering) of as many persons as possible, and this meant that a shifting measure of consequences could be applied in particular cases. There could be no predetermined principle beyond this, but it was asserted to be, even if not just a calculus in practice, an objective measure and not a mere subjective judgment.

Alongside ethical systems built about duty or utility, those that employed intuition and ethical egoism (e.g., Henry Sidgwick), as well as those who were shaped by the acid of Schopenhauer and Nietzsche's will-to-power, were part of the specifically British background against which Lewis and Farrer's analysis played out. The intuitionists, which included Sedgwick and G. E. Moore, often agreed in practice with classic utilitarians on social policy; where they disagreed was the grounds for such decisions.[9] Moore, for instance, held that there is no one standard of happiness, such as pleasure; there are many ideals, each with its own intrinsic value, and they are simply recognizable each as a good state or object. In arguments such as Moore's or H. A. Prichard's, the good is immediately recognizable and therefore indefinable.[10] In 1936, another major voice was added to this conversation: the logical positivism and emotivism of A. J. Ayer's *Language, Truth, and Logic*. Ayer insisted that the claims of duty or utility (or virtue) are not facts, only emotive values. Human beings do not have free will, even if they experience something like freedom, that is, noncompulsive action.

Unlike Kantian, utilitarian, intuitionist, emotivist, or volitionist theories, by the beginning of the twentieth century an appeal to virtue ethics was a decidedly minority position, yet one explored by the renewed importance of Thomas Aquinas in Roman Catholic intellectual life, and consequently a position against which the other approaches could define themselves. Lewis and Farrer's interest was unusual, but not entirely alien to Anglican circles.[11] Farrer's advocacy for aspects of virtue ethics was mostly in the context of other arguments within philosophical theology, and he must have seemed a tad sectarian. Lewis, on the other hand, at least with works such as *Abolition of Man*, was trying to engage a more general public, yet he also had to address deontology, utility, and subjectivism. A virtue-based ethic, for the Kantian deontologist, was too subject to exceptions and too bound to the elusive search for circumstantial happiness. For the utilitarian consequentialist, its stress on the individual's character would seem to miss the point of how happiness is achieved. For an emotivist, such as Ayer, virtue ethics was simply emotional language, having no verifiable basis in physical reality.[12]

In the following, I will first address Farrer's defense of ethical decisions and character, then come in short order to Lewis's corresponding defense of traditional ethics. Farrer's ethics were a predictable extension of his views on analogy, as well as nature and grace. He had to answer philosophical objections that either, with a high view of human ability, ignored the need for grace or, with a low view, denied free will altogether. Farrer considered it a "Gideon predicament" of Christian thinkers to have to shrink their argument to thin naturalist claims because there was a serious danger in reducing a moral argument to simply what "we have decided" (*RF*, 131). "In making our 'decision' we are not expressing our royal pleasure as joint sovereigns of a moral universe"; instead, ethical judgment matters because human dignity makes itself felt by decision-makers (*RF*, 132). Virtue ethics posited an observable set of activities, but also a practical means of reasoning about the goods endemic to such practices. It gave Farrer a more precise means of describing the right action, events, and wisdom in non-Christian cultures and yet also a structure within which they were not only preparations for the True Myth made fact in Christ, but also in which they were the cardinal virtues of cultures that the grace of the supernatural virtues might empower unto salvation. If Farrer was never a true Thomist in regard to ethics, he was nonetheless drawn to natural decision-making with a supernatural end in view. What virtue ethics had to distinguish it, and arguably why Farrer found it attractive, was a way of describing the trajectory of oscillating human becoming (such as that which Erich Przywara valued), as well as being preparatory for the theology of theosis that Farrer and Lewis prized.

In his first great book, *Finite and Infinite* (1943), Farrer set out to build a case for the reality of free will and for the objectivity of moral goods (i.e., the objects, experiences, and states of character) that persons attempt to achieve. To make this case, Farrer had to answer not only the standard objections from neo-Kantians, consequentialists, and intuitionists, but also the objection from emotivists that would (in practice at least) reduce human choices to biological and psychological determinism. Farrer argued that to intend an action is to be conscious of what one contemplates to do, and this ethical good is external and beyond the self. Even if the descriptions "beyond," "above," and "below" are analogies or verbal images, the continuity of the self, and something like causation, allows one through memory to narrate one's actions, past and present (*FI*, 107–8).

Admittedly, we do often act from habit, and even at times from what the psychoanalytic skeptic would charge with being obsessive compulsion, and Farrer acknowledged that the language of "strength" or "weakness" or "energy" of will is analogical and metaphysical to a degree that the positivist would only allow as emotion. Nevertheless, such language *as a narrative* is closer to human experience than a determinist one.[13] Will and action are necessarily treated as equal if we are going to take "moral heroism" and the continuity of our actions seriously. Our own stories demand they be, so Farrer took a teleological stance. The will does tend toward the perceived fitting, good, or correct action. We have preferences and aversions, and yet we also commit ourselves to certain future courses of action in line with or in opposition to them, and it is the projected action in question that we pay attention to rather than the particulars of each step—what we will is an integrated course of action. And this is true not only of moral decisions, but also in many of our day-to-day tasks (*FI*, 108–26).

At the same time, the desired good is objective. Will is "an appetite for the good," even when the choice is a knowingly imperfect or morally deficient one.[14] There is still some good present even in the most banal or wicked circumstance. Against Kant's categorical imperative,[15] Farrer insisted that moral decisions called for situational awareness, yet in turn, he refused to be baited by the consequentialism of utilitarian ethics. The universal good can take many forms in particular circumstances. Kant, Farrer admitted, was no moral intuitionalist, yet he did understand "that morality had reference both to (projected) actions, and to entities (persons)," in other words, persons and objects are real. Yet the universal cannot always be plotted ahead of its actual application in circumstances. As Aristotle argued, the bad person still has perceived goods in mind, and in the case of a tyrant, can achieve "a truly terrifying consistency" (*FI*, 146–57).

Farrer concluded that it is reasonable to see in our lives a scale of will. At its shadowy base are desires that are opaque to our apprehension, while at the top are levels of obedience that mirror the artistic experience: "Creativity appears to be a certain identity of judgment and action, whereby we do not judge actions or projects as they arise, but express our judgment in making them what we make them" (*FI*, 167).[16] Taken together, this suggests that reductively atomizing the various aspects of our moral action is counterproductive: "The more we come down to the detail of life, the more absurd it is to think out and judge our projects; action and thought and judgment lie in one another; we think and judge in acting. But this does not mean in any sense that formed desires and habitual dispositions take control; we may create the individual structure of conduct for its worth. Or, of course, we may not" (*FI*, 166). The bodily basis of will and instinct, of one's personal interest and that of a social world, calls for some investigation into a "super-pattern" of intentional unity across space and time, for "*character is the policy of choice*" (*FI*, 191), and "there is no opposition between character and freedom, since freedom in a non-intuitive self supposes character" (*FI*, 195). A more settled character does not preclude freedom, Farrer insists, because even an older person can be thrown into challenging new circumstances, and yet when this is not the case, "the choice of age, we suspect, is the choice to believe and to do, with less choice as to what; its course is set. And therefore, in a manner, it has a full possession of its ends" (*FI*, 196). Freedom need not always be a matter of will, provided that our wills can become settled in admirable action.

In short, Farrer argued that (1) we act with certain good ends in mind; (2) the narratives we tell about ourselves assume ends-oriented actions; and (3) if we are motivated by certain desires, habits, and a sense of duty, we work these out in practice in specific situations. If a bare belief in free will is thin and weak without a larger faith, determinism is a rival "faith," built upon a number of reductive theories of existence. Both existential and positivist pictures would seem to offer a more assured and minimal set of explanations. Neither, however, can be fully satisfying. Each fails, in Farrer's estimation, because neither can account for the wonder that arises in the presence of that which outpaces understanding, that which can only be gestured at in the very inability of language to name, even as we act upon it to our spiritual and moral sustenance.

Just as Farrer felt it necessary to defend free will and natural decision-making, so Lewis thought that a justification of traditional morality must be on grounds other than that of social utility or pragmatism, and he likewise was concerned with answering the charges of emotivism. But whereas Farrer was concerned with a clear defense of free will and ethical action, Lewis's concerns were with the origins of moral values. Lewis was wary, and not only of an equation of the aesthetic and the ethical. He was also concerned with those who called for a return to Christian ethics on the grounds of societal preservation. As he would argue in *Mere Christianity,* "We shall never save civilisation as long as civilisation is our main object. We must learn to want something else even more" (*MX,* 119). A true return of Western civilization to Christianity would not be to just its ethics because the traditional codes held by all cultures were quite similar: "Did Christian Ethics really enter the world as a novelty, a new, peculiar set of commands, to which a man could be in the strict sense *converted?*" (*CR,* 46). Christianity, instead, asserts that the sinner has failed in keeping the natural moral law and cannot do so successfully without grace. For similar reasons, Lewis had the demonic Uncle Screwtape praise Reinhold Niebuhr's *Interpretation of Christian Ethics* (1935) as an example of the tendency of some to make Christianity socially expedient: "He recommends his own version of Christianity on the ground that 'only such a faith can outlast the death of old cultures and the birth of new civilisations'. You see the little rift? 'Believe this, not because it is true, but for some other reason.' That's the game" (*SL,* 124–27).[17]

This did not mean, however, that the merits of various ethical systems should be left unassessed. In his essay, "On Ethics," Lewis made a weak, negative argument for natural law, broadly construed, if not a full-blown Aristotelian or Thomistic one. He insisted that one cannot choose a code of conduct for pragmatic reasons alone; there is no outside neutral space from which to make such judgments, for as soon as one judges, one has already entered the realm of duty and conscience. Lewis also distinguished between the injunctions of such systems (Stoic, Aristotelian, or Christian) and the philosophical ideals that structured them, such as the Kantian categorical, the utilitarian calculus, Thomistic *prudentia,* and so on. He argued that these diverse theories tended to cloak something more basic: actual ethical practices overlap greatly, even when theories are wide apart: "The philosopher's or theologian's theory of ethics arises out of the practical ethics he already holds and attempts to obey; and again, the theory, once formed, reacts on his judgement of what ought to be done" (*CR,* 45).

Not unlike Farrer, Lewis borrowed aspects of natural law without setting out a completely doctrinaire position. For example, he rejected the notion of a preservation instinct for the species. The parental desire to protect one's own children is obvious and well attested, but the maxim against taking human life in general is one of a larger set of cultivated injunctions. These a person learns in order to apply them in varying situations. "Thou shalt not murder" is natural only in that it is nurtured through sources of authority and influence. Even if they have their basis in some kind of biological impulse, rival appetites still need adjudication. After all, the impulse to kill one's enemies was also natural and universally felt. A sorting out of impulses needs moral law (*CR,* 49–52). For Lewis, the moral law is "something which makes a kind of tune . . . by directing the instincts" (*MX,* 23). Ethical systems that try to build their ideals on supposed racial and evolutionary traits are conducting a sleight of hand. Scientific humanism, Marxism, and Fascism draw from the traditional morals that preceded them: "And all the specifically modern attempts at new moralities are contractions. They proceed by retaining some traditional precepts and rejecting others: but the only real authority behind those which they retain is the very same authority which they flout in rejecting others" (*CR,* 53).

At the same time, Lewis did believe that some modernist approaches, such as that of Nietzsche or Sartre, tried to cut themselves entirely from the moral reasoning of particular cultures, and thus they could be charged with reducing historical practices to the purely arbitrary. In "*De Futilate,*" for example, Lewis sought to answer the despair of evolutionary fatalism, while in another essay, "The Poison of Subjectivism," he joined Farrer in opposing ethical emotivism. In both essays, Lewis was concerned with those who would reduce a sense of truth and reality to operant conditioning. Not unlike his critique of psychoanalytical treatment of symbols, he charged such theories with substituting a poor set of ethical reasons for a richer one.

Lewis insisted that a universe saturated with reason had valid inference as one of its hallmarks, and reality has ultimate Reason and Wisdom and Goodness behind it, or else we cannot make judgments about our world failing to live up to these (*CR*, 62–69). The shape of this rationality, however, is dependent upon what has come before, and any progress in a society has its measure in categories taken from past generations. It is a *depositum fidei*, and yet one in which clarification and correction of the pursuit of the good can be rationally worked out.

This rational decision-making ability, then, was fixed on traditions of moral instruction. Lewis understood that a tradition of ethical action is not so calcified that it cannot adapt itself to new eras and circumstances and yet remain within its tradition and its resources of reflection. But because the development of morality happens within a tradition, it can only be judged within a practice of enquiry: "The outsider who has rejected the tradition cannot judge them" (*CR*, 77). One need not conclude that the ancient moral traditions were incommensurable to one another, for they shared a great common approach and similar moral impulses (*CR*, 76). What they together opposed, however, were the modern systems who were living parasitically off their traditional capital. As Tracey Rowland points out, a project of natural ethics and natural law can *only* occur in a certain kind of practice and tradition. It is not a context-free project, even as it makes universal claims (2003, 118).[18] Lewis would concur because the neo-Kantian, utilitarian, emotivist, and reductionistic approaches were built on isolated fragments of ancient tradition.

Lewis and Farrer, then, shared a modified defense of free will shaped by virtue ethics. For Farrer, this meant ethical action, while for Lewis it meant defending moral traditions. Each held to a model of natural moral reasoning that involved tradition, as well as practices that cultivate ethical sentiments. As such, they were concerned with practical rationality that could be nurtured through moral education.

MORAL SENTIMENTS AND PRACTICES IN LEWIS

C. S. Lewis's argument for a Tao, a natural law cultivated within traditional cultures, was constructed within a hierarchy of nature and grace. *The Abolition of Man*, though not an argument for theism, much less for Christianity, made the case for a common heritage of ethical principles and practices. It is true that the book does not speak to the eschatological telos that ultimately guides and orients the natural law (Dyer and Watson 2016, 31), yet from the larger perspective of Lewis's faith, it is these natural virtues toward which grace is extended. Christian salvation builds upon common natural law and is an answer to human failure to keep it. It is not surprising that Lewis's broadcast apologetic began with an appeal to the common morality in order to address the need for Christian atonement, and his third set of BBC addresses, "Christian Behavior," assumed the same general framework of nature and grace, which he expanded upon and clarified in the 1953 published version in *Mere Christianity*. According to Lewis, general ethics is concerned with "fair play and harmony" between persons, with the internal harmony of the internal self, and with the purpose of each person's life in general. It is in considering the latter that the Christian difference in moral understanding most comes to the surface (*MX*, 71, 73–74). Virtues are formed in us, not just for the quandaries and dilemmas of this world, but also because eternal beatitude requires a certain quality of person (*MX*, 77–78).

For an ethical issue, therefore, Lewis could make a case that was not automatically an appeal to Christian dogma. For example, in addressing whether human beings have a "right of happiness," he considered an instance in his own neighborhood. It was a story of adultery, divorce, and the subsequent marriage of the lovers, set against a background of war injury, sacrifice for another's illness, and the suicide of an abandoned spouse. Lewis granted that in the excuse made for the lovers (i.e., "they had a right to happiness") there was a germ of natural law, something higher behind civil and domestic law (*GD*, 317–19). Lewis insisted that natural law was necessary for civilization. The questions of rights, power, and sexual fulfillment, in such a case, were practical ones. In their neighborhood, no one who defended the lovers was suggesting that freedom allowed for any and every action to be committed regardless of harm. It would be the end of any civilization not willing to uphold restrictions upon certain impulses. The issue under debate, then, was whether the lovers who abandoned their spouses were justified based on their own happiness at the expense of others. Lewis strongly dissented, arguing that an unrestricted right to divorce on such grounds would have horrible effects for women specifically and for domestic life in general (*GD*, 322).

Lewis's approach to general ethics has at times earned him a designation as a deontologist, yet this is problematic. Gilbert Meilaender has pointed out that Lewis could effectively be called a "cognitive nondefinist" because he held that moral judgments are true, not reducible to aesthetics or emotions, and yet such judgments are tacitly basic. The human person must be brought into harmony with the moral injunctions of the Tao if one is to make good decisions (Meilaender 1988, 188–89n18, 214–16). At first glance, this may seem a step away from Farrer's prudential emphasis, yet Lewis had the same end result in mind. For example, in his 1940 address to an Oxford pacifist society, "Why I Am Not a Pacifist," Lewis made a distinction between the sense of conscience as conviction and conscience as rational moral judgment. The first always demands from us obedience, while the second can be altered with rational examination (*WG*, 65). Moral judgment includes weighing one's experience along with those that of trusted authorities; discerning which moral intuitions are properly basic; and shaping intuitions according to reasonable patterns. These aspects of moral reasoning show up in particular realities that make moral questions necessary; in sentiments/convictions as to what is good and evil; in rational deliberation about specific actions; and in reliance upon trustworthy authorities, which, given the high possibility of human corruption, are a necessary corrective (*WG*, 65–70). Each of these reveals something about practical moral reasoning.[19] Lewis was not really putting forth a method for ethical enquiry; rather, he was outlining out the elements that make up good reasoning once it is internalized in the ethical actor.

Lewis, in *Abolition*, was arguing for natural law in the older classic or medieval sense, even if in a more negative or restricted fashion, and he was also rejecting ethical naturalism in the Enlightenment and modern positivist senses. Lewis held that the Tao is objective; it stands outside us. We cannot begin with our experience as the test of what is right and wrong. As he had argued in his earlier essays, there could be no advances in ethics outside the Tao itself (*AM*, 46–47). We argue *from* rather than *to* the Tao. We can be educated into it and learn to develop and clarify it, but we cannot make moral judgments outside it. Our "moral platitudes" are self-evident within each culture's moral imaginary; they are *intellectus*; that is, they are rationally perceived as true, and not merely subjective. Judith Wolfe observes that in Lewis's ethics, "*what* people consider 'good for its own sake' is as unchangeable as the fact *that* they orient themselves toward a good" (2018, 98). Only when we accept these foundational moral truths do we practice *ratio*, the procedural debate as to how to pursue the desired good in practice (Meilaender 1998, 199–200). All this is self-evident to those who reside within the Tao because the natural law is cultivated through studying moral examples and narratives. Yet this participation is not guaranteed by birth. One has to be educated into it. The moral law itself is not an instinct or a set of desires—rather, it guides us to adjudicate rival desires with a higher set of judgments (*MX*, 25). These are not for Lewis simple social convention, though they are learned from parents and authorities.

For this reason, while arguing for the Tao, Lewis was not at the same time bothered by the differences across cultures, for we cannot assume identical values outside of particular contexts. Lewis argued in his *Preface to Paradise*

Lost that the "doctrine of the unchanging heart" is dangerous as an exegetical method because we tend to ignore the nuances of particular historical contexts and thereby misinterpret the literary work. "It is better to study the changes in which the being of the Human Heart largely consists than to amuse ourselves with fictions about its immutability" (*PPL,* 64). Attempts at abstract universals inevitably misguide us in literature. We understand the universal only by paying attention to the particularizations of human instances (*PPL,* 65). The same can be said for ethical applications in various times and places.

It was not uncommon for Lewis as an Anglican apologist to muster a compendium of authorities when making an ethical argument. His appeal to just participation in war was built upon a florilegium of mostly Western cultural texts, along with the *Bhagavad-Gita,* followed by an examination of the statements of Jesus regarding treatment of one's enemies and how they are best interpreted (*WG,* 80–88). In *The Abolition of Man,* Lewis mustered a similar short florilegium of thinkers and traditions that value the cultivation of moral attitudes (*AM,* 16–19). When he was criticized for this in "Christianity and Culture," Lewis defended it on the basis of his Anglicanism, yet he also asserted that it was a natural principle: one consults the wise when seeking rational evidence, just as one asks an expert in mathematics to check one's figures (*CR,* 14–20, 26). The appendix in *The Abolition of Man* is simply one more of such collections.

Lewis charged, too, that the modernist reduction of the natural world was "to treat a thing as mere Nature" and was, thus, already limited as a moral means of enquiry. It shrank the natural world to that which was quantifiable, efficient, and without value. This quantifiable world made ethical reason impossible. There is no purely biophysical measure by which to adjudicate our various instincts because if there is not a telos, there is no final purpose for existence (*AM,* 69–73). There can be no evolved hierarchy of instincts that allow us to choose in a consistent and principled way one instinct over another, no "infinite regress of instincts." "Our instincts are at war," that is, our wills are divided (*AM,* 34–36). Nor can one reduce ethic decisions to utilitarian consequences. Lewis's objection to "The Green Book" (i.e., Alec King and Martin Ketley's *The Control of Language*) was that the authors reduced all ethical feeling to subjective emotions; King and Ketley's emotivist ethics dismissed traditional value judgments as nonreferential and untrustworthy, yet they brought in numerous nontraditional modern values under the guise of calm rationality and social science. In effect, they taught the young reader to shame any values but the authors' own. Their language of nature, Lewis charged, was to justify the control of some over others.

If Lewis refused the reduction of law to emotional training, he did understand that ethical dispositions have a partial psychological basis. *The Abolition of Man* is built upon "the possibility of having certain experiences which thinkers of more authority than [students] have held to be generous, fruitful, and humane" (*AM*, 9), and thus the role of proper education is "to inculcate just sentiments" (*AM*, 14). "Just sentiments" as a term may have had some limitations for its original audience, but it seems better than other terms such as "moral feelings" or "moral emotions." Lewis held that the moral narrative in literature was "one which *merited* those emotions" (*AM*, 15). If an object or event deserves particular emotions, then the object gives itself to the person, and the person in turn learns to reinforce rather than repress such holy receptions (*AM*, 28). It is such fundamental moral intuitions, shared by traditional societies, that ground the claims of natural law (Dyer and Watson 2016, 126–27).

It is possible in Lewis's fiction to see how the cultivation of just sentiments aligns with a theory of virtue. Like Farrer, a defense of freedom and therefore free will is part of Lewis's ethical concern. Societies that practice slavery cannot have flourishing participants because people cannot act upon the good through particular judgments nor are these cultivated in an active culture. Indeed, the slave society must deny free will and creaturely dignity to all but a few. In *The Silver Chair*, for example, Underland is an enchanted city, quiet, orderly but without joy. "Her will is not to be questioned but obeyed" (*SC*, 122). Its inhabitants, under the Green Lady's spell, must repeat the same banal statement: "And few return to the sunlit lands" (*SC*, 130). Prince Rilian is unable to see that the Lady's future role for him is as a puppet king to a tyrant (*SC*, 138), and only when her spells are broken can he make moral judgments again. Once he is free to assess situations, he can decide what is the best thing to do (*SC*, 150). The inhabitants of Bism, of the Really Deep Land, can now joke, tumble, and set off fireworks. They manifest again the marks of good persons and the good society. Other examples of this are present in *The Silver Chair*. An incapacity for the good exists in the progressive school that Eustace and Jill attend. Cruelty and cronyism are treated as psychological cases for study. The giants of Harfang too are seemingly blind to the basic right to life of talking stags or of human children. Neither stag nor human is truly free to act. Likewise, in *The Lion, the Witch, and the Wardrobe,* Tumnus the faun recovers virtue only when he realizes that his pledge to enslave a daughter of Eve for the White Witch is fundamentally wrong: "Of course I've got to. I see that now. I hadn't known what Humans were like before I met you. Of course I can't give you up to the Witch; not now that I know you" (*LWWR*, 17–18).

In contrast, the ordered society of Malacandra in *Out of the Silent Planet* is hierarchical yet free. It does bear a superficial similarity to an enslaved Underland. The *hrossa, séroni,* and *pfifltriggi* each have their particular roles: the first are poets and hunters, while the others are herdsmen scientists and artisan technologists. Yet each is at peace with the lot in life they are given, for they cultivate from birth the virtues necessary to the good life. While Oyarsa rules under God, and while the *eldila* are angelic messengers, the obedience they require is not accompanied by a repression of ethical action. It is true that Whin tells Ransom, "It is not a question of thinking but of what an *eldil* says," yet this is a considered view confirmed by a lifetime's judgment. To do otherwise is "cubs' talk," and Whin reaches this conclusion precisely by measuring Hyoi's death against their actions: "I have been thinking. All this has come from not obeying the *eldil*." Ransom ought to have done differently and must now be on the road (*OSP,* 83, 82). Likewise, the honor and forgiveness that Hyoi extends to Ransom is by naming him *hnakrapunti, hnakra-*slayer. It is a title that takes on value when set within a culture that prizes the heroic as an ideal and within a hunt that is an ethical practice cultivating courage and adventure. This is how the *hrossa* practice being truly sentient, that is, being *hnau* (*OSP,* 82).

Something similar can be seen when Eustace enters the alternate universe of Narnia. He enters an Aristotelian world yet one in which slavery is a vice. The *Dawn Treader,* in particular, is a world not defined by the selfish relativisms of technique and situational pragmatism in which Eustace has been trained. Life aboard the ship is defined by skill and its accompanying quality of made work. Each person has a role by which he is defined and for which he is held accountable. The quality of artisans and the moral quality of persons are seen in numerous moments together. Their actions are conducted with deliberation in circumstances that are unusual or trying, and the telos of their quest, that of adventure, imparts a life defined by persons who quest.[20] Such a life requires courage and endurance and is defined by practices that value honor. No one can set themselves above its good, yet that good is not an absolute one. Caspian cannot abdicate in pursuit of it, and his own subjects would be justified in defying him to force him to honor his role: "You shall not please yourself with adventures as if you were a private person" (*VDT,* 209).

Adventure is, nonetheless, arguably the chief good of the quest that repeatedly defines and clarifies other ethical actions. Reepicheep becomes its defendant, though not always to the expected outcome. When the crew balks at entering Dark Island, it is the mouse that rejects this on the basis of nobility and adventure. To do otherwise is "no little impeachment of all our honours," and once he argues from this position, the others are won over. Caspian is forced to concur, "All right! If you put it that way, I suppose we shall have to go on" (*VDT*, 152–53). In similar fashion, when others would stay away from Aslan's Table for fear of its enchantment, Reepicheep insists that he will stay for it is "a very great adventure" (*VDT*, 169). As such, to face the task requires courage in the face of understandable fear, a courage he must exercise as well when invited to drink and eat of the table (*VDT*, 173).

As Adam Pelser points out, emotional, practical, and imaginative cultivation is not the same as emotional conditioning (2017, 21). The emotions are part of an educated response to something that is independent of the respondent. It remains good whether the person is capable of recognizing it or not. The Duffers are placed under the magician Coriakin because they are not ready to be "governed by wisdom instead of this rough magic" (*VDT*, 137). They must be forced to do the most basic tasks necessary for their own survival, and while they have some semblance of authority and self-protection, they are unable to pursue any greater good. That Reepicheep is capable of recognizing the good in adventure and that others are able to see this are moral conclusions built upon cultivated values. One cannot draw a practical conclusion from facts alone (*AM*, 30), and some things must be self-evident for reason to advance (*AM*, 40). Practical reason begins with the preservation of traditional societal ethics, and it cannot be enacted without a fundamental trust in the "ultimate platitudes" that form its guiding structures (*AM*, 32, 49). The crew of the *Dawn Treader* hardly questions its chief ends of honor and adventure or its chief goods of skill, courage, and endurance.

Yet this can go terribly wrong as it does in Lewis's fictional country of Calormen. There the moral platitudes of a culture are too often used to support a slave state that rationalizes its abuse of others. The fisherman who found and raised Shasta overrides the boy's desire to learn of the northern lands by appealing to values such as "Application to business is the root of prosperity" or warning that such questions "are steering the ship of folly towards the rock of indigence" (*HB*, 3). Admittedly, the sayings of the Calormene poets can offer insight into moral duplicity. The Calormene lord who proposes to buy Shasta sees through the fisherman's manipulation and warns, "He who attempts to deceive the judicious is already baring his own back for the scourge" (*HB*, 5). But while wisdom here may help the wise to adjust to a certain kind of world, it is a world built upon power and exploitation. Lewis does not necessarily treat such maxims as simply the values of another culture. They have a fundamentally different telos, and it shows in their poetry. Ahoshta observes to the Tisroc that the poetry of Narnia and Archenland is "all of love and war" and not "full of choice apophthegms and useful maxims" (*HB*, 113). Further-more, though Calormenes can produce a noble warrior such as Emeth (in *The Last Battle*) and can develop the admirable skill of storytelling, one that Ara-vis possesses and for which Bree has cultivated a taste, in general the heroic society of Narnia is treated as a superior culture. Calormen's values of utility and personal power corrupt not only its hierarchy but also the possibility of virtuous existence. It is one in which economics and profitability reduce per-sons to less than true ethical actors. Thus, it renders people less free.

MORAL SENTIMENTS AND PRACTICES IN FARRER

If Lewis for the most part could assume certain aspects of a moral anthropol-ogy necessary for his defense of human freedom and openness to natural law, Farrer within his philosophical circles found it necessary to argue more explic-itly for an anthropology that undergirded character ethics. Almost fifteen years after *Finite and Infinite*, Farrer would return to the matter of practical ethical reason in his 1957 Gifford Lectures, *The Freedom of the Will*, and Farrer would make an even stronger case for the role that moral desires played within ethi-cal decision-making. As a Gifford lecturer, he was charged with making a natu-ral (i.e., philosophical) argument about God, not one proceeding from divine revelation. Farrer would further develop an anthropology that made character ethics possible, and here, too, he would tender an analogy with artistic practice that advanced the implications of his views of myth and analogy. Because hu-man motivations and desires shape moral actions, determinism was a serious threat to any theory of a developed, perfected ethical judgment. Farrer had to address head-on not only A. J. Ayer's emotivism and G. E. Moore's antinatural-ism, but also the soft behaviorism of Gilbert Ryle's *The Concept of Mind* (1949), in which Ryle sought to erase the distinction between physical and mental ac-tion. Ayer's rejection of free will was based on the possibility of noncompul-sive action; we are determined, yet we feel free. Ryle contended that motives for actions are really just dispositions to behave in certain ways. Human beings are perhaps a sort of "higher mammal," for which there is no need to posit a free will. There is no "ghost in the machine." Emotions, thoughts, and memo-ries are all observable behavior, while volition is a category mistake, attributing outward behavior to a nonexistent inner state (2000, 21–29).

Against this position, Farrer sought to make the case for freedom and free will, for without them, the practical reasoning and character of virtue ethics were empty categories. He did this, however, by accepting (at least initially) some of Ayer and Ryle's limitations. Farrer began his argument with observable actions and patterns rather than by trying to investigate too closely the mind or brain-body problem. For this, he set up a scale of models of human action. The description that can be made of the emergent action of an athlete, he showed, is more difficult to make of the silent thought of a mathematician or more difficult still with the person who imagines herself to be singing or speaking but is not. Farrer concluded that the manner in which we describe such thought is analogically drawn from bodily behavior: "The shadow of doing, which is thought, must be interpreted by full-blooded doing. . . . we make the interpretation instinctively" (*FOW*, 39).

Doing so, however, would seem to limit us to two languages of description—one of synaptic action and one of bodily responses. Here, Farrer navigated a path that was neither given over to epiphenomenalism nor to some other form of psychological parallelism, for he was more interested in how the personal explanation of human action operated.[21] There is a difference, he maintained, between how we respond to a determinist explanation and that of a moral rebuke. The latter, even if painful, can renew our resolve to change, while the former leads to frustration or passive despair or stoic ennui (*FOW*, 119). Christ's injunction to pray to not be brought into temptation only makes sense, Farrer held, against this background (*FOW*, 116–17). A person with an earth-shattering decision on her hands hardly thinks in terms of determinism (*FOW*, 134). Explanation, Farrer would insist, is itself a form of free action, and the idiom we use is found in the action, too. We simply cannot help describing ourselves as active, decision-making beings. By making this kind of appeal, Farrer was essentially striving to out-narrate Ayer and Ryle, rather than trying to disprove them in detail. There are better ways to describe what we are doing and intend to be doing. Through our language, we describe occasions instead of causes. And thus, we are left (and justly) with analogies. To assert that "we see what we are up to" is metaphoric and holistic, but Farrer would insist that this is an entirely helpful way of describing human action and motive.[22] There is no need to compulsively atomize every detail.

It is with a narrative of moral decision-making that Farrer then returned in *The Freedom of the Will* to the components that make virtue ethics a possibility, for he was going to set out why *phronesis* or *prudentia* better explains how humans conceptualize the world and how they adjust their conceptions with new encounters. Farrer began by crafting a historical analogy to the causative model of Aristotle. Given the times, this was a surprisingly gutsy move, one calculated to underwhelm some readers, yet by doing so he further developed the need for practical, analogical language. He argued that the old

Aristotelian physics arose out of a psychology that is still useful. Humans do not normally separate out our phenomenal experience of subject and object; instead, we interact with the world as it manifests itself to us, not unlike a conversation: "A deliberate reaction to our environment is a sort of comment upon it, and a decisive action is a sort of practical conclusion" (*FOW*, 202). Animals, including human animals, form and use ideas. This formation and usage include both unconscious and conscious interest, along with personal responses, which are bridged by being inclined to something and concomitantly to developing that action (*FOW*, 232). And this is so even against the background of our psychological biographies and sociological generalizations about our conduct. We act because we interact.

As a result, moral decision-making and character formation go hand in hand (*FOW*, 269). John Underwood Lewis has pointed out that Farrer's ethics has what some consider a fundamental paradox: Farrer does believe the law of God to be objective, yet human beings are still self-judging creatures (1983, 142). An ethics of rule alone, Farrer suggested, cannot predict new circumstances entirely: "Moral self-judgement is not essentially a habit of blaming past actions, but a habit of imposing on one's conduct the law of one's mind" (*FOW*, 263). To do this, one needs reasoning, practices, and a shaped character. Farrer traced this pattern through four stages: from public law to custom, to formal or tacit agreements, to personal resolutions or rules, and then to the need "to act as the circumstances require" (*FOW*, 277). Even if we accept Moore's contention that any good is only valued for itself, the *Principia Ethica* can be seen as a kind of commentator on the one aspect of Aristotle that Moore ignored—that the good is what each person pursues with his or her choices. Of course, the happiness of each person has to be evaluated on a case-by-case basis. But this still suggests that we need a final orienting good by which to test the other goods we pursue and develop. Without a true telos, aspiration is just impulse: "For aspiration is always endeavouring to be right aspiration, and to respond to objects, or pursue aims, intrinsically meriting it" (*FOW*, 306).

For Farrer, moral *prudentia* is comparable with poetic inventiveness.[23] The poet is deeply involved with the various decisions at hand in any work of art; she has cultivated the standards of the practice, much of it now tacit, but her own development of them is in response to the claims that the developing object makes upon her sensibilities. Such poetic (or moral) invention does not lead to Sartrean existentialism: "We are free, and free to make our lives, but always in response to claims; claims which we may be psychologically free, but not morally free, to ignore" (*FOW*, 301). These, in Farrer's judgment, must be offered by theology and not philosophy. "We make answer that moral policies are at the service of reverence and love," and become practical as soon as we ask what and whom it is we revere and love: "For it is no trifling difference, whether we value our neighbor simply for what he is, or for the relation in which he stands to the will of God; a will establishing his creation, and intending his perfection" (*FOW*, 309). Only within the larger framework of revelation can one begin to find a meaningful pattern.

BEING SHAPED FOR THEOSIS

While Farrer and Lewis, then, engaged the theoretical debate concerning metaethics and sought to defend character, free will, and ethical traditions, they were also concerned with dramatizing the actual principles and practices of an ethical person. They both strove to use language that not only made their audiences feel the import of the moral encounter, but also that modeled the drama of character formation. Here again, at the heart of their ethical injunctions, rather than simple defenses of natural law, were imaginative engagements with the teleological journey that their soteriology implied. Lewis and Farrer's practice reinforced their theoretical reasoning. While descriptive words and accounts are not enough to effect ethical change, they are nevertheless a necessary element in guidance, discernment, and wisdom. Well-chosen language names the situation in question; it gives it significance by providing insight; and in dramatic form, it embodies ethical reflection with narrative exemplar. Thus, by reinforcing their audience's stock of ethical reflections, Farrer and Lewis taught *prudentia* in preparation for daily life. Lewis's theological fantasies, such as *The Great Divorce* and *The Screwtape Letters,* bridged ethical reflection and fictional engagement by creating narrative forms that called for explicit Christian moral analysis, and they allowed Lewis to keep it aesthetically and narratively interesting by using satire and fantasy. Farrer, as a priest, was more likely through his sermons to shape and inspire others, yet he, too, could recommend "tales" to describe the character of a life and to offer "the implicit formulation of a policy" (*FI,* 158), and he could employ the occasional extended anecdote or narrative of a life. This dramatic emphasis of both writers, then, highlights the importance of cognitive and emotive modeling, especially within their broader picture of Christian salvation.

This emphasis can be seen in Farrer's interest in French phenomenology. A phenomenology of the ethical pursuit is part of what attracted him to existential philosophy, though of a Catholic and not a Sartrean sort. In attending the Gifford Lectures of Gabriel Marcel, Farrer was particularly impressed

with the poetics and dramatics of the French philosopher. For a BBC broadcast audience in 1951, he praised him as beyond compare because Marcel was
able "to make us taste and feel our human existence, to lay out and analyse
the structure of our living without letting go the vividness and pathos of it,"
and in that, it was the philosopher's "special gift is to make us see personal and
spiritual realities" (RF, 164, 165). Farrer felt that Marcel was able to focus on
what matters to each of us in life. It was not simply rhetorical skill for which
he was honoring the Catholic existentialist; he found in him a methodology
that took seriously the high drama of experience. Marcel's method was not to
be systematic in exposition but to disrupt empty language: "He never trusts
the form of words, but practically breaks it against the things" (RF, 169). Farrer highlighted Marcel's explorations of hope and the creative will, journeys
that lead one to goodness and divine sovereignty (RF, 170). One suspects
that Farrer might have aspired to this method himself, or, if not quite Marcel's genre-bursting high-wire elucidation, at least his recovery of philosophy
as the work of wisdom and hope.[24]

For both Lewis and Farrer, the teleological character of life hangs over its
suspended shape. It is hope that emphasizes both being and becoming; indeed,
hope allows one to see our essence and development as analogically held in
tension. While both writers could speak of ethical decisions, it was really ethical living that was closer to their intellectual convictions and emotional gravity.
The temporal character of existence is not pointillist but flows into the future,
and this charges the present moment with seriousness. As Lewis pointed out,
virtue (or vice) is a settled character that forms and becomes an *esse*: "To be the
one kind of creature is heaven: that is, it is joy and peace and knowledge and
power. To be the other means madness, horror, idiocy, rage, impotence, and
eternal loneliness" (MX, 86). This ultimate outcome in being either a "heavenly" or "hellish creature" assumed not only that life has a narrative structure,
but also that its account is based in a reality that God beholds and is involved
in shaping (MX, 107, 127). Farrer stressed, too, that choosing between happiness and piety is a false dichotomy; both are found when we set our hearts on
knowing God (CF, 130). That we have an eternal end shapes our lives here, not
just in their particulars, but in their general existential import, and since death
comes to all, believers must not hoard their lives but spend them with "a certain recklessness." Only then do they live, for immortal life is what one should
desire; this shapes principle, and thus do we surrender to the death of the cross
(FO, 183, 185). A surrendered life in its cruciform pattern likewise shapes what
one may justly claim as beautiful, for "even in the midst of this life the crucifixion of the will is immortality and glory" (FO, 187).

Since Farrer paid attention in his theory to the freedom of the will and to our desires for what we perceive as good, it is not surprising that commitment and resignation of the will were key aspects of his ethical preaching. Commitment was at the heart of his sermons, and yet for Farrer, resignation to God's will meant experiencing God's goodness as a profound and divine mystery (*BM*, 83). The rhythm of the suspended middle of becoming is marked by both active and passive movements of the volition. In abandoning ourselves to the will of Christ, obedience in the present is "to have [Christ] on earth" (*BM*, 90). The heart is drawn to commitment and resignation. To live and die for Christ gave Paul "a motive, a cause, a something, on which to employ his will, to spend, and to be spent," so, too, we should set out reasons for finding out what Christ is about and "embrace it with a good will" (*EM*, 96–97). For Farrer, the active, continual commitment of the self is drawn into a relationship of submission, and spiritual obedience like love is at once active and passive for it transcends the distinction between freedom and subservience. Such a commitment of heart and mind imparts a unity with Jesus "and enters into that divine fire, which warms the heart of the world" (EM, 162).

The fictional setting of *The Screwtape Letters* shares with Farrer's sermons the quality of embodying ethical awareness and teaching discernment. Lewis's Uncle Screwtape understood that experience is to attend to the present and eternity: an ideological fixation upon the temporal future is really a counterfaith and a demonic antihope, and Screwtape offered advice on how to use the latter to undercut the former (*SL*, 75–77). Ethical reflection is a key aspect of prudential development. For example, it is not only the context of the looming reality of another war that obviously hangs over the demon's "patient," it is also the spiritually dangerous but seemingly mundane encounters that need a renewed gravitas of attention. The acerbic and cynical wit of a group of intellectuals from which the patient seeks approval, or the dry and fusty tone of the congregants at the church that he attends, these are as serious in matter as world war. Such situations have the tendency to keep the young convert distracted rather than penitent, and this is high drama if the reader has the eyes to see it.

Self-examination, however, is not meant to be an invitation to myopia, but a spiritual practice that points one away again toward the other and his or her goodness. Lewis must also guide the reader toward a subject for meditation other than the self. He held that the country of the Beatific Vision gives us a foretaste of what we practice now, and this kind of reflection is a movement away from the self's failure and toward the promise of divine beauty. The humble person will not be thinking about herself at all (*MX*, 114): "But they do not call it goodness. They do not call it anything. They are not think-ing of it. They are too busy looking at the source from which it comes" (*MX*, 130–31).

In 1956, Farrer spoke of this movement toward forgetfulness. In his ser-mon, "Radical Piety," he encouraged a Trinity College Chapel audience to consider what it meant to be intellectually honest: Is the life of the intellectual complacent and parasitic, and what do we do to avoid it being so? Paradoxi-cally, the journey to habits beyond the self requires some self-examination. "I am a great shutter of windows," Farrer admitted, "but there are some voices which get into the mind itself, and will not be excluded" (*EM*, 98). Farrer re-called how an ex-Communist and Russian exile had faulted Farrer and his Oxford crowd for being "pluto-aristocratic intellectuals," and how this accu-sation had stung. As a teacher he recollected that students from South Africa had made the same charge over the years. Such moments (as he asked of his listeners) forced Farrer to weigh a life of institutional privilege against Jesus and the prophets' warnings against riches. And the priest concluded that dif-ficult work is one form of mitigation: "You can work. . . . You are here to train your powers for all sorts of uses . . . at least you can get on with the training" (*EM*, 100). When work, like prayer, is not enjoyable, then its shaping of our character is more likely to be at hand. Discipline accompanies the true dis-cernment of one's vocation and life purpose: "Ah, dare I live with the crucifix before my eyes, and dare I die with the crucified to meet—I do not think my regret on that day will be for the opportunities of pleasure I have neglected" (*EM*, 101–2). This is Christian mysticism, but it is also a future-oriented hope that determines a life's course of action.

This transcendent obedience could in fact be distorted by encouraging more myopic self-examination. Lewis wrote of the formation of our charac-ter, "Knowledge can last, principles can last, habits can last; but feelings come and go" (*MX*, 99). He understood that the very act of commitment carried with it a doppelgänger-like parody of itself. "Keep them watching their own minds," counsels Screwtape, "and trying to produce *feelings* there by the ac-tion of their own wills" (*SL*, 16). Lewis offered that submission was one part staying focused upon God and one part tutoring the bodily self to a practice that even circumvents its weaknesses. The will becomes a center of virtue only when it is shaped by habit; and only then does one's character address the Bible's concern with the heart (*SL*, 28). The loss of real, positive pleasures is not necessarily what the Christian means by setting aside self-will; rather, when those pleasures undercut becoming who and what we truly are, only then are they to be dealt the death blow (*SL*, 64–65).

Yet, as Lewis understood, the limitations of our self-awareness make self-examination tricky. Consider Screwtape's advice about gluttony. The patient's mother, in her fickle concern with delicacy, is really more a glutton than many an overeater: "But what do quantities matter, provided we can use a human belly and palate to produce querulousness, impatience, uncharitableness, and self-concern?" (*SL*, 87). There are many such means by which a cloak of respectability can be cast over a sinister character. Different historical eras have particular sins to which they are blinder than others (*SL*, 32). Temptation is only superficially about the immediate act in question; its deeper matter is that of the character being crafted by repeated actions. Screwtape understands that the pretense of civil mores can mimic true virtue, all the while encouraging real vice. Flippancy, unlike pure fun and laughter, can appear as if it were joy, though not forever (*SL*, 53–56).

Farrer, too, could preach that true submission to the will of God comes with loss: "For we do not learn what dependence on God is except through having our self-dependence broken in the mill of life, slowly and painfully" (*FO*, 171). Farrer, like Lewis, understood that certain pretenses to virtue could be practical forms of disobedience, and his calling college-age students to discipline was itself a matter of formation. The society that maximizes fluidity of social and economic movement instead of a stable commitment to Christ is to be feared (*EM*, 92–103). Likewise, in the academy, there are false motivations—often conceit and complacency—for refusing, in a show of humility, to judge what is outside our discipline. Sincerity requires a ranking of goods, which is not the same as the temptation of unfair valuation (*FO*, 203–4). Farrer also insisted that the desire for leadership in collegiate life could be a mask for pride, and teachability might be written off as docility, while a reorientation of our pursuits means a profounder drama still: "God is the very world of opportunity to his saints" (*EM*, 45–46).

For Lewis and Farrer, character formation did include cognitive reflection and conceptual discernment, and its center is the life of the Son of God. It is understandable that Farrer would choose Christ's temptation in the wilderness as a Lenten text. In *The Triple Victory*, Christ's three encounters place the drama of salvation before the reader, who also may act within Christ's action. Our thinking after Christ's thoughts is imperfect but far better than our own thoughts: "What impels a man into a new train of action . . . upon which he stakes his life?" Farrer asks (*TV*, 25). Lewis also understood that the habit of faith must be cultivated before temptation. He called Christ the "only complete realist" because of the strength of temptations that he resisted to the end (*MX*, 124–25). If Christ is the fullest incarnate example for the reader, other wisdom is also formative. It is with the full experiment of the trial in mind that Lewis has Screwtape warn Wormwood of the law of undulation and dark night dryness (*SL*, 37–40), and yet with equal candor, the reader is let in on an open secret: that courage is "the form of every virtue at the testing point, which means, at the point of highest reality" (*SL*, 161). The reader who shares Lewis's desire for spiritual formation is schooled by such matter. Commitment and resignation follow from a repeated attempt at self-awareness and self-forgetfulness. This is the same rhythm of the suspended middle and of grace; thus, for the Christian to reach a place where one is reduced to the small hope of meeting only the next temptation is itself a training in humility and radical dependence (*SL*, 69).

Both writers meditated upon free action and divine enablement. Farrer was anxious to let his communicants know that the Christian narrative is a necessary element to faithful practice. Integrity of mind is impossible without the cross of Christ to conquer sin, and the desire for chastity is "something worthy to convince the intellect and attract the heart" (*FO*, 205–6, 208). Potential to act in certain ways only comes with the necessary framework to make it explicable. At the same time, for Farrer, this is more than the conceptual. It is an actual strengthening by sacramental means. Here again, the relationship of grace and nature is not a forced one. The supernatural gift of faith is not alien to human nature and brings us into a relationship with "*my* God to each of us" and never abstract but as "the God of . . ." (*SB*, 26–27). Freedom is in God because God is the source and overflow of all newness (*SB*, 33).

Given a background of faith and freedom in Christ, Screwtape's analysis of free will and virtue is not quite right. The senior devil understands that for humans to be free lovers and servants requires something other than demonic absorption, and that God will not do for them what they must do themselves: "Desiring their freedom, He therefore refuses to carry them, by their mere affections and habits, to any of the goals which He sets before them: He leaves them to 'do it on their own'" (*SL*, 7). But this is hardly the whole picture. The young convert is assisted in moments of prayer by a blinding light that Wormwood cannot penetrate, and Screwtape himself is utterly reduced to frothing rage in trying to come to terms with the order of sacredness that surrounds the Christian family of the patient's fiancé: "The whole place reeks of that deadly odour. . . . They guard as jealously as the Enemy Himself the secret of what really lies behind this pretense of disinterested love. The whole house and garden is one vast obscenity" (*SL*, 119). Screwtape is unable to comprehend that love transcends freedom and service and that grace makes us more ourselves than less so. But through his reversal, the reader is invited to intuit just that, even if the rhythm of God's freedom and ours can only be implied in analogy.

Of course, particular narratives can make ethical generalizations under-standable in multiple ways (MacIntyre 1998, 311).[25] One of Lewis's most ex-tended examples of this invitation to freedom is in the character of Eustace. Eustace has been malformed ethically in his "modern" experimental school, which is run along lines that Lewis condemns in *The Abolition of Man*. How-ever, life aboard the virtuous society of the *Dawn Treader* had already begun to harden Eustace, and his life as a dragon gives him a sense of his own moral shortcomings and some idea of how he might contribute to the good of the ship (*VDT*, 65, 83–85). The sanctification of Eustace is a key example, if not the book's chief example, of grace's role in perfecting nature. Eustace cannot peel away his own dragonish hide—at least, no more than a few layers. It is Aslan who must tear it away, and the procedure is excruciating while it lasts. Yet it is not as if Eustace does nothing. Even as a dragon, his "character had rather improved" (*VDT*, 83), for he had begun to learn the pleasures of being of use to the community, while after his painful regeneration, he still "had re-lapses. There were still many days when he could be very tiresome." Eustace will in time attempt valiant action, such as attacking the Great Sea Serpent, and even if he is at moments still a know-it-all, it is more out of habit than in-tention (*VDT*, 100, 102). "The cure had begun" (*VDT*, 93). Cruciform virtue, then, is both nature and grace at once.

For the theist, death is not the end, life is not complete here; we await beati-tude. This was a key conclusion of both Farrer and Lewis. In Farrer's sermon, "Remembrance Day: On Hugh Lister," he employed an implicit narrative to hold together a radical life. A priest who started out as an engineer, then be-came a worker priest in the slums; who helped organize and lead a success-ful strike; who contracted tuberculosis and went to recover in a sanatorium, only to return to the slums to work among the poor; and who then chose in World War II to fight in battle while helping design a new infantry carrier, and then dying in battle on a reconnaissance—all this Farrer says describes a man who was "a heroic, hearty," able to accept delight, who "cared for the will of God," and who was proof that "lovers of God really exist" (*BM*, 118). Lister was someone who made an offering of his life, but was hardly aware that he did so, for he was focused outward and not inward.[26] Farrer does something similar in his "Commemoration of Charles Linnell 1915–1964." He suggests that a life like Linnell's is a kind of bridge between this world and the eternal future, and he describes Linnell as someone who served well in his calling, who didn't try to be artificially influential (and therefore naturally was), and whose celibacy was simple and a matter of service to his parents, then to his parishes (*CF*, 214).[27]

For Farrer and Lewis, the final end of humanity can be achieved only by being on the road to sanctification, a way that is costly and even painful, but love offers no other kind of freedom. The nature of hope is one of expectation, and this expectation guides the decisions we make now, the settled character we hope to achieve, the practices of self-examination and self-forgetfulness, and the continual surrender of the self. In this, the virtue of humility, a virtue not understood well by the classical world, is central. To act within Christ's action is to be finally turned outward from the self and, thus, to dwell upon the beloved and that always and ever again.

·✦5✦·

HISTORY

What might have been is a vain speculation. Change a single historical fact, and you escape as by a magic door from the world of actualities. . . . Historians who know their trade will have nothing to do with that will-o'-the-wisp, the might-have-been. At the very most, it is a piece of trick-lighting to bring out the shape and colour of what actually occurred.
—Austin Farrer, *Saving Belief*

I do not suppose that the sixteenth century differs in these respects from any other arbitrarily selected stretch of years. It illustrates well enough the usual complex, unpatterned historical process; in which, while men often throw away irreplaceable wealth, they not infrequently escape what seemed inevitable dangers, not knowing that they have done either nor how they did it.
—C. S. Lewis, *English Literature in the Sixteenth Century, Excluding Drama*

In his 1954 inaugural address as the Cambridge Professor of Medieval and Renaissance Literature, "De Descriptione Temporum," C. S. Lewis drew an analogy between the work of historians and that of flower arranging: "I am less like a botanist in a forest than a woman arranging a few cut flowers for the drawing-room. So, in some degree, are the greatest historians. We can't get into the real forest of the past" (*SLE*, 3–4). Perhaps he was thinking of his own *English Literature in the Sixteenth Century Excluding Drama,* which had been published just two months earlier. According to Lewis, the practice of history is an antiquarian display, rather than an axiomatic science. The best one can do is attractively exhibit examples from the past, enticing an audience to examine them closely. His confidence here appeared rather low in the scope, even veracity, of history, yet what he was condemning were metahistorical law-like theories. Austin Farrer could sound a rather similar note: "History has no middles, just as it has no beginnings and no ends . . . History just goes on and on. Very likely it will stop, but we do not know when." While Farrer held to a larger meaning of history in Israel and in Christ, he knew this would hardly satisfy those looking to organize nonsacred historiography: "Most of the lines which merit the attention of historians," he confessed, "passed by on other roads" (*SB*, 69). He worried, too, about reducing the past to deterministic cycles: "History in general does not have a centre, but the secret history of God's providence in the making of any one creature has a centre" (*SB*, 70).

Farrer and Lewis wrote much of their historical texts to assist with literary or biblical appreciation. Lewis's work in history was that of Medieval and Renaissance literature, which he ranged over not only in *English Literature in the Sixteenth Century*, but also in such texts as *The Allegory of Love* (1936), *The Discarded Image* (1964), and in conceptual studies gathered in *Studies in Words* (1960, 1967).[1] Most of his literary histories were winsome attempts to build knowledge and sympathy for the classical and Christian past in a manner that trusted historical characterization and narrative. His posthumously gathered lectures also evince this concern. Farrer, as exegete and theologian, sought to address the interpretation of New Testament texts, and in the middle of his career, he adopted a figurative approach to the historical meaning and intent of the Gospels. This approach included his *A Study in St Mark* (1951) and *St Matthew and St Mark* (1954), but also his late *The Triple Victory* (1965). Clearly, his goal was more than literary understanding. In particular, Farrer rejected the search for a Jesus of history behind the gospel accounts, and, in turn, he defended the typological imagination of Judaism as a legitimate form of historical thinking.

Lewis and Farrer were working in different fields and thus focused on differing problems. Unlike their similar views as to myth, analogy, and even ethics, their individual approaches to history can best be described as parallel, though they shared some important convictions. Each had some concern with historical method, as well as how best to answer metahistorical theories. Lewis seriously doubted even a theistic vision of universal history, except for the broadest view of time and apocalypse, and thought such views had cultural and political dangers. Farrer shared these cautions: metahistorical claims were untenable, with the exception of providential sacred history. Just as their positions on myth, analogy, and ethics had to address viewpoints within and without the Church, so their work with history had to address religious and secular theories. Here, Lewis and Farrer's chief interlocutors were often fellow Christians, who were also weighing modern viewpoints as to historical understanding, historiography, and metahistory. Both men ultimately focused on the personal aspects of history, recognizing that narrative and agency are one of a piece. That both shared a sense of the personal in history speaks yet again to their focus upon a thick, supernatural universe, even in this most temporal of subjects.

LEWIS AND HISTORICAL SYMPATHY

In 1940, C. S. Lewis had been studying the Roman Catholic historian and social critic Christopher Dawson's *Beyond Politics* (1939), and he wrote his brother Warnie that Dawson was particularly good at teasing out the historical differences between freedom and democracy, the former being an English ideal that supported the individual against the overreach of the political community, and the latter being a French ideal that justified communal imposition upon the "honour and idiosyncrasy" of the individual. Lewis drew several conclusions from Dawson's book. First, he noted that these ideals had their own lineages—the English viewpoint had its roots in English Nonconformity and in English aristocracy, while the French notions could be traced to Jean-Jacques Rousseau and the Revolution, and in the same way, the French Revolution was the ideological parent of not only a conformist democracy, but also of modern dictatorships.

Secondly, Lewis thought the historical difference explained why conscientious objectors were allowed in England and not in France, as well as why some, such as his brother and himself, could be strong on personal freedom but not as invested in the rhetoric of corporate democracy. And thirdly, Lewis also reached the conclusion that "the Whig alliance between great aristocrats and dissenting tradespeople" was something other than just mere pragmatism, for they shared a common faith in certain classic ideals (*Letters*, 2.398).

In his remarks to Warnie, Lewis was himself practicing historical explanation and understanding. He supposed that convictions which he and his brother held were traceable to older social traditions and beliefs, and, in turn, that certain current practices, such as the treatment of pacifists during World War II, derived from older ideas. Furthermore, Lewis regarded Dawson's history as offering a better explanation of the past, namely, that a spiritual principle and tradition once held aristocrat and freeman together, despite some systematic tensions. A letter like this to his brother shows that Lewis could be drawn to historical explanation, and he was obviously interested in its political implications. This might seem at odds with his later flower-arranging analogy and its skepticism, yet this disparity is a reminder that he could have more than one view of history in mind.

History for Lewis was a lifelong concern. The practice of even literary history could be highly contested, and he addressed more than once the nature of historical judgment and what best practice entailed for historiography. He did recognize that the term *history* could be employed in numerous, overlapping ways, and this referential complexity said much about the limitations of human scholarship. *History,* as Lewis observed, can mean:

1. "the total content of time: past, present, and future";
2. "the content of the past only, but still the total content of the past, the past as it really was in all its teeming riches";
3. "so much of the past as is discoverable from surviving evidence";
4. "so much as has been actually discovered by historians";
5. that "which has been worked up by great historical writers"; and
6. "that vague, composite picture of the past . . . in the mind of the ordinary educated man" (*CR,* 105).

Lewis thought the first two definitions were closed to human ability. Given that the total content of the past is available only to God, the past as it really was can function only as a limit idea, otherwise unattainable. It is the surviving evidence and the discoverable past that form the substance of actual historical investigation and the warrant for claims that historians make. Lewis thought that the conceptions making up definition 6 explained the absolute importance of history writing and teaching (i.e., definition 5). The space between what has been discovered, what has been written, and what the ordinary reader thinks about the past is the impetus for historical creativity, and while the distance between the historian's culture and audience and that of the past may defeat good historical work, it also signals the conditions for its true power.

Peter Burke has argued that the modern enterprise of critical history is built upon three of its senses: (1) the evidence, which can be critiqued; (2) the anachronism, which stands between us and a differing past; and (3) the explanation, which depends upon natural or human causation (1969, 13–40). All three senses were part of Lewis's own historical reasoning. The sense of anachronism was particularly of concern to him, so much so that it shaped how he treated historical evidence and explanation. In his *A Preface to Paradise Lost,* he warned readers that variances must be studied with "the effort of the historical imagination" (*PPL,* 72). If part of the joy of researching and reading history came with cultural difference, the cross-cultural and cross-era barriers nevertheless remained. This was the crux of Lewis's own historiography. He sought to navigate the difference between past and present, while at the same time encouraging sympathy (or at times antipathy). He saw cultivating students' historical imagination as a key aspect of his teaching and writing, and he was committed to helping readers appreciate the context of classic texts. He observed, "To judge between one *ethos* and another, it is necessary to have got inside both, and if literary history does not help us to do so it is a great waste of labour" (*ELSC*, 331).

In his 1957 "Is History Bunk?" Lewis argued that the goal of historical investigation is a synchronic picture: "We want to know how such stuff came to be written and why it was applauded; we want to understand the whole *ethos* which made it attractive" (1986, 104). Daniel Danielson has praised Lewis for having talent for Wilhelm Dilthey's ideal of *Nacherlebnis*, the reexperiencing of historical eras (2010, 43–44). Lewis understood that historical periodization was a model rather than an assured set of facts, and yet if one were to imagine why things were significant to the past, one needed a setting by which to assess them (Patrick 1985, 127–28). "Though 'periods' are a mischievous conception they are a methodological necessity," Lewis observed (*ELSC*, 64), and he quoted with approval popular British historian G. M. Trevelyan's maxim that "periods are not facts" but "retrospective conceptions that we form about past events, useful to focus discussion, but very often leading historical thought astray" (*SLE*, 2–3).[2] And though Lewis weighed in against the ontological reality of historical periods, he also recalled fondly how Trevelyan taught him about Walter Scott, who taught, in turn, to Thomas Macaulay the historical sense of "feeling for period" (*SLE*, 217–18).

Arguably, Lewis learned from Trevelyan an ideal for the writing of history. In 1902, J. B. Bury's first address as the Regius Professor of Modern History had advocated a strong objectivist approach to gathering and ordering the archives and data upon which to base a scientific history. Bury, like others before him, wanted history to be practiced as a natural science: "To clothe the story of human society in a literary dress is no more the part of a historian as a historian, than it is the part of an astronomer as an astronomer to present in an artistic shape the story of the stars" (1973, 214). He argued for the strongest criterion, that of law: one has to offer evidence by which one can be assured that (a) caused (b), and quite possibly that (a) always causes (b). Trevelyan famously answered Bury's positivism with a rousing defense of history as persuasive art, "not merely the Accumulation and Interpretation of facts, but also the Exposition of these facts and opinions *in their full emotional and intellectual value* to a wide public" (Trevelyan 1973, 230). History's audience needs help bridging the cultural gap between their context and the period being described: "The motive of history is at bottom poetic," and this poetic is one of similarity arrested with surprising difference. Both the scholar and the reader are "enthralled by the mystery of time, by the mutability of all things, by the succession of the ages and generations" (Trevelyan 1945, 18).

This was something Lewis understood well. His treatment of history drew off the same anthropology as his virtue ethics. We expect human freedom to surprise us at times, even as we also learn to size up persons and their typical actions. General judgments about agency are character-based, and character is assessed by an action's context. Understanding the past need not commit one to suprahistorical law-like patterns. All one needs is a working model as to what cultures in a definitive time shared in common, and this is tested against the actual evidence that has survived from the past. Periodization is neither equivocal fiction (since it reports real behaviors and beliefs), nor is it univocal certainty (i.e., it cannot claim to know all that can be known or why), so no portrait need ever obtain univocal purity, nor need it give into equivocal despair; instead, new descriptions can continue in each generation of historians and critics.

As a result, period judgments do attempt to represent a real gap between the past and present, something Lewis embodied at times in his fiction. For example, in the third installment of his Space trilogy, *That Hideous Strength,* Lewis pictured the challenge of understanding the past. The scholar Arthur Dimble recognizes that in meeting a sixth-century Merlin, the community at St. Anne's were encountering "an age," a period that had been divided between Roman Christian influence and those regions still under pagan Celtic control: "He could see it all. Little dwindling cities where the light of Rome still rested—little Christian sites, Camalodunum, Kaerleon, Glastonbury—a church, a villa or two, a huddle of houses, an earthwork. And, then, beginning scarcely a stone's throw beyond the gates, . . . Little strongholds with unheard-of kings. Little colleges and covines of Druids. Houses whose mortars had been ritually mixed with babies' blood" (*THS,* 230). Tellingly, Dimble pictures the past in archaeological terms, going over known sites, and imagining what they must have been like. Yet such historical understanding falls rather short of the reality.

The shock of surprise is one Lewis intended both for Ransom's household and for that of the reader—that a cultivated man like Merlin would eat with his hands, demand oil for his hair, or consider that Jane Studdock (for her use of contraception) is deserving of a merciful decapitation. Merlin's self-estimation is that of a just, even merciful man. Dimble observes, "We've all been imagining that because he came back in the Twentieth Century, he'd be a Twentieth Century man. Time is more important than we thought" (*THS,* 279), and not just in terms of judicial penalties. In the novel, the failure of historical imagination goes both ways. Merlinus Ambrosius is stunned at the lackluster way moderns dress and live, yet they have exquisite dishes and windows, and a bath fit for a king. Merlin has to completely alter his political and spiritual landscape: he must accept that his allies are the Saxon English, instead of the ancient British; that Christendom is torn into factions; that there is no Christian prince; indeed, that there is no Christian emperor (*THS*, 289–90).

Lewis understood that certain conceptions of the world could stand in the way of readers appreciating the past. He noted, for instance, that some judgments about historical texts were almost inevitably altered by cultural taste, and he drew attention to this in his *English Literature in the Sixteenth Century*. He noticed that the premodern love of rhetoric "is the greatest barrier between us and our ancestors" because moderns have no taste for it, yet if that were ever to change, "the whole story will have to be rewritten and many judgments may be reversed" (*ELSC*, 61). As Lewis observed, a writer's prose can take on different resonances because the modern reader likely values certain aspects, for example, mediocre "Drab" prose can acquire interest for moderns who distrust ornament (*ELSC*, 272). Equally, he noted that the modern taste for the novel is at odds with an earlier world's love for interwoven tales based on tradition (*ELSC*, 332–33). Lewis also understood that sympathy across periods was at times problematic, and that even translations were not free from limited perspective. He thought, for instance, that there was a gap between Homer's original texts and George Chapman's "Half-Stoical, half-Machiavellian, idea of the Great Man." Chapman's reworking of Homer imagined a moral teacher and a model for civic responsibility, "which never crossed the real Homer's mind," while such mistakes Gawin Douglas would not make in translating Virgil, though Lewis thought neither translator revered his poet less than the other (*ELSC*, 517–18).

At times, Lewis himself could not or would not make the sympathetic jump, either to an era's tastes or to its ethic. He himself confessed, "If the medieval approach is alien, that of the Renaissance seems to me sometimes repellant" (*SLE*, 129). "It is difficult to think oneself back into a taste which could have enjoyed such writing," he wrote of the *Narrenschiff*, a Renaissance set piece in the literature of folly (*ELSC*, 126). He acknowledged this same difficulty with the English satires of the 1590s, which are, "in the aggregate, a weariness" (*ELSC*, 477). His attitude toward Thomas Cartwright in particular was vivid, ironic, and scornful (*ELSC*, 447–50), and Lewis could even take a tilt at the "New Ignorance" of the Golden Age and its treatment of the medieval, which he blamed on the age's own prejudices (*ELSC*, 370).

HISTORY IN LEWIS'S PRACTICE AS CHARACTER,
PERIOD, AND MORAL JUDGMENT

The very idea that one can bridge historical mentalities raises the question as to what historical periods actually are. Do they have any reality in and of themselves, or are they better acknowledged as simply conjectural tools? Neville Coghill once commented that C. S. Lewis's "Protestant certainties," his use of complete or final words, as well as his antithetical absolutes, provided for Lewis "a committed force, an ethic on which his ramified and seemingly conciliatory structures of argument are invisibly based," and yet Coghill also thought that they robbed Lewis of "certain kinds of sympathy and perception" (Tandy 2009, 85). To later generations, what we judge to be perfectly objective about the past may indeed be the most obviously biased readings on our part.[3] Arguably, however, despite or perhaps because of his strong tendency to generalize, Lewis did not place absolute faith in his historical narratives. The case can be made that they were to be argued with, supplemented, and even overturned.

To explore this in detail, I will focus on three examples of Lewis's methods of history writing, which included offering an overall plot; developing characters and corporate quasi-characters; and making analogies with the present to invite readerly judgment. Paul Ricoeur has contended that a temporal and open shape is why history shares with fiction a narrative structure. Typical plots and standard characters help describe historical periods and behaviors, and they assume some measure of teleology and essence respectively, even if only as organizing devices. "Plot, in effect, 'comprehends' in one intelligible whole, circumstances, goals, interactions, and unintended results" (Ricoeur 1984, 142). We generalize human action and context in order to make an analogy between the past and the present. Historical periods, which function like quasi-characters as much as contexts, are unavoidable because it is the nature of explanations to include background (Ricoeur 1984, 152–53, 226–30). Given his alliance with a position such as G. M. Trevelyan's, it is not surprising that Lewis would use typical types and narratives to describe the past. "Change is never complete," he observed, "And [yet] nothing is quite new; it was always somehow anticipated or prepared for" (SLE, 2).

Lewis's essay "Addison" (1945) stands at the center of his professional career and is a good example of his practice. "Addison" is as much about Alexander Pope and Jonathan Swift, the Tory satirists, as it is about Joseph Addison, the Whig essayist, and being so, it offers not only literary assessments of the three men, but also the sociocultural contexts that supported them. "Participatory belonging," as Ricoeur put it, is one of the necessities for judging an historical character's intentions (1984, 194). Lewis took rather complex positions on the writers and their conversation. The boisterous, even acerbic sarcasm and fun of Pope and Swift were threatening but defensible as schoolboy "high-spirited rowdiness" (*SLE*, 154). Addison's civil conversation, on the other hand, even when humorous, would never be marked by a lack of polish or urbane control. Lewis employed such generalizations to describe differences across cultures for his audience. Consider the following passage:

> All through the century which Addison ushered in, England was going to attend more and more seriously to the Freeports, and the de Coverleys were to be more and more effectually silenced. The figure of the dear old squire dominates—possibly, on some views, corrupts—the national imagination to the present day. This is indeed 'to make a man die sweetly'. That element in English society which stood against all that Addison's party was bringing in is henceforth seen through the mist of smiling tenderness—as an archaism, a lovely absurdity. What we might have been urged to attack as a fortress we are tricked into admiring as a ruin. (*SLE*, 156)

According to Lewis, Addison was part of a cultural change that continued up to the present, and Lewis pictured an eighteenth-century world in which sentimentality was growing in explanatory power, becoming the tacit ideal of a populace, and thus slowly shifting what was deemed reasonable behavior.

Historical periods are made up of practices that divide the world in certain ways, and the era brought about by Addison helped shape the modern world. Lewis asked his 1945 English audience to consider whether being the inheritors of this shift, they had not been corrupted. Words like *archaism* and *lovely absurdity* offered an audience a position of moral and chronological superiority, yet Lewis also called them to account. The gap between themselves and the traditionalism of Swift and Pope was far wider, and something had been lost. Lewis did not treat Addison or Richard Steele as cynical manipulators; indeed, he thought they could not have foreseen the entire effect of their work; they were part of a change in imagining the world that was wider than themselves.

In the "Addison" essay, common human experience allowed Lewis to examine historical changes and yet treat them as commensurable for his audience. The contemporary present was alike yet different than the past, and this could be sympathetically navigated. None of the three men in question were entirely tied to their period, yet each was representative of it. Addison, Pope, and Swift were subject to an eighteenth-century stress on "rational piety," that is, a belief that the sensible person observes the local faith without any unnecessary perplexity over dogma. Yet the three men did not respond alike. While Pope, the Roman Catholic author of "Universal Prayer," was the least subject to the pressure of a culturally shared faith, and while Swift's version was full of Christian angst and pain ("Swift still belongs . . . to the older world"), Addison's calm acceptance was "historically momentous" (*SLE*, 157, 160). Lewis tied this change in faith to another change—that of good breeding—and he observed that this shift gave the lie to treating standards of mannerly behavior as universal, even while assuming that his 1945 audience shared a standard of propriety that arose with Addison's generation.

The differences between the three men, therefore, signified not just their individual styles and personalities but fundamental shifts that reached forward and backward in time. Lewis could argue for historical threads, connecting Swift and Pope to the hilarity of the medieval and yet also to the narrowness of Renaissance humanism; in turn, he could connect Addison to the coming Victorians and to Romantic views of the medieval, and yet still prize him as a classicist who "touches hands with Scaliger on the one side and Matthew Arnold on the other" (*SLE*, 162). Lewis's final defense of Addison was rather telling: "I fully admit that when Pope and Swift are on the heights they have a strength and splendour which makes everything in Addison look pale; but what an abyss of hatred and bigotry and even silliness receives them when they slip from the heights! The Addisonian world is not one to live in at all times, but it is a good one to fall back into when the day's work is over" (*SLE*, 168).

It was this kind of characterization that easily reflected the trade-off between an assured picture of the past with the knowledge that the picture can be corrected. How, then, given this trade-off, could Lewis's use of historical periods function so confidently?[4] In 1956, for example, he addressed the Zoological Laboratory at Cambridge on the topic, "Imagination and Thought in the Middle Ages." Lewis summarized high medieval conceptions of the cosmos, including its size, its orderly nature, its hierarchical pattern, its natural and supernatural inhabitants, and its triadic organizing structures, the latter which encompassed aesthetic, ethical, social, and metaphysical elements. Such a project involved generalization, as Lewis himself admitted, but to simply encapsulate was not enough. He also set out to shape his modern audience's imagination, in this case one made up of mostly Cambridge scientists.

At several points, Lewis offered a different master metaphor than the one he expected that his audience held without much question. In particular, he wanted to counter a picture of religion as primitive evolutionary residuals, as well as a determinist view of interstellar space as an empty and infinite terror. To confront the first, Lewis admitted to something of an historical genealogy of certain beliefs, but only to seriously discount its value: He conceded that one *might* trace back the medieval belief in angels, demons, and fairies through a long series of written texts until one reached an ancient Attic world, and such a world *perhaps* could be said to approximate the prelogical world posited by anthropologists, but such was as distant from the highly bookish milieu of medieval intellectual culture as that of twentieth-century Britain (*SMRL*, 41–43). Lewis stressed, "Characteristically, medieval man was not a dreamer nor a spiritual adventurer; he was an organizer, a codifier, a man of system" (*SMRL*, 44). While the world of the troubadour was closer to the oral, prelogical one, Lewis insisted that it was not the center of high medieval culture and that current interest in them was a product of eighteenth- and nineteenth-century Romanticism. As heirs to this approach, moderns exaggerated the boundless ineffable as a key to medieval culture, rather than its actual textual and logical practice. Lewis suggested that it was better to understand the systematic and orderly mind of the medieval by paying attention to Gothic cathedrals, Aquinas's *Summa*, or Dante's *Commedia*. Rather than prelogical and intuitive, the medieval mind was credulous yet always about harmonization.

To appreciate this approach, especially when it comes to cosmology, moderns have to revisit their own inherited image of the universe, for to understand the medieval imagination "the motions of the universe are to be conceived not as those of a machine or even an army, but rather as a dance, a festival, a symphony, a ritual, a carnival, or all these in one" (*SMRL*, 60). In essence, Lewis treated a high medieval conception as a social imaginary and invited his audience to entertain its analogical, emotional, and aesthetic states of being. His appeals to the codifier and the systematizer were ones he hoped would engage his audience of researchers, yet he also asked that they envision the medieval universe as a "great, complex work of art" (*SMRL*, 49). He urged them to allow for the differing analogies that medieval science would have appealed to, such as an object's desire for its end. Lewis understood that his audience was only too aware of how analogies describe scientific phenomena, and he insisted that an analogy shaped one's response to the universe, "whether you fill your universe with phantom police-courts and traffic regulations, or with phantom longings and endeavours" (*SMRL*, 50).

To speak of the Medieval era as he did before the Cambridge Zoological Laboratory, Lewis had to employ a highly overdetermined set of data, and he wove together a rather complex picture that reinforced his generalizations, and because he was a literary critic and historian, he drew from numerous texts to build this portrait. He was aware that the picture he offered was colligative, even at points conjectural. That all of this relied on assertive simplification did not seem to threaten Lewis, and that such was a composite did not surprise him or really endanger his project. He openly acknowledged that "most people would now admit that no picture of the universe we can form is 'true' in quite the sense our grandfathers hoped" (*SMRL*, 62); rather, the question was which models suggest a more beautiful, humane existence. This was not just an admission that the science of the Ptolemaic universe was wrong; it was also an admission that even modern world pictures represent shifts in mentalities. He wondered before the scientists present for his second lecture, "What our own models—if you continue to allow us models at all—will reflect, posterity may judge" (*SMRL*, 63). Such an ending perhaps feigned helplessness for a literary scholar like Lewis, but it did offer a pungent question.

As both the "Addison" essay and the Cambridge address model, Lewis did not use historical character and period for bridging only the sympathy gap between current audiences and the past; he also invested historical periods with ideological importance. Periods can include moral judgments, not only as analogies to the present, but also as genealogies of contemporary successes and failures. Lewis's willingness to treat periods as ideological quasi-plots was clearly evident in *English Literature in the Sixteenth-Century*'s introductory chapter, "New Learning and New Ignorance." The title signaled a controversial stance, for Lewis rejected a Whig history of unidirectional progress. He did not have high praise for the Ciceronian rhetoricians of the new humanism or for the Puritans who followed in their wake, and he recognized that because British education was the descendant of Renaissance classicism, it was difficult for some to entertain a less than exemplary notion of the Ciceronians. Indeed, the standard language of periodization—Ancient, Medieval, Modern—arose from their self-appointed rejection of the centuries before them: "And what can *media* imply except that a thousand years of theology, metaphysics, jurisprudence, courtesy, poetry, and architecture are to be regarded as a mere gap, or chasm, or *entre-acte?*" (*ELSC*, 20) Lewis charged the humanists with losing the ability to read the ancients because as rhetoricians they held to a thin standard of Latin style and decorum. Their rejection of scholasticism and medieval romance was fundamentally a fear of being considered vulgar, rather than any seriously engagement with metaphysics (*ELSC*, 20–30).[5] But then, Lewis speculated, "Perhaps every new learning makes room for itself by creating a new ignorance" (*ELSC*, 31). Such was as close as Lewis came to an historical axiom.

Lewis also allowed this principle to shape his discussion of the period. He made similar observations about high magic, the new geography, the first stages of European colonialism, the new political theory of the divine right of kings, the changes in modern authorship, and the growth of Puritanism. He highlighted these to counter traditional and contemporary misconceptions: "Modern parallels are always to some extent misleading. Yet, for a moment only, and to guard against worse conceptions, it may be useful to compare the influence of Calvin on that age with the influence of Marx on our own" (*ELSC*, 42). The problematic historical analogy was still a useful structure. Lewis held that the first Puritans were the radical left wing of their day, both in their doctrinaire passion and their insensitivity to the horrible implications of their systems: "We may suspect that those who read it with most approval were troubled by the fate of predestined vessels of wrath just about as much as young Marxists in our own age are troubled by the approaching liquidation of the *bourgeoisie*" (*ELSC*, 43). Just as the hard-core Marxist is surrounded by fashionable dilettantes, so Calvinism had had both its radical center and its less serious fringe (*ELSC*, 44). Yet Lewis acknowledged that the humanist and the Puritan could often be the same person. Both considered themselves the cultural new wave, hoping to sweep away the old corrupt standard. Calvinism shared the determinism of Renaissance astrologers and the period's high value for the human person.

Given such strong, even antipathetic positions on the period, it may still seem surprising that Lewis understood periods to be fictional, yet it is not too surprising. "'Periods' are largely an invention of the historians. The poets themselves are not conscious of living in any period and refuse to conform to the scheme" (*ELSC*, 106). Throughout *English Literature in the Sixteenth Century*, he provided examples of those who did not fit the model in question, who functioned as transitions, as test cases, as unexplained anomalies, or as variations on a theme—each acting to both affirm and give the lie to the model or tradition in question (see *ELSC*, 464, 469, 476, 481, 523, 531). Perhaps aware that his own portrait of the period had been one-sided, Lewis apologized that he offered "no model of neatness," for "it is too neat, too diagrammatic, for the facts." The historian, he warned, "must beware of schematizing" and must remember that individuals could combine opposed positions: "a Protestant may be Thomistic, a humanist may be a Papist, a scientist may be a magician, a sceptic may be an astrologer" (*ELSC*, 63).

Consequently, Lewis's narrative historiography may be said to be one that in seeking to bridge the distance between his contemporary audience and the past, it trusted in ethical reasoning even as it wore its judgments with a modicum of humility. He knew they were made to be replaced. If he could be convinced of historical judgments, such as Christopher Dawson's, and if he could seek both sympathy and antipathy with the past, he nevertheless understood that there were limitations as to what one could say with certainty. Austin Farrer's approach to the Gospels, likewise, sought to defend their authors as serious first-century Jewish writers, yet as a philosophical theologian and biblical critic, he also worked to place this understanding within the Christian doctrine of scriptural inspiration. At face value, this made Farrer's project seemingly less flexible, yet in practice this was often not the case. To this project, we now turn.

FARRER AND THE MIND OF THE EVANGELISTS

Gerhard Ebeling once observed, "Wherever historicity is not taken seriously, there is also a failure to take really seriously either the text of the Scriptures or the man to whom this text must be interpreted" (1967, 28). Ebeling's point contains a great truth, as well as a great point of debate. The history of twentieth-century biblical criticism, especially its criticism of the Gospels, was a debate about both history and form, and it was a debate that Austin Farrer could not avoid. The nineteenth-century quest for the historical Jesus (and its counterpart in the 1950s) had at its heart the desire to locate a Jesus independent of the biblical witnesses. However, nineteenth-century lives of Jesus, such as that of David Friedrich Strauss or Ernest Renan, tended to produce a human Jesus whose authentic teaching was suspiciously like that of ethical liberalism. As George Tyrell said of Adolf von Harnack, "The Christ that Harnack sees . . . is only the reflection of a liberal Protestant face, seen at the bottom of a deep well" (1909, 44). It took Albert Schweitzer's *The Quest for the Historical Jesus* (1906) to place before the world a more arresting image of Jesus as an apocalyptic eschatologist who expected the end within his lifetime. Schweitzer's Jesus was perhaps no more miraculous than those of nineteenth-century liberalism, yet for many it put to rest an approach that decontextualized the life of Christ. After Schweitzer, the quest went into decline until the 1950s, and neoorthodox theologians, be they conservatives, such as Karl Barth and Emil Brunner, or more radical, such as Rudolf Bultmann, would downplay, even discount, any attempt to speak "objectively" of Jesus and his message.

Even given this public retreat, the quest had been about verification and originality, and these concerns did not go away. That these were necessary for sound historical judgment was hardly questioned. The rise of modern critical history continued to stress the testing of sources and independent confirmation: And the parallel search for an objective, critical methodology did not spare the study of Christian scripture. Discrepancies between parallel passages in the Gospels raised questions about their historical accuracy. Determining which gospel was written first, and in addition to oral accounts, whether the gospel writers influenced one another, was important as a means of uncovering the original events. Likewise, a distrust in the miraculous, as well as a sometimes strained standard of credulity, meant that critics would attribute some or much of the gospel materials to legend, myth, or doctrinal interpolation. And the dating of the Gospels was often an important key to determining where they fell in terms of early Christianity. Along with the quest for a Jesus were close examinations of the veracity of the texts. Four approaches in particular were important, and Farrer interacted with them to some degree. These included source criticism, form criticism, redaction criticism, and tradition criticism.

Farrer's approach to the gospel of Mark, as well as to Matthew and Luke, made him a transitional figure between that of early form and source criticism and that of later rhetorical and redaction criticism. All approaches took dissimilarity (or discrepancy) as a key impetus for interpretation, yet they were divided upon what grounds one could establish coherence. Source criticism was not only about sorting out originals, but also concerned with reconstructing material behind the received texts. It sought to establish the veracity and therefore believability of claims—either to the state of the evidence or of the eyewitness's actual proximity to the supposed events. In his *A Study in St Mark* (1951), for example, Farrer opened by describing the aspirations of the old source criticism. Such critics had hoped that Mark's gospel, in being the first, was "somewhat nearer to the fountain-head from which tradition flows," and thus would provide access to those eyewitnesses who were most pure as historical evidence (*SSM*, 3–5).[6]

For the New Testament at least, the Synoptic problem was the key expression of source analysis. By the twentieth century, the majority hypothesis was the Two-Source Model, namely that Mark was written first and based on oral, even written sources. Matthew and Luke in turn, both used Mark, but also a lost document, Q, which was the basis for what they shared but clearly did not derive from Mark. B. H. Streeter in 1924 had argued for a four-source answer, positing not only Mark and Q, but a Proto-Luke (which was built up from Mark and Q) and M (an additional source for Matthew) (Neill and Wright 1988, 132–35). In "On Dispensing with Q" (1955), Farrer argued that not only was there no need for Streeter's hypothesis, but Q itself could be forgotten. Once we accept that Luke used not only Mark, but also Matthew as a source, and that, while Mark is Luke's chief source, Matthew had been consulted and adapted, it follows that Luke is a real author with independent purposes in composing his gospel.[7]

Form criticism, on the other hand, while having similar concerns as source criticism, was more focused upon exploring the *Sitz im Leben*, the cultural situation in life that gave birth to the forms. Works such as Martin Dibelius and

Bultmann's located a space between the Gospels and their pericopes. This meant treating the Gospels as folk literature, rather than as cultured literary products, and as having been compiled from oral anecdotes without concern for style. Form critics assumed that these accounts were from superstitious communities given to embroidering the actual events, even fabricating legends. But source critics saw each tale as serving an anthropological purpose that could be ascertained scientifically. Of course, all this was the case once one was able to untangle the hodgepodge; and there was hardly a consensus to that.

Farrer would go on record as to this matter a number of times. He insisted that form criticism led to too strong a trust in human reason, a positivist skepticism, and an atomism that did not recover the history it sought (*IB*, 21–22). He complained that the approach only showed that the author of Mark wrote in anecdotes, not that he had compiled them (*SSM*, 22–24). Farrer insisted the "study of the large has the priority," for pattern takes hermeneutical precedence (*SSM*, 22–23). Mark's gospel is not a compilation of fragmented pericopes. Form criticism reduces the evangelist's "free inspiration" (*SSM*, 22) and ignores the obvious: that Mark "builds up his own rhythms" (*GV*, 113). In the end, Farrer simply refused to see Mark as a clumsy compiler: "If he modified tradition, was he bound to introduce detectable anachronisms *at every stroke*? No doubt he occasionally does, or so it is commonly thought—but always?" (*IB*, 18–19).

Redaction criticism, promoted by German critics Günter Bornkamm and Hans Kozelmann, would come after Farrer's first two gospel books, but Farrer's work represents one of its precursors. Redaction criticism based its findings on the textual world assumed by source and form criticism but tended to see the gospel redactor (that is, editor or compiler) as making creative choices that reflect a theological vision. Instead of seeking to uncover the original event or early stages of witness, redaction criticism turned to the final product—the texts themselves. While rhetorical or composition studies would treat the gospel as a literary whole, redaction criticism still tended to acknowledge that the earlier stages influenced the final outcome, and this presumed history nuanced the choices that the gospel writers were judged as making. So, for example, Matthew or Luke deliberately altering or reorganizing Mark's gospel would lead to different conclusions than reading Mark as truncating Matthew.

As an alternate path to form criticism, Farrer looked to the symbolic approach of R. H. Lightfoot. Lightfoot, one of the strongest British advocates of form-critical approaches, developed them to such an extent that some, in retrospect, have considered him the first redaction critic (Kealy 1982, 141; Perrin 1971, 21–24). Farrer thought that what made Lightfoot's approach valuable, if not per se as modern critical history, was that it offered a window into Mark's mind. In Lightfoot's approach, the history that is Mark's forces us to pay attention on Mark's terms (*SSM*, 6–8).[8] Thus, in Farrer's reading, Lightfoot's approach escaped the dilemma of the Jesus of history by focusing upon how the redacted text was itself a history (though of an ancient and not a modern sort) (Neill and Wright 1988, 282–83).

Farrer acknowledged the desire for independent collaboration of the gospel accounts, but he insisted that the closest we were ever likely to find were other Christian accounts: "Christians were the only people sufficiently interested to memorize or record the Christian facts while there was still living witness to them" (*SSM*, 203). Even given this strong emphasis on the final whole and its treatment as a conscious singular product, the question of authenticity and veracity remained: How much of the evangelist's gospel could be trusted to do justice to the historical occurrences, especially given its deliberate literary shaping? The state of this question paralleled the debate over the Jesus of history and the Christ of faith, particularly in regard to the preaching and teaching of the early Church. In some versions of tradition history and dogmatic development, the actual events behind the faith of the Church become secondary. Is the gospel writer to be understood (and to what extent allowed) as an original writer, rather than simply reflective of post-Easter ecclesial viewpoints? And what is the exegete to make of the authority of the writer, apostolic and inspired by God?[9] Does the authority of the account, then, reside with the inspired author, or with the history of divine encounter that the text reports with more or less accuracy? Or does final authority rest with the Living Church, be that Anglican, Roman Catholic, or Eastern Orthodox?

Farrer always considered these matters within the confession and dogma of the Historic Church, and his assumption of a single end for nature and supernature shaped his hermeneutical values, as well. The gospel witnesses are read within the faith community; they are judged to be inspired witnesses and their reception is part of the faith of the second-century Church. However, the history attested to in the Gospels is real history and not a mythic account with no relationship to the world. The inspired apostolic narratives are what they are because the supernatural life of God in Christ flowed out of him and into them, and this is rooted in the real past: "Development is development, and neither addition nor alteration," and that development is inspired and works its way out through the apostolic teaching and mission (*GV*, 41–42).

In one of his later writings, "Infallibility and Historical Revelation" (1968), Farrer had to face the other side of this question; namely, is doctrinal development itself infallible? He insisted, over against his Roman Catholic counterparts, that making infallible, dogmatic claims based on fallible historical judgments was dangerous because they remain open to further confirmation of disconfirmation (*IB*, 157). "What I have to point out is that to admit primitivity as a judge or as a control is to submit to scholarship or historianship; and the scholar or historian is fallible; his work is endlessly corrigible, or subject to revision" (*IB*, 158). Farrer went so far as to argue that correctable scholarship would likely carry more weight for most than a Magisterium: "The links of infallible authority would be less effective in binding us to our origins than would the most fallible procedures of historical science" (*IB*, 159). He concluded that in terms of Church dogma, infallibility was "a regulative idea" and not itself incorrigible (*IB*, 163). Farrer's approach to the Gospels, then, was to treat the inspired authors as real authors, as actual persons with literary and theological ideas and with intelligent, even calculating choices as to how to embody these in literary narratives, and yet they were still inspired by the Holy Spirit, and thus, they were sources of Christian kerygma, for they were apostles and yet of their culture.

FARRER AND HISTORICAL REENACTMENT

Taken together, source, form, redaction, and tradition criticism asked of Austin Farrer serious reflection upon the nature of history itself. Farrer had to examine whether historical understanding with regard to the Gospels would take the same shape as secular history. In a position not unlike C. S. Lewis's, he insisted that even profane history is not the product of scientific positivism. "All historical writing involves the use of the imagination. . . . we have to appreciate the laws of [the historian's] imagination, and the assumptions he makes about the pattern of events" (*SSM*, 182). By "laws" Farrer meant a set of normative practices rather than something axiomatic. Because Farrer's general model was humanist, he insisted that there was no singular method for establishing historicity or accuracy. And equally like Lewis, Farrer argued that the historian does not begin with a "set and ready-made method" because the subject matter of history is human action. As such, history requires personal understanding and subject only to personalist approaches: "There is no method for dealing with the unique. . . . No historical generalisation is more than a pointer" to the singular human deed.[10] The historian has to range over not just records of stated intentions, but also the actual actions and contexts, and intentions and actions may be at odds with one another (*CF*, 38).

This was a general approach Farrer shared with historical idealism. In his broadcast tribute to R. G. Collingwood, "Thought as the Basis of History"

(March 20, 1947), he recommended a number of texts by the late philosopher and historian: *The Idea of History, The Idea of Nature,* and *Principles of Art,* perhaps because these were approachable reading for a general audience, and he also mentioned Collingwood's final work (presumably *The New Leviathan*), though this work was less solid to Farrer's judgment. Most of the broadcast was a brief eulogy to Collingwood's "truceless war" with academics whose pedantic work he had judged as having no relevance to life. Farrer summarized Collingwood's chief points about history and thought:

- "History is a developing science, and it has reached no final form today.... history has just come of age."
- "The historical process is moved on by one thing alone, by thinking." And this is so even given psychological or economic forces. "The moving power in history is thought."
- History is reconstructed by working with the surviving evidence, critiquing accounts which often lie, contradict, or omit key information, and this reconstruction requires rethinking "the thoughts of dead men."
- Such thinking is difficult and requires considerable effort "to avoid cooking the result," yet it is possible.
- "Unless thought can be brought alive again, there can be no history." Otherwise, the surviving objects do not have historical significance. (Farrer 1947, 424–25)

Farrer asked himself, then, if he agreed with Collingwood's conclusions, and he was not sure. Farrer was firm that he could not concur with Collingwood that thought and effort alone were enough to change the human predicament. For the Christian, it could not be so because divine action was key to the larger movement of history. Farrer also noticed a particular dilemma in Collingwood's thought: the question of "the permanent unity of mankind," which Collingwood's historicism would seem to deny. After all, Collingwood's view of reenactment depended upon that held in common by the present historian and by the past culture, yet his approach threatened one with a flux of historical relativism. And unity of understanding and divine providence were not the only difficulties for Farrer in the historian's system; likewise, how did Collingwood account for the universal nature of human responsibility? All people are related to the unchanging God, which Collingwood presumably held to be a truth of reality (Farrer 1947, 425).

When addressing these problems, Farrer had something like the suspended middle of Erich Przywara in mind. Historiography cannot be reduced to purely subjective storytelling, or to even a quasi-idealist account of thought. Eventually, in its theory and practice, history has to appeal to a qualified critical realism. The world is something tangible, even given that the past is no longer present except in archives, archaeology, and memory. Farrer agreed with Collingwood that there is a difference between the language of causation when it describes the considered action of human beings and when it signifies the supposed regularities of physical reactions:

> Casual explanation is and can only be an interpretation of natural interactions by the clue, or the model, of our own interferences with our environment, and its interferences with us. To understand the world never was, nor conceivably could be, to construe it as patterns of *phenomena*. It must be construed as an interaction of real existences carrying on business as it were out there in space under their own names. (*RF*, 210)

Farrer's point was that the language of efficient cause is itself analogous to human formal cause. Even our attempts to describe the regularities of natural phenomena draw from analogies with our own active, choice-laden behaviors. The language of historical description is causal, but of a very human sort. History cannot be written with the same confidence that the hard sciences claim, yet quasi-causal analysis is at the heart of historiography given that agency and narrative are intertwined. In fact, as Collingwood had pointed out, historical casual thinking was an ancient idea and preceded early modern positivism. At the same time, Farrer insisted, a true sacred history, while it recognizes human freedom, also must accept the double agency of humans and God. The Creator is at work, and analogical that it may be, there is no better way to describe the First Cause than that of personal causation: "No; the theist sees behind all causes the personal agent, the Creator, the supreme archetype of his own efficacity" (*RF*, 217).

For Collingwood, historical reenactment was neither the actual past (which is gone after all) nor a mental copy, but the ideas of the past conceptually rethought. The historian must reenact the thoughts (i.e., contexts and decisions) of historical actors in order to understand their actions. Thus, the history of ideas and deeds are tied together. Ideas occurred within settings with certain ends in view. Generalizing across particular activities means that we cannot generalize universals from historical conditions because human behavior is not reducible to conditioning. Yet truth does survive into the present, and we connect with it in the present, even as thought is historically dependent, and ideas must be understood within their contexts. Historical science must resist positivism, for even statistics require interpretation (Collingwood 2005a, 213–31).

in the history behind the text had its dangers. "It does not seem as though the theory of revelation by divine events alone is any more satisfactory than the theory of dictated propositions," Farrer had written in *The Glass of Vision* (*GV*, 39). Farrer proposed in the Hulsean sermon to explore "the true nature of historical enquiry" and its relationship to the New Testament (*CF*, 36). He had in view the question of the historical Jesus and the debates about the Synoptic problem, but especially the increasing issues with form criticism, and he opened by commending the Cambridge theological faculty's attention to "the plain historical and positive method of enquiry." Farrer observed that a historian's philosophy became more important the more obscure the subject was. If numerous source materials were available, such as with the reign of Victoria, then "the capable historian will make a tolerable job" regardless of theory; and when such was the case, method remained a matter more for the philosophers than practicing historians. But once one moved to the remote past, this became fraught with danger (*CF*, 36–37).

Like Dodd, Farrer acknowledged that to read the New Testament was to encounter Paul, Mark, and John's views, yet in studying these we may yet come to know the Christ to whom they were responding (Dodd 1938, 27–28; *CF*, 40–41). As I discussed in chapter 2, "Myth," this was a position that Lewis shared with him. Farrer also set forth this view in *The Core of the Bible* (1957). There, he discussed how Paul's earliest epistles to the Galatians and the Corinthians exhibited the manner in which the infant Church conceived of Jesus. The same, he felt, was true of the Evangelists. Despite their differences, they were all directly referring to actual events. Such writers were not attempting historical biography as the twentieth century understands it, yet "certain incidents, being the turning-points of the history, keep their true historical positions" (1957b, 10).[12]

In his Hulsean sermon, Farrer insisted that Jesus must be understood as a first-century Jew and not as a nineteenth or twentieth-century ideal, yet Farrer was quick to stress that Jesus was not reducible to his context. Having a context in mind was not the same as declaring Jesus's actions typical or predictable: "For what Christ did was certainly not obvious, any more than what Socrates did when he provoked the court to condemn him was obvious" (*CF*, 39–40). "No rules, forms, or principles of historical procedure can see us through such a task" that pretends to operate "independently of our estimate of what we can see Jesus of Nazareth to do" (*CF*, 43). And this was the case because the character of Christ transcends all other persons. Here, Farrer was making a point that exceeded Lewis's about how historical figures can defy period expectations. Farrer was insistent: "We cannot establish what happened, we cannot establish the bare historical facts, without a personal understanding of Christ"

(*CF*, 42). The Christian does not believe that Jesus was only a Jew, but the Incarnate Son of God—our historical judgments about the accounts are, therefore, based on what we believe the Divine Being can and would do in history: "If we lay down the dogma that Gospel history is just like any other history, we are committing ourselves to the proposition that Christ is just like any other man" (*CF*, 44), which is what many a textual critic had done.

Farrer insisted that introducing a shadow account behind Mark's record solved nothing, as if Mark could be expected to decontextualize the original anticipation of first-century Jews and Christians. Instead, he made the case that Mark was mirroring the actual hope that Paul referred to in his epistles to the Thessalonians. The human Jesus's own eschatological expectation, Farrer argued, did not have to have in mind an exhaustive time line as to what his prophecy pointed (*SSM*, 358–64). The maturation of theological understanding happened within the New Testament writers themselves because they were inspired. There is simply no measure by which we can judge how quickly, or under what consistent conditions, ideational change and complexity takes place, as if there were a sociological covering law for such matters.

The same is true for its opposite. The supposition that premodern people, without a critical sense of historical evidence, were simple and credulous is arrogant and deceptive, as is the claim that doctrinal complexity could only arise through a long period of random formation: "The hypothesis of unrestricted accident is unnecessary and (what is more to the point) untrue" (*SSM*, 368–69). Mark's gospel could be expected to be not only historical and theological, but also "historico-theologico-parenetic" (*IB*, 14–15). Even if one, for analysis purposes, could tease apart the historical and theological elements of the narratives, they were not conceived with modern critical and positivist assumptions in mind. Their authors would not have separated out their history and their theology from their persuasive technique. Farrer would, thus, conclude that the attempt to get to the actual event behind the accounts was finally misguided, if not shaped by an ideological commitment. "Impartiality towards the Gospel story is really impossible: believers through love of God may be over-indulgent to the witnesses: unbelievers are afraid of God, and evade the evidence. Of course, what else could one expect?" (*BM*, 111)

Farrer insisted that neither the author of the Gospels nor his readers would have assumed that the miracles chosen to be recorded were the only ones that happened; the stylized patterning was, nevertheless, not simply made up; they were drawn out of the events and shaped to impart a truth about them, and they were patterned primarily upon typological symbolism: "Prefiguration is his form of historical thinking" (*SSM*, 183), and this patterning is one that no historian would use without theological commitments: "It belongs to history viewed as divine revelation" (*SSM*, 184). This is essential to understanding Farrer's whole project. He was rejecting objectivist, positivist claims for history, including a need for cause-effect sequences (*SSM*, 187–88). Mark, and all New Testament writers, Farrer would insist, reason historically but not in the same way a modern historian would (*SMSM*, vii). A thick metaphysical understanding was an interpretive essential.

Still, Farrer insisted that the writers were "realists after their own manner" since they had to work out their beliefs about divine providence in light of numerous oppressions and deportations (*SB*, 74). "Idols of the historical imagination" assume a continual chain of moments that in themselves have limited meaning, for "nothing can have any significance for what preceded it in time" and what comes after "is bound to be a diminishing factor" (*SSM*, 185). Yet this is what figurative typological understanding found convincing. The ante-type by divine plan explains more deeply what prepared for it, and what comes after it takes on additional resonances, even centuries apart. Farrer spoke of Mark's typological history as a kind of metahistorical force: "he feels in his bones the power of one historical phase to beget the next" (*SSM*, 184). But this is not the same as the evolution of religious consciousness. Farrer, thus, treated seriously the proposition that time is not exactly linear or reductively horizontal but "presented for interpretation" (*SMSM*, 15).

Near the heart of the debate over gospel history, then, was the difference between a critical historiography and a faithful submission to theological truth. Farrer also held with Collingwood that all historiographical judgments were based upon extrapolating from our own experiences. "Functions of existential decision" are what make up our narrative commitments to a particular interpretation of past events, and this is certainly the case with judgments about the historicity of Christ (*FS*, 91). Farrer argued that there are two ways to approach the Bible: one is "as a sacred collection . . . read out as carrying apostolic authority in the Church in the second century," while the second is as a first-century text, whose material is subject to close historical erudition. The sacred approach, Farrer said, was open to a twentieth-century person "with great enjoyment and substantial profit," while the second was hopelessly technical and closed except to the professional (1957b, 12). The first approach assumed not only personalism, but also supernatural purpose and assistance. In addition, interpreting with predetermined historical theories is reductive and suppresses the setting out of which human action takes place—another insight Lewis affirmed. We cannot devise a singular historical method because all human action is "personal and unique" (*CF*, 38). Farrer argued that the "pattern of hiding and opening" asks the reader "to reason from analogy." The Resurrection of Christ is the ultimate hidden, then open, event in the text (*SSM*, 226). In this, the authority of biblical revelation takes precedence in a way that a historical text would not (or should not) otherwise do. To understand Christ, we must place him in a first-century Jewish context; yet to truly understand him we must be given spiritual understanding via the Holy Spirit, for Jesus is not just a human being, but the perfect God-Man. We cannot understand the Gospels without understanding Jesus, and we cannot understand Jesus without the Spirit, and there is no receiving of the Spirit except through the Church.

Thus, despite their widely differing fields of works, Lewis and Farrer shared a basic trust in personalist accounts of history and sought to help their readers understand historical texts. Admittedly, Farrer's work with inspired scripture meant that he would not judge the Evangelists as fallible in quite the same way that Lewis could speak of his historical subjects, yet both men still positioned their approaches over against more positivist attempts at an historical science. This shared concern was not the only matter in historical interpretation in which they concurred; they also cautioned against large meta-accounts of history, and if Farrer's cautions took place against a biblical background, Lewis's were nonetheless also concerned with theological accounts and what they might portend.

LEWIS AND THE DREAD OF AXIOMATIC HISTORY

The decades from 1930 to 1960 saw much public dispute among philosophers, theologians, historians, and public intellectuals about the larger meaning of history. While the debate itself was hardly new, two world wars, the rise of Marxist and Fascist theory, and the general search for an objective standard of history had all encouraged sustained thinking about the topic, even among the general population. Writing in 1949, historian E. Harris Harbison could observe a hunger for meaning among the young veterans returning to universities after the war: "They made it clear to advisers and teachers that they were looking for answers. . . . Somewhere in history, many of them thought, the answer to how it all came about was to be found" (1964, 8). The debate among specifically Christian thinkers gravitated toward large suprahistorical questions not only about determinism and freedom, as well as relativism and historicism, but also about the relationships of sacred and profane history and about last things. Certainly, the prolonged discussion about the historical reliability of the scriptures was a significant part of this debate, as was the consideration of the nature and method of critical history. Yet the question as to whether there were axiomatic laws and the related question of whether history has a predictable direction were of central importance because they seemed to offer a meaning, if not a myth, that would explain national change and suffering.

C. S. Lewis distrusted theories of historical change, including Christian ones: "I do not dispute that History is a story written by the finger of God. But have we the text?" (CR, 105). He also worried that the search for historical laws would lead to a devaluation of the eternal claims upon our moral realities. Screwtape advised Wormwood that "the general Evolutionary or Historical character of modern European thought" has made it easier for moderns not to take seriously their own sin (SL, 138). False views of history, "hazy ideas of Progress and Development and the Historical Point of View," enable tempters to delude their patients into believing themselves superior to the childlike, superstitious ages of the past (SL, 46). And such a historicist approach could achieve its demonic end in two ways: (1) by reducing all ethical reflection to relativism, so that the student or researcher would never ask if a claim in the history of ideas was true, or (2) by declaring historical findings as worthless twaddle, "as the most ignorant mechanic who holds that 'history is bunk'" (SL, 150–51). Lewis had to hold at bay both a historicism that led to relativism and a strong distrust of history as a worthless exercise, and this was certainly present in Screwtape's advice. In the first case, rather than asking whether something is true, the tempter focuses the scholarly "patient" on establishing what an idea's intellectual pedigree was or what it illustrated about the development of an author's corpus. In the second case, perhaps with the more general, uneducated "patient," the relativism of historicist methods could lead one to conclude it has no real value for day-to-day existence. History is just a load of contradictory claims; nothing is sure except the pragmatic power of the moment.

Lewis considered how to respond to both these outcomes. After World War II, he wrote enthusiastically to Christopher Dawson about the historian's first Gifford Lectures, Religion and Culture (1948), which Dawson had sent to Lewis. Lewis admired Dawson's treatment of Hegelianism and evolutionary developmentalism, as well as his work "on the Humanists ... [which] seems to me particularly sound," and he remarked to Dawson that the book made for "the most exciting kind of reading" because it "also was strangely 'corroborating,'" though Lewis admitted this to be a subjective response (Letters, 3.1584). Having previously now met, Dawson and Lewis were on a personal basis, but the latter was hardly just being polite. Dawson's approach to natural theology and humanist culture struck a chord in Lewis because it resonated with views that he held as a literary historian. Yet none of this, Lewis would insist, required historical laws.

In October 1950, Lewis published his essay "Historicism," in which he condemned the pursuit of historical, developmental causes, giving a stipulative definition for "historicism" that would have surprised some of his audience (Bebbington 1990, 180; Ritter 1986, 183–87).[13] It may have surprised Dawson. Instead of decrying the cultural relativism associated by many with historicism, Lewis described it as "the belief that men can, by use of their natural powers, discover an inner meaning in the historical process" (CR, 100). Here, he was particularly concerned to disassociate Christianity from suprahistorical theories, and in this case Lewis's more immediate interlocutor was another fellow Christian. That February, he had likely listened to Father Paul Henry's Denecke Lecture at Lady Margaret Hall, and the Jesuit's claims were ones that Lewis both learned from and yet questioned.[14] Henry's talk, "The Christian Philosophy of History," reviewed fairly well the state of the question circa 1950, and concluded that, apart from the Church and its understanding of Christ, for many Christian thinkers "there is no historical knowledge which can raised to the level of a philosophy of history or in which can be found the meaning of history" (Henry 1952, 421–22). Henry argued that this was true across confessional lines, Protestant, Catholic, and Orthodox, and was the case because only Christianity (along with Judaism and to some extent Islam) offered a directional view of history. Enlightenment Progress was just a secularized heresy. Yet Henry wanted to moderate this claim, pointing to directional or "providential" destiny in Roman histories. To these, Lewis agreed and added Norse examples. But whereas Henry thought Roman historians were still incapable of drawing from their Virgilian strains any universal axioms and, thus, that the patristic and medieval vision of history was groundbreaking, Lewis was suspicious of such visions. Even the Augustinian vision of Two Cities he distrusted, and he charged that Dante's imperial vision of history in De Monarchia was a Roman neopagan derivative, rather than anything Christian (CR, 103–4).

Henry noted that within the shared Christian theology of history, there were divergences. All agreed that the Incarnation changed everything, that its historical reality created a before and after, and therefore, a beginning, middle, and ultimate end to history (Henry 1952, 428–30). Yet even given this consensus, Christian thinkers disagreed over what this meant for historical action and involvement. For one class, which Henry labeled as "eschatological," there can be "no Christian humanism," since human progress is a moot point and only the awaited eternal destiny matters; while for the other class, "incarnationists," human progress is real and possible, since history is the "natural and necessary milieu" of Christ's "spiritualized and resuscitated body" (Henry 1952, 431–32). Henry associated himself with this second class. Lewis, on the other hand, judged such conclusions to be Hegelian; they require the activist to know which events are aligned with the expected, providential destiny. "If history is what the Historicist says—the self-manifestation of Spirit, the story written by the finger of God, the revelation which includes all other revelations—then surely he must go to history itself to teach him what is important," yet Lewis complained, "How does he know beforehand what sort of events are, in a higher degree than others, self-manifestations of Spirit?" (*CR*, 109)

Though in the delivered address, Henry did not always name names, he did draw particular attention to Karl Barth and Emil Brunner, as well as Oscar Cullmann's important *Christ and Time*. Henry's 1952 notes suggest that he had a wider gamut of authors in mind, including Dawson's 1929 *Progress and Religion* and his *Beyond Culture*. Henry's fellow Catholic is an important inclusion because of how he would come to dissent from Lewis. Dawson shared with Austin Farrer and Lewis a strong stress on a single end for nature and supernature, and this allowed him to locate in his historical theory a fundamental energy learned from Augustine's Two Cities. The Catholic view of human nature is that of a being compounded of spirit and matter, held in tension with one another yet interpenetrating as well: "The supernatural is not the contradiction of nature, but its restoration and crown, and every faculty of man, whether high or low, is destined to have its share in his new supernatural life" (Dawson 2009, 262–63, 281).

It was not the hierarchy of nature and supernature over which Lewis and Dawson disagreed, but over how Dawson identified that hierarchy. For Dawson, it was a historical principle that could be identified using sociological and anthropological findings. Despite his high praise of Dawson's work, Lewis distrusted the social sciences to which the historian appealed. "The mark of the Historicist," Lewis complained, "is that he tries to get from historical premises conclusions which are more than historical; conclusions metaphysical or theological or . . . atheo-logical" (*CR*, 100–101). Perhaps this was what concerned Lewis most with Henry's distinction between the eschatologist's theology of history and an incarnationist vision. Lewis worried that reading history in an axiomatic fashion had enabled dictators to claim for themselves the hand of destiny, and theistic versions had been no better in their abuse of power. Such opened the door for any "quack or traitor" to "woo adherents or intimidate resistance" to tyranny (*CR*, 110). Lewis stressed instead that which individuals are most important from God's perspective is not something to which we are privy. They represent an entirely secret history of sainthood.

The next year, in his essay, "The Christian View of History," Dawson in response to Lewis argued that historicism (i.e., metahistory) was not the same as material or idealist dialectics, and that German liberal Protestantism and Idealism had muddled things. He gave Lewis credit for opposing positions that mistook their own philosophy for Christianity, yet he insisted that a Christian understanding of history was compatible with an Augustinian model of time and society: "For the Christian view of history is not merely a belief in the direction of history by divine providence, it is a belief in the intervention by God in the life of mankind by direct action at certain definite points in time and place" (2002, 245–47). Dawson argued that the typological history in the Old and New Testaments was the framework out of which patristic doctrinal development naturally took place. In this, Dawson was assuming dogmatic guidance by the Holy Spirit, a position not unlike Farrer's. Augustine's vision of history and the various Christian efforts at universal history that followed were attempts to understand what the past meant in light of the promised eschaton. Such endeavors did not, however, of necessity commit a historian to their every conclusion. If anything, the doctrine of the Two Cities allowed one to find a general principle of cultural energy without committing one to specific predictions. For Dawson, it was clear that metahistory was not universal history and that sociology should play an important role (2002, 307–10). General, law-like estimates were neither by nature conclusive nor unadaptable. And, if nothing else, the Christian directional vision broke through the fatalistic (or positivistic) claims of historical cycles.

Lewis, on the other hand, discounted any pretense to a science or philosophy of history, even though he affirmed a general theological shape to its course. History, he held, is an interpretive study of the particulars; it cannot be an attempt to explain the deep causes or developmental pattern of historical forces. The normal means of historians, he insisted, included inferences of unknown events from known ones or even future outcomes from past ones, though he thought the latter misguided, even if allowable. Suprahistorical laws, on the other hand, could not be advanced without comprehensive knowledge. No one can know the totality of history because we do not know most of the past, nor has the future happened: "The philosophy of history is a discipline for which we mortal men lack the necessary data" (*CR*, 110). Lewis feared even conjectural metahistory was a threat to free agency and to the foundations of moral decision-making. He could warn that "Fascism and Communism, like all other evils are potent because of the good they contain or imitate. *Diabolus simius Dei*" (*Letters*, 2.327), and he disapproved as well of Marxist-inspired Christian movements and recognized that Marxism was only one of several secular theories of history that could trace its historical origins to Christian millenarian hopes.[15]

Lewis was wary, too, of the cyclical theories of Oswald Spengler and Arnold Toynbee. Each imposed a totality upon all the particulars. Spengler claimed to have found eight high cultures that had moved through a life cycle of birth, maturation, and death, while Toynbee had identified nineteen full civilizations with four abortive ones by which to map out his theory. In "De Descriptione Temporum," Lewis spelled out his objection to such approaches: "I am not, even on the most Lilliputian scale, emulating Professor Toynbee or Spengler. . . . I know nothing of the future, not even whether there will be any future. I don't know whether past history has been necessary or contingent. I don't know whether the human tragi-comedy is now in Act I or Act V; whether our present disorders are those of infancy or of old age" (*SLE*, 3).[16]

In "Historicism," Lewis drew an analogy with a departed father's old drawer, forgotten, then recovered, which contains an assortment of documents, most with no clear value to the family. Lewis insisted, "I think the real historian will allow that the actual *detritus* of the past . . . is very much more like an old drawer than like an intelligent epitome" (*CR*, 109). Historical evidence is often a matter of chance. Admittedly, if such a claim were taken in isolation from his other considerations of history, it would render impossible his own practice. In Lewis's defense, the object in his particular sights was that a predictive (and thereby oppressive) model of the future could be discovered from the past, not that moral universals are undiscoverable or even that a larger transhistorical narrative could be advanced. He was taking a position that he hoped guarded against political abuse and tyranny. Yet his stress on moral universals certainly carried with it questions with regard to historical judgment. Moral judgments must be made within history, even if they are acknowledged as objective and given for all traditional cultures. Lewis, after all, affirmed a transcendent Tao, and this was what he most feared historicism would corrupt.

FARRER AND TRANSHISTORICAL JUDGMENTS

In the 1960s, Austin Farrer also returned to larger questions about the nature and meaning of history, especially trans-era judgments. Like Lewis, Farrer engaged the wider cultural debate about the meaning of history, and he too was distrustful of claims to uncover a pattern and destiny in secular history. Farrer's early career interest in Eric Przywara and his interactions with R. G. Collingwood's works are only two examples of how he interacted with these wider concerns involving suprahistorical societal patterns, historical law, and human freedom. Farrer was less sure about some of Collingwood's suppositions in these matters. For example, progress and decadence for Collingwood were judgments of mind in a specific period based on specific problems and assumptions. There is no forward, backward, cyclical, or wave-like law of history. Histories are narratives told with rational plots that make sense for the teller. In Collingwood's understanding, it was meaningless to ask whether happiness has increased or decreased because we cannot determine such a thing; we can only assert whether our own convictions and commitments are worth holding, and any judgment of progress (or regress) follows from these. Collingwood suggested that one could argue that political systems simply reflect the psychological needs and concerns of a period; therefore, change appears as progress to us since it fits our socioeconomic needs (1995, 118–19). And Collingwood could insist on this, even when in works like *The New Leviathan* he contended that Christendom was a historical necessity to stay Fascism's spread in the world.

This latter notion Farrer found a bit ridiculous. In *The Glass of Vision,* he had asserted that Collingwood's approach "calls on us to rally round the Athanasian Creed and save scientific civilisation" (*GV,* 87), while in his 1963 address to the Voltaire Society, he worried that Collingwood's position was one of social pragmatism: "that the world-picture proves its validity by its ability to organize the terrestrial phenomena," and that "the little baroque heaven at the top right-hand corner" will remain for only socially useful reasons (*RF,* 209–10). Any religion would do in such an analysis, and this despite Collingwood's prizing of Trinitarian thought as a high point in the history of ideas. Still, Farrer agreed with Collingwood that persons are not autonomous individuals without any debt to their sociocultural settings.

Like Lewis, Farrer, sought to respond to metahistorical models without embracing either relativism or nihilism. In one of his Deems Lectures, "Revelation and History" (1964/67), he interacted with Dean of York Alan Richardson's 1962 Bampton Lectures, published as *History Sacred and Profane* (1964). Richardson's book was one of several recent works that had taken a longer look at the debate over a Christian meaning of history.[17] Richardson and Farrer had much in common. Richardson was in the loose sense a Liberal Catholic of the Anglican tradition of Charles Gore, and Richardson shared with Farrer the conviction that the Resurrection of Christ was a physical event and not just a spiritual one (Richardson 1964, 212). Along with that, they also shared a critique of Karl Barth's, as well as Rudolf Bultmann and Paul Tillich's, removal of the biblical narratives from actual historiography (Richardson 1964, 233). Like Farrer, Richardson believed that historical facts are a hybrid of actual past events and an interpretation of them (Navone 1966, 36–37), and Richardson stressed that the history of Israel was one of divine encounter. In addition, he agreed with Farrer that the Evangelists were historians in their own right (Richardson 1964, 237–38).

At the same time, they did disagree. Farrer, in particular, critiqued Richardson's argument that the history of Israel (as contained in the Old and New Testaments) could be history in exactly the same sense as any other history. Richardson insisted that "Israel's history *is* our history, the history of mankind," and that its story models, in light of World War II, a "discernment of a divine imperative in history" (Richardson 1964, 226). Richardson's claim was not unlike that of Collingwood: that the problems of one's age shape the history that one chooses to research and compose. Yet he reversed Collingwood's order, arguing that Israel's ubiquity should have prepared the suffering millions to learn a lesson. Or, at least, that the parallel was an analogous *Einfühlung*, a cross-cultural and pan-historical empathy that taught something (Richardson 1964, 231). Essentially, Richardson removed the distance between sacred and profane history, making all history potentially sacred in its revelatory lessons. As Farrer had previously noted in his "Creed and History," such a viewpoint raises not just a question of revelation, but also of theodicy, of what Providence is actually up to: "In general, the difficulty of following the trace of God's providence in history is that we cannot presume to fix the goal of his purpose" (*SB*, 73). One could ask instead if the events of history meant anything. Are they, as Max Plowman famously remarked, just "one damn thing after another"? Perhaps, after all, history is random and pointillist? "Can the thinker who utilizes the *empirically achieved data* of historical study stand, as it were, outside the historical process and see pattern or meaning in the whole historical process itself?" (J. Connolly 1965, 41).

Richardson's argument, Farrer pointed out, would lead us to hold that all historiography uses myth to frame forces larger than human control. The economic historian and the historian of theology share in common "diagrammatic or mythical fictions" that mark out the future of "successive acts and destinies of creatures" (*FS*, 95–96). And up to a point, Farrer had no problem with this: "The revelation is what God does in the history, could we but see the drift of it" (*FS*, 96). Yet, what Farrer granted to salvation history he would not grant to public, political history. He may have had historian Herbert Butterfield's musings and cautions in view.[18] Farrer warned that the historian who thinks to discover a pattern of providential or axiomatic history already faces a dire dilemma: "You might trace several trains of events which looked providentially ordered towards the emergence of the British Empire," yet at the same time, "perhaps you think that the Empire was a mixed blessing to mankind;

and so you might hesitate to write a modern sacred history on the theme of God's work" (SB, 73).

Richardson, because of his notion of "disclosure situations," extended to such moments a covering law of crisis and commitment: "There occurs at certain 'historic' moments the discernment of a meaning which provokes a response to what is discerned, an acknowledgment of an obligation, a commitment to an overriding purpose" (1964, 223–24, including 224n1). Even granting this to be a general truth, it nonetheless troubled Farrer with regard to freedom and historical direction. He insisted that to equate divine disclosure with all other historical judgments was too risky. The term *metahistory* implied "a cant term for sacred historians," and he argued that even if one granted it to God's doings in history, this failed to realize that without divine revelation, we cannot know what they are.[19] Even if one limited disclosure events to all other crisis moments that demanded particular nomic reconstructions (such as the late war), this raised numerous questions about upon what grounds, if any, God discloses his plans.

Again, Farrer struck a note, which he shared with Lewis. God is past explanation, unless he deigns to reveal himself: "The only history we have is of what he does in and through his creatures, if only we see the pattern, or grasp the whole" (FS, 95). This strong awareness of double agency put Farrer at odds with Richardson. The law-like nature of reality is actually divine choice, continuously so. Yet such reality, if we are to know it as personally caused, requires more than historical analogy. Farrer pointed out that one does not discover the meaning of divine revelation in an inductive manner. The Christian starts, having already read "the final pages" (SB, 61). Farrer was willing to concede to Richardson that in one sense, Israel's history was no different than any other people's history—God's providence may be up to many things, yet these are not discoverable by some sort of metahistorical set of axioms. Instead, Israel's purpose has been made known, through the prophets, and perfectly in Christ. "Secular history gathers its criteria from a flat-rate survey of humdrum humanity. But the man of discernment knows that whatever he is dealing with in Christ, it is not this" (SB, 81). National history transcends simple biography, even while a biography depends to some extent upon a history of a people or period (FS, 88–90). That the national faith of Israel was typological was surely an important aspect of the providential ordering of history, and yet as a typological response, it was not a general metahistorical assessment of crisis points in its history. It was a response to an active figure of a particular and singular nature—the Incarnate God-Man.

"Christ's life, then, may be called the centre of history, only in the sense that the horizontal movement of human affairs was uniquely touched at that point by a vertical inflow from above" (*SB*, 69). Farrer's point was that sacred history as a theological and philosophical grasp of the direction and purpose of salvation is not the same as historical judgment by historians. Away from the political deeds of public history, the obscure Jesus was and is the true nexus of reality. Jesus, by some not regarded at the time as terribly important to history, only became so by profane standards once the Church rose to political power in the Empire, and yet he is history's secret core: "However far from the focus of public history Jesus moved, the human existence of Jesus was a focus drawing the world into itself" (*SB*, 70). The critical practice of the historian would seem strangely tone-deaf in the world of worship. To enter the world of Christian worship (for example, in the praying or singing of the Psalms) is to enter a world where people cry out to God for deliverance and are answered, where kings fail or succeed based on obedience to the prophetic warnings. Does the historian who enters such a world just "think that the biblical picture is an old-world legend, illustrating sound spiritual principles by means of gross historical distortions?" Farrer wondered (*SB*, 71–72). In liturgical experience, the historical becomes remembered not as a past event alone, but also as one currently present and participated in at that doxological moment.

In other contexts, nevertheless, Farrer still had to consider what human capacity played in revelatory disclosure. He sought to refute the objection that prophecies about future events that historically occurred had to be actually written after the fact, while those that turned out not to be true were clearly written ahead of the matter. Farrer thought this an obvious case of special pleading. In his "Messianic Prophecy and Preparation for Christ" (1961), Farrer argued that prophecy was a middle step between historical events and the actual Advent of Jesus. "History narrates the rise, decline, and fall of Davidic monarchy; prophecy declares that what has failed as a human experiment must triumph as a divine visitation" (1961b, 3). Likewise, in his essay "Mary, Scripture, and Tradition" (1963) he addressed historical understanding and theology. If one position was that natural (i.e., physical) events arrive into our experience before theological interpretation, and a second was that theological interpretation can arrive without natural experience, a third position was to acknowledge that natural experience and theological understanding arrive in some measure together. Farrer held that the second position was actually just a species of the third. Thus, "according to the first, no physical event can be accepted as credible except by a stern application of physical or at least natural criteria," while in its opposite, "we may accept as Christians what as mere naturalists we might reject." Farrer understood that those holding the naturalist perspective might think that the supernaturalist one opened "a floodgate to superstition," while a naturalist position simply was incoherent in regard to what Christianity believed (*IB*, 116).

Taken together, then, Farrer's defense of the unity of the Gospels was ultimately about meeting Jesus, a true historical Jesus we encounter through the minds of the inspired Evangelists, and their accounts were typological history in a form that made sense to ancient Israel. Farrer held that agency and narrative belonged together, and thus, his considerations of the nature of history were ultimately to defend that fundamental human presupposition. Lewis and Farrer shared a fundamental caution not only about positivist models of history, but about any metahistorical model that would seek to exalt natural temporal models of history, especially to that which only the supernatural doctrine of inspiration could aspire.

THE PERSONAL IN HISTORY

Given that C. S. Lewis took a character-driven and narratorial approach to literary history, and given that Austin Farrer worked to defend the Evangelists as actual writers, and given that both also distrusted macrolaws of history, it is not surprising that both held in common a commitment to personal history as the central meaning for history and even historiography. This was an emphasis that they shared with Herbert Butterfield. Lewis had read Butterfield's *Christianity and History* lectures (1949) with some sympathy (*Letters*, 3.5), and their warning against invoking the judgment of history, especially without careful academic study, was an emphasis that Lewis shared. For Butterfield, the personalist aspect of history is a Christian one, and a surer guard against violating the dignity of the individual than historicist or Marxist visions. He stressed the "'Now' that is in direct relationship to eternity," and that what matters most is the individual's standing before God in the immediate (Butterfield 1950, 28–29, 66–67), and concluded, "I am unable to see how a man can find the hand of God in secular history, unless he has first found that he has an assurance of it in his personal experience" (Butterfield 1950, 107). Historical examples and contexts, for Lewis, were applicable to each reader's "holy present," that which is not subject to laws of history but to transcendent standards and divine encounter. Lewis insisted in "Historicism," a year after Butterfield, that the "primary history" of personal revelation is what truly mattered, and it was that fundamental accountability before God that rendered any human story significant:

> I mean the real or primary history which meets each of us moment by mo-
> ment in his own experience. . . . What MacDonald called 'the holy present'.
> Where, except in the present, can the Eternal be met? If I attack Historicism
> it is not because I intend any disrespect to primary history, the real revelation
> springing direct from God in every experience. It is rather because I respect
> this real original history too much to see with unconcern the honours due to
> it lavished on those fragments, copies of fragments, or floating reminiscences
> of copies of copies, which are, unhappily, confounded with it under the gen-
> eral name of *history.* (*CR*, 113)

This is another passage in Lewis's essay that, if left to itself, would seem to undercut many aspects of his larger project. Historical judgments, parsed thus,
would be highly relativistic.

Of course, these were hardly Lewis's practical conclusions. In his Narnia
tale *Prince Caspian,* one can see how the stress on the personal still might work
itself out in practical ways. Memory, individual and corporate, is an important aspect of the past; indeed, it is almost its sole basis in the novel. Narnia
under the Telemarines is a world divided between the official history of the
conquerors and the repressed history of Old Narnia. As such, the dry school
history is dreadfully boring, while the half-hidden history of Narnia is buried
in old fairy tales (*PC*, 213. 42–43). The Telemarines do not remember their
own ancient origins on Earth (*PC*, 230–32). Even among the Old Narnians,
not all is remembered. Trumpkin does not believe in Aslan, while Nikabrik
remembers the White Witch not as a tyrant but as a power that might yet
be summoned (*PC*, 178). Doctor Cornelius as a half-dwarf has gone under-
ground among the humans, while the pureblood dwarfs have all but forgotten
that half-dwarfs exist (*PC*, 53). It is the beasts, like Trufflehunter, who "don't
change. We hold on" (*PC*, 71), as the bulgy bears too recall their right to be a
marshal of the lists (*PC*, 197–98). Such diverse history might be the conflicting narratives of master and subaltern were it not that one is actually true.

The four children, also, when they return, are as much dependent upon
memory, as they are the archaeological ruins, to document the Narnia they
remember as adult kings and queens. The shape of Cair Paravel, the location
of the orchards, and the gold chess piece are not just evidence of the past,
they embody the personal memories of each of them. "Do you remember?"
is the repeated basis for their shared history (*PC*, 25, 117), and Lucy can look
upon a favorite constellation as "Dear old Leopard" (*PC*, 121). Yet the children have the unsettling experience at Aslan's How of an ancient site that was
built after their time in Narnia (*PC*, 96, 172), and geological history can prove

their suppositions false. The ancient river Rush is now a gorge (PC, 130), as Cair Paravel is now an island. Peter, Susan, Edmund, and Lucy are in a sense embodied history; their presence and their memories testify to Narnia's true past. In the end, however, it is the arrival of Aslan that changes everything, for he is the Lord of Narnia and of its history. It is he who vindicates the old nurse for her tales.

In light of Herbert Butterfield's lectures, one can read Lewis as concerned with protecting individual dignity against predictive systems that would absorb the person, that would treat our memories as insignificant. In "World's Last Night," Lewis insisted that the final *parousia* is "a sudden, violent end imposed from without," an end to the play that we cannot read, being that we are in it (WLN, 101). Our not knowing what the future holds offers us dramatic freedom: "The playing it well is what matters infinitely" (WLN, 106). Indeed, affirming only a general providentialism keeps the historian "from writing a great deal of nonsense" and "to get on with the story" (ELSC, 148). This "getting on with the story" was key to Lewis's experience as a literary historian. When we read Lewis's descriptions of the historical process, we find we are reading phenomenological accounts, and his analogies of the drawer, the floral arrangement, or the personal encounter, as well as general descriptions of the history's limited purposes, are descriptions of researching and writing from sources. Because Lewis feared that axiomatic causality undercut human choices in the past, he stressed what little historians knew and described a more epistemically cautious procedure.

Yet this call to epistemic hesitancy hardly stopped Lewis from expressing wide historical claims. For example, he shared with others such as Christopher Dawson a commitment to a macrohistorical narrative of the West, one in which the modern world has fallen from some measure of the goodness of its past. Lewis's "De Descriptione Temporum" is likely his most well-known example of this metanarrative. There, Lewis was able to express caution toward historical judgments and also to paint a tragic narrative. He admitted that there was "no great Divide" (SLE, 3) in terms of human nature, but considered several possible breaks—between the pagan and Christian worlds, between the Dark and High Middle Ages, and between these and the Enlightenment. Lewis argued that the deepest shift took place in the mid- to late-nineteenth century with radical changes in politics and aesthetics, as well as with the general rise of a post-Christian Europe (SLE, 4–8). He half-mockingly labeled himself a living fossil of "Old Western Culture," able to give some sense of this bygone era to twentieth-century students (SLE, 12). Lewis, like Doctor Cornelius, embodied a living Christian past many would simply like to forget.

Of course, this claim was a ruse. Lewis was as much a person of his time as his hearers, but his appointed moniker did highlight two aspects; namely, that he was a scholar of the literary past who loved it and that he was one invested in the consensus of Nicene Christianity. This was not to conclude that Lewis idealized all things ancient and medieval, but he did establish himself as their sympathetic defender and an exegete of what he believed most compatible with Christian truth. His history of the centuries since the High Middle Ages could pinpoint numerous changes that prepared for his nineteenth-century fault line. So, Lewis's jumbled drawer could be assembled into a rather wide narrative of historical accountability and blame.

This same return to personhood and its place in history was essential to Farrer. In "Creed and History," he argued that a Christian understanding of history was that of "cosmic personalism." And Trinitarian personhood is the source and life of human personhood, as history is a communal enterprise: "Mind is a social reality. The characteristic act of mind is to discourse" (*SB*, 63). Since mind is structured this way, it is typified by "real discourse between persons," the fictional conversation carried on by an individual with herself is always "mimic dialogue," and this is the case even when we acknowledge that each person is an individual focal point in time and space (*SB*, 63–64). We are all, no matter how often alone, "*plurifocal*" beings, that is, we are shaped by multiple and often untraceable historical streams (*SB*, 65). None of us is accounted for without a broad background of numerous influences.

In putting it this way, Farrer was attempting to tease out not only the differences between professional critical history and personal history, but also between the agency of our histories as we experience them and that of God's agency. Here, Farrer sounded a note similar to Lewis's. People have "personal centres" for their own histories, yet most are not regarded by public accounts as terribly important. Seldom, if ever, can those passing through the events of their lives know what they portend. And yet God's constant double agency, shaping our own freedom, is also personal. God offers each of us an encounter, and this encounter is deeply historical in nature: "He steered many sequences of cause, many lines of influence to their meeting place in you or in me . . . [T]he secret history of God's providence in the making of any one creature" also has a unique center (*SB*, 70–71).

When Farrer wrote this, he had been reading Lewis's *Perelandra,* and the passage echoes the vision of the Great Dance that Ransom receives near the end of the novel (*SB*, 68). To Tor, Ransom wonders that all that has come before is but the beginning: "Or do you make your world the centre? But I am troubled. What of the people of Malacandra? Would they also think their world was the centre?" (Lewis 1944, 183). The answer that Ransom receives is that every experience is at the center of the cosmic plan; its design is that overarching. At one level, both human and divine aspects are experienced as entirely the same, and yet we cannot forget this if we are to get the matter of freedom and determinism correct, for God does not himself have "a history" as we do. History, like Time, is his creature. Farrer would have no process-style God in this. That most of us do not see the pattern places severe limits upon what history can claim to accomplish, and yet this need not be cause for despair. If all history is in one sense revelatory at an existential level, it does not follow that every subjective reading of that history is equally valuable. In a cosmically meaningfully sense, all things are at the center, including the center of history.

Both Farrer and Lewis, then, were deeply concerned with historical narratives that were treated as the real products of human imaginations, in particular human cultures and contexts. Both practiced approaches that helped their readers come into sympathy with those of the past. Both affirmed a broad Christian vision of salvation history, but otherwise distrusted any sort of axiomatic set of laws, either at the suprahistorical level that Marxists, Fascists, or metahistorians like Spengler and Toynbee espoused, or at the infrahistorical level as source and form critics assumed. Farrer and Lewis shared, too, an assumption that despite the fallibility of broad historical judgments across eras, individual texts had something of their authors' worldviews and beliefs about them, and that this was communicable. Both men held that historical causation should be understood more as human agency is understood—that is, interpretively. And thus, both also believed that at the center of every history, if one had the eyes to see, one could proclaim of the Creator, "Blessed be He!" (Lewis 1944, 183–85).

·✦6✦·

THEODICY

I've read your book with great enjoyment. . . . Of course admiration is not
always agreement. . . . How do people decide what is an emotion and what is
a value judgment? Not presumably just by intersection wh. will certainly be
hard put to it to find a value judgment chemically pure from emotion . . . I find
however that the problem of animal pain is just as a tough when I concentrate
on creatures I dislike as on ones I cd. make pets of. . . . I loathe hens. But my
conscience would say the same things if I forgot to feed them as if I forgot to
feed the cat. . . .
—C. S. Lewis, Letter to Austin Farrer, December 29, 1961,
in *Collected Letters*

The light Lewis casts on omnipotence derives from the intrinsic character of
the world's structure; the light he casts on goodness, from a consideration
of the highest personal benevolence. How are the two discussions related to
one another? If the requirements of world-structure are so inexorable, what
scope is there for a free providence in distributing pleasures or pains? If pains
are the natural rubs of a world-structure bearing sentient creatures, what need
have we to view them as instruments of a disciplinary providence?
—Austin Farrer, "The Christian Apologist" in *Light on C. S. Lewis*

Austin Farrer would outlive C. S. Lewis by four years. In one of his last remaining years of life, he found it important that his first public observation
on Lewis in print would be a critical examination of the weaknesses in Lewis's
theodicy. While he had commended Lewis in more than one sermon,[1] Farrer,
when asked to contribute to the 1965 collection, *Light on C. S. Lewis*, chose to

focus on one of their stronger disagreements. In doing so, Farrer still came to praise his dead friend far more than to damn him, and his essay, "The Christian Apologist," examined *The Problem of Pain* to show the great strengths of Lewis as an apologist. Farrer observed that the book combines philosophy and theology for the educated layperson, not for the specialist, and for those encountering the problem of evil in a formal way for the first time, Lewis's style was all to their benefit (*Light,* 33–36). Farrer noted with approval that the majority of Lewis's argument reasoned from God's use of pain for sanctification, and that this led Lewis to the rhetorical heights in praise of God's eternal purposes, as well as to a heroic, hopeful call for the reader's self-examination. At the same time, Farrer did add some caveats, and these cautions tell us as much about Lewis and Farrer's shared theodicy as about their differences. As we shall see, Farrer worried that *The Problem of Pain* indulged in too much moralism and that it tended to overlook the nature of the physical world. He thought that Lewis's speculation on Satan created more problems than it solved, slipping into the realm of fairy tales, and while he admired Lewis addressing animal pain, he found his conjectures unconvincing. Farrer lamented that Lewis's fantasies "should furnish the public with excuses to evade the overwhelming realism of his moral theology!" (*Light,* 40–42).

Because Lewis and Farrer shared so much in regard to the value of myth, the meaning of language about God, the purpose of virtue ethics, even a trust in the Gospels as history and a distrust in metahistorical theories, their differences in regard to theodicy are instructive. As a close comparison of Lewis's *The Problem of Pain* with Farrer's *Love Almighty and Ills Unlimited* shows, both men centered upon the salvific nature of the created order and upon the crucial role of the Incarnation; they, nonetheless, had differing opinions about the meaning of the Adamic Fall (which they agreed was at some level mythic) and about the role of the demonic (for which Lewis had a more vibrant role, by far). Strangely, what divided Farrer and Lewis was how to engage evolutionary history and the physical, biological world, especially in regard to animal pain. Yet, in the last analysis, this difference had to do with how best to imagine what they agreed upon—free will and redeemed personhood. Given that, beyond their two chief theodicies, Farrer and Lewis also addressed the question of evil in a personal manner, it is not surprising that they shared a concern as to how evil is answered in human experience.

BEGINNING WITH GOD

C. S. Lewis's *The Problem of Pain* (1940) was published near the center of his career,[2] while Austin Farrer's *Love Almighty and Ills Unlimited* (1962) was released near the end of his. Despite the difference of over two decades, both Lewis and Farrer understood these two books as representing differing positions, and in light of Farrer's critiques, it is not going too far to see his book as being written partially with Lewis's in mind. At the same time, their differences must be set within their largely shared belief system. They certainly held similar views about the Christian life, soteriology, and suffering. Both held that the Christian life is a call to moral development and that sanctification which begins in this life is completed in the next. Both rejected seminal theories of original sin and stressed the atonement of Christ as being redemptive but not necessarily propitious (Lewis, *MX*, 57–60, 1960b, 118; Farrer, *FO*, 23–25, *SB*, 102–7). Both looked to the grace of the Christian life, especially the Eucharist, as central to this change (Lewis, *MX*, 62, *WG*, 94; Farrer, *LIB*, 49, *WL*, 60–62, *FO*, 149–51),[3] and each saw productive suffering as an essential aspect of that change, a position in the spirit of Irenaeus.[4]

However, they argued to these shared concerns within theodicy in quite different fashions, at least in *Problem of Pain* and *Love Almighty*. It is tempting to claim that Farrer's theodicy in *Love Almighty* is structured from the bottom up, while Lewis's in *Problem of Pain* is from the top down, and while this is basically true, the picture is more complex. They both relied on a "lower" realm to build their case—Lewis's being anthropological and Farrer's more generally biological. It is that fundamental difference in emphasis that defines their disagreement, for the substance of Farrer's charge was that Lewis overemphasized the soul-making of suffering at the expense of how biological competition already offers a world that assumes pain and death. Farrer's critique of Lewis has been remarked upon by others. John T. Stahl, for example, has argued that Farrer underestimated Lewis's awareness of the biological component in human suffering (1975, 234–35), while Robert MacSwain has expressed greater sympathy with Farrer's critique because Farrer recognized that much evolved competition seems to have no moral purpose (2008, 38–39). Nevertheless, I want to argue that the role which explicit Christocentric theology played in Farrer and Lewis differed more in emphasis than in essential particulars. The basic flow of their theodicies showed them engaging objections from the modernist distrust of a good and powerful God whose world is suffused with pain and evil. Yet neither one was really defending God, so much as setting forth the Christian understanding of God's nature, action, and character, and this overshadows their disagreements.

How each man began his book reveals something about his concern with God. The theist who believes that God is omnipotent and all-knowing, as well as absolutely good and wise, confesses a God who can act and does act with complete understanding and fittingness. That material reality too often seems to give the lie to this conception of God becomes a deeply important matter. Arguably, modern theodicy shifted from a focus upon how to suffer well, to whether God is just, to whether God even exists. *How long, O Lord?* is a different question from *Given evil, what kind of God?* or even *Given evil, is there a God?* Yet these concerns can overlap, and Lewis and Farrer agreed that the problem of evil for a Christian theist can only be addressed with the right kind of God and world in view.

In *The Problem of Pain,* Lewis started with what he would have thought as an atheist, calling attention to a universe in which animals compete with other animals, end in pain, and the human animal, having achieved consciousness, dreads death and disaster: "All stories will come to nothing; all life will turn out in the end to have been a transitory and senseless contortion" arising out of meaningless, "infinite matter" (*PP,* 13–15). Why would such an absurd world have imagined a good God at all? Lewis built his case upon the phenomenology of Rudolf Otto's Numinous. Otto's *The Idea of the Holy* argued that the fundamental human experience of the divine was in three interrelated emotions: *tremendum, mysterium,* and *augustus. Tremendum* is to be dazed and endangered by the dynamic force and plentitude of the divine. *Mysterium,* on the other hand, experiences a magnetism and saturation before the *fascinans* (the awe, desire for, even love) of divine otherness, the *totaliter aliter. Augustus* is the resulting sense of desecration and transgression before divine holiness (Otto 1958, 13–17, 23–29, 50–57). That such is powerful, attractive, and yet separate brings out in human consciousness a sense of our weakness, desire, and corruption.

This mixture of dread, awe, and guilt before the divine was important to Lewis's analysis of the religious impulse. He argued from Otto's model that since all cultures share such a basic view of a fearful and mysteriously overwhelming divinity, this phenomenon may be said to imply both the existence of the supernatural and the reality of divine revelation. All developed religions, Lewis suggested, (1) have a sense of the uncanny in the world, (2) have a sense of the moral law and right and wrong, as well as a sense of obeying or disobeying it, and (3) recognize that the numinous is the guardian of right and wrong. Lewis dismissed as misguided the anthropological and psychological attempts to reduce these to prehistoric projection: "We do not know how far back in human history this feeling goes. The earliest men almost certainly believed in things which would excite the feeling in us if *we* believed in them, and it seems therefore probable that numinous awe is as old as humanity itself" (*PP*, 19). At some point, regardless, human beings found their dread and awe combined with their consciousness of their fallible responsibility.

Lewis did not stop there. Along with Jewish belief in the providence of a just God, he noted that Christians add the Incarnation, that the numinous became one of us, a moment that for Lewis had all the startling particularity of history, "that willful, dramatic anfractuosity," which "not made by us" strikes us suddenly like a punch in the face (*PP*, 25). Of course, Lewis argued, the Incarnation is noumenal in its power, but it is more, for Christ is more. Lewis's direction, almost from the beginning of his theodicy, was to already arrive at the nature of God's interaction in a world and to help his readers reimagine their world picture. As Philip Tallon notes, Lewis, in writing *The Problem of Pain*, did not restrict himself to the "mere theodicy" of arguments from the natural world and natural reasoning but sought to explain the larger picture of Christian understanding (2008, 199–200). This was because Lewis's worldview rejected purely sentimental or psychological views of shame and guilt. Shame, he insisted, offers an existential protection against moral relativism. The *mysterium tremendum* is not an evolved vestigial emotion worth jettisoning, but a clue to the character of God and of ourselves (*PP*, 56–57).

Farrer also took the trouble to stress the nature of the Christian God and distinguish him as such from rival views of the universe. In *Love Almighty*, he early qualified his approach: he was not proposing to deal with God "as an explanatory cause, but as a saving power," that is, we must recognize "the Maker in his works" when we are "engaged with the action of a Saviour" (*LA*, 12). Farrer did insist that given his parameters, he was not attempting to justify particular evils—this was not a pastoral work, and yet one must still develop something of a taxonomy of differing evils. Our experiences of pain and suffering are too diverse to lump them all together. Farrer's rhetorical method was to explore numerous options, often with a faux interlocutor (a method he also used in other books), only to show either how they could be partially answered or in order to illustrate their limitations (*LA*, 19, 25–29, 33). In this, Farrer was not trying to break new argumentative ground; rather, he was working to set out what made the Creator and Savior of Christian theism different from other cosmological rivals.

First, in light of theodicy, with what kind of God are we dealing? Farrer set out basic arguments for the single-source origin of the universe, and he pre-

sented evil as privation ("the parasite of a good") (*LA,* 22), that is, as an explanation for how God's good creation can nonetheless contain evil. Farrer thus
sought to eliminate another key objection—that God is the author of evil. At
the same time, he was concerned that since God is the single source of the universe, we should also eliminate rival spiritual powers. If Farrer sought to remove
Manichean dualism from the table, he was also opposed to Gnostic theories
of creative intermediaries whose faulty works the high God must repair. "The
God we encounter is the author of a marvelous and vital elaboration in natural
being, effective on many levels, and open to our actual knowledge" (*LA,* 46).
Thus, Farrer was answering two cosmologies that had threatened Christian
theism for far longer than arguments from atheism (Larrimore 2001, xxi–xxiv).

   Farrer also stressed that one must begin with a correct view of the world in
question. As he moved on to discussing stellar matter and its beginnings and
endings, he employed, for the first of several times, the machine-maker metaphor for God, only to argue for its failure. Theodicy is, among other things,
a question of world analogies and cosmic imaginaries. We cannot see the
universe as a failed machine. This was one of the mistakes of early modernist theodicy, such as that of Gottfried Wilhelm Leibniz's "best of all possible
worlds." Farrer thus entertained and rejected the idea of an undifferentiated
"preexistent intractable matter" (*LA,* 41) since it would neither be divergent
nor resistant, indeed, would be unimaginable. It could speak neither for nor
against a divine Creator. Humans can only conceive such things, Farrer believed, by invoking analogies from the crafting of material, but the theist's
problem was not the potter's clay with which the Craftsman began.[5] So, in
turn, it was rather unwise for natural science in investigating the world to apply ideas of perfection in design, then in turn refuse the analogical imagination
its finding of God in the world (*LA,* 45–48). Only with this base of complex
creation and a recognition of a good God in place would Farrer work his way
forward to eventually end his theodicy with a meditation upon the purpose
and direction of human salvation.

   Lewis, too, distinguished a Jewish and Christian understanding from monist
and Manichean alternatives, though for differing reasons than Farrer. Beginning with anthropological evidence of the numinous allowed Lewis to engage
rather quickly omnipotence and omni-benevolence, as well as concepts of free
will and of human proclivity to acts of evil. At the center of Lewis's theodicy
was God's love, which was not the same thing as easygoing tolerance, for he
maintained that God's purpose is to remake humanity. The moral law by its
very nature can only make demands upon us if there is something like distinguishable good and evil, and in turn, that the good is ontologically basic. "It is

either inexplicable illusion, or else revelation" (PP, 22). The world is a moral world, and arguably a moral God is at its center.

Thus, while Lewis began with moral anthropology and Farrer began with a divine cosmology, they, nonetheless, shared certain concerns. Both stressed the unique purpose and plan of God for humanity, as well as how the nature of humanity in a world of pain and suffering ties into this plan. However, the road map that the two men offered branched off in differing directions from this shared concern. A simple review of their core chapters shows this:

Farrer	*Lewis*
Physical accident	Human wickedness
Animal pain	The fall of humanity (including Adam)
Humanity redeemed	Human pain and hell
Adam and Lucifer	Animal pain (including Lucifer)
Griefs and Consolations	Heaven

In *Problem of Pain,* Lewis moved quickly to focus on sin, the fall of human-ity, and the meaning of human pain along with the possibility of damnation. His consideration of animal pain was, by its very nature, a digression before returning to the telos of heavenly existence. Farrer, by contrast, in *Love Al-mighty* would work upward from the cosmic material to biological interac-tions to animal pain to finally human suffering and redemption. Only then would he engage humanity's fall into sin and the purpose of individual suf-fering and martyrdom.

What this pattern shows is that natural evil was of far greater concern for Farrer, at least in terms of a formal theodicy. If they both began with the nature of God in relation to evil, they had differing points of emphasis in regard to the world itself. For Farrer, the place of animal pain was architectonic to human suffering and redemption in a way that it was not for Lewis, yet both writers had to address it and in light of twentieth-century views of biological origins.[6] This meant that theories of evolution had to be taken seriously by both and played an important role in engaging Genesis's picture of the primal Adam.

EVOLUTION AND THEODICY

C. S. Lewis and Austin Farrer understood that some account of the natural world and of physical pain was necessary to understand suffering and theo-dicy, and being persons of the twentieth century, each believed that such an account must interact with evolutionary theory. It may help here to put their shared understanding within a larger historical context—first, in regard to the kind of theodicy that arose from the early modern era, and second, the kind of world being imagined. Modern theodicy, as an intellectual project, was a product of the Enlightenment stress on system and foundational certainty, and, as I noted above, modern theodicy sought to explain or defend God's action or perceived inaction in a way that historical earlier responses would have left more open-ended. Classical formulations of the trilemma of an all-knowing and all-powerful God who does not eliminate evil were more concerned with recommending either, like Sextus Empiricus, blissful indifference, or like Marcion, a dualist vision of a good God and a lesser evil one. It would take an eighteenth-century version such as David Hume's to argue that the trilemma rendered belief in God irrational (Larrimore 2001, xx–xxiii; Neiman 2002, 159–69).

One of the outcomes was a set of models that, in deistic fashion, regarded God as a disengaged Creator whose purpose in designing a mechanistic world should include an understandable (i.e., not mysterious) purpose for pain and disorder. In early versions of this, a well-designed construct of the universe was deemed compatible with a Creator, for the Creator was understood to be either the force behind the universe's mechanistic movement, or at least the force behind the active principles located in gravity, but this expected compatibility did not hold in the late eighteenth and nineteenth centuries (Roger 1986, 277–95). It was not arbitrary on Lewis's part that the opening epigram for the first chapter of *The Problem of Pain* is Blaise Pascal's warning against trying to prove God from the natural world: "It is a remarkable fact that no canonical writer has ever used Nature to prove God" (*PP*, 13). The design argument, put forth by such as William Paley, never quite held. Modern theodicy had to adapt once evolutionary reasoning entered the picture. The early modern shift in the cosmological imaginary from an ordered cosmos to an impersonal universe likewise led in the nineteenth and early twentieth centuries to conceptions of wilderness and the sublime, as well as to an evolutionary stress on the "dark genesis" of our humanity. The universe could no longer, for many, be considered a well-designed cosmos favoring human meaning or purpose (Taylor 2007, 335–51).

This was certainly Charles Darwin's own conclusion in *The Origin of Species,* where he mustered examples of "thousands of drones" born only to mate and be destroyed and queen bees who with "savage instinctive hatred" eliminate younger rival queens (2003, 192). He stated this even more clearly in his correspondence: "There seems to me too much misery in the world. I cannot persuade myself that a beneficent & omnipotent God would have designedly created the Ichneumonidae with the express intention of their feeding within the living bodies of caterpillars, or that a cat should play with mice" (1993, 224). Surely, a Great Designer could have perfected a better system than one so wasteful and wretched. Furthermore, with the evidence that predation had occurred before the human species existed, a literal Adam and Eve became increasingly problematic and the first eleven chapters of Genesis no longer taken seriously as history by many (Kelly 2002, 172–82).

Post-Darwin, for such reasoners, humans are not the noble, godlike creatures that they once imagined, and the higher impulses of the human species are judged to be only evolved psycho-sexual mechanisms. The "best possible world" of the Enlightenment that undergirded theodicy, thus, found itself running up against a view that stressed the biological and psychological irrationality of the evolved self, though both imaginaries warred against the older cosmic, creational view. In either case, for many we were no longer the imago dei. The problem of evil became yoked to evolutionary developmentalism. This search for a rational and airtight theodicy in a well-planned cosmos gave way in part to an evolved and essential irrational universe that questioned if God could exist. The search for certainty, however, remained, even as the millennia of natural history asked further questions of a Creator.

Neither Lewis nor Farrer was suggesting that Christians could bring about a clear (or safe) merger between Christian theodicy and evolutionary models of the world and humanity. Nor was either man attempting what in the analytical tradition of philosophy would call a "defense," as opposed to a full theodicy.[7] For Farrer, a natural, "modern" theodicy was never enough, for his starting point was always revelatory in the last analysis (Oliver 1988, 288–89). Neither man was attempting a natural, rational case that would answer the logical problem of evil, and neither was attempting to engage the problem on existential grounds alone. Instead, both invoked the larger theological resources of the Christian faith, even as they invoked certain philosophical assumptions and conjectures.

What each assumed was that humanity can attempt a map of its best efforts, and this being true of its models of the universe, it follows it is also true of its explanations of evil. Lewis and Farrer understood that in a post-Enlightenment era, scientific models represent a search for explanation bounded by assumptions and family resemblances across representations, yet neither was willing to suggest that such attempts were purely nominalistic. Farrer compared the process to a "sieve" for a range of facts that science can test and interpret. He observed that natural "laws" simply do not "*exist*," for they are attempts at approximation, and yet we need their help to imagine the world (*LA*, 21–23). The language of scientific "laws" is really just that of "generalities and averages," which we abstract from patterns in the world. They are "fictions of human understanding" (*LA*, 98). Moreover, Farrer felt, one does not need to look to natural science as a method of establishing theological belief: "We can do little more than remind ourselves that the outline sketch our science provides is coloured in by the vigorous existence and lively interaction of innumerable energies" (*LA*, 38).

Lewis, in similar fashion, in *The Discarded Image* could talk of "tastes in universes," since each historical era has its own conceptual model of the cosmos: each worthy of some respect, for each reveals some aspect of human imagination: "No Model is a catalogue of ultimate realities, and none is mere fantasy. Each is a serious attempt to get in all the phenomena known as a given period" (*DI*, 222). Yet unlike their strong opposition to metahistory, Lewis and Farrer felt that natural evolutionary history was best taken seriously up to a point. Farrer thought that the evidence for evolution was less assured than some might wish, and yet it was foolish to try and oppose it. Earlier models of spontaneous generation and of a mechanistic world were functionally no better for theological matters (*LA*, 42–43). A theodicy that accounts for developmental models must avoid the Scylla of being tied too closely to a current scientific theory and the Charybdis of rejecting in poor faith all scientific models.

Despite Farrer's concern with Lewis's use of "fairy-tale" stories in theodicy, both employed theological exploration that admitted to imaginative limitations and possibilities. In doing so, they were, I suspect, refusing the Enlightenment insistence on exhaustive knowledge. At the same time, by having to work within received notions of evolutionary history, they both undertook biological models of the human past that blurred the line between physical and spiritual suffering, as well as the line between humanity and the physical and biological world. For both men this meant that theodicy was a matter of reimagining the world, including the evolutionary world, according to the Christian metanarrative. As Wilson and Hartt observe, Christian hope for Farrer offered a different epistemology of life. Simple emotional consolation and the broader purpose of salvation have differing ends to their investigation of the cosmos and its struggles (Wilson and Hartt 2004, 111). Sean Connolly, too, calls attention to a similar emphasis in Lewis's teleology. Human virtues and desires have an eschatological direction (S. Connolly 2007, 60). Thus, despite their wide differences in approach, both Lewis and Farrer set forth a version of the free will argument, that evil exists because God desired that humans may make real, significant choices.

Lewis's evolutionary "just so" story in *The Problem of Pain* is an example of placing an evolutionary narrative within a larger theistic one. He sought to merge aspects of Adam and Eve, their paradisal existence, and their fall into sin with standard views of human evolution. But it is important to remember that his account was a supposal of what *might* have happened. He was clear that he was offering a possible history, not a cosmic legend such as Reinhold Niebuhr's "symbolical representation of non-historical truth" (*PP*, 77n1). Lewis treated the Genesis account as doubly mythic and historical in its shape and intent without affirming the particulars as an actual documentary account. He supposed that God perfected the human form for millennia before visiting the creature with consciousness. Only with the latter did the proto-human become an actual human being. Lewis imagined this Adamic creature as subject to death and pain but not to moral and spiritual bondage. Not unlike Augustine's picture of the unfallen Adam, such would be in complete control of their bodies and wills; sleep would be chosen; they would be in a constant state of praise; the animals would be playfully subject to them; and they would in no way act out of self-will: "I do not doubt that if the Paradisal man could now appear among us, we should regard him as an utter savage, a creature to be exploited, or at best, patronized. Only one or two, and those the holiest among us, would glance a second time at the naked, shaggy-bearded, slow-spoken creature, but they, after a few minutes, would fall at his feet" (*PP*, 79). Lewis thought that we could not know how many of these beings existed or how they morally fell—it could be a literal fruit tree. Regardless, at the center of that collapse would be an attempt to become gods, to indulge in acts of self-will false to their creaturely condition. With their fall, they became subject to biochemical desires that overpowered their wills; "these uneasy rebels became the subconscious as we now know it" (*PP*, 82).

Of course, it can be asked whether Lewis believed in a singular prelapsarian couple, and the question is not easily answerable. There is nothing in Lewis's understanding of Genesis or of Paul that obligated him to such, yet even a cursory familiarity with his corpus reveals the imaginative centrality that the original couple had for him. Both *Perelandra* and *The Magician's Nephew* feature Adamic stories of great importance. In *The Magician's Nephew*, Frank and Helen mirror the unfallen couple. Chosen by Aslan to be the first king and queen of Narnia, they are given the task to "rule and name these creatures, and do justice among them, and protect them from their enemies when enemies arise" (*MN*, 151). It does not matter that the cabby and his wife are uneducated; they can work the earth and pledge to do what is right, and as they pledge themselves, they grow more regal, and Frank's voice in particular takes on a country nobility. The original Edenic glory is given them, even as an echo.

In *Perelandra*, Tor and Tinidril are set in a higher register. Ransom, upon beholding them, says he has "never before seen a man or a woman," for they represent the unfallen antetype that on Earth is present only in broken and splintered types (Lewis 1944, 176). Ransom reflects that in looking upon them, he sees that the true definition of *animal rationale* is before him. The Adamic parents of Perelandra become the integral key to both the *eldila* and the beasts: "They closed the circle, and with their coming all separate notes of strength and beauty . . . became one music" (Lewis 1944, 178). Frank and Helen, as well as Tor and Tinidril, are pictured as figures of nobility, of original promise, so they are not that far removed from Lewis's Adamic Cro-Magnon; they all represent a holy ideal.

This ideal is also present in some of Lewis's poetry, for example, "Adam at Night" (1949) and "Solomon" (1946) (Lewis 2015, 340, 362–63). While we have suffered an Arcadian loss in our makeup, the Adam figure is capable of real insight. In "Solomon," the ancient king is seeking to recover "the Adamite state / And flame-like monarchy of Man" (lines 23–4). In "Adam at Night," the unfallen man is free from a daunting consciousness of death. He can sleep without dread or fear, and while he sleeps, he enjoys a psychic unity with Earth, which establishes his rule over it (stanzas 2–5). The poem ends picturing Adam and Eve as truly free in every aspect: "Collected now in themselves, human and erect, / Lord and lady walked on the dabbled sward, / . . . . The Earth's strength was in each" (lines 29–30, 32). If such stories and poems do not answer whether Lewis believed in a single original unfallen couple, they do show why he held that something like them must have existed. Their existence grounds a fundamental split in human consciousness. Thus, whether prehistorical figures or noble prelapsarians, they are deserving of awe and wonder. Or, as Aslan observed to Prince Caspian, "You come of the Lord Adam and the Lady Eve. . . And that is both honor enough to erect the head of the poorest beggar, and shame enough to bow the shoulders of the greatest emperor" (*PC*, 233).

As then to that primal dishonor, Lewis, as was Farrer, was less inclined to shift the blame for human wickedness primarily onto Adam and Eve, though they provide stories for reflection. For Lewis, the divinely revealed "myth" of the paradisal Fall was to teach us that we are a bent race in need of a renewal that we cannot accomplish ourselves. The Fall explains our need for recovery, not so much where original guilt belongs. Because the higher capacity

of humans is broken—that is, because of "a radical alteration of his constitution, a disturbance of the relation" between animal and spirit—we must address the healing of our splintered capacities (*PP*, 83–84), yet we are too far
gone to save ourselves. Lewis insisted that this was not the doctrine of total
depravity; we are still capable of great good, even though our wickedness is
more than sufficient to destroy us: "If our depravity were total we should not
know ourselves to be depraved," he insists in a note that draws off his objections to positions such as Karl Barth's (*PP*, 66).

Moreover, Lewis was careful to locate his understanding of sin within dogmatic tradition. Following an argument that he perhaps first encountered in
G. K. Chesterton's *Everlasting Man,* Lewis asserted that we can know little
about prehistoric humanity, and we are mistaken to argue that indigenous
groups are vestiges of a less evolved humanity. We are also mistaken to claim
that much of what we call sin is a biological holdover from prehistory (*PP*,
73–74). As did Augustine, Lewis held that the first and great human sin was
self-will, one that moderns are as subject to as any generation, for we easily
regard our fellow persons as things for our use and manipulation, yet Lewis
also opined that this understanding did not need the seminal view or the fed-
eral theory of sin to recognize that humans were a "spoiled species" in need
of help. Just as the quantum world is distorted by a picture, so the reality of
human nature is not easily explained by mental abstraction (*PP*, 85–87).

The two temptations of Digory in *The Magician's Nephew* do not so much
represent the spoiling of a species as embody its trouble and its hope, for Digory fails in the first and succeeds in the second. Significantly, roles are reversed here. After all, Frank and Helen are not the only Adamic parallel in
the novel. Polly is more like Adam; she often sizes up the situation and sees
what must be done, while Digory, like Eve, desires knowledge and is driven
by *curiositas*. In Charn, it is their quarreling about gender that propels Digory
onto ringing the forbidden bell and awakening Jadis. But this is no original sin
per se; the two are human (and therefore fallen) children. Digory's actions
arise from an already self-driven temperament, and they lead to Jadis coming into Narnia at its creation, rather than afterwards. While she has already
wrecked ruin on another world, it is Digory's choice that allows evil to enter
an unspoiled world, and it is a choice he has made many times before, if on a
less global level. When Digory is confronted by Aslan for what he is done, he
indulges in the same blame-shifting that Adam and Eve attempt in Genesis.
Only when Digory admits that he was not pretending can he fully confess,
"I've spoiled everything" (*MN*, 147).

The roles of Eve and the serpent are also played out in the novel. As a character, Digory is still capable of great good, though without the task and memory of Aslan, he will not be able to mitigate some of his first fallen deed. In the garden he must refuse the apple of life for himself, and the White Witch's temptations are on the basis of good for another, that is, his dying mother (*MN*, 176–77). Jadis's deceptive logic is not unlike the form the temptations of the Un-Man take in addressing the Green Lady. Tinidril, too, is continually offered a tragic vision of sacrificing herself for the unnamed good of her unborn descendants: "Shall I go and rest and play ... while all this lies on our hands? Not till I am certain that there is no great deed done by me for the King and for the children of our children" (Lewis 1944, 112). Both Digory and the Green Lady must eventually receive help to survive this onslaught: the compassionate command of Aslan in the former story and Ransom, the representative of Maleldil, in the latter.

One can argue that Farrer's project in *Love Almighty* was partially seeking to fill out Lewis's understanding of evolved human pain and particular moral fallenness. As I set out above, Farrer began with a personal, involved, intentional God and established him as sole creator of the good universe, so while not claiming *creatio ex nihilo*, Farrer nonetheless rejected resistant cosmic material or weak subcreations as an explanation of the problem. In his own manner, Farrer even invoked the symbol of Adam in *Love Almighty*, albeit latently, for a human is "a talking beast," one in whose "speech lies his reason" (*LA*, 106). If Lewis invoked the mythic side of the Edenic account for imaginative purposes, Farrer appealed to a theological deep structure that still bore the shape of his theism's picture of a fallen world. This in part meant recalling humans are the imago dei. Locating reason at the center of personhood allowed Farrer to integrate mortal capacity with salvific change.

A human is an animal created for eternity, whose final telos is the Beatific Vision and relationship of love. Part of the reason we can know this, according to Farrer, is because our personhood transforms our experience of animal pain and simple consciousness by altering our animal sensation, emotion, and actions: "The world laid bare by reasonable discourse opens a field to all our powers. Not knowledge only, but love and delight find equally their objects" (*LA*, 109). Thus, we begin to tally up and talk about the universe. Justice and charity—in being rational and shared—become matters of speech; and our shared speech gives us shared narratives of our experiences. We are given this rational speech by the divine Logos. This is not to say we can effectively imagine how God is remaking us; we are left to wonder what the exact role of physical suffering is, especially since not all seem able to profit from it. Nevertheless, our end is "the completion of Christ's Incarnation" in the bringing up of all that into his perfection (*LA*, 130).

Even if one argues that people "suffer and perish as animals," while "they are redeemed and saved as rational persons" (*LA*, 113), the physical and moral state of humans is expressed in varied gradations. For Farrer, there was no clear line between our physical circumstances and our spiritual ones, and yet as a Christian, one still affirms the change with a divine destiny in mind. Farrer could conclude that ancestral sin was environmental rather than seminal, and that, as a doctrine, the lapsarian state did not remove individual responsibilities nor the need for forgiveness and transformation. He seemed to distrust a too literal Fall precisely for the same reasons Lewis invoked it. It would make sin prehistoric and savage rather than willful and modern. This did not mean, however, Farrer thought, that we do not each inherit a culture and environment of sinfulness that we take on and replicate; something has happened in our past. A stress on original sin, however, made theodicy a historical question rather than a current one. This was not to say that sin had not increased death's pain and made it bitter; it had. But whether we suppose or not the existence of a primordial Adam, "Sin is ours" (*LA*, 157).

Even material decay must have a larger purpose. Lewis had felt that the competition and decay among vegetable matter was not of necessary evil (*PP*, 135), while Farrer concluded that this needed better integration within a theodicy. Free will has a larger, natural, and evolved context. Farrer began with conflict in the biological world, including that of vegetative matter. He classified three kinds of imaginable "misfit" between or within living systems: (1) *a misfit in form*, as when an organism does not fit its soil; (2) *a misfit in relations*, as when two species compete for the same nutrients; or (3) *a misfit in matter*, as when a plant is ingested by an animal. Each, according to Farrer, could be judged as a mismatch between biological systems, and it is impossible to imagine a world without these conflicts. It would mean a loss of biological vitality, for nature is a number of interacting and conflicting systems (*LA*, 55). God, it would seem, has created creatures to act, and they act upon each other within a "diversified field of force," which involves "interactive energies" (*LA*, 56). Farrer, thus, rejected the machine model inherited from the Enlightenment for a more ecologically dense one.

Farrer even argued that humans cannot work out what a truly better world would be, though we still tell such stories. He, too, like Lewis, used analogical supposals to explore the possibilities and help his readers reimagine what such a world might be, but as often these were to show what we *cannot* imagine. For example, Farrer considered two pictures: the first, a hierarchical picture in which God fills in the levels of the universe from the top down; the second, a universe in which all objects are drawn to God but protected by the screen of physicality in order to remain free. The first model does not explain why God would need to create a world. After all, God in his freedom could go in infinite directions—horizontal as well as vertical. On the other hand, the second model might be a world in which we begin with the smallest of atomic materials then build up further and further in perfection, and this could explain our need for suffering and its possibilities, yet it too is not entirely successful (*LA*, 75). In the end, our best response is to be grateful for what and where we are, and Farrer encouraged his readers to do so: "To regret the universe is either morbidity or affectation" (*LA*, 61).[8]

Farrer's own "answers" were, thus, often presented as partial pictures that overlap without offering a complete solution. Like Lewis, Farrer was seeking to set forth Christian theology as a way of reimagining theodician issues: "We have propounded dogmatically what we could not establish argumentatively; but we trust that, even without the supporting arguments, our conclusions will have commended themselves to the reason" (*LA*, 100), and this in full awareness that these, even then, might not entirely answer the objections of the heart. If Lewis looked more to the mythopathic quality of original Eden and the tragedy of a lapsarian condition, Farrer looked to the rational condition of human nature that the doctrine of the imago dei implied, and in turn his examination of a world of organic competition sought to imagine better the role that human decision-making and therefore self-will played in its painful condition. Given all this, both men had to consider the reality of animal pain as well.

ANIMAL PAIN AND THE SATANIC

Since C. S. Lewis and Austin Farrer were each committed to the proposition that animal pain and death (indeed human physical death) occurs in biological history before human moral failings, they both felt that theodicy must account for animal suffering, or at least attempt to do so. In some ways, Lewis's chapter on animal pain is the least satisfying one in *The Problem of Pain*, yet one can also make it out to be more than Lewis wished it to be. It is really a set of conjectures rather than any solid claims, though obviously some were dear to Lewis. Lewis himself admitted the reality of animal pain is horrible (and as an antivivisectionist, he sought to relieve it), yet he thought it was horrible in part because there was no direct Christian reflection that one could draw upon (*PP*, 129). This is a strange assertion since he proceeded to draw from theology a number of speculative ideas in the remainder of the chapter. He summed up the issue in three areas of concern: "What do animals suffer?" "How did disease and pain enter the animal world?" "How can animal suffering be reconciled with the justice of God?" (*PP*, 130–31). As to the first, Lewis held that consciousness, and reflective consciousness at that, is necessary for an awareness of good and evil. Higher mammals seem to have some capacity for memory and sentience, but Lewis did not extend to them anything like the reflectivity that makes pain actual suffering. Such creatures have no "self" in the human sense, and to read too much into their responses to pain, he argued, is a species of "the pathetic fallacy" (*PP*, 131–33).

Lewis's own answer to his second concern—that of the origin of animal pain—was far more conjectural. Given that geological history and the fossil record suggest that animals lived and died long before human existence and that many were carnivorous, Lewis conjectured that a prehuman Satan who rebelled against God could be the source of animal predation and violence (*PP*, 134–35). Lewis defended this supposition as having a long pedigree in Christian tradition, and he judged materialism's dismissal of the demonic as without foundation. Materialists had no evidence to the contrary; the demonic simply did not fit comfortably into current "climates of opinion" (*PP*, 134). Lewis also explored this in his fiction. Many of his demonic figures have a hatred for life. The Un-Man in *Perelandra*, left to itself, rips open the backs of frogs or shreds vegetation if nothing else is at hand. The Macrobes behind the N. I. C. E. inspire a program of animal experimentation that is actually animal torture. The Deplorable Word of Jadis destroys even insect life on Charn. The prehistoric aspect is also echoed in *Out of the Silent Planet*. Ransom discovers that the Oyarsa of Thulcandra had invaded Malacandra millennia before life existed on Earth. "It is the longest of all stories and the bitterest" (*OSP*, 110, 120).

Outside fiction, such conjecture was the sort of thing that bothered Farrer the most, and not just in response to animal pain. Farrer had a number of objections against popular and personalist readings of Satan, including how the supposition of Satanic temptation impacted human morality. Farrer argued that an Adamic Fall did not need to posit Satan as a literal cause, nor in turn did a demonic explanation of evil need a literal temptation of Adam and Eve. He was especially concerned that these two doctrines should not be used to blame-shift responsibility onto God, and he concluded that a literal Satan was not a necessary element of theodicy except as an image of larger psychotic, disturbing evils. Farrer held that we cannot really imagine a spiritual power like devils except in human terms, and that such dark angelic powers were not essential to explaining human actions in general. In turn, the belief in a literal Satan left open the question as to why God would allow such powers to roam through the universe. "Lucifer expresses our sin, he does not explain it" (*LA*, 142).

At the same time, Farrer admitted our emotions need these pictures if only to name "a sort of cunning" (*LA*, 147). Satan, he suggested, represents "a sort of rebelliousness in things," and as such it was better to see the demonic as a force "overruled by Providence" than that of an angelic servant of God's (*LA*, 164). Interestingly, in the same year as Farrer wrote this, he could also talk as if the devil were indeed a personal force. He observed that Satan tries to convince us that our actions are not entirely under our control, that is, "my sober, working self is off the job" (*LIB*, 65). The demonic lord becomes a co-partner with human choice in sin, not so much the cause as the excuse. He represents a deception that as one grows more corrupt, one can still do good: "This is the revelation of God's righteousness, that he rejects (and it costs the death of his Son) the lies of the devil. For the devil says that I can remain essentially good, and therefore worthy of my Creator's love, in spite of my sin; and his saying this is the unrighteousness, or crookedness, of the devil" (*LIB*, 67). Thus, Farrer still had a place for such imagery.

As to the third concern—that of justice—Lewis admitted that there seemed to be no obvious compensatory function for an eternal life for animals. He wondered if domestic animals might continue in some way "in" their masters, while wild species might continue as a kind of Platonic gathering figure in which they all exist in one living archetype still free to roam in paradise (*PP*, 136–41). Both supposals for an animal future suggest a semifederal "interanimation" or "mystical togetherness" (Creegan 2014, 99). A singular representative was not a hard-and-fast rule either. Lewis had two such creatures romp and play together in the purgatorial antechamber of Paradise in his *The Great Divorce* (1946, 33). He conceded in other places that these were not dogmas; they were only attempts to widen the human imagination as to what could be. Given the omni-benevolence of the Creator, "the appearance of divine cruelty in the animal world must be a false appearance" (*GD*, 168). Better, then, "to liberate imagination" and to at least encourage "a due agnosticism about the meaning and destiny of brutes" (*GD*, 169).

Nevertheless, Lewis in some of his poetry playfully explored an eschatology for animals. In "Pan's Purge" (1946) he imagined an animal apocalypse not unlike the one in *That Hideous Strength*, though on a cosmic level (Lewis 2015, 342). "On a Picture by Chirico" (1949) and "Such Natural Love Twixt Beast and Man" envision a healed cosmos where animals are treated with fairness and peace (Lewis 2015, 362, 417). The first of these even has a kind of arcadia and utopia for horses in which they leave behind the atrocity of human wars and civilization:

> These are not like the horses we have ridden; that old look
> Of half-indignant melancholy and delicate alarm's gone.
> Thus perhaps looked the breeding-pair in Eden when a day shone
>   First upon tossing manes and glossy flanks at play.

> They are called. Change overhangs them. Now their neighing is half speech.
> Death-sharp across great seas, a seminal breeze from the far side
> Calls to their new-crown'd race to leave the places where Man died—
> (lines 13–19)

These are animals who are healed of fear and sadness, and what awaits them is arguably compensatory, yet certainly it is a renewal of animal life, and even as their half-speech indicates, it extends to their exaltation. The same might be said of Strawberry, the coach horse, becoming Fledge, the first of winged horses in Narnia, or even of the talking animals of Narnia in general. In offering such conjectures whether in poetry or prose, Lewis's goal was to diminish hard-and-fast materialism—not to rationally disarm it entirely, but to out-narrate it with a better world.[9] Even if the purpose and answer to animal suffering is not spelled out clearly by dogma, it still could conceivably be imagined.

Farrer, two decades later in *Love Almighty*, attempted a more detailed analysis of animal pain within the larger framework of biological existence, and thus, he also sought to address Lewis's second and third concerns. Animals, Farrer noted, as systems "both suffer damage, and inflict it," and thus undergo aches and agonies at some level (*LA*, 77). Animal life is about avoiding pains and accepting pleasures (*LA*, 79). Farrer, like Lewis, did suggest that we could too readily impose human personification upon animal existence, but where Lewis used these limits to suggest what we cannot know, Farrer used them to suggest how problematic the issue was, for nonhuman animals appear to have less to offset their pain. We really cannot speak about the balance or overbalance of good and evil in an individual animal's existence without projecting our human experiences onto it. Farrer argued that it was a mistake to treat "Nature" as a singular system when it was actually a whole series of natures with species interacting with and within one another. Do we really even know what a "timely death" for an animal is (*LA*, 81–83)? A number of caveats, then, Farrer judged as important: (1) the suffering of animals does not have the same potential "justifications pleaded" for human existence; (2) humans can achieve something like "heroic endurance"; and (3) human reasons can be used to transcend some aspects of prolonged suffering in ways that, as far as we can tell, animals do not have open to them (*LA*, 84–85). Here, too, Farrer's position was not entirely unlike Lewis's. Other animals, even higher mammals, apparently do not have the same kind of reflective self-regard, yet Farrer was left still wanting to know what the justice of God *might* mean to other mammals.

Farrer suggested that God does do more for individual creatures than we could possibly work out through scientific observation. Farrer argued that a cosmic theodicy could note that such pain was as a step in evolution toward human self-reflective agency. At the same time, there likely remain goods that God has conceived for other species that are meaningful to them in some sense of the word (Hebblethwaite 2007, 59). Pain within normal instinctual existence is "justified," Farrer asserted, if we understand by it the ways in which animals learn to adapt to danger and the manner by which they become food for others. (This does not, however, apply to the human torture of animals. Farrer insisted that when we do encounter the case of the prolonged suffering of an animal, we should have the compassion to end it in one way or another.) Nevertheless, we are simply limited in our understanding—humans cannot ask for natural foresight to avoid every instance of prolonged animal pain nor can they know why God designed a world that has occasions of it. In the world they do have, human beings cannot expect "perpetual miracles" to avoid such animal pain (*LA*, 87–89). None of this, however, Farrer insisted, was promoting a "mere Deism" in which God left the universe to run on its own. The sustaining and creating work of God are the same (*LA*, 94).

Farrer argued for the guidance of God within creative evolution, yet he was careful to avoid a God of the gaps or that "the overplus is Providence" (*LA*, 96). The action of God is hidden; we cannot measure it, for it is present at every moment in every way. Again, Farrer looked at the limits of the artist analogy, and he listed four ways in which God's care could be said to be present for his creatures: he makes them to shun destruction. He designs them to flee any pain or harm. He makes death something they do not resist for long when it arrives, and finally, he gives creatures (e.g., humans) who can feel compassion the obligation to help end the suffering of animals when possible. "It must never be forgotten that God is the God of hawks no less than sparrows, of microbes no less than men" (*LA*, 97–104).

Farrer in other places reflected, as well, upon the hiddenness of God and his actions in the evolutionary history of species. Like Job, humans are unable to uncover the action of God in the process of development, and yet Jews and Christians confess God has been acting all along, as the end result of amoeba and cedar and gazelle all testify (*WL*, 6–8). What makes God's agency so profoundly beyond us? God knows all directly and utterly: "he feels from both sides the interplay of forces" (*GND*, 80). Human limitation in the world is unable to draw this unity together, yet it is there in God's acumen (*GND*, 82), and we cannot grasp the infinite attendance of God in every way at all times: "The works of God are not irrational, they are endlessly intelligible; but that means there is always more and more for us to understand in them" (*GND*, 87). Thus, a decent agnosticism as to what God is up to with animals is warranted. Lewis and Farrer may have disagreed upon how conjectural pictures were best used, but in the end they agreed that theodicy was as much about softening the atheistic resistance to greater meaning as it was in helping their readers imagine a more charitable purpose for the cosmos. While clearly Farrer thought that Lewis's conjectures were less than helpful, Farrer's own suppositions were not of necessity hard-and-fast claims, though they were based in biological evidence. If Lewis's approach was more mythic, Farrer's aspired to current science, but not in a way that divorced its meaning from the wider theological possibility. Thus, both Lewis and Farrer had to admit how little we can know.

EXPERIENCING EVIL

Such mystery also extended to human suffering. It goes without saying that the problem of evil is not simply a philosophical or theological issue; it is also an existential or personal one. Austin Farrer and C. S. Lewis explored the phenomenology of evil, though Lewis did so in far more detail, and both writers understood that how persons are conscious of their own psychological and bodily experience says much about how they are able to understand the Creator. What, then, must one make of the human experience of suffering itself? If animal suffering is an evolving step toward human consciousness, is our being subject to dread and vice understandable? Does human awareness of evil possess anything beyond absurdity and the unfathomable? Michael Ward has argued that as one of Lewis's first apologetic works, *The Problem of Pain* does not fit seamlessly together, and that Lewis's more mature theodicy included not only Lewis's journal after the death of Joy Davidman, *A Grief Observed*, but also Lewis's five sonnets on suffering from the 1940s (see Lewis 2015, 423–24).[10] Ward insists on this because he judges Farrer as overlooking the "cry of dereliction" of Christ's death on the cross in Lewis's theodicy, especially in later works, such as *The Last Battle* (Ward 2010, 208–16). There is much justice in what Ward has to say. At the same time, in Farrer's defense, he did understand these elements were part of Lewis's personal suffering and his theology, and Farrer thought that Lewis after Joy's death would have written *The Problem of Pain* with much the same convictions, but certainly not in the same way: "It is not much good to tell a man laboring to conceive the Providence of God in spite of the evils rampant in his Creation, that if after prolonged bachelordom he makes a blissful marriage and loses his wife in a couple of years by an agonizing disease, he will then (should his faith survive) have reason to tell himself that nothing further of the sort is likely to shake it" (*Light*, 32). Upon what basis, then, did Farrer make such a judgment? The Farrers, after all, were quite close to Joy, and Austin had been present during Joy's long struggle with cancer, performed her funeral, and been with Lewis afterwards. Was Lewis's experience of grief itself a radical extension of his theodicy, or more like a confirmation of it?

The charge is sometimes made that rational, philosophical theodicies cannot do justice to the problem of evil because they artificially abstract evil and suffering from the actual experience of sufferers.[11] To treat the manner in which humans suffer as a logical dilemma is to flatten the way consciousness receives the overwhelming events that are atrocities, natural disasters, and personal violations or bereavement. Theodicy is more like a "meaningful order, or nomos," that, as "a shield against terror," orders our psychic breakdown before the destabilizing nature of experienced evil (Berger 1969, 19–27). In his introduction to *The Problem of Pain*, Lewis assured his readers that he was not operating as one who wished to downgrade "serious pain" as anything "less than intolerable" (*PP*, 9–10). Certainly, his own life up to that point had given witness to that— the death of his mother and father, as well as his experience in World War I, to name only the most obvious events. And he also stressed that *The Problem of Pain* was intended to address only "the intellectual problem" (*PP*, 10).

Farrer would make a similar caveat in *Love Almighty*. He was addressing the "theoretical problem only" and not the "pastoral, medical, or psychological" aspects of the "practical problem" (*LA*, 7). Yet as William M. Wilson and Julian N. Hartt point out, Farrer was not bifurcating the theoretical problem from the practical problem as if they had no relationship whatsoever (2004, 110–12). "Trouble is, indeed, the acid test of virtue; but only because its tendency is to destroy it," Farrer could observe (*LA*, 15). He understood that the actual experience of evil is a far more debilitating event: "Evil commonly strikes us not as a problem, but as an outrage. Taken in the grip of misfortune, or appalled by the violence of malice, we cannot reason sanely about the balance of the world. Indeed, it is part of the problem of evil that its victim is rendered incapable of thought" (*LA*, 7). A general recovery in the face of the evil event has to precede any debate over theory. This did not mean that epistemic answers were simply academic; they also could shape and form our ability to make sense of grief and intense pain.

Farrer noticed that our own epistemic limitations shape deeply why we long for an orderly understanding. Humans "experience imperfection and precariousness in ourselves," and not in our theories. So, for similar reasons, we come to God not looking for a descriptive model that settles logical confusion, but for one who acts upon our behalf, "a rock on which to plant our feet" (LA, 12). Practically speaking a cosmic theodicy that addresses questions surrounding the natural world, and yet one that never addresses the conflict between God's goodness and tangible moral evil, does not reflect the actual concerns of believers. It is upon the basis of a need for order and a responsibility to reflect actual religious worldviews that the theologian must be careful not to fall too quickly back on the paradoxical. We all need a nomic structure. As Farrer noted, "It is always our duty to find as much sense and order in things as we can" (LA, 15).

Farrer could admit in a sermon that an offer of sense and order could be overplayed by the Church. An appeal to divine wisdom and sanctification amid pain is asking for the counterobjection, "but here's a man simply broken to pieces, physically and morally; and it isn't his fault" (BM, 6). Farrer's response as a priest to such was not to keep insisting on theoretical order, but to turn to the sacramental and devotional experience of God. Some situations are not meant to be made sense of by rational organization but to be experientially addressed over time. "The new marvel God makes will organize the old chaos and draw it into a new pattern" (BM, 7), and this is made in us as Christ's Resurrection life works itself out and at a cosmic level. For this truth, Farrer was still willing to appeal to "the shattering paradox" that merges old and new creation by bringing eternity into the temporal world.

Farrer also recognized that because of human consciousness, our "pain-experience" is different from that of animals. "We never know a naked pain, we always take it as something—as a thorn, as a sharp intruder, as a danger, a cruelty, an outrage; as burning, tearing, chafing, or disabling." We always experience pain as an imposition upon our order and process it within the field of our beliefs (LA, 108–9). In a sense, pain, especially significant pain, never arises in our experience without a great struggle or injustice, and Farrer further understood that persons have different capacities to undergo suffering. "The world is more full of limping souls, who shuffle somehow about," neither psychological sound nor pathologically broken (LA, 112), and this was not only at an individual level. It was true of communities, too. Farrer took as an example a poverty-stricken community worn down by the "unrelenting pressure of material need"; such, he observed, would develop a truncated view of existence, and all who grow up within that culture would inherit its shrunken social imaginary (*LA*, 113). This communal suffering could be particularly in view when a leader, such as a school administrator or priest, is called upon to remember the numbers of soldiers killed in battle, or for that matter, to pray for the souls of the global martyrs in the news. Farrer noted of the lists of the remembered dead that "our imaginations are broken against the obstacle of a hideous arithmetic" (*FO*, 153). For better or worse, the world is interdependent and the experience of evil includes these larger horrors. Yet what humans find impossible is possible to God, who knows every name and every story.

Farrer preached on a similar theme, in this case imagining a naval commander who respects God but thinks it unseemly to pretend to love him. The commander comes closest to loving God when one of his children is brought back from death's door. While at service singing a psalm about the great deeds of God who saves us from death, tears stream down the commander's visage, and he reflects how foolish it has been not to love God. But then comes the challenge: "If we cannot help feeling the hand of God in the recovery of a dear endangered life, but overflow with thankfulness; why not be equally ready to feel the direct stab of divine cruelty in the boy's falling ill? And suppose—for boys do die—the boy died?" Everyone does die in the end (*CF*, 172). The commander could respond that the two things are simply not the same. "Bad things don't reveal a cruel God; they hide from us a God of love" (*CF*, 173). While true in a sense, Farrer insisted that what is needed is the gift of a larger love, one which realizes that sanctifying love extends beyond whether our day-to-day existence is full of positives. Farrer insisted that this was Job's dilemma, and that it could only be answered in the cross of Christ (*CF*, 174–75). Job equated God's love with the blessings of wealth and family that he had received, then lost. But in Christ's sacrifice another definition of love is present, one in which the ultimate destiny of our temporal, changing personhood is reflected.

Many of these same themes were present in Lewis's experience. When he wrote out his *A Grief Observed* he had come to understand that his personal suffering was not only a theodicy, but also a kind of anthropodicy of consciousness: "Reality looked at steadily is unbearable." Why is there such a thing as "the terrible phenomenon called consciousness?" (*GO*, 28). Why are humans the kind of creature who can respond with horror and disgust and not just basic fear? Even though Lewis had made a case for the real good of consciousness, he understood that in a postlapsarian state, it was a mixed blessing, even at times a seeming curse. In *A Grief Observed,* Lewis explored four areas that are prevalent in a phenomenology of grief: (1) grief's bodily conditions; (2) the doubling of the self that a consciousness of grief brings; (3) the self-deception that often accompanies change; and (4) how grief shape one's view of God. Each, Lewis discovered, has the ability to disrupt the theological and existential structure of one's belief.

In the opening of *A Grief Observed,* Lewis began not with a challenge to the justice of God, but with a close description of grief. These first paragraphs show Lewis carrying out both aspects of the word *observed* in the title—to examine the grief he feels, but also to enact it as an inevitable, even auto-affective response. He notes how grief's bodily aspects—"fluttering," "restlessness," "yawning," "swallowing"—as well as that of dullness and distance between oneself and the social world, were phenomena that happened to him and not at his invitation (*GO*, 3–5). As the journal goes on, he continues these close descriptions of the way grief can dominate a person. He notes his disgust at self-pity and that "the laziness of grief" led to being unkempt, disorderly, and repulsive to others. He also reflects that shame and decency are intertwined, noting how the boys responded with a sense of the indecent to his talking about Joy ("H."), and he realizes that he could be an embarrassment to himself and others, "a death's head" (*GO*, 10).

Lewis notices, too, how the temporal and spatial conditions that held him and Joy together were disrupted by death, and he describes not only the feeling of "empty successiveness," which is akin to numbness, even emptiness or sterility (*GO*, 33), but also how grief gave him "a vague sense of wrongness, of something amiss" (*GO*, 35). Because he realized that depression crept into everything, including his experience of the natural world and mechanical objects, Lewis understood that the suffering body has a silent power that one cannot ignore; one is literally vulnerable to oneself, and yet by this, the body is more effective in awakening one to reality than are the various rationalities of the mind (*GO*, 40).

Along with bodily suffering and disturbance, Lewis experienced what Farrer described—the way evil can disrupt our rationality. Our intense desires can have a strange doubling in that they increase our yearning rather than satisfying it (*GO*, 45). Lewis also noted a doubling within himself—one part trying to assure the other. With this multiplicity of self came a realization that conceptualizing grief already carried the possibility, even the certainty, of a failure of language: "The thing itself is simply all these ups and downs: the rest is a name or an idea" (*GO*, 12). He even questions the bodily and psychological purpose of his journaling: "Do I hope that if feeling disguises itself as thought

I shall feel less?" (*GO*, 33), and he experiences a constant doubt about the efficacy of his thoughts: are any of them a true insight into reality?

A doubling of consciousness also had other kinds of distortions it could offer Lewis. The doubling of the self is attached to the nature of memory. In *The Problem of Pain*, he had praised the material aspect of embodiment as making individuality and society possible. Because they have bodies, human beings can have both inner and outer worlds. "You are enabled not only to *be*, but also to *appear*" (*PP*, 31). There, Lewis had reflected on the moral uses of pain; that it may expose our self-delusions as to our goodness (*PP*, 92–95); that it may uncover our pretenses to self-sufficiency (*PP*, 95–98); and that it may assist us in pursuing the good when our motives are invested elsewhere (*PP*, 98–102). But now he discovered that our bodies could carry with them destabilization. The inner and outer worlds are not so separate. Bodily memory is at the center of grief, for one is subject to it whether one wishes to be or not. He found that the all-pervading nature of Joy's absence was not localized in any particular place or object, and he observed that one could not share someone else's pain or fear and that even lovers have been trained in "complementary" or "opposite" feelings and not shared bodily experiences (*GO*, 13). As a result, he fears a false memory of her, and Lewis continued throughout the journal to struggle with how memory could distort her reality, and yet it was also memory that helped him recall that Joy's presence had been the continual bodily closeness of another person. "The rough, sharp, and cleansing tang of her otherness is gone" (*GO*, 20), he lamented. Grief fragments our mental and bodily order. Before such experiences, our mental clarity, organization, and habits are all dislocated.

Lewis came to notice that grief took on a particular shape precisely as it impacted one's general experiences. For example, the death of one's spouse by its "tragic figure" extended how one could receive loss; even the shape of mercy and lament was altered, as was hope (*GO*, 50). How one endures the very pattern of the volition must be different (*GO*, 52–53), for the temporary lessening of sorrow does not mean the loss of it. Grief can come upon us unannounced and unexpected, almost as if for the first time, once again auto-affecting us with its imposition (*GO*, 56). Grief will not allow us a stabilizing structure to make sense of things. Lewis came to understand that grief requires a long narrative of change. It is not a "state," mimicking permanence, but a "process. It needs not a map but a history" (*GO*, 59). And grief, he realized, could continue to render happiness unseemly, as if mourning were the only decent response to the world (*GO*, 60–61).

For Lewis, the test of reality, not unlike what he proposed in *The Problem of Pain*, was a strange comfort. It is difficult to let in the fullness of reality.

Our limitations of our very selves, our senses, our intellect and memory, and the horizons of our perspectives all work to close us off from the real, though perhaps precisely because reality is simply too much for us. We can hardly bear it because it will not allow us the delusion of our self-deception: "All reality is iconoclastic" (*GO*, 66). At the end of the journal, Lewis describes an experience of Joy's mind strangely without feelings in the traditional sense. However, for Lewis it was a state of consciousness and a phenomenal perception for him. He found her mind's presence to be "an extreme and cheerful intimacy," and Lewis wondered if there was any other way to experience such except by one's own bodily experiences and imagination (*GO*, 73).

Lewis closed the journal, reflecting "how wicked it would be, if we could, to call the dead back!" (*GO*, 76). Decades earlier, in his fourth and fifth sonnets upon the nature of loss, Lewis had made a similar comparison. There, a bee, upon being trapped inside a room, is beating itself against a clear windowpane wanting to escape into the light and to "the laden flowers." The ones who catch the bee to release it outdoors doubtless cause all kinds of rage, terror, and despair in it, but there is no other path to "where the quivering flowers stand thick in summer air" (Lewis 2015, 424, lines 4.14, 5.12). Of course, *A Grief Observed* was also a journal of Lewis's own doubts and fears about God, and this invoked a fourth aspect of the phenomenology of grief. He noticed that even how we trust or distrust God is shaped by the reception of suffering (*GO*, 42–43). After Lewis's first exploration of what it felt like to pray and not receive a sense of God's presence, he had begun to doubt the character of God and to experience silence as truly silent, not as a silence that speaks or even as an absence that draws one to God.

Along with this, there was the question of our natural capacity to receive divine assurance. Lewis asked himself, "Perhaps your own passion temporarily destroys the capacity" (*GO*, 46), and he surmised that grief mirrors phenomenal deferral because it "comes from the frustration of so many impulses that had become habitual" (*GO*, 47). Eventually, he came to realize about both Joy and God that love was its own mode of understanding, whether presence or absence itself predominated. "Praise is the mode of love which always has some element of joy in it," including gratitude to God for giving the beloved, even if for only a season (*GO*, 62). Lewis concluded that knowledge of and love of God are one and the same; they could not be truly experienced as opposites (*GO*, 72, 76), but, then, the character of love, as Lewis long had taught, was never simply gentleness, but a "lord of terrible aspect" (*PP*, 40).

As Lewis's "Five Sonnets" remind us, *A Grief Observed* was not the first time that Lewis explored the experience of suffering in print, even if his journal was among the rawest. Lewis's novel *Till We Have Faces* is another personal theodicy that examines the nature of grief and how it divides the sufferer from the divine. Part I of the novel is written near the end of Orual's life, and it represents her memories of her love for and loss of Psyche, a loss she blames upon the gods. She begins her bitter testament against them by complaining that "Terrors and plagues are not an answer" (*TWHF,* 3), and she ends it by asking, "Why must holy places be dark places?" The gods, she concludes, are "obnoxious to man" because they will not give an answer, that is, an accounting of themselves that makes any sense (*TWHF,* 249–50). Along the way, Orual learns of herself that she has been divided into "two halves," a rational half that the Fox has cultivated in her, one that puts its trust in a natural theology of divine order and harmony, and another half that finds the smell of the holy in bloody sacrifice and ritual (*TWHF,* 151). In this division, she represents a modern theodician dilemma, one in which a noumenal awareness of the *mysterium tremendum* is unable to be combined with a project like Leibniz's. For Orual, any hint of the best of all possible worlds is quickly ruined: "The gods never send us this invitation to delight so readily or so strongly as when they are preparing some new agony" (*TWHF,* 97). She has led a life that disrupts her ability to trust anything the gods might offer her, and yet she finds in a civic life of hard work an ability to often deaden the pain she feels.

But, more than this, Orual's demand for a theodicy is also a coming to terms with her own jealousy and possessiveness. In part II, she must now recount "the gods' surgery," for she has come to understand that her testament of rage was also a means to uncover her moral disease (*TWHF,* 254). Here, as in Lewis's later *A Grief Observed,* the god is the great iconoclast. The lord of terrible aspect comes to judge her in the end, and what she learns unmakes her accusations. Eleonore Stump, in her recent *Wandering in Darkness,* argues that the promised unity with God in the Beatific Vision makes suffering potentially worthwhile, for the suffering necessary to purify the person enables that unity's fruition. This does not mean that the person completely lays aside all his or her desires, but that these are subsumed and transformed within the ultimate desire for God: "When one of those in union is a perfectly loving God, the human person in that union can wait in trust even while he is grief-stricken over the loss or absence of something he had his heart set on. In such circumstances, both the waiting and the trust become a kind of giving back, which is part of the mutuality of love" (Stump 2010, 446–47).

I do not believe it is anachronistic to suggest that something similar to Stump's model happens in the life of Orual. Her account of her life is one of a noble queen who learned to govern fairly justly and wisely, at least by the light of her culture. Yet she also learns that she has suffered on behalf of Psyche, that the breaking of union that she brought about between her half-sister and the god, along with its consequences, she has carried about in herself so that Psyche may undergo her trials without terror. She gains, too. some measure of sympathy for the lifelong suffering of Bardia's wife and even the loneliness of Redival, which she had ignored, and Orual learns that she is Ungit, a being whose love demands and drains others. Yet Orual's suffering is also redeemed: "You also are Psyche." In this last vision she receives the beauty she had been denied all her life, and this beauty is tied to the divine union: "I know now, Lord, why you utter no answer. You are yourself the answer" (*TWHF*, 308). Her desire for an answer and the experience of her life's suffering are enfolded into one another. Orual, thus, receives an answer not unlike the one Lewis would receive at the end of *A Grief Observed*. The problem of suffering is answered not by harmonic models, but by a divine narrative. As Farrer pointed out, it is one thing to claim that the promise of infinite good will one day engulf all our grief and pain, it is another to say that this knowledge can help us now: "Any Christian can say the first; only a sufferer can venture the second" (*LA*, 170).

Lewis and Farrer both shared an understanding that the personal problem of evil, while certainly not divorced from the theoretical one, had to be lived out over time. Both understood that grief and pain have the ability to bodily and psychically fracture the human self, and that theoretical answers were of little use in the thick of this rupture. Yet Farrer and Lewis also looked to the answer of heavenly union as that which would transcend any sorrow.

HUMAN PAIN AND THE LAST THINGS

In *The Problem of Pain* and *Love Almighty and Ills Unlimited*, C. S. Lewis and Austin Farrer understood human salvation within a cosmic framework, and this had important implications for their theodicies, both in these books and in other works by them. Farrer's conclusions in *Love Almighty* were based around Christian hope—that the eternal state clarifies and explains the suffering of this world, including that suffering which appears as without purpose. He stressed that the final blessed "last and universal end which God has disclosed," by doing so, in our temporal existence, grants us a potential flourishing in this world (*LA*, 165). Lewis, in turn, devoted chapters in *Problem of Pain* to both hell and heaven. Rather than focusing too much upon the actual nature of these eternal realms (if indeed, hell can be referred to by the language of being), his primary focus in each chapter was the eternal state of human beings. Yet this focus also had important ramifications for how one lives life now.

Both men needed to examine a human being's negative refusal to become oriented toward Christ. As Lewis noted, if hell is intended to be a warning and an assurance that the worse sins will not escape judgment, that the incorrigible horror will have to face the truth of its conditions, then the reality of heaven is a pointer to our "utter satisfaction" in the presence of God (*PP*, 147). Hell is the consequence of a universe in which people may choose against God. Lewis thought that the images of hell in scripture were addressed to human will rather than curiosity. We do not really have to know what hell is like, only that it is everything we do not need. The horror should remain, even if we cannot say with any authority as to what it actually is. For Lewis, hell could be seen as retributive punishment, yet the real emphasis he placed upon it was the final consequence of human freedom. It is a matter of the self left to turn in upon itself. "I willingly believe that the damned are, in one sense, successful rebels to the end; the doors of hell are locked on the *inside*" (*PP*, 127). Those who object to the supposed disparity between an eternal hell and a temporal set of sins should consider whether the hell changed the person involved. Perhaps it is some final state of changeless loss of even personhood—what remains is not an entity as we would recognize it. It is a state of something defiant, if even that, though that defiance might no longer be recognizably human (*PP*, 118–28).

Rather than in *Love Almighty*, Farrer's specific reflections on hell and heaven were in his next book, *Saving Belief*. Like Lewis, Farrer defined hell more by its empty state: "Hell is simply something to be shuddered from, not anything that gives shape to your Christian existence. Heaven shows the meaning of everything; hell shows the meaning of nothing" (*SB*, 151). Farrer downplayed all this more than Lewis. In Farrer's mind, hell was at best a nagging warning that "the loss of heaven is a real danger" (*SB*, 153) rather than the heart of Christian meditation. Farrer focused more on the justice of hell, as well as the language of "eternal fire," and he did wonder whether such eternal fire itself need imply that the punishment was unending, though he was reluctant to take a hard-and-fast position.[12]

If Lewis and Farrer both considered whether hell might imply human impersonality, for each the ultimate end of human salvation is theosis (or divinization), the ongoing exalted state of the glorified believer. Just as theosis was central to their reflections upon myth and analogy, and just as it was the hypergood that drove their ultimate concern with virtue ethics, so it was with such a telos in view that both held that suffering could enter an eternal framework that offered to transcend it.[13] Lewis most famously discussed this in his war address, "The Weight of Glory," while Farrer evoked the doctrine in a number of his sermons. Lewis spoke of those being redeemed as "a society of possible gods and goddesses" (*WG*, 45).[14] Farrer, too, waxed upon the theme: "The end of man is endless Godhead endlessly possessed, but that end flows back in glory on our mortal days" (*EM*, 4). Both recognized that personhood and theosis are tied together. The structure of the physical universe makes personhood possible, which in turn makes glorification possible. Personhood requires faith and hope, agency and growth, and an orientation of the self away from itself and toward the other, especially toward God. For Farrer, trust (rather than Cartesian certainty) marked the personhood necessary for divinization for we are oriented toward God in Christ (Slocum 2007, 43–44; Hebblethwaite 2007, 81–83). Lewis, in turn, held that glory is the consummation of personhood, a gift of grace yet a gift of personal transformation and the healing of the broken self (Sutherland 2014, 141). Farrer was careful to stress the limits to theosis; we do not become the triune God himself, for God cannot divinize us beyond what is the potential of our natures. To do so would be not to perfect us but to annihilate us (*GV*, 36). A similar restriction was present in Lewis's corpus, such as his picture of the next stage in human evolution being beyond biological change. Evolution is superseded because we take in the *zoe* life of God; we do not become God himself (*MX*, 140–41, 185). Theosis is first and foremost a relationship, a turning of the soul toward the exalted Christ (Habets 2014, 123), and because this is so, human change is a movement of our selves' orientation.

For both men, theosis and suffering were part of a singular movement of the heart and body. Lewis distinguished the physical warning that we experience in our nerve endings from the distress we feel before physical pain, as well as before other kinds of mental, social, and emotional suffering. The Great Surgeon uses pain for three broad purposes: (1) to teach humans that pride and self-centeredness are not sufficient (*PP*, 93); (2) to show them that their lives are not their own (*PP*, 95); and (3) to enable humans to rise to a love that is chosen for itself rather than its pleasures alone. Our desires are not often oriented to what is best for us; thus, our pain can be a way of teaching us to make God our final good (*PP*, 98–100). Humanity was born for much, much more, yet our self-surrender inevitably involves some level of suffering in order to get there. Pain is the necessary shadow side of *phronesis* and of character and, therefore, of happiness.

For Lewis, humans are given opportunities for growth in goodness and pity. Given that God uses suffering to get through to them, it does not follow that they should avoid eliminating pain and poverty. Humanity should work to eradicate these, even though one may recognize that aspects of them will continue until the end of creation. Suffering is something between God and the person, not between persons and other persons, especially of the political sort. And God has not created a world that is entirely without pleasure and joy. Arguments that appeal to the sum total of pain ignore that each of us experiences most pain individually (*PP*, 110–17). Lewis was, of course, not invoking a soul-improvement Pelagianism. The cross of Christ, for Lewis, was the ultimate embodiment of these lessons, especially in its purest form, and the cross was working itself out in every sacrificial act of Christ's followers. "The sacrifice of Christ is repeated, or re-echoed, among His followers in very varying degrees, from the cruelest martyrdom down to a self-submission of intention whose outward signs have nothing to distinguish them from the ordinary fruits of temperance and 'sweet reasonableness'" (PP, 104).

Farrer, like Lewis, understood that there is a divine tutorial role in human suffering. In more than one place in his corpus, Farrer's stress on the "double agency" of God and free action put this in perspective. The energy of living creatures, he stressed, desires to express itself and not be checked, and because this energy comes from God, it must be recognized as his. The need to express our pride, and also to restrict it when it neglects others or especially God, is part of the matrix of agency (*CF*, 51). Yet we should be careful not to read Farrer's strong model of Providence as mitigating or overriding human free will. God does not "overrule" but "uses" and "persuades" (*GND*, 88), and "it takes infinite God to exercise a particular providence" (*TV*, 55). Just as Farrer avoided a God of the gaps in his scientific descriptions, so he avoided a puppet-master God in his theology of agency. The Universal Cause creates at every level, every moment; the only differences are in the experience of the individual creatures being touched by God in some manner (*GND*, 69). Freedom is in God because he is the source and overflow of "all newness"; thus, we are not determined but finally set free: "One is no more enslaved by dependence on him than one is enslaved by the habit of breathing" (*SB*, 33).

Indeed, the creation is bathed in God's infinite choosing. "God is known in being obeyed. Do anything for God's sake, with all your heart, and your will is the prolongation of God's will, the two are in one line; the channel between God and you is cleared and opened, and the Maker descends into his creature" (*BM*, 104). Farrer stressed that double agency is at the heart of our salvific experience, for "a man is never so truly himself as when his action is God's. 'The more truly it is God, the more truly it is I.' That is where God and man come together" (*BM*, 126). "God makes the world make itself" so the world's multiplicity possesses a kind of "free-for-all" variety (*GND*, 89–90), and yet we deeply underestimate the divine agency unless we see its center, which is caritas: "His love is an endlessly generous choice" (*GND*, 100). Thus, our freedom and God's freedom meet in a journey leading to a final transcendent transformation.

If both Farrer and Lewis saw love as the final goal of our sanctification, they also worked at ways to picture the state of this final bliss. Lewis stressed that the "vale of soulmaking" will not end until it is remade, and for now we are continually lessoned by God that this is not the final state of creation (*PP*, 108). We must learn in this world to pay attention to and enjoy the aesthetic of heaven (Tallon 2008, 205–6). Human agency has as its telos our eternal, infinite relationship with the Triune God. In Lewis's vision, a kind of evolutionary recapitulation happens in history, though of a spiritual sort: Jesus draws up our humanity into himself, and by this, humans draw up the rest of creation. Lewis pictured the new humanity as the "next step" and one unexpected in human evolution. Christ is the New Man, the forerunner of what will occur in all the redeemed (*MX*, 170, 184, 186–87).

For Farrer, likewise, this promise of bliss is a communal reality. Theodicy is answered in the incorporated status of us all (Oliver 1988, 294). Farrer argued in *Love Almighty* that the *Corpus Mysticum,* the mystical Body of Christ, is what the Church is building now in this world. At the Day of Judgment, we will confront the resurrected Christ and his saints, for the core of paradise is the Israel of God now gathered in his Church. The divine life of Christ radiates through his earthly and bodily acts and this is extended in the life of the Church now. The mission of the Church is to complete Christ's Incarnation (*LA*, 130). The final crux of a world of pain is to either conclude that there is no Maker, or to receive such pain "as God's invitation to succor his world" (*LA*, 188). The beginnings of our theosis in this life are always those of a witness to and a confrontation with Christ. Even anonymous Christians may recognize whom they have prepared for on the Last Day (*LA*, 125–27).

What, then, did Lewis and Farrer conclude about those who have no saving knowledge of Christ? For Lewis and Farrer, the one who comes to faith on the Last Day still meets the living Christ as the way of salvation, and on these terms, the exclusivity of the Christ or the *Corpus Mysticum* is not denied. Farrer noted that we cannot escape our physical cultural and sociolinguistic heritage, nor can we know explicitly the full shape of this heritage in us. Our faith is placed in God's work upon us, and this includes biological and cultural knowledge and existence. Farrer held that the argument for universal salvation seemed to undercut the process of sanctification, as well as the seriousness of any spiritual warfare. It may even mitigate against the eternal continuation of our character and personalities in any meaningful manner. In turn, Farrer considered the argument of 4 Esdras that the remnant few were simply the natural result of how God works, that God is content to get the few who are willing and able to accept salvation. But Farrer questioned this conclusion: was this not to treat the proclamation of the gospel as if teaching played no real role in instruction and conversion? The Anglican priest held out hope that a Last Day conversion might be possible, wondering if Christ preaching to the dead in 2 Peter implied a chance to repent for those who had yet to hear (*SM*, 154–57; *LA*, 113–29).

Lewis also allowed for the possibility of the anonymous Christian coming to faith outside the normal channels of the Church or perhaps by having an opportunity to decide after death. He stressed that the question was an open one, and not a dogmatic certainty; however, given that the Body of Christ is the vehicle of Salvation, it is only to the Church's advantage that God would add to them from beyond its tangible borders: "Every addition to that body enables Him to do more" (*MX*, 65). Lewis admitted that there could be an unbeliever "in a state of honest error," yet he warned that more often such persons were in "dishonest error" (*GD*, 111) and considered intellectual misjudgment a real evil that compounds its evil over time (*PP*, 116). *The Last Battle* is perhaps Lewis's most developed consideration of this possibility. The Calormene warrior Emeth has served Tash all his life and desired to meet him after death, even in the face of fear and dread. Yet after death it is Aslan he meets, and Aslan receives him. Aslan tells him that all the good he did in Tash's name is acknowledged: "Child, all the service thou hast done to Tash, I account as service done to me." In turn, Aslan instructs Emeth that all the evil done in Aslan's name is actually done for Tash and "by Tash his deed is accepted" (*LB*, 205). Even after Aslan disappears, Emeth is now possessed of an abundant desire to behold the Lion again. In knowing the truth by his real name and face, his desire for truth (Hebrew: *emeth*) is now even more fecund. In a sense not unlike Orual's, the meaning of Emeth's life—his service to Tash, his vocation as a warrior, his disgust with his superior's hypocrisy, his long commitment to the truth—reaches its narrative completion in his meeting with Aslan, and the final good now awaits him in the real world (perhaps the real Calormen) of eternity.

What, then, do our human desires tell us about our final end in God? Both Farrer and Lewis saw the Resurrection as a promise of the transformation of our very selves. As Farrer noted, God's providential knowledge of human beings and of their future implies that humans can learn to trust his work upon them, for "the evidence of his heart in my heart" (*WL*, 78–79). Farrer was careful not too quickly to divide sinner and sin in the calculations of God, for the sins of a person are not somehow separable actions that have no relationship to his or her true self. "The Christ who dies for men makes no comfortable distinction between the sin he hates and the sinners he loves; so, he dies to make them the thing he loves in them. He kills them in his death, to bring them alive in his resurrection" (*LIB*, 67). The answer to the problem of evil is a narrative assurance of the future and present love of God. Farrer reminded his audience of the thinness of human will and of human independence and of the corresponding need to love God and others: "I am commanded to love, and love is not at command and yet I know where the currents of charity run, and I can strike into them." This, too, was double agency, for willed actions are personal and yet at a level below consciousness they are ever empowered by the agency of the Triune God (*WL*, 23–24, 27–28). Freedom is not found in autonomous action but in embracing God's will/love and in being part of his offering: "No one is free but he who embraces the will of God, and shares in the *great energy* of love which makes and rules the world" (*LIB*, 55), and in embracing this, we come to understand by faith that the "suffering that [God] approves, and himself undertakes, is redemptive" (*LA*, 172). Farrer stressed that this love shaped the experience of human suffering even at the phenomenological level: "The more we love, the more we feel the evils besting or corrupting the object of our love," and yet in turn a focus upon and an experience of "besetting harms" could bring home to the person how valuable are the goods of existence which they seek to degrade and cancel out (*LA*, 188). Resistance to evil could be joined with the mercy of God and have a higher purpose.

Like Farrer, Lewis drew a connection between the transformation of human experiences and their end purpose in God. Lewis's chapter on heaven in *The Problem of Pain* was but one version of his most characteristic apologetic—that our desires tell us what we are as a species, and that a desire for eternal paradise suggests that perhaps we were made for it (*MX*, 120; *WG*, 28–32). This argument from desire, while not phenomenological per se in its formulation, nonetheless lent itself to an approach that paid close attention to the personal consciousness of experience: "Heaven offers nothing that a mercenary soul can desire. It is safe to tell the pure in heart that they shall see God, for only the pure in heart want to" (*PP*, 145). Lewis argued that we are each unique persons whom God must treat individually in order to prepare us for a relationship with him as their first love. As fitted for a heaven that meets their unique eternal shape, "the secret signature of each soul" is destined for a unique articulation of divine love (*PP*, 146). In this sense, human desires are not so much present experiences as unsated desires for a future experience that no current experience will entirely satisfy: "The thing you long for summons you away from the self" (*PP*, 149). Lewis appealed to Revelation 2:17 and the receiving of "a new name" as a promise of this individual reception and change. Or, as he remembered in *A Grief Observed*, the biological pains of the human animal must give way to something far more divine: "'Now, get on it. Become a god'" (*GO*, 72).

The character of Caspian in three of Lewis's Narnian Chronicles is illustrative of this end. It is easy to forget that readers experience only select moments in his life. He begins as a young prince who by the help of Aslan leads Old Narnia to freedom, and a few years later, he goes in search of the seven missing lords, travels to near the End of the World, and wins the hand of his bride. Yet the longer period of his grief is only seen and heard of from afar. For ten years, he suffered from the tragic death of his wife and the disappearance of his son. After losing over thirty others to the quest to recover his son, Caspian on one last journey goes in search of the answer, only to be met by Aslan and turned back to meet and bless his son at the moment of his own tragic death. Yet this is not the end. In Aslan's Country, Eustace and Jill are allowed to behold Caspian in his beatific state (or rather, the beginning of it), while Rilian must bury the body of his father, mourn, and go on to rule in his stead. In that eternal country, the ancient body of Caspian is renewed by blood from the great Lion's paw, and it takes on an age that cannot be easily described, except as very young. It is Caspian's resurrected body, one able to embrace and kiss, for "one can't be a ghost in one's own country" (*SC*, 213). The delight, even the humor, that the three experience with Aslan is emblematic of the promised joy, a joy that does provide a better end to a life of grief. Caspian is now one renewed, and he even helps the children for a moment in their own troubled world.

At the same time, if Judith Wolfe is correct, while Lewis's eschatology was far more oriented toward the destiny of individuals, his stress on the Cosmic Dance was one way that Lewis imagined the corporate, symphonic aspect of divine life in God (Wolfe 2012, 112–15). Lewis, in *The Problem of Pain*, ultimately appealed to the Triune relationship as the foundation of love—love is in community, a union with distinctions (*PP*, 149–50), and he took the position that the soul has an intermediate state that will be the mold (that is, the form) for its resurrection body, and this reflection allowed him to think more about the mutual giving of glory that happens not only in the Trinity but also in the redeemed creation. In that Great Dance, the self will no longer be imprisoned but allowed to enter into a grand *perichoresis* of "Love Himself" and of "Good Himself" (*PP*, 151).

Keeping in mind this cosmic telos in Christ shows how even among some of their greatest disagreements, the shared witnesses of Farrer and Lewis were far more united than divided. Both had to account for evolutionary and developmental models of the world and of humanity. If they disagreed, even strongly disagreed, upon the particulars of animal pain, Satan, and Adam, they nevertheless shared a strong trust that the experience of evil, while it said much about the limitations of the human condition, pointed one to a radical good purpose in suffering. Such suffering could reveal the radical love of God, a transformative love that prepared one for a divinized state in eternity. Even if Farrer took more seriously the competition of the cosmic and biological worlds, when set against a modernist background that distrusted and denied a heavenly eschaton, their shared concerns across their disagreements still take on renewed importance.

Farrer described the death of Lewis as an extension of his life: "The life which Lewis lived with zest he surrendered with composure. He was put almost beside himself by his wife's death; he seemed easy at the approach of his own. He died at the last in a moment. May he everlastingly rejoice in the Mercy he sincerely trusted" (*BM*, 47). One suspects Lewis would have written the same of Farrer. Both understood their end in God, and both learned to face hardship as part of the promise of that final telos. Their diverse theodicies together suggest that a world of suffering can nonetheless be imagined, narrated, and received as a world of love, or rather, a world with infinite love as its final end.

·+7+·

APOCALYPSE

The vision of the universe which she had begun to see in the last few minutes had a curiously stormy quality about it. It was bright, darting, and overpowering. Old testament imagery of eyes and wheels for the first time in her life took on some possibility of meaning. And mixed with this was the sense that she had been manoeuvered into a false position. It ought to have been she who was saying these things to the Christians. Hers ought to have been the vivid, perilous world brought against their grey formalized one; hers the quick, vital movements and theirs the stained glass attitudes. That was the antithesis she was used to.

—C. S. Lewis, *That Hideous Strength*

See, then, with whom we unite, and whose supplicating voices support our prayers here: certainly when we gather before the altar we know that they who are with us are more than they who are with our enemies.

—Austin Farrer, "Holy Angels" in *The End of Man*

C. S. Lewis once wrote to Dom Bede Griffiths that he was worried at the prospect of Communist or Fascist ideologies being absorbed by Christian thinkers, for then "the abomination will stand where it ought not." He argued that the two ideological movements were parodies of the truth, and they had arisen because of a historical and spiritual need that the West had left unsatisfied. But he also insisted this did not change that they were great evils, and one should be wary of their penetration into "a Leftist and a Rightist pseudo-theology" (*Letters*, 2.327). Lewis was alluding to Jesus's prediction in the Olivet Discourse that the "abomination of desolation" would be "standing in the holy place" as a sign of the cosmic end of things (Matthew 24:15), and Lewis's reference was one he could expect the priest Griffiths to catch, yet it was perhaps more than shorthand for dangerous heresy; it also represented for him a means of conceptualizing history, a way of framing the ever-present threat. Austin Farrer, too, took apocalypse and a final end seriously, also interpreting its fearful imagery as a vital lesson for the present age. He warned that the individual's conscience and God's judgment are not separate, and that they speak to the present social and political order:

> In particular, when nature breaks forth in singular disasters or when the madness of man is permitted to break loose in war and its attendant horrors, we ought to see that the angels who are the motive-forces of nature and the controllers of history are warning us of what the arm of the Almighty cannot for ever withhold. . . . And if you still think that God will build into the stainless city any that loves or works a lie, rather than cast him on to the everlasting fires without the gate, I advise you to look into your consciences. (*RI*, 34)

Farrer insisted that this was the voice of the Church in every generation. Apocalypse is a warning that we must examine our lives, for we cannot evade forever the evidence that speaks against our age. That he made this observation in a biblical commentary in no way made it a perfunctory analogy between first-century and twentieth-century concerns; rather, an awareness of the last things shaped his understanding of world war and its metaphysical consequences. The apocalyptic was a warning in every generation as to what may come of its sins.[1]

In such matters, Farrer and Lewis were hardly alone. Richard Overy has recounted the widespread sense of crisis in Britain in the period between the world wars and in the years directly following World War II. Overy describes it as a "morbid age," afraid of the fall of civilization, marked by metaphors of diagnosis and cure, and yet frustrated by an inability to turn the tide of cultural change (2010, 3–5, 366–74). The language of decline, despair, and apocalypse were shared by religious and nonreligious alike, and that such language was invoked suggests the apocalyptic was more accessible to those on the margins of institutional Christianity than its other beliefs. What was it, then, about apocalypse that made it a ready set of images for Lewis, Farrer, and their generation?

In order to understand why eschatology in general and apocalypse in particular were important to both men, it helps to have a larger picture of the genre, for each took advantage of its potential. While scholars of apocalyptic literature disagree on any exact list of the genre's characteristics, they do share many overlapping descriptions. Apocalyptic literature seeks to make a point

about the *eschaton,* the final end of all things, and to do this, it often mirrors
and critiques current events and cultures. Likewise, the end of the world can
be pictured as a cataclysmic reconfiguration, yet this need not lead to fatalism.
Its struggle between sharply defined good and evil at the cosmic level also represents for many a call to resist opposition and persecution. Apocalypse is also
deeply intertextual. It employs canonical imagery and stories, and by doing
so participates in a tradition of apocalyptic writings and predictions, as well
as sharing in a larger theological and scriptural collection of received works.
It employs language that we associate with the mythic; this includes a heavy,
patterned use of the figurative, allegorical, and symbolic, and apocalypse also is
delivered and understood within a liturgical setting of sacred time. Therefore,
it transcends history, even as it also speaks of a coming future. In addition,
apocalypses offer a vision of the destiny of humanity and especially of God's
people, and the large sweep of history is revealed by its visions. Apocalypse
too is an answer to the problem of evil, one in which a just God answers evil
decisively and makes all things new.[2] One might add, following Frank Kermode, that apocalypse imparts a certain phenomenology of experience: its
sense of an end carries with it notions of crisis, decadence, and catastrophe,
as well as narrative in which not only is the individual "directed-toward-the-
End," but so is history, for the transcendent kairos of significant time rises
above and informs the typical experience of chronological time. Ironically,
then, apocalypse can order our world, providing both an ending and a new
beginning in the midst of what otherwise seems threatening and without order (Kermode 2000, 29–31, 46–49, 94–96).

In popular discussions, interpretative questions surrounding the apocalyptic
literature of the scriptures, especially that of Daniel, Ezekiel, and the Revelation of John, have frequently centered on discerning the prophetic timetable,
as well as uncovering the meaning of events such as the Millennium. There are,
of course, other approaches to this material from the historical to the literary,
and these often treat it as more symbolic and universal.[3] An emphasis on the
symbolic does have the advantage of focusing on what audiences can gain from
the texts in any age, and in doing so helps address particular times and places.
Such readings serve, too, as models for apocalyptic texts that are post–New
Testament, including those that are intentionally fictional in their imitation
of apocalyptic themes. Farrer and Lewis in the 1940s, 1950s, and 1960s crafted
works that employed apocalypse as a countermove to the modern age. Over
against a disenchanted world that had lost its engagement with divine fullness
and that had dismissed mystery for the comprehensible and controllable, Farrer
and Lewis made gestures toward a thicker, more vertical world, and found that

the apocalyptic provided mythic intuitions of the cosmic. As Charles Taylor has observed, in the modern world, people imagine themselves as less vulnerable to supernatural forces; indeed, for the secular, disenchanted world, such powers will likely not be acknowledged at all (2007, 7–14). The apocalyptic, on the other hand, offers a less protected self, one more subject to forces beyond the self and one less inclined to maintain a disciplined objectivity before that which overwhelms. On such terms, even a secularized apocalyptic retains echoes of the dreadful and the cosmic and reminds us that we are subject to great energies beyond our stable selves and societies.[4]

Lewis's fictional accounts, such as *That Hideous Strength* and *The Last Battle,* and Farrer's interpretative commentaries, such as his *A Rebirth of Images: The Making of St. John's Apocalypse* and *The Revelation of St. John the Divine,* were written with broadly differing purposes: the former seeking to tell a good story with a cultural critique, the latter to assist a fuller understanding of the biblical Revelation of John. Nonetheless, they each understood apocalypse as a way of answering the modern world, and, in addition, wrote essays and sermons that reflected on its meaning within modernity. Arguably the seed of their apocalyptic works arose within the context of World War II. Lewis's *That Hideous Strength* fleshed out apocalyptic themes in his earlier two science fiction books, *Out of the Silent Planet* and *Perelandra*—each in its own way a war book—while Farrer's first commentary referenced the war in several instances as emblematic of its themes.

Indeed, the apocalyptic pulls together many of Lewis and Farrer's shared concerns. Both spent time reflecting upon myth and metaphor because each understood these to be means by which language engages a reenchanted world. Such a world is not entirely suspicious of hierarchy and revelation, for it finds these necessary to imagine powers beyond itself. The cosmic, moral struggle at the heart of apocalypse also addressed Lewis and Farrer's concern with ethics, and the angelic and demonic powers so prevalent in its literature, as well as its corrupt world powers (e.g., the Antichrist, the Beast, false prophets, imperial Babylon), form key elements in that cosmic struggle. The matter of history is also present, for cosmic judgment is part of history's end, and therefore its pattern, yet the Last Judgment is a judgment upon history itself, a final disruption that brings its corruption to a sudden end. Certainly, the symbols of Last Judgment and millennial bliss have shaped the metahistorical, social aspirations of Western society, not only its liberal democratic trust in Progress, but also in Marxist and Fascist hopes for a utopian state. Theodicy, too, is inherent in the apocalyptic because evil is answered in full and the righteous are rewarded with eternal bliss. As committed Anglicans, Farrer and

Lewis's experience of time and eternity was rooted in liturgy, which provided a history that was not historicist, and both insisted that theosis was not only an answer to human suffering, but also the very orientation of our images and myths. Together, apocalypse in their hands sought to hold the horizontal hope for the future within the greater, vertical eternal reign of God.

A VERTICAL WORLD

Austin Farrer understood that there is a difference between abstractions and "the impact of the whole fact" (*IB,* 5). It is one thing to theorize models of reality, be they biological stressors, socioeconomic relations, or psychological instincts, and quite another to recognize how a reality claims you personally: "You have to throw the door open, however mysterious, or terrifying, or overwhelming the body of fact may be that tumbles in" (*IB,* 5). The apocalyptic is such a world, one that overwhelms by its pictures and narratives, yet this symbolism is also a call to self-examination. Farrer was wary of theological approaches that downplayed its moral warnings: "Don't let the Christians say that Antichrist will never come. There is no guarantee that he will not; it is the true realism to make your reckoning with the assumption that he will" (*EM,* 133). As Farrer neared the end of his career, he was especially concerned that if Christians jettisoned the doctrine of eternal life, they would even lose a sense of God's control of the universe.[5] Farrer insisted that without the Beatific Vision, people have no "direction for their total thought about existence," no final end that clarifies both "Divine purpose" and human response to God (2020, 117). The orthodox God outstrips any process theology because he superintends every aspect of creation: "Beginnings and endings tie up together." They do so in that the universe, which by constantly "smashing itself the whole time," is ever going out of existence. Without divine action, the whirlpool of subatomic existence is ever ready to end, and without an eschatological sense of divine action, a belief in divine judgment would be lost (*RF,* 189–90).

C. S. Lewis addressed this matter, as well. He warned against theological positions that sought to downplay the promised end as only a personal encounter with one's own death. He thought in particular that the influence of Albert Schweitzer's *The Quest for the Historical Jesus* had reduced Christ's apocalyptic predictions to "little more than...a local 'scare,'" even though he acknowledged that this may have not been Schweitzer's intent (*WLN,* 94). Lewis stressed that the apocalyptic was not just a species of general poetic insight and wisdom. For both Farrer and Lewis, the apocalyptic should confront us with our age's pretensions; its demands upon our imaginations speak to human will. The apocalyptic does not leave us alone with ourselves. As a literary form, it speaks to each person's conceptions of his or her time. It confronts them with the possibility that the established order of things can end, indeed, is deserving of an end, and the individual must face the reality that he or she may be complicit with the corrupt order.

As such, apocalypse does not leave its audience simply entertained, or rather, at the very least, it *should* not. Moderns may want a gentler, assuring message, yet we require something more arresting if we are to see ourselves in our actual state. Lewis could speak of the "doctrine of the Second Coming" as "the medicine our condition especially needs" (*WLN*, 106), for it challenges the modern assumption of technological control over nature and over one's own environment. Farrer noted, too, that "Each new generation seems to bear the hope of purity because it has not yet been tried," and, in setting out, it hopes to create a new and noble order, yet such a generation, too, "fails when it is put to the test, for it is not Christ. Solomon built the temple, and then proceeded to apostatize at leisure" (*RI*, 256). Both Farrer and Lewis were suspicious of notions of Progress that promised a gentle, enlightened utopia. Lewis was particularly careful to answer those who thought evolution guaranteed a civilization always improving. He insisted that an apocalypse rendered suspect any attempt to predict the course of history or any assurance that modernity was safe from a sudden end. "Watch, watch, is the burden of his advice," he insisted. "The Return is wholly unpredictable" (*WLN*, 107–8).

Farrer and Lewis were both careful to avoid predictions as to when and under what conditions the end might come, for both assumed that the genre's chief value was in its mythic form, that is, in its ability to reshape our embodied imaginations and consciences. Some theorists have read the apocalyptic genre as self-assured in its predictions about the future, though these insist that this second assurance does not necessarily follow from a first trust in the images' power (Koch 1970, 28–33). It was, after all, not a matter of dispute that apocalyptic texts speak with self-assurance, and yet such assurance was not the same as a belief that one possessed an objective account of the universe. The imaginative power of the apocalyptic need not commit one to a timetable in order to demand of its reader an imaginative reorientation, that is, a lived, existential preparedness. What it does is reinvoke a vertical world in which the self cannot protect itself from the cosmic powers that would overwhelm it. Apocalypse forces us to terms, at least imaginatively, with a transcendent world outside our control.

Consider the following two accounts:

How little it appears in the true panorama of heaven and earth! The outbreak of Antichrist is the last convulsive struggle of the old serpent, his head already smashed in by the woman's Seed, the Son of Eve and of Mary. In heaven above a spacious liturgy unfolds, where prayers are incense, angels are ministers, and Christ is the living sacrifice; the face of Fatherhood and Mercy himself is there to heed the world's desire. They pray, he grants: so step by step as the liturgy progresses divine judgement spills over the lip of heaven on the head of earthly evil, and loving-kindness pours on faithful hearts. (Farrer, *EM*, 133)

Both were filled with some passion, but what passion they did not know. They came to the front door and as they opened it a sight met their eyes which, though natural, seemed at the moment apocalyptic. All the day the wind had been rising and they found themselves looking out on a sky swept almost clean. The air was intensely cold, the stars severe and bright. High above the last rags of scurrying clouds hung the Moon in all her wildness—not the voluptuous Moon of a thousand southern love-songs, but the huntress, the untameable virgin, the spear-head of madness. If that cold satellite had just then joined our planet for the first time, it could hardly have looked more like an omen. The wildness crept into Jane's blood. (Lewis, *THS*, 191)

Neither one of these—neither the hermeneutical meditation in Farrer's sermon nor the narrative account in Lewis's novel—obligates one to an entirely predictable future in our world, though the vision forecasts the possibilities and, thereby, gives us a foretaste of them now. Perhaps this goes without saying in the case of the novel. We expect it to offer us a fictional *as if*, which we may experience in numerous ways with possible applications. While we are in the world of Lewis's science fiction, we accept the unfolding danger of that world, observing the above presumably as the characters do. We are invited to enter imaginatively and sympathetically, and only in conjunction with this, either as we read, or perhaps afterwards, do we begin to reflect on its implications for our own lives and our own world. For the character of Jane, the madness of the moon has symbolic associations from classical mythology, and these are absorbed up into the higher key of apocalyptic fear, yet neither of these dictates the exact nature of an objectified, stadial future. What it offers instead is the possibility of a significant, widening moment. Colin Manlove calls this pattern in Lewis "a method of dislocation. His characters are constantly having their assumptions about the world widened or reversed"

(258). And this is the case for the reader as well. Lewis was seeking to widen his readers' world, to open them to the possibility of the metaphysical, as well as their own state in such a world.

This stands as true for the meditation by Farrer. The word-pictures of apocalypticism are multilayered and, as Lewis and Farrer both held, are participatory and liturgical, yet this polyvalence is not relativistic; it is bound by the center who is Christ. Christ is the child of both Eve and Mary, the seed threatened by the great Dragon, yet he is also the Lamb, whose sacrifice anoints the martyrs and renders judgment upon a resisting world. Farrer was particularly drawn to how Christ holds together the varying imagery of the Revelation of John. Christ is the Dayspring, the Incarnate and Great Amen, "the faithful witness, the prince of martyrs," the Warrior Word, the Divine Glory of God personified, "as the Lord of Sunday," and the Harvester, alongside the vine of vengeance (RI, 98, 280–81; RJD, 197–99, 66, 68, 166–67), and as Edward Henderson puts it of Farrer's understanding, "Christ lived the dialectic of images" (1982, 72). Because this is so, the fecund imagery of apocalypse can be applied without complete hermeneutical determinism, and the symbolic tradition of reading John's Apocalypse has as much to do with this layered polyvalence as with its trust in the cosmically eternal. In the above, Farrer's congregation is gathered to hear his sermon. They are invited to see themselves as part of the great cosmic liturgy and to recognize that this liturgy is an eternal perspective upon their earthly existences. Christ is at the center of this drama, and the last acts are already assured, even if their manifestation is one the congregants (and all persons) await.

Lewis, in "Transposition," a sermon delivered for Pentecost 1944, also explored how the apocalyptic opens up into a larger, cosmic world. Why, he imagined some asking, is our knowledge of the eschatological state dependent upon "selections from terrestrial experience (crowns, thrones, and music)," and why must the mystical union of heaven be pictured as "that of human lovers" and "the old familiar act of eating and drinking" (WG, 94)? Lewis's answer was that of "transposition," that is, that "if the richer system is to be represented in the poorer at all, this can only be by giving each element in the poorer system more than one meaning" (WG, 99). In a hierarchical cosmos, the lower system participates in the higher one. Rather than being simply symbolic, the pictures provided by the lower are sacramental.[6] Transposition without material existence would likely be Docetism, and certainly Gnosticism (WG, 102, 112), for transposition aligns with an orthodox emphasis on the goodness of the material world and on Christ being both God and human. It is even arguably the case that transposition helps explain why the final divine state is able to receive the human person at all (Habets 2014, 117–19). The Incarnation is the bridge-point for the eventual theosis of redeemed humanity because Christ himself is (to quote Athanasius) "the medicine of immortality."

It follows that Lewis saw the vertical thrust of transposition as opposed to the horizontal faith of developmentalism (*WG*, 112). The developmentalist, according to Lewis, "explains the continuity between things that claim to be spiritual and things that are certainly natural by saying the one slowly turned into the other," while, in contrast, transposition's theory of history is more typological: "I am saying that the Spiritual Reality, which existed before there were any creatures who ate, gave this natural act a new meaning" (*WG*, 112). Part of Lewis's rejection of metahistorical laws was that he concluded that history itself is not judgment; rather, a verdict will be rendered upon history from outside it. The temporal and the horizontal take on a more permanent meaning because they are within an eternal transcendent-reality. The Last Judgment must be reckoned with; it cannot be treated as unknown or without import.

Farrer's choice of a title for this first commentary on Revelation, *A Rebirth of Images,* recalls his treatment of the Gospels and history: "The rebirth of images can be studied everywhere in the New Testament, but nowhere can we get so deep into the heart of the process as we can in St. John's Apocalypse" (*RI*, 17). Since images are a key aspect of human consciousness, their transformation is crucial in tracking salvation history. Hans Urs von Balthasar thought that Farrer's title summed up well the process of rebirth that the Old Testament images had undergone in the Revelation of John. At the same time, he thought Farrrer's subtitle, *The Making of St. John's Apocalypse,* led down a false road—an attempt at method obscured the revelatory power of what had happened (von Balthasar 1994, 4.46n4). There is some justice in this critique. Farrer in both commentaries argued that John's apocalyptic vocabulary was the "common property of the Church," as it was employed by many New Testament authors, including Jesus (*RJD*, 4–6). He also held that John writes "in character" as if he were a prophet such as Ezekiel or Zechariah (*RJD*, 49) and that he derived his images for the messages to the churches by going back over what he had written from the first vision of the exalted Christ (*RJD*, 70, 92). R. G. Collingwood's historical theory of reenactment is also present here. Farrer imagined John the revelator working around the patterns to produce a mental fusion of sources (*RI*, 312–13), and Farrer saw John's vision as the work of a skilled writer, thinking with pen in hand, and argued that this was so because God's control is not an alien control (i.e., grace does not violate but elevates nature) (*RJD*, 24–26).

Farrer set out to uncover the deep patterns—the creation week, the zodiac, the Jewish liturgical cycle, the Gnostic Pleroma, Jewish numerology—by which the author generated numerous meanings and allusions, yet though Farrer never entirely jettisoned this approach, by his second commentary sixteen years later, he had radically pared down the patterns.[7] At the same time, he never jettisoned the belief that the images, though reworked by the author of the book, were also of a great and divine power, for Farrer always recognized that the Apocalypse had a way of calling its readers to encounter. For Farrer, the rebirth and the making could be one and the same. While he stressed Christ's role in taking the classic images to himself and transforming them, Farrer nonetheless held that the early Church fathers also unpacked these new meanings. This was another example of why the images could not be removed from the process. There was no ethical distillation that can be detached from the myths, for they are servants to the spiritually transformative encounter. This was especially true of the apocalyptic, which speaks to the future inbreaking of God: "The Apocalypse writes of heaven and things to come, that is, of a realm which has no shape at all but that which the images give it. In this room the image may grow to the fulness of its inborn nature, like a tree in a wide meadow" (RI, 17).

Still, for Farrer, the images of the apocalyptic future were not bound in quite the same way as the rest of the New Testament. The Gospels and epistles were responding to the history of the Incarnate Christ. The Revelator, on the other hand, was looking forward to the promised hope. "We know all the time what the great discovery is going to be; it is like reading a mystery tale after having looked up the final few pages" (SB, 61); what we don't know is how it will unfold in the meantime. Apocalypse manifests both the polyvalent nature of symbols and their determinable limitations. They cannot mean anything and everything, for they are flowing out of the master images taken by Christ to himself; at the same time, they are not theologically exact statements, for "exact prose abstracts from reality, symbol presents it" (RI, 19–20). This left much for the exegete to do. Farrer's own work acknowledged the great debt that the British study of the apocalyptic owed to R. H. Charles, and he saw his own generation's work to be that of ordering the details culled by Charles and others into a literary, creative explanation (RI, 9).[8] Farrer was quite willing to acknowledge not only the Jewish origins of the symbols, but also those that shared pagan origins. For example, Farrer held that the Beast is a mockery of Christ but also likely drawn from the Babylonian goddess Tiamat (RJD, 52–55). Likewise, the background to Revelation chapter 12 uses a basic story pattern—the true prince and the usurper (RJD, 141).

Scholars have pointed out that since Albert Schweitzer's work, the terms *apocalypse* and *eschatology* have become somewhat muddled. Eschatology, properly speaking, for many centuries simply meant the last things—human death, the general resurrection of the dead, the judgments of God, as well as the final states of heaven and hell. But with Schweitzer, the term in twentieth-century theology had been stretched to encompass the prophetic and apocalyptic, especially as it included imagining the end of history. As a counterthrust, this inclusion was answered by a sharp separation of the prophetic from the apocalyptic, then in mid-twentieth-century theology a slow merger of the two. As Old Testament scholarship came to understand, the prophetic expectation of Israel's vindication in the future by Yahweh merged with the awful and hopeful events of the Last Day (Neill and Wright 1988, 210–12). And, as did Lewis, Farrer stood in that transition. Even if one wanted to see the eschatological as that which followed after the apocalypse, the sense of an ending could not be denied in any period of human history. The temporal always stands under the judgment of the eternal, and yet it is the expectation of a final verdict that should keep Christian theology from entirely subjectifying the promised conclusion. The eternal nature of the drama is one that speaks into the hearer's consciousness in every age.

This was something that Lewis and Farrer absorbed from the apocalyptic genre itself. The apocalyptic can be understood as awaiting the future, which manifests itself in kairos moments along the way (McGinn 1979, 9). Kairos is that sense of the fullness of time, not as time is measured in day-to-day sequential experiences, but in those moments of intensive, eternal meaning (S. Connolly 2007, 109–12), and for both Lewis and Farrer, this intensive eternality is in Christ. Kairos moments, as manifestations of the eternal, do not leave the self unaffected. The spilling over of judgment in Farrer or the nightmare clarity of the moon in Lewis suggests the inbreaking of the eternal into the temporal. Because the apocalyptic genre engages the future, even as it also invokes an eternal world, its ultimate orientation is as much *beyond* time as *awaiting* the future. While apocalypse is full of horizontal predictions as to how the political powers will arise and fall, these are expressed in symbolic ways that make their lasting value more vertical. They suggest that history's true meaning is found in its relation to the fullness beyond us. They also suggest that there is a fundamental need in human beings for such imagery.

By its symbolic pictures, the apocalyptic shapes our imaginations in ways that are more associative than propositional. They are God's myths, as Lewis had pointed out, and as Farrer insisted, the inspiration manifested by John was not at all like "a modern bishop sitting down to compose something edifying for the lay people to read during Lent" (*RI,* 21). The symbols, familiar to John's audience, had an immediacy that did not demand explication until after their initial imaginative impact. Nonetheless, it was the task of a writer such as Farrer to do just this—to explicate in order to open readers again to what may be still on the horizon of their future, that is, an awaiting crisis and the sense of an ending. Such an explication did not, however, mean that one could simply tease apart the symbol and its reality. Lewis insisted that we cannot know if all is symbol or if all is analogy, and we are not in a position to decide which parts we really need: "You cannot know that everything in the representation of a thing is symbolical unless you have independent access to the thing and can compare it with the representation . . . [W]e must take our ignorance seriously" (*CR,* 165–66). We cut ourselves off from what riches the symbols offer if we insist on treating them as a coded timetable. We also cut ourselves off if we think we can reduce the apocalyptic symbolism to mere morality. Instead, Lewis insisted, only in the final state of glory would we have enough knowledge to know what is symbolic and what is literal. To do otherwise is to accept the false assurances of modernity.

JUDGMENT AND PARODY

Not surprisingly, this countermodernist thrust in the apocalyptic literature is often seen as morally compromised. Apocalyptic texts, it is charged, incline readers to fanaticism and a general *ressentiment* of the ethical Other. At times, the apocalyptic genre is criticized for its moral binaries, the complaint being that the apocalyptic is a too-simple world of good and bad forces, which are easily distinguishable, unlike real human beings (Adams 1990, 137–38). The case is made, too, that apocalypse enables religious violence and oppression. That they have enabled these is indisputable; that they should do so is more questionable. Cyril O'Regan has noticed that the apocalyptic as a motif may take three broad forms: (1) *pleromatic fullness and disclosure* (offering a theological picture of apocalypse); (2) *kenomatic emptiness* (arising out of a sociocultural critique of apocalypse's dangers); and (3) *the metaxic between* (that is, in looking to history, also critiques institutional Christianity) (2009, 7–32). The sum of O'Regan's analysis is to show that kenomatic critiques of apocalypse are not necessarily more ethical than pleromatic ones; indeed, the apocalyptic "demands a hyperbolic ethic" even as it may also "say no to the secular culture that says no to Christianity" and yet also it may still critique forms of Christianity that have justified abuse in the name of apocalyptic metaphors and images (2009, 115, 128).

What is often overlooked in the complaint against apocalypse is the aesthetic purpose in its stark contrasts. It does picture a world of seductive wickedness, yet it also offers a picture of the good, which calls us with its beauty. And this has numerous possibilities that may work themselves out in a culture. Audiences are invited, perhaps even called, to imagine a beauty beyond themselves, and the sharp contrast does not necessarily lead to our demonizing the political, the racial, or, for that matter, even the religious Other. What it can do is rediscover deeply held moral absolutes and recover resistance to the immoral. That it may also "name the powers" does not of necessity lead to oppression. Hans Urs von Balthasar observed that human beings even in the post–Christian age cannot quite throw off an orientation toward the absolute, and in being unable to do so, "the pathos of the world stage becomes grotesque, grimacing, and demonic." As such, the apocalyptic names the refusal of horizontal modernity to acknowledge its vertical aspirations (von Balthasar 1994, 4.71–73). Demonization may be culturally self-inflicted.

Austin Farrer admitted that the calls for vengeance in the Apocalypse of John and the physicality of its symbols could be "embarrassing pictures" (*RJD*, 4), and he recognized that, of the bloody and violent end of Christ's foes in the text, many modern Christians would want such passages to be about the death of "enmity" rather than of "enemies," and yet Farrer noted that John would have none of that. "Advent is the fulfilment of hope" (*RJD*, 198), and this meant a literal end of that which is destructive. The angelic announcements of woe in Revelation 14, for example, are "a gospel for the saints" (*RJD*, 164); they assure the suffering martyrs that an end will come, and that a clear verdict will be delivered upon evil. Farrer also understood that the "pagan reader" could locate in the Apocalypse a resentment of humanity, yet Farrer did not strive to lessen the offense but placed it in the context of divine defense: "If you persecute the saints, they will cry to God, and their cry will return on you in a rain of fire" (*RI*, 134).

While he acknowledged the complaint that in John's text the two Christian witnesses are the cause of the plagues, Farrer argued that the judgments that come upon the great powers are consequences endemic to their corrupted state. The enthronement of the Harlot is the condition of her judgment (*RI*, 55). In similar fashion, the Beast is both instrument and object of judgment (*RI*, 259), his "fatally limited reign" encoded in his 666 (*RI*, 260). Without the violent imagery, not only is hope for a fitting end compromised, but evil's nature is compromised. Such imagery calls into question the self-definition of imperial powers that promise all is well. Even if the martyrs' actions seemed helpless against "the imperial power," Farrer stressed, they were to be honored as faithful (*RJD*, 86). He noted, too, that John's audience needed shoring up by a "revelation of their membership in God's heavenly congregation," and they were to be warned that their spiritual compromise was part of the "degenerate city-culture destined to destruction." They were assured, though their actions seemed helpless against the "imperial power," they were to be honored as faithful (*RJD*, 86), for martyrdom is not defeat but victory (*RJD*, 154).

Certainly, Lewis did not shy away from using the violence of the genre for fictional purposes. In *The Last Battle,* Tash consumes both the ape Shift and the Calormene captain Rishda Tarkaan. In *That Hideous Strength,* all Belbury's key figures meet a grisly end that echoes both the fall of Babel and Odysseus's killing of the suitors. Yet there is the sense that these brutal deaths are endemic to the violence and corruption the characters had embodied. Shift and the Tarkaan had dared to call upon Tash, so it is Tash they meet as his "lawful prey" (*LB*, 166). It is Hardcastle who begins the killing spree, and it is the tortured animals that rise up and take vengeance. Straik and Wither's sacrifice of Filostrato, as well as Wither's subsequent killing of Straik, follow from their adoration of the Macrobes. Frost's suicide is similar: a horrifically buffered self, he has long been a creature subject to a power other than reason. Even Mr. Bultitude's destruction of Wither and the ghastly head ("the best deed that any bear had done in Britain" [*THS*, 279]) has a poetic, moral suitability. As Sanford Schwartz observes, for Lewis, human rationality is not to be unseated from its animal affective and biological existence (2009, 124–25). Bultitude's consciousness represents Owen Barfield's "ancient unities," in which friendship and instinctive desire are not separated, and his immediacy of experience mimics the absolute and has "no prose" (*THS*, 258, 303). That the bear makes an end of an experiment in postmaterial humanity mirrors the bodily rejection of a rationality divorced from its biological anchor, as well as a perversity in speech and form that had enabled it.

Lewis understood, however, that such fictional characters were somewhat one-sided. Mark and Jane Studdock represent in the novel two more complex, multidimensional persons, subject to corruption and with the opportunity for conversion. Mark's refusal to step upon the image of the crucifix is not a singular or heroic moment, but part of an extended change that is affected by his humiliations at the N. I. C. E. His experience in the perverse "Objectivity" room makes him long for the normal (*THS*, 296). Jane's turn toward community at St. Anne's is a slow process, one worked out among conflicted aspects of herself. It is their shocking encounters with the extremes of evil that push them both toward renewal. Apocalyptic binaries shape not only the consciousness of the novel's readers, but also Mark and Jane as characters. Their consciences are addressed by morally stark examples.

This approach did not commit Lewis to a simple binary view of humans or history. He could observe during World War II that "one of the things we learn from history is that God never allows a human conflict to become un-ambiguously one between simple good and simple evil"; rather, one has to face that one's own meanness could, under differing circumstances, grow into an equally amoral brutality, for no person is "so different from these ghastly creatures" (*Letters*, 2.391). Mark and Jane are not Lewis's only examples. In *The Last Battle*, Emeth the young Calormene, whose lifelong service to Tash is received by Aslan as service to himself, is a corrective to the belief that all representatives of the imperial power are completely evil. In turn, the refusal of the dwarfs to believe is a reminder that not all Narnia is unreservedly for Aslan. Hingist serves a similar purpose in *That Hideous Strength*. The skeptical chemist is a moral traditionalist and has a genuine commitment to truth's objectivity.

Yet the adjectival qualifier "ghastly" in Lewis's letter is not only a moral judgment but also a warning. The Reverend Straik may have represented for Lewis one of those ghastly warnings, a kenomatic model of religious misuse. He was "a good man once," as Professor Dimble observed (*THS*, 219), yet he now embodies the faults set down to the apocalyptic imagination—a call for violence and a social utopianism that is willing to do anything and work with anyone to justify its goals. Straik points out to Mark about the N.I.C.E., "The feeblest of these people here has the tragic sense of life, the ruthlessness, the total commitment, the readiness to sacrifice all merely human values" in order to bring in the techno-utopian Millennium (*THS*, 77), and yet it soon becomes apparent that that Millennium is the creation of posthumanity, "the Son of Man," which Straik imagines as a godlike being (*THS*, 175–76).

Filostrato's own "hygienic" hatred of biological life takes on similar tones. He, too, is a caricature, and of an ideology that Lewis was sure had terrible consequences. Filostrato's mad belief is not so much sexual as postsexual, for he is a gnostic believer that the body can be disposed with. His own worship of a race of lunar beings that are expunging the organic from the surface of the moon is a sinister myth, apocalyptic in its own right. Filostrato is also devoted to a deathless power, which will finally be concentrated in one immortal "king of the universe" (*THS*, 176). Straik and Filostrato, then, represent two versions of the "abomination standing where it should not" that Lewis feared. Both epit-omize the millennial or utopian imagination run riot, for both desire to create a Beast whose wounded head is healed, so that the whole world might follow it (Revelation 13:3–4).

A wounded head is but one example of the apocalyptic use of parody. Parody in the apocalyptic also complicates its supposedly simple binaries. Rather than merely picturing an absolute good and an absolute evil, the symbology of evil derives its power from a grotesque imitation of the good. As Farrer pointed out, in the Revelation of John, the nature of the kingdom of darkness is its blasphemy, its violating mimicry, and its reduction of the holy. Farrer read the seven kings as a parody of the Genesis week and the Beast as a parody of Christ, its wounded head returned from the Abyss being a parody of Christ's cross and resurrection, "the quintessence of demonic unreality" (*RI*, 288–90). The Dragon, the Beast, and the False Prophet are not so much mimicries of the ontological Trinity as of "the triad of revelation," the Father, the Messiah, and the prophetic ministry, which the Spirit empowers (*RJD*, 156). Yet, among the seven heads of the Beast, one currently exists, while another has passed, and a third is yet to come. Farrer interpreted this as a "defective parody of God's eternal being," of the One who Was, Is, and Is to Come (*RJD*, 184).

Farrer speculated, as well, that the false death of the Beast is a commentary on first-century Jewish notions of the first and second death. As he pointed out, not all deaths in the Old Testament are penal; some are restorative in their discipline, preventive of further sins, or even "heroic and meritorious." The seeming recovery of the head of the Antichrist is a foul inversion of this, a false resurrection, not of life but of that which is already annihilated or destined for annihilation (*RI*, 290–91). In turn, the second beast spoken of in Revelation 13 is a blasphemous John the Baptist, parallel with an Egyptian magician, or is a false Elijah (*RJD*, 155–56). The Queen of Babylon, too, is a parody of the Woman of heaven (*RI*, 81). Like Lewis, Farrer did not read this formal structure of parodies as a simple demonization of the imperial powers that threaten the Christians. Nor is this a simple dichotomy between Christians and pagans. As Farrer noted, the false forms of worship in the seven churches of chapters 2 and 3 are repeated thematically throughout the Apocalypse (*RJD*, 83). The powerful disturbing imagery of the remainder of the book was to be not only encouragement that persecution would one day end, but also a strengthening of Christian loyalties to their membership. "They were to understand that the tolerant laxity of a complacent Church was the inebriating cup of the great harlot, the degenerate city-culture destined to destruction" (*RJD*, 86).

One of the dramatic and aesthetic purposes of the Revelation of John is to make the failure of these shadow parodies obvious, and not just in the dramatic overthrow they receive at Christ's hands, but also in their distorted form.

They are always sinister, kenomatic reversals, and the rhetoric of their signs and wonders is empty for the faithful reader. In *The Last Battle,* Shift the ape, Rishda Tarkaan, and the cat Ginger are obvious parodies of the misuse of religious revelation. They each claim to speak for Aslan, or Tashlan, or finally Tash. The proverb, "he is not a tame lion," is used to parody the apocalyptic God, using the language of fear and judgment to exploit the Narnians. Shift takes upon himself the gaudy garments of wealth and demands in Aslan's name an endless supply of nuts. Together, he and Rishda invoke Aslan as a pretext to enslave the talking horses, as well as to demand forced labor with a threat of religious terror. Yet they are all three unbelievers who, in toying with demonic powers, receive in themselves the final end of such flippancy. Farsight the Eagle foresees as much. Observing Rishda's own surprise and fear, he asks, "How will it be with him if they really have come?" (*LB*, 145).

The Last Battle, then, served as one of Lewis's metaxic critiques. He recognized only too well how the apocalyptic could be used as a justification for oppression. Shift, Rishda, and Ginger are intended as flat characters, yet we still learn how political religion can distort and manipulate a populace. "True freedom," pronounces Shift, "means doing what I tell you" (*LB*, 39). As Farrer pointed out, political religion is a parody that is idolatrous; its "gods are worshipped as the support of established power" (*RJD*, 152), while the end of Babylon's reign is an end to slavery (*RI*, 295). The rot in political religion is how it seeks to imitate the divinity of the Father, but it has no true or lasting authority or even power. Farrer noted that there is no true hierarchy among Satan, the Beast, and the False Prophet, so neither is there any true unity (*RI*, 286). Shift, Risdha, and Ginger are using one another; not even Rishda is the final authority. Their own counsels finally end in their destruction. Indeed, their ultimate implosion arises because they make the pretense of the vertical, thick cosmos, all the while believing only in the thinner, horizontal world of political and economic exploitation.

In *That Hideous Strength,* parody is even more pronounced. The entities of Belbury and St. Anne's on the Hill mirror one another throughout the novel. Both the N. I. C. E. at Belbury and the community at St. Anne's are subject to and interact with the *eldila,* that is, with angels and demons. The goings-on are not explainable by the surface-level actions of bureaucracy at the institute or by the domestic goings-on at the manor house. The wounded director, who is responsible to his masters, the planetary Oyéresu, is parodied by the wounded Head, who is a mouthpiece for the demonic Macrobes. The community at St. Anne's, despite the director's distrust of the rhetoric of equality, is run on deeply democratic grounds, and these are gender-balanced in their division of labor and cordial in their humor and interchange. The members of the household are each indebted to others and subject to one another in a dance of complementary gifts, and the implication is that much of this is rendered possible by being under the various cosmic powers that visit Ransom. The N.I.C.E., in the language of Wither, gives lip service to elasticity and family, but in fact is built upon Fascist absorption and loss of identity.

Many of the members of St. Anne's are also parodied by those under the sway of Belbury. The powerful and serious Grace Ironwood is mirrored by the dominatrix Fairy Hardcastle; the knowledgeable professor Cecil Dimble has his counterpart in the soulless Professor Frost; and the selfless, upper-class Dennistons have their counterpart in the myopic Lord Feverstone. This mirroring also works itself out in the way each group functions. Just as St. Anne's has its office of the skeptic in McPhee, so the N. I. C. E. has its religious fanatic in Streik. The former maid Ivy Maggs becomes an equal member of the manor community, while her husband is requisitioned as a criminal to be experimented upon by the institute. Mr. Bultitude, Baron Corvo, and the three mice all form a part of St. Anne's, too, personalizing one of Lewis's possible scenarios for animal and human life, while at Belbury a menagerie has been collected for sadistic vivisection.

Thus, Lewis used apocalyptic parody to picture a kingdom of light and one of darkness. St. Anne's pictures true membership, a freedom found in the interchange of obedience and love, while Belbury embodies all Lewis feared of the inner ring, the shifting favor and shame, the ruthless self-service without loyalty to principle. It becomes rapidly clear to Mark that Belbury is a set of inner rings and that real authority is based on fear and coercion. All the techniques of modernity in regard to tyranny and superiority are on display—no due process, sadomasochism, police brutality, loss of the rule of law, obfuscation as a form of manipulation, and loss of individuality. Paradoxically, it is St. Anne's that respects free will, while the N. I. C. E. uses compulsion. St. Anne's values tradition and marriage, truth-telling, fecundity and the organic, and this is materially manifested in a garden home with its historic architecture and its respect for philology, logic, medicine, and literature. Belbury, with its modernist planning, its idealization of hygiene and eugenics, and its institutionalization, is a place of empty rhetoric, which enshrines both sadomasochism and the destruction of the organic. Belbury shares with the Calormenes a willingness to cut down ancient forests and to exploit the natural world with no regard for a traditional ecology of village and cultivated valley. In St. Anne's, the books are actually read; at Belbury, the library is a meeting place for the inner ring.

That Hideous Strength also employs two countervisions of history, the various dystopian agendas of the N. I. C. E. and the secret history of England, whose soul is divided between Logres and Britain. The particular distaste of Lewis for "historicism" is an assumed undercurrent, as is his preference for Romanticism, which with its paganism is at least a healthier path than that of brutal modernism. The worlds of Belbury and St. Anne's offer Mark and Jane conscious choices as to whom they will commit themselves. The old Christian world is past—not only the Edwardian one, which has some residual Christian (or at least theistic) elements, but also the far older world of Christendom, which the fifth-century Merlinus can remember. Merlinus must receive the news of the change itself as an apocalypse. Christendom is divided; the poison of the West has spread everywhere (*THS*, 289–91). If St. Anne's is a parable of what the Church could and should be, Belbury is what Lewis feared the new British national planning would actually accomplish. It was a portrait of the Babylon to come. Yet in the end, St. Anne's triumph is "a restitution of the 'high' romance mode that overwhelms its dark Gothic double" (Schwartz 2009, 130).

This same kind of universal judgment upon history was one Farrer found in the Apocalypse of John. Babylon was to be contrasted with Zion, for the two cities represent fundamentally opposed social imaginaries. Yet while Zion is not, in the last analysis, an earthly kingdom, Babylon is representative of the inevitable divisions between the urban centers and the military powers that occur in every imperial project. Zion's experience is a common one, found among many an empire. "The relation between city and monarch is not a stable marriage, but a shabby love-affair disgraced by quarrels and darkened by murderous violence" (*RJD*, 187). The urban centers, which are synonymous with civilization itself (*RJD*, 190), make a pretext of freedom, but are actually propped up by "irresponsible armed despotism." And this despotism maintains its power by idolatrous deceptions, its tyrants upheld as gods. The Great Babylon is literally stripped and eaten by her kings and merchants in a great parody of the Marriage Supper of the Lamb. She is only a great "hive of material culture," and in being so is unable to rise to the transcendent plane that Lady Zion inhabits (*RJD*, 187). If Babylon was for John the revelator a reference to the splendor and comfort of Rome, as Farrer observes, "He had not seen London or New York" (*RJD*, 190). Ancient Greece and Rome had lost its cultural heights and its republican virtues, so might the great urban postwar cities of modernity. As Farrer was wont to stress, however, "By praying that the world may come out black and white, so as to be ripe for judgment, we need not express the criminal desire that any soul capable of repentance should persist in sin" (*RJD*, 225). To name the powers did not amount to wishing, even secretly, that no enemy might repent or that no reversal could ever happen.

HOPE AND THE HEAVENLY LITURGY

If the apocalyptic genre provided both C. S. Lewis and Austin Farrer access to a thicker, vertical world, and if the parodies and violence of this genre offered a counter to modernity, it still remains to ask what positive benefit such pictures offered both writers. I would argue that this can be summed up as the virtue of hope, though each man examined Christian hope with differing points of emphasis. In this section I will explore Farrer's basis for hope in some detail before coming to Lewis's.

As Farrer noted, the final logic of the Apocalypse of John is that those who may be martyred have a hope that great injustice will be redressed (*RJD*, 206), and yet, as Farrer also understood, it is not so difficult to believe that God rescued Daniel from the lions; what is harder is why the divine pattern is so often martyrdom (*BM*, 163). In 1951, Farrer for the BBC reviewed Gabriel Marcel's Gifford Lectures, *The Mystery of Being*, and he was especially drawn to the philosopher's discussion of hope. While his views preceded Marcel's work, the resonance between the two was obvious (*RF*, 168–70). For Marcel, faithfulness to the future imparts a measure of receptivity to what it still has to offer, including the opportunity for creative engagement. It follows that caritas is the posture of absolute availability, of engaged receptivity, and it gives us a readiness to encounter, engage, and move beyond the inertia of despair. To love someone, as Marcel notes, is to insist, "Thou, shalt not die" (2001, 2.153), and yet to exist in this world marked by death is to suffer the opposite. Hope continues in spite of disappointment. Indeed, real hope may be only discovered in the face of numerous failed expectations, and its very quality is one that resists despair (Marcel 2001, 2.147–62). In a world ruled by death, "all hope is a hope of salvation" (Marcel 2001, 2.180). As Farrer summarized him, "Hopefulness is the opposite of an attitude which expects nothing of life, the opposite of listlessness rather than alarm" and yet by some lights, "hope is not reasonable foresight of good to come" (*RF*, 168). Hope is only of real value in a certain kind of world—a world that transcends time even while that which is desired has not yet arrived. Because hope waits, hope acts.

Farrer noted in Revelation that the plight of the martyrs is what marks the invocations and responses of the heavenly court. The worship of heaven in the book is transcendent yet also concerned with the injustice that the people of

God have suffered. This dual aspect mimics the nature of hope itself. The transcendent element is able to rise above persecution because it looks to the eternal peace of God, and yet the Church's hope also looks to a "harvest" of vindication and restoration (*RI*, 82–83). "The Advent is the fulfilment of all hope," that is, it is the content and aspiration of all the liturgical prayers and visions of the book (*RJD*, 198). Farrer argued that the Sabbaths of God in Revelation, those pauses between various aspects of divine action, represent the "eternal repose" of God out of which not only do his acts arrive, but also toward which they find their complete resolution (*RI*, 70). Farrer found in such an understanding a theology of history that held together both the vertical and the horizontal:

> The eternal rest of the seventh creation-day is the womb out of which issues the work of history. . . . Is not God's sabbatical rest from the work of history the womb out of which a greater work comes? God rests, perhaps, from the guidance of his first creation, but this rest is itself the changeless act of uttering a new creation, and filling it perpetually with himself. God is not inactive through the eternity of the World to Come. (*RI*, 70)

Hope is praxis, yet praxis is born out of an expected end, and this tension between expectation and transcendence is what organizes the eschatological energy of Christian hope.

It is not that one only hopes for the day after the last day, but that hope is expressed in concrete, sacramental ways in the present. Robert Boak Slocum describes this emphasis in Farrer as an eschatological one: "Heaven is available now in an already-but-not-yet kind of way" (2007, 31). In the heavenly liturgy, worship and judgment both become realities. The unity of praise and work here are aligned with the pattern and rhythm of worship there. Such a unity marks a vertical world, one where the division between heaven and earth is thin and the distinction between natural and supernatural is not so important, yet at the same time, the liturgy is awaiting the final end when all is put to rights. It is "a pattern . . . of celestial liturgy performed by Christ and the angels," and it does not equate to history as we might know it (*RJD*, 23). The light of the heavenly liturgy is a gift to hope—an assurance of justice and the recognition of glory, for the Church's desires will be fulfilled. Yet the revelation remains a hope while it can be seen in the heavenly and awaited in the temporal world.

Farrer observes that the last messages of the Apocalypse in chapter 22 are "a sharp contrast of severity and tenderness side by side" (*RI*, 187), and yet this could be said of much that Farrer analyzes. The worship in heaven—that is, the divine incense-liturgy—is marked by tenderness for the martyrs of God and by severity in the plagues that fall upon their persecutors. It is both a "liturgy of Alleluias" and "the liturgy of judgment" (*RJD*, 192, 17). The prayers of the people for vindication are answered "by making a burnt-offering of her enemies with outpoured fire of heaven" (*RI*, 166). As Farrer stressed, John keeps returning to this key theme—that judgment is a "liturgical situation" (*RI*, 167). The worship of the earthly Church in every age is joined with cosmic awareness of her sufferings, and her prayers for redress are received by God within the nexus of corporate devotion. Farrer also noted how many other aspects of the book are liturgical in form and shape. He associated the sealing of the 144,000 with baptism, as well as seeing baptism reflected in the great sea of glass (*RJD*, 105, 171). In similar fashion, he located in the heavenly praise of chapter 17 the "primitive Christian sense of eucharistic prayer, and of its invocatory power" (*RJD*, 182) and reads the passage itself as a Great Thanksgiving prayer (*RJD*, 196). To enter into worship is to enter into a cosmic world, one larger than the buffered self will allow, and a world that makes kairos manifest in sacramental manner.

Yet one still waits. Farrer noted that the book of Revelation is often marked by "the sign of incompleteness," suggesting that incomplete or broken patterns in the text are a way of gaining insight and a means of building up to a final climax (*RI*, 86–89). There is a pattern of delay, frustration, then fruition (*RJD*, 15–16). In part, this is because the "the convention of vision" is that of static "stills," which can be traced through a deep intertextuality of four kinds: stories, history, allusions, and repetitions or cycles. The static visions act as panels in a storyboard whose gaps must be filled in; there is no continual movement, only iconographic pictures that demand reflection (*RJD*, 56–58). But it is also the case because the Apocalypse works its dramatic tension by disjunction and conjunction, and this is more than dramatic convention. It is a matter of human limitations in receiving the transcendent. The heavy symbolism and analogies that structure Revelation are not just a generative pattern that John uses to create the work; they are also the medium that enables insight. Farrer's views of analogy and the "suspended middle" of the human condition come into play here. The symbols are an *already-not yet,* and this manifestation, which is yet also still a promise, is the very shape of hope.

As Farrer observed, the heavenly temple can only partially be described because it is "no picture for the eyes" (*RI*, 164). The ark is a secondary symbol—God's glory is primary (*RJD*, 139). Farrer thought it significant that in Revelation 11:19 the cosmic Holy of Holies is opened by Christ so that all who read the vision may see, yet that an ark is there at all is surprising in light of Christ being the antetype of the tabernacle. There will be no temple except the light of Christ in the New Jerusalem, so what does such a vision portend? Farrer theorized that it represents the Church as "an incomplete 'Israel.'" Such a structure combines the earthly and the heavenly seat of worship, being of both worlds and therefore belonging to neither entirely. The saints of God are simultaneously candles in the celestial temple and martyrs upon Earth (*RI*, 135–36). "We may all be High Priests, to appear before that indwelling God; and yet this is not to enjoy the Beatific Vision" (*RI*, 137). Instead of a temple, there will be the glory of a new creation, and in this God's presence will radiate with full splendor. Until then, to love is to hope.

This love and hope suggest that the vertical world that Farrer prized in the apocalyptic genre is a window into the transcendent, which is already a real presence in the liturgy. In the text of Revelation, Farrer noted that the true sacrifice in heaven is also the Eucharist. What the Church experiences on Earth is its more temporal manifestation (*EM*, 34). "This is the 'Church' in which all Christians really worship, whether the walls that close them round are in the house of Prisea or in the house of Stephanas. The walls melt, and leave them in the one congregation before the great Throne" (*RI*, 105). The earthly and heavenly worship, then, are one and the same, and the last texts of the book that offer fellowship with Christ "equate the advent-hope with the presence of the Christ in the eucharist of the ecclesia" (*RI*, 187). And it is Christ who must finally be the end and energy of the Eucharist. Farrer, in particular, extended a liturgical and typological reading to Revelation chapter 15 in which the glory of God as an overwhelming sacrificial smoke enters the heavenly sanctuary. Farrer saw the heavenly temple and its events as both Christ and Passover; the heavenly temple is dedicated with God's glory just as the earthly one was, yet this great light who enters it is also the crucified Christ (*RI*, 157).

Nor is this unusual. In the new Moses, who is Christ, "law, prophecy, and pattern are all one" (*RI*, 247). For John the revelator (and for Farrer), Christ is the Sabbath rest of God yet also the eighth day of creation; God's continual upholding of his creation is the new thing that he is now doing, with its beginning and end in the new heaven and earth to come. Likewise, the White Rider in Revelation, according to Farrer, is Good Friday Christology; indeed, each Christophany in the book is a scene of great worship in the heavenlies (*RI*, 70–76). "The cross reveals the End" (Slocum 2007, 33), for Christ is the final substance of all hope. And the promised theosis of redeemed creatures is centered in who Christ *is*, for "'Christ-in-us'" is "now 'the hope', but then the substance 'of glory'" (*RI*, 252). It is this hope that justifies the harsh and violent imagery of the apocalyptic genre. In Christ's victory as the faithful and true witness, the victory of the saints is made complete; it is the "triumph of

Advent" (*RJD*, 197). In the Apocalypse, hope is synonymous (or nearly so) with the hope of the martyrs. They need not despair in this world, for justice does exist for their suffering, and this justice was, is, and always will be Christ.

If Farrer's formulation of hope helped him hold together the vertical *already* with the horizontal *not yet*, this same tension can be found in Lewis's reflections upon eternity and apocalypse. Arguably, Lewis's own Christian hope was deeply intertwined with his understanding of transposition. Not only did it ground his trust in a vertical, transcendent world and provide him a counter to theories of metahistory and developmentalism, it also held together his trust in the transcendent with an expectation that the eschatological end promised great glory. Lewis openly admitted that the concept of glory had been problematic for him as a new convert. It seemed to promise either a kind of special status at the expense of others (which he judged as a temptation to pride) or a strange luminosity, "a kind of living electric light bulb," which he thought absurd (*WG*, 36). Yet Lewis came to understand that the first really meant the childlike desire for God's approval, while the second was describing something trans-sensory that would radiate one's entire being. In *That Hideous Strength*, one of the transvaluations that Jane Studdock undergoes is when she comes to realize that what she had always judged as the domesticized sterility of Christianity, as "fat Mrs. Dimble saying her prayers," was turning out to be a realm of great power and glory. "The old ring-fence had been smashed completely. One might be in for anything. Maledil might be, quite simply and crudely, God. There might be life after death: a Heaven: a Hell" (*THS*, 231). The actual eternal reality, while it may use the stuff of natural existence, was hardly mundane, once one began to experience it in a greater totality.

In "Transposition," Lewis offered the example of an artist who is imprisoned with her child, and the only knowledge of the outside world that the child has are the artist's pencil sketches. However, when the mother explains that the greater world is not made up of pencil marks, the child is confused, even skeptical. This is analogous to Jane's original views of Christianity with its "horrible lithographs of the Saviour," and its "embarrassment of confirmation classes," and "the nervous affability of clergy-men" (*THS*, 231). Yet Lewis argued, as one comes to know what these represent, they are not unfounded pictures of the reality. A fine artist can portray with shadowed sketches the sun, a cloudy sky, or the human body in a manner that makes them strongly present to us (*WG*, 115). The immortal condition will turn out to be like, and yet far greater than, the imagery we now possess. Lewis argued that this was equally true of the Old Testament: "Because the lower nature, in being taken up and loaded with a new burden and advanced to a new privilege, remains, and is not annihilated, it will always be possible to ignore the up-grading and see nothing but the lower" (*RP*, 116). The transposition of the Old Testament in its various imagery, even when violent or spiteful, offers higher meanings for which it prepares. Indeed, that which is most distasteful may be the most necessary if one is to prepare for the greater realities promised.

Lewis understood that liturgical life was partially for putting one in touch with the supramundane reality via the sacramental life. This included the way that scripture held a place in worship. In *Reflections on the Psalms,* he looked at several psalms that are read messianically by their place in the Anglican liturgical cycle. He began with the figure of Melchizedek in Psalm 110, who in his numinous mystery was from outside the normal channels of the Abrahamic world (*RP*, 122–23). There is no other figure that he can be said to anticipate other than that of Christ, nor does any other personage in turn make sense of Psalm 110. That this is a Christmas psalm within the Anglican liturgy—as are Psalms 45, 89, and 132—is important. Each takes on new meaning within this yearly worship, even as it also helps fill out the worship themes themselves. The type and antetype are mutually clarifying.

Lewis noticed something similar with Psalm 68, which is chosen for Pentecost (*RP*, 125–26).[9] As the Apocalypse of John models, the Israel of God is type to the Bride of Christ, the Church. Christmas is "the arrival of the great warrior and the great king. Also of the Lover, the Bridegroom, whose beauty surpasses that of man. But not only the Bridegroom as the lover, the desired; the Bridegroom also as he who makes fruitful, the father of children still to be begotten and born" (*RP*, 130). The last few pages of *Reflections on the Psalms* show Lewis reflecting eschatologically on Psalm 90 in the light of 2 Peter 3:8. "One day is like a thousand" to God because he is eternal, beyond time, and, being eternal, may meet us at any moment of any length. God meets humans at any moment equally and with equal attention. "Hence our hope finally to emerge, if not altogether from time," as Lewis observed. The human condition will always be sequential at some level, yet neither will "mere succession and mutability" dominate it, for the redeemed will find that discomfort and surprise with age and change will contain a real truth about the eternal condition (*RP*, 137–38). In this way, Lewis shared with Farrer a trust that the heavenly liturgy was connected with the divine one, yet at the same time, it could not substitute for its final, eschatological glory. If the truth could not be removed from the myth, as Lewis was wont to point out, neither could its symbolism be said to substitute for what one hoped for by it.

For Lewis, this meant that hope and spiritual preparedness go hand in hand, and that moral imagination requires symbolic understanding. At the same time, Lewis admitted that he found the raw idea of judgment more an expedient than the apocalyptic symbols of catastrophe, mostly because this expectation spoke to his will, while the other could only appeal to his emotions. Preparedness and attentiveness are training for what is to come. They involve learning to see our actions in the light of that last and final judgment. Such preparedness is not, however, without its own transpositional understanding. Lewis thought that the verdict of heaven when revealed would turn out to be what "in some dim fashion we could have known" already (WLN, 113). The final verdict will be like the overheard opinion of those we love and value. Lewis's trust in how myth prepared for fact has an analogous relationship to how he sought for his fictional works to prepare for the actual apocalypse and eschaton. Even though the stories from the science-fiction trilogy are, well, *fiction*, it is not going too far to realize that they, too, act as symbols that transpose Lewis's hope into an earthly key.

In a letter to Sister Penelope, CSMV, Lewis noted the irony that only two of sixty reviews had any sense that Christianity played a role in *Out of the Silent Planet*. He observed, perhaps somewhat wryly, that such fiction could play a role in evangelism: "any amount of theology can now be smuggled into people's minds under cover of romance without their knowing it" (*Letters*, 2.262). The apocalyptic, while most pronounced in *That Hideous Strength*, certainly played a role in all three volumes of the trilogy. In the first novel, musings about the great "celestial year," which had begun in the twelfth century (*OSP*, 151), only foreshadow the predictions of Tor, who in ten thousand rotations of his planet will gather with others to lay siege to Earth and overthrow its Dark Lord. In that siege, all the plagues and catastrophes of the Apocalypse will take place, though they arise because "the evil things in your world shall show themselves stripped of disguise." Then Earth will be made whole, healthy, and beautiful again (Lewis 1944, 182). In the third novel, the dystopian state that the N. I. C. E. could bring is as much a damning indictment of modern subjectivism and irrationality as it is of a techno-behaviorist philosophy, for its outcome would be that "Hell would be at last incarnate" (*THS*, 200–201). But lest one forget, this fear, even this potentiality, is a prerequisite to its overthrow and the renewal of all things earthly.

While the vision afforded to Ransom at the end of *Perelandra* can be said to ground elements of Lewis's ethics, it also represents his liturgical trust and cosmic hope. If it is not a picture of the celestial court or the heavenly temple, it is nevertheless of the eternal, cosmic order of things. It mirrors both Dante's final vision in *Paradiso* and Augustine and Monica's at Ostia. Temporal existence is left behind, even reason is overwhelmed with the grandeur of love and order without reminder. In the vision, every aspect of the cosmos is central to the plan, and none is inessential. "There seems no plan because all is plan," so every movement itself appears to be what is most important. Likewise, every band of light is itself key, and when one turns away, it becomes reoriented in another pattern, and this is repeated infinitely. And at the culmination of his vision, Ransom beholds that at "the very zenith of complexity, complexity was eaten up and faded," and he comes to "a simplicity beyond all comprehension," which draws him with longing into its stillness (Lewis 1944, 186–88). Complexity and simplicity, comprehension and incomprehension, pattern and that which transcends pattern, together reflect the ultimate impulse of hope in that they are analogies of that which one still awaits.

In similar fashion, the "Descent of the Gods" in chapter 15 of *That Hideous Strength* connects the temporal world with the cosmic one, even as it foreshadows hope for the last things. The Oyéresu are Neoplatonic gods and Dionysian angels, and they represent not only planetary powers, but also the virtues as archetypal realities. Just as John in the Apocalypse must be repeatedly warned not to kneel to angels, so Ransom must forbid Merlin to do so when the powers arrive, for though they partake of aspects of the divine, the transcendent uniqueness of Maledil is never violated. All the members of the household experience Meaning, Charity, Fortitude, Gravity, and Festival both in experience and memory. The order is important, too. Glund-Oyarsa, King of Kings, must come last, for he is closest to God, too often "confused with his Maker" because of the kingly spirit he subordinately radiates. It is with his presence that Ransom and Merlin are "momentarily caught up into the *Gloria* which those five excellent Natures perpetually sing" (*THS*, 324). The two experience heavenly worship in a form analogous to the worship that John portrays in the chapters of his Revelation, for the angelic powers have come to bring judgment upon the evil at Belbury. These grand visions of Eternity prepare the heart for what is still to come, for what can be hoped. In that sense, Lewis's fictional creations are parallel with Farrer's commentary and with the images of John that each writer drew upon.

THE SENSE OF THE ENDLESS

Near the conclusion of *That Hideous Strength*, many of the principals of St. Anne's debate the justice of the destruction of Edgestow and Bracton. Mother Dimble asks, "Aren't Merlin and the eldils a trifle . . . well, *wholesale*. Did *all* Edgestow deserve to be wiped out?" (*THS*, 369). Some, such as McPhee, see it as comeuppance and a warning, while others such as Mark Denniston and Grace Ironwood see it as the natural consequence of evil deeds. The Dimbles themselves disagree as to whether any may be counted as innocent. But Ironwood also offers a strange, eschatological analysis, noting that "nearly everyone except the very good (who were ripe for fair dismissal) and the very bad, had already left Edgestow" (*THS*, 370). The apocalyptic binary is yet again employed here; however, it is more complex than one might first notice. From one perspective, the circumstances of the deaths of the very evil and the sainted good are the same, yet phenomenologically, the actual arrival of their deaths is entirely opposite.

And while theodicy is near the heart of the issue, the related question of the good death is also at hand. All the parties in the debate assume that the noble death of the very good is to be admired, even (though this is implied) that such a death is the "ripe" fruit of a sacred life. Because Austin Farrer and C. S. Lewis took seriously virtue ethics, they also assumed that a telos shaped the meaning and outcome of a life, and because they understood the exalted state of divinization as an orientation for ethics and an answer to theodicy, they each saw the promise of eternal life as having what Joseph Pieper called "the character of being-directed-towards-the-End" (Kermode 2000, 166). And not just as a fictional or ideational requirement for the logics of virtue and theodicy, but as that which truly is, so much so that to attempt to offer an explanation of human life without it is to offer a truncated and ultimately false definition.

Farrer certainly understood the problem that both resurrection and the heavenly state posed for the modern imagination. In particular, the physical location of heaven seemed an absurdity in light of modern views of the universe, as did the notion that a body, which had long dissolved back into the elements, could be reconstructed. Farrer sought to approach this limitation from both analogical and dogmatic grounds. He argued, for example, that a natural revulsion against death is different than the sense of one's potential immortality, as is the desire for those one loves to continue happily ever after. Natural revulsion humans presumably share with other higher animals, while the intuition of eternity "involves imaging the future in a way animals presumably don't" (*SB*, 136). This intimation was one Lewis obviously shared. It is not insignificant that in *The Last Battle*, Ginger recedes to a dumb beast, and his fate is comparable with those at the N. I. C. E. banquet who lose the capacity for rational speech. The loss of rationality is a precursor of hell, while rationality is a sign of eternal existence. Lewis was sure that hell was, at the very least, the self left truly to itself, yet the biblical imagery of destruction might also imply the loss of selfhood, even the nadir of nonentity (*PP*, 123–27).

By way of contrast, heaven represents the final good state, what the human person is meant for. Lewis's argument from desire often took the form in which given that the desire for the eternal cannot be fulfilled in this life, another life must await (*PP*, 148–50). However, it is not a Christian idea that the immaterial part of humanity is guaranteed immortality by its nature, nor was Lewis suggesting as such. Farrer himself was careful to stress that the human soul is not immortal, for in Christian theology, the resurrection of the whole embodied person is a gift of grace. The human intimation of immortality is rather a sign that the gift is offered (perhaps uniquely) to human beings, at least as individuals. "It's where the road goes" because Christianity does not hold together without it (*SB*, 140).

Farrer also argued that heaven is the inevitable result of a relationship with God. The beauties of this life will continue in the heavenly state for our present joys are a foretaste to come, and this condition of beauty includes human joy, for it contains the perfection of our relations and our possible creative actions. Heaven is where God bestows his action and presence (and for all eternity), and thus, heaven can only exist as God so chooses. Farrer pointed out that Albert Einstein's theory of relativity made space itself a nexus of interactive energies, and thus heaven as a space could exist without interacting with the temporal, material world. He also stressed that as the faithful are attached to a living Christ, so the gift of resurrection will be theirs because their continuing existence is connected to his eternal being (*SB*, 145–46).[10] Lewis, too, had sought to address the difficulty of the spatialization of heaven. He pointed out that the "New Nature" of Christ's ascension, as well as that of the bodily and spatial state of the next life, was hardly comparable to a localized vision of heaven that some seemed to hold, not because it would be immaterial, but because it would be transmaterial. The new creation would not be a "formless Everywhere-and-Nowhere," but neither would it be like the decaying mortal condition of this universe (Lewis 1960b, 156, 162).

None of this, as both writers understood, need erase the cost and trouble that death brings, nor did they deny that apocalyptic endings carry with them a sense of dread and trepidation. All of human life is fleeting; no human civilization is guaranteed infinite longevity, and the end of the physical universe is scientifically inevitable. Lewis observed that "what death is to each man, the Second Coming is to the whole human race" (*WLN*, 110). All persons have a sense of fear before knowledge of the first, and knowledge of the second should put an end to utopian fantasies. Michael Ward has described how Saturn, the planet of contemplation, grief, and death presides over *The Last Battle*. A martyrs' book, every chapter until chapter 12 is one of failure on the faithful's part. Betrayal, deception, and even coldness undercut any attempt Tirian, Jewel, and the children make to turn the tide. As Ward notes, until near the end of the book, the novel is one of Aslan *absconditus* (2010, 204). Only in death are they finally rewarded for their pains. The end of Narnia is almost surreal in its apocalyptic symbolism. Father Time, who is Saturn, announces the cataclysm; the stars descend from the sky; all the talking animals pass through the door either to eternal joy or to rational reduction; the great dragons and lizards ravage its vegetation; the Great Wave buries all; the moon burns; and Saturn squeezes the life from the Sun. As Tirian knows, it is only right to mourn the death of one's world (*LB*, 198).

That expected ending can also shape how one lives one's life in the present. Farrer's sermon, "The End of Man," contrasts two science-fiction style endings for the world with the Christian hope of heaven and theosis—the first, a total nuclear apocalypse with no survivors; the second, a biological adaptation of the human species to such a point that it is no longer human, though able to survive in an alien world. He noticed that these popular scenarios share an intuition with theology—that the end of humanity is both an abrupt and final end to history and a promise of an entirely new state. Farrer's point was that while Christians accept that the present world will someday cease to be and that the human species will be changed in a radical manner, this knowledge now also changes the death that all can expect in this world. If "God is the end of man," then the character of God's intention is that of love, and the actions planned for eternity involve an exalted state for humans. Just as an expectation of a science-fiction apocalypse could shape the mind and actions of those who entertain it, so the expectation of theosis may be expected to transform "whatever Christians do for love of God or love of one another" (*EM*, 4).

Farrer understood that John also treated the Millennium as the reward of the martyrs, and yet Farrer rejected the view that Mount Zion is equivalent to it (*RI*, 50, 171–72). Rather, Mount Zion, the eternal community of the faithful, is what comes afterwards. There is a pattern in John's Revelation "of that miraculous providence is that it finds its fulfilment in man's final blessedness" (*RJD*, 111), yet Farrer observed that "a sleeping volcano overhangs the millennial kingdom," and he saw the Millennium as something of a late Jewish addition that John the author absorbed, yet one that does not deeply disturb the larger pattern (*RI*, 172–74). Nor was Farrer sure that the Millennium was as central and fundamental a belief as heaven. He argued that while John believed in a literal millennium, Paul seemed to have not foreseen it or mentioned it (*RJD*, 203–4). But even John, Farrer insisted, knew that one could know less about the Millennium than about the final state of glory (*RJD*, 207).

If as Frank Kermode (among many others) notes, that every death offers a personal "recurring *parousia*" (2000, 25), the possibility of our deaths opening out into that which is endless makes the promised arrival more than an event. Rather, it is the opening up of an infinite emergence of ever increasing and improving events. Farrer understood it as a failure of imagination that many saw the picture of singing in heaven as "eternal sameness." But, he stressed, if the new song is ever new, then the "wonder of it never stales" (*BM*, 107–8). Instead of imaging the future as a machine that must finally break down, one should imagine it as a violin, whose potential for music is "a manner open and infinite" (*EM*, 2).

In *Perelandra,* the narrator Lewis recalls Ransom arguing with McPhee that the eternal state of immortality is one in which the sexual and gastronomic desires are engulfed in a condition that does not negate but saturates them. Lewis realized that the divinized state was more than an extended life for the resurrected person; it also implied a spatial and temporal reality that, while still like the current world, also exceeded it, a state "too *definite* for language" (Lewis 1944, 30). In *The Last Battle,* Lewis pictures this energetic state as one not only in body, but also in space and place. It is a state of speed. The faithful Friends of Narnia never grow tired in their racing onward; as the repeated refrain declares, they always continue "further up and further in" (*LB,* 213–20). They can ascend to heights without fear or without even the vertigo of physical finitude, and they find that "the inside is larger than the outside" (*LB,* 224). Kermode argues that while spatialization requires metaphor, that experiences of the eternal cannot do so (2000, 178), but Lewis's last Narnian tale would seem to require exactly that. The final vision of the New Narnia is equivalent to the New Jerusalem of John's Apocalypse. The true, real, eternal Narnia can only be described by a rushing recognition of the old one.

For this reason, the connection of the old universe with the new one, if to be talked about at all, does require some familiarity of imagery. As Farrer stressed, the new Earth will have continuity with the old one. "That a primitive Christian might think of the world what he thought of his own body; raised again and transformed, yet without loss of individual identity" was something that no modern Christian need reject (*RJD,* 213). The theme of rulership, which is stressed in the New Testament, affirms a connection with the governmental structures of the past, yet it could be said that the lordship of those in the city is shared; "all that are not lost are fellow-kings" (*RJD,* 223). Farrer wrote that visions of the exalted state of the saints are "a glimpse of final bliss," which "cannot help being an anticipated conclusion to the whole apocalypse" (*RI,* 39). Because this is so, the structure of Revelation is one of mounting climaxes, each one building up to the final Last Judgment and New Heaven and Earth; the intermediate judgments foreshadow the final one; and the Last Judgment is "the climax of climax" (*RI*, 40, 43, 58). Such requires continuity as well as change.

The same can be said, then, of everlasting life. Just as nothing good in Narnia is lost in the true and eternal Narnia, so nothing of value in England is truly gone. *The Last Battle* ends with "Chapter One of the Great Story," a tale whose conditions portend that each new moment exceeds those before it, and yet in its infinite variety, it neither displaces the good that has come before nor loses continuity with it. Both Lewis and Farrer looked forward to the Beatific Vision, a visionary beholding that is active in its implications, for the endless bliss that awaits is ever improving. Such final continuity was, is, and will be that of Christ himself. "The face that we shall see is the face of Jesus," Farrer preached in hope (*BM*, 13). On the last page of *The Chronicles of Narnia*, Aslan no longer appears as a lion. As Christ becomes manifest, the beauty that follows, Lewis insisted, cannot be described for it transcends the written word (*LB*, 228). For both Farrer and Lewis, the refusal to set a timetable to this hope meant that the symbolism of apocalypse is a special kind of myth, a myth (that is an analogy, archetype, or poetic) that invites its readers to fill the present with the beauty of Christ, who is calling to them both from the vertical eternal and from the horizontal future, a future that in no way ceases to be creative in the present, and a present that in its eternality is ever calling the faithful forward. In such an understanding, the world becomes thick again, cosmic not only with warning and danger, but also with transcendence and ever-increasing love.

CODA

C. S. Lewis described the Christian way as neither rejecting the present world with its limitations nor concluding that our desires for more than this are deluded. Yet despair can be a temptation. Secular modernity, as well as painful existence, can work against eternal hope. As Lewis insisted, "I must keep alive in myself the desire for my true country, which I shall not find till after death; . . . I must make it the main object of life to press on to that other country and to help others to do the same" (*MX*, 120). Austin Farrer, looking to the Incarnation of Christ, affirmed the same desire. "The heart and focus of humanity is there with God; and when we lift up our hearts, and put them with the Lord, we recollect what we are, and where we truly belong." The glory of kings is a sign of the glory of Christ, which awaits us, for "his purpose is the purpose of our being. The wonder of it never stales" (*BM*, 108). It is this wonder that grounded the work of Farrer and Lewis.

The diverse topics that I have explored in *The Shared Witness*—myth, analogy, ethics, history, theodicy, and apocalypse—have been informed by five central themes, all of which draw their imaginative conviction from Lewis and Farrer's desire for eternity. Firstly, in the midst of the twentieth century, each writer continued to uphold the *hierarchical and transcendental character of existence,* a world picture that informed not only the purposes of myth and analogy, but also those of ethics and history. Secondly, both men also affirmed *an eschatological orientation* that gave a shape to their ethics, theodicy, and views of sacred history. Thirdly, this transcendental and eschatological world recognized *the limited and yet open character of human beings.* To be human is to be personal and tentative, and narrative makes sense not only of myth and analogy, and ethics and history, but also that of theodicy and the apocalyptic. These emphases upon hierarchy, eschatology, and the personal were, fourthly, part of *a classic vision of nature and grace* by which Farrer and

Lewis navigated general theories of myth, language, ethics, and history, even while affirming the single divine end that their Christian faith proclaimed. Thus, fifthly, *Christian hope in theosis* served for each writer as a fundamental affirmation of all the rest, for it put into practice a sacred and liturgical reality. Lewis and Farrer were narrating a world of luminous apexes, and they turned in hope to a luminous end. This expectation took varying forms: a telos of apocalyptic hope; an answer to the problem of evil; the end, which is beyond temporal history; a supernatural fullness that informs virtue; and the completion of analogy and myth in Christ.

While these ideas carry with them universal significance, we cannot forget that this shared witness was within twentieth-century modernity, a world perceived by many as desacralized and afloat without moorings. Both men as committed Anglicans sought to preserve this greater apex of grace. They wrote and taught during a period when English Christianity was waning, even if briefly rallying. It was a period of ecumenical conversations and doctrinal divisions among Protestants and Catholics, as well as traditionalists and moderns within and without Anglicanism. Additionally, it was a season in which institutional Christianity still had an influential voice in the academy and the culture, though no longer a hegemonic one.

There is both continuity and discontinuity between their time and our own, or perhaps I should say *my own* as a twenty-first-century citizen of the United States. As Shmuel Eisenstadt pointed out in the year 2000, there are "multiple modernities" (Berger 2014, 68), and the story I have sought to recount in this book would look very different told by other persons in other places. It is always hazardous, in my judgment, to speculate too much as to how persons in the past would respond to contemporary situations, but given that Lewis continues to be read with profit by many, as Farrer is by a more select audience, it remains an open question what their broad shared witness says to one's current world. Admittedly, ours is a world that is still coming to be, but I do think Lewis and Farrer leave our own era with questions worth asking.

"A SPIRITUAL SUPERNOVA"

Charles Taylor has described the cultural trend that progressed from deism and humanism to the secularity of the mid-twentieth century as a kind of "nova" that spread from the elites into many other areas of life. The more complex, multireligious world that has arisen in the last seventy-five years he compares to a "spiritual super nova, a kind of galloping pluralism on the spiritual plane" (2007, 299–300). Whether we consider this a product of post-modernity or late modernity or something farther reaching than either, the assumption that the future belongs to a desacralized world is no longer a majority position. At the same time, a naked public space is often still a procedural expectation, even if it takes different forms in regard to varying spiritual beliefs. Near the end of his career, Peter Berger argued that there are two kinds of pluralism in the contemporary Western world—a pluralism among various religious groups and a pluralism between those groups and that of secularity, and Berger suggested that what defines the contemporary world is that all of these exist as options alongside one another and that they can be combined by the same individual in varying manners, though not without tension (2014, 53–58).[1] Such a world, Taylor observes, is marked by (1) the drive for individual authenticity; (2) a highly personal mixture of religious options; (3) a defense of this mixture as a matter of unarguable and unopposable choice; and (4) a strong stress on "mutual display" as a way of signaling those choices and their personal authority (Berger 2014, 480–81, 513–14). There are reasons, as discussed in chapter 1, to suggest that such a world was in the making long before Lewis and Farrer, but certainly it was gaining strength in their England. Both were speaking to people who already felt free to pursue religion or not to pursue it in less than purely institutional terms, "a large 'floating vote,'" as Lewis called it (*GD,* 250).

At the same time, one does not need a sociological theory of inevitable secularization to recognize historically that the pressures of secularism were real for Farrer and Lewis on a number of fronts, especially within their intellectual worlds, as were the variety of Christian responses to those pressures. And that experience does have something to say about navigating varying positions even in contemporary pluralist settings. Farrer and Lewis were both committed to engaging charitably their intellectual and cultural opponents in environments that allowed for academic debate and public apologetics. The Oxford Socratic Club, though a student organization, represented that impulse at its best, and Lewis's leadership and Farrer's support showed how much they valued this kind of engagement across belief systems. Such an academic world was different from what has been called a "subaltern counterpublic," a religious community that provides protection for its members from secular or pluralist pressures (Ammerman 2014, 96). Yet there were some similarities. Farrer certainly understood that his mission as a tutor-priest was to buttress the wavering convictions of students, as it was also to make a credible showing for the faith where many saw it as problematic. He could urge of the faith, "If it is anywhere, it must be everywhere, like God himself. . . . You must be able to spread the area of our recognition for him . . . widely as your thought will range" (*CF*, 60). Lewis, too, understood part of his mission as protecting the faith of less educated Christians: "To be ignorant and simple now—not to be able to meet the enemies on their own ground—would be to throw down our weapons" (*WG*, 58). Both men were examples of the complexities of faith in a heterogeneous set of contexts. In this sense, it is worth considering if their trust in transcendence, eschatology, and the human center, as well as in nature, grace, and theosis, can continue to offer an alternative to desacralized public spaces and ideologies, as well as to a plurality of sacred traditions and sects.

Though the case has been made that the division between the eternal and temporal worlds in Christian thought and practice eventually led to modern secularism,[2] the category of "nature" in Farrer and Lewis's beliefs was not necessarily reducible to secularity; indeed, as I have tried to show, the overlapping distinctions between nature and supernature provided both thinkers a way of negotiating and answering the pressures of modernity. Given especially that the world of pluralism is for many a world in which the supernatural is at best wholly immanent in otherwise natural experience (and chosen experience at that), can a system of belief like theirs be effectively heard in our own day?

Perhaps it goes without saying that the topics that Lewis and Farrer engaged are not confined to mid-twentieth-century European concerns. Certainly, their positions also remind us that there is not a singular impartial position from which to engage issues of myth, ethics, history, and theodicy, and yet the answers that Farrer and Lewis asserted also show how it was possible to retain some flexibility and adaptability; that is, their Christian convictions were capable of listening and learning from others even in the midst of debate. For this reason, the questions they brought to their context are of importance to our own as well. Admittedly, the account that Lewis, and to a lesser extent Farrer, assumes—one in which other belief systems are preparatory for the truth in Christ—is a claim not calculated to go down lightly with many pluralists or traditionalists of other religions, but neither was it in their own day. What it does raise is the issue of whose theory—that is, whose world structure—will be employed at any one time when analyzing what are (problematically) called world religions.[3] What Lewis and Farrer help us to remember is that a "neutral" sociological analysis exists in no more impartial space than does a religious one, and indeed, it may leave out key aspects of reality. If the position they held runs the risk of arrogance, it is not automatically inclined to it. It may indeed be worth still taking seriously.[4] I would argue this includes the twenty-first-century postsecular academy.

THEOSIS AND THE POSTSECULAR

The promised future of theosis, as Austin Farrer and C. S. Lewis understood, is a "desire for a true country" and "the purpose of our being" believed upon in this world. Impulses like these have at times been appropriated by those who do not share their supernatural trust and yet who see in them valuable motivations with this-worldly outcomes. In the last twenty years or so, this has been one of the chief concerns of postsecularity. As Colin Jager has observed, postsecular approaches have committed themselves to making more problematic old models that insisted "there is no such thing as 'religion' in the world" except that it arises "for historically specifiable reasons" (2018, 415). *Postsecularity* is admittedly an ambiguous term, and it remains to be seen what staying power it has. Whether there is even an actual "postsecular turn" is still debatable. Depending upon the definition—not unlike the *modernity* in *postmodernity*—the *secularism* in *postsecularism* has hardly gone away. For some, postsecularity will seem but a cover for the reintroduction of fundamentalism (Milota 2018, 539), while for others it will strike them as nothing more than secularity with new terminology (McLennan 2010, 12). But for those who would employ the term positively, postsecularity is an analysis of natural and historical realities that need scholarly nuancing because older approaches have bifurcated the world too easily.

For many, the postsecular simply rejects the secularization thesis, while for others it seeks to respect the religious diversity of the global and postcolonial world. Jürgen Habermas's use of postsecular advocates such a position (2008, 29). In similar fashion, the postsecular can include the tracing of how Western secularity grew up within and perhaps at the expense of Christianity, so much so that they are irrevocably intertwined (Calhoun, Juergensmeyer, and VanAntwerpen 2011, 5–14). For others, postsecularity recognizes the diversification of what secularism was and has become, and these seek to take seriously the twenty-first-century pluralistic world. Talal Asad (2003) in many ways set the terms of this debate.[5] Yet again, for others, postsecularity seeks to take seriously religion and spirituality without affirming its actual supernatural content. The language of transcendence, teleology, metaphysics, and the life of the spirit are reinterpreted within social, evolutionary categories. Some judge these as achievements of human cognition and culture that contain necessary aspects of human psychology, social ritual, and evolutionary adaptation. Craig Calhoun can speak of a "secular transcendence," that is, "a transcendent experience of the beauty of the world that does not depend on

fusion with something beyond the world." For Calhoun, there is an experience of a world that is greater than the self with all its limitations, but it need
not be a testament to the numinous (2012, 357). And charitable as William
Connolly's term "mundane transcendence" may be, he, too, admits that his
is "nontheistic gratitude for the . . . plurivocity of being" (1999, 159).

It is possible, then, to entertain whether these approaches are but new examples of Erich Przywara's suspended middle. A complex part of reality is
limited to one set of its aspects—that is, the sociobiological and political—
and the luminous apex is downgraded to its anthropological, preternatural
components. Craig Bradshaw Woelfel has stated the problem well:

> The first and most serious question about religious experience is whether or
> not it is, in fact, truly transcendent experience or not—that is to say, whether
> it originates from and is "closed" or bounded by the self and can be explained
> by entirely immanent means: or whether it has its origins in something ob-
> jective and outside the self, by virtue of which the subject in fact experiences
> something beyond individual subjectivity or even the material world. (2018, 22)

And this stands as the case whether we mean psychological and/or aesthetic
experience. It remains an open matter as to whether scholarly investigations
of religious experience must begin with reductionistic assumptions and methods, and in doing so declare "out of the picture those possible engagements
with something beyond the human" (Woelfel 2018, 32). This is what Lewis
and Farrer worked to overcome in their own context, though with different
interlocutors.

Of course, both Lewis and Farrer lived and worked in spaces that asked
of them to negotiate the secular and religious. Their sense of the luminous
apexes did finally seek to leave students and readers with a strong challenge
to take seriously "the signals of transcendence" (Berger 1970, 52–67). Now,
what again may their approach say to the contemporary academy? To begin
with, we must acknowledge that the need to complicate religion and secularity is in part because they are bifurcated by many. Nancy T. Ammerman has
observed that in the United States, for example, many are both secular and
religious at once, and are able to negotiate which to enact under which circumstances (2014, 99–103). Yet, as has been stressed by others, it does not
follow that such negotiation is always a good thing. Sometimes the result is a
faith that increasingly defines away its essentials. There is a line of demarca-
tion for Christianity in which the humanist project of human flourishing is too
limited. On these terms alone, something essential is lost to the picture that

faith offers (Taylor 2007, 654–55). This was the repeated conviction of both Farrer and Lewis, and it influenced how they engaged the debates into which they so often entered. Farrer certainly understood that in his own time, the "notorious 'scandal of particularity' . . . the unique importance which Christ's intervention bears for the Christian" was an offense for those who preferred a natural explanation for all religion (*CF,* 24).

Each of the six topics that I have explored in this book were debated by multiple parties and from multiple positions. The interpretations of Lewis and Farrer were argued from transcendent frameworks, though at different points of pressure and concern, and yet each was potentially subsumable under immanent or material views by their opponents. This is what made them debatable. In some of these, such as the practice of history or the nature of ethical judgment, Lewis and Farrer undertook their positions on grounds they partially shared with their nonbelieving counterparts. Lewis's theory of history he held along with other colleagues, while Farrer's concerns were with showing that the Gospels could still be considered divine texts while accommodating other redaction theories. While both wanted to make the case that the actual view of history held by the Evangelists was more open to the miraculous, they nevertheless insisted that the Gospels were history, and thus had marks that were historiographical. In the matter of ethics, while their ultimate positions owed much to their theological assumptions, each sought to engage others on matters of tradition, character formation, moral judgment, free will, and moral creativity—all positions partially open to those who did not share their faith. Their interpretations of myth and theodicy were also shaped by their nonbelieving interlocutors, and they learned from them as a result. Anthropological and psychoanalytic theories had to be partially absorbed into their thinking, as did evolution into their theodicies.

The postsecular still seems to be divided among matters of politics, epistemology, and hermeneutics, and yet these do have intersecting relations to keep in mind. If one concludes like Habermas that the public space is better off by not losing the insights of religious persons even on their own terms, then one begins to admit as well a wider definition of what an otherwise secular discourse can risk (Calhoun, Juergensmeyer, and VanAntwerpen 2011, 19). This stands to follow for any academic institution, professedly religious or secular, that has power over what and who can speak or publish. In similar fashion, if one concludes that transcendent discourse is a good thing but is finally a natural human adaptation to a large ecological habitus—that is, an "immanent naturalism"—then the basis for allowing that wider religious discourse is presumably still an intrasecular one (McLennan 2010, 18–19). And then the goods in question that can be presumably found are also shaped by this risk and expectation. We are more willing to openly assert what we hold to be the case in situations that reward it, as we are more willing to participate in projects that help advance what we most value.

My guess is that for many, Farrer will seem *too* Anglican, *too* theological to enter into a clearly postsecular debate, but I think the better entry points would be his treatments of religious language, science and the problem of evil, and assuredly the apocalyptic. Farrer in his day did address nonbelieving societies. Obviously, he would be a welcome partner in some interreligious dialogues. On the other hand, Lewis is still well known enough that postsecular usage is not only conceivable, but likely. Lewis's choices of science fiction or fantasy were not premeditated apologetics, even if he discovered their possibilities as such—they first and foremost flowed out of his own imaginative loves. They do provide an opportunity for something like a postsecular conversation in part because science fiction and fantasy are already genres in which questions arise that can trouble a purely horizontal and buffered existence.

As I sought to show in chapter 7, the apocalyptic and the eschatological are especially suited for challenging the secular, even as they can be subject to post-secular questions. These insights, too, can be appropriated by those who see in them a natural human (even communal) desire for a heavenly wholeness on earth. Ernst Bloch (1885–1977) did as much in Lewis and Farrer's lifetimes. Bloch's atheistic apocalypse longed for a Marxist and deeply poetic home-land. In Bloch, the new heaven and the new earth were finally a variant of the Communist utopia, but a warm one that drew on all human hopes and long-ings for the good and beautiful. That Bloch helped theologians like Wolfhart Pannenberg and Jürgen Moltmann rediscover the centrality of eschatology to their work is not surprising nor even ironic.[6] He helped them to see what was already theirs. The best case one could advance for the postsecular reception of Lewis and even Farrer would be this kind of mutual appropriation.

I would like here to return to a passage from Lewis, which I examined in chapter 7. I would contend that it models the sort of experience that some postsecular theorists are drawn to because it can be understood in more purely mundane or immanent terms:

> Both were filled with some passion, but what passion they did not know. They came to the front door and as they opened it a sight met their eyes which, though natural, seemed at the moment apocalyptic. All the day the wind had been rising and they found themselves looking out on a sky swept almost clean. The air was intensely cold, the stars severe and bright. High above the last rags

of scurrying clouds hung the Moon in all her wildness—not the voluptuous Moon of a thousand southern love-songs, but the huntress, the untameable virgin, the spear-head of madness. If that cold satellite had just then joined our planet for the first time, it could hardly have looked more like an omen. The wildness crept into Jane's blood. (Lewis, *THS*, 191)

For Akeel Bilgrami, a recovery of proper human agency is to recognize that there are external values calling from the natural world, that there is "a self-standing benevolent ethical order," though it need not be transcendental per se. These values phenomenologically summon humans to an accountability beyond themselves, yet such callings are not arriving from a sacred order. For Bilgrami, one can be an atheist and yet still affirm that not all natural values can be appropriated or assessed by science. This is what a reenchanted response to the world would entail (2010, 156–57). The omen-like quality of the natural world is calling in some sense with its values to Jane. Even more than Bilgrami, Connolly strikes me as expansive, for he is drawn to the manner in which, at key moments of wonder, creative awareness and possibilities arise out of our otherwise ordinary experience. Connolly describes this process as "mundane transcendence," that "any activity outside conscious awareness that crosses into actuality," whereby it can offer fruitful forms of productive action and thought that transcend normal durative time (2010, 131–34). There are parallels here with kairos time. The *why* of such moments arise from a direction not entirely explainable, though neither closed off from explanation.[7] In a reading like Connolly's, one need not conclude that the fecund creativity that arises from this experience, even the wildness in Jane's blood, need be transcendent or noumenal.

And such moments, others would contend, might even arrive unbidden and seemingly unfruitful and yet still be full. Simon During argues that one can experience the beauty and fullness of the world with neither any debt to the transcendence or even any moral grounding. The experience may come unbidden— "spiritual gravity may inhere in the self-emptying contingencies" of history and place, when even these seem bereft of any higher meaning (2010, 124–25). Here, I do not wish to assume that I know how Bilgrami, Connolly, or During themselves would actually read this passage, but their essential points—the external call of the world's value; the fecundity of mundane transcendent moments; and fullness, even in self-emptying moments, could be said to each describe some aspect of Jane's experience. Even the apocalyptic could be read as a creative response to a thoroughly human and unsacred kairos of significance.

And this is where Lewis and Farrer have something to contribute to the discussion, for they take seriously the transcendent as existing beyond the immanent, the mundane, or the neurobiological. As they each modeled in their reflections, kairos moments are one way of holding together the eternal and eschatological within our limited, fragile experience. Such moments call readers to attend to this possibility in every age. One suspects that Lewis would conclude that immanent transcendence is actually a longing for the transcendent glory of one's true country, while Farrer would not be surprised that the transcendent God would use the immanent sense of things to reveal himself. Lewis rejected the claim that Christian dogma could be "*merely* poetry" (*WG*, 117). Instead, doctrine is a kind of map summarizing the actual journeys of Christians through a real spiritual landscape (*MX*, 135–36). Farrer also called it a "very wicked thing" to say that faith was only poetry (*RF*, 24), and both writers were suspicious of the social usefulness of Christianity. Utility and poetry must be based, in the last analysis, in God.

From their Christian perspective, Lewis and Farrer each in his own way argued that there can be no complete definition of human life without an eschatological telos. Theosis as hope shapes the way we love and can only be truly perceived in this world via analogies with our temporal experience. The good death of the martyrs and the sense of the endless together follow from this understanding. The doctrine of nature and grace treated such experiences of immanent or mundane transcendence (or of extrinsic values and unspecified fullness) to be preparatory for identification. For one thing, they help us see that such moments can arise in persons who do not confess transcendence or teleological ethics, even those who consciously reject them as valid options. This was, of course, what Lewis was assuming about Jane. But immanent readings such as these call on those who do affirm the transcendent to give a better account of the human experience of a greater world, even the temporal one.

Admittedly, none of this lessens the debate between a radical transcendence and a mundane one, but it does ask how much reciprocity is possible and under what conditions. At times such scholarly and academic debate can seem to some to be anything but productive. Kevin Seidel describes the disappointment well: "They turn their scholarship into shovels and start digging out new lines of inquiry only to find themselves in another trench of what is by now a tired battle between the religious and the secular" (2018, 473). There is much truth to this; the hypertheoretical world of scholarship can seem arid, even vapid. However, sometimes uncovering old trenches can provide worthwhile history.

Charles Taylor described the impulse behind his *A Secular Age* to be an open conversation in which a broad spectrum of religious and nonreligious persons "eschew mutual caricature and try to understand what 'fulness' means for the other" (2010, 318). Armand Nicholi's popular course at Harvard, which compared Lewis with Sigmund Freud, is an encouraging example of this sort of thing. Nicholi's book, *The Question of God: C. S. Lewis and Sigmund Freud Debate God, Love, Sex, and the Meaning of Life*, and the PBS series that resulted from it, model one way such respectful engagement can take place. One can hold out hope for a more generous and receptive set of conversations, of cross-pollination that all parties would find helpful. In such an ideal, a postsecular academy could become a more hospitable place in which varying viewpoints learn to dialogue productively. Academic hospitality can take on different forms depending upon who hosts the table, even as each host practices self-examination. Over thirty years ago, Alasdair MacIntyre argued that in the presence of incommensurable traditions of moral judgment, those in the university have two tasks worth undertaking: (1) "to advance enquiry from within that particular point of view" that one holds along with its ethical and theological history; and (2) to enter into the debate with one's rivals and seek on the grounds of one's own position to explain their deficiencies (1990, 231). For MacIntyre, this meant the close reading of texts and historical contexts that surrounded them.

Farrer's understanding of nature and grace appreciated the goodness of his non-Christian neighbor. In a sermon entitled "Nice and Worldly" (and "The Charms of Unbelief" in *A Faith of Our Own*), he could imagine how those believers at chapel could depart with commitment to their faith, but after a pint with a secular friend wonder whether such a winsome friend really needed the faith after all. Farrer concluded that such friends were living out some aspects of God's intentions for the temporal creation, and because they were, Christians should pray and work for the happiness of their counterparts. At the same time, the reality of our deaths, Farrer stressed, also called us to account for our futures. The Christian, in light of that future, is preparing not only to live, but also to die: "We see then that there is no getting to God without passing through the fire" (1960c, 15; *FO*, 18–19). This extends to the way both Lewis and Farrer understood the nature of liturgy. According to Farrer, in John's Revelation, judgment is a liturgical situation. And for Lewis, the experience of the liturgy is reflective of the human suspended middle, for it is transpositional (that is, sacramental). It connects to that which is above and beyond, even as it also condescends to our limitations in speech and body. Farrer also understood that celestial liturgy brings together apocalypse and theodicy, for it gives a sense of that which is beyond our understanding.

There was something quite self-aware when Lewis noticed that his own belief was weakest after he had successfully argued for it. At such points, one can only be refreshed, he observed, "by falling back continually from the web of our own arguments . . . into the Reality" (*GD*, 103).

Lewis and Farrer realized that Christ is at the imaginative center of the hope in which both invested themselves. The possibility of hope, especially advent hope, is that when Christ returns, all is made new, yet for now, this hope acts upon that which it has yet to receive in its fullness. Even the encounter with Christ is already-not yet.

In the debate over myth, Lewis and Farrer found echoes of the Myth Become Fact. In analogy, they discovered their limitations but also evocations of glory. In the pursuit of virtue, they found common ground with others, which also called for eternal aspirations. In history, they found methods worth testing and an encounter with Christ worth defending. In theodicy, a shared trust in salvation structured their diverse responses to evolution and human suffering. In apocalypse, they evoked symbols that would offer hope in a greater cosmos and end. Theirs was an openness to an arresting strangeness and a beauty that never ends. "Now get on with it. Become a god," said C. S. Lewis (*GO*, 72). "And then we shall be cured of our self love," said Austin Farrer, "and shall love, without the power of even turning from it, the face that is lovely in itself, the face of God" (*CF*, 122). What they have to offer is a cosmic vision, a call to personal devotion, an academic and at times public apologetic, and finally an invitation to liturgy. The world to which they held, one may refashion, reject, or receive.

But, regardless, they invited others to join them.

NOTES

INTRODUCTION

1. For example, each man interacted with Samuel Alexander's *Space, Time, and Deity* (1920). From its two volumes, Lewis learned ways to critique Idealism. Farrer, on the other hand, thought it poorly argued, though he admitted there were a "good many acute and sensible passages in it" (Curtis 1985, 28).

2. Farrer's wife, Katherine, or Kay, also offered advice on Lewis's *Till We Have Faces* (see *Letters*, 3.589–90), and Lewis responded to drafts of her mystery novels.

3. Farrer (1979b, 383–86). Also printed as "'In His Image': In Commemoration of C. S. Lewis" (*BM*, 45–47).

4. See MacSwain (2008, 22–45).

1. MODERNITY

1. For a discussion of this, see "Interpreting Orphans" (Lundin 1999, 6–64).

2. Robert MacSwain, in "Correspondence and Documentation Related to Austin Farrer's Baptism" (2012, 241–76), publishes letters between Farrer and his father, a Baptist theologian, on the former's conversion.

3. A thorough discussion of the matter can be found in the *Journal of Inkling Studies* (Oct. 2011): 9–123.

4. *The Glass of Vision* was released in a critical edition, along with important critical essays, in 2013 as *Scripture, Metaphysics, and Poetry: Austin Farrer's* The Glass of Vision *with Critical Commentary* (MacSwain 2013a).

5. Ann Loades discusses their disagreement upon the issue of theodicy, and she believes that Farrer's chapter "Griefs and Consolations," in his *Love Almighty and Ills Unlimited,* has Lewis's *A Grief Observed* in mind (2004, 34–36).

6. Scholarly discussion of Lewis's role as an apologist includes Gehring (2017), Mills (1998), and Menuge (1997).

7. Maurice Cowling would declare them "one of the most remarkable public performances in twentieth-century England" (McIntire 2004, 201).

8. Bishop Hensley Henson could say of England that "the nation as such is certainly not Christian, to speak of national Christianity is to use a phrase without precise meaning," and yet the English coronation showed that English identity still looked to Christianity and remarkably "should desire that its ordered life should continue in the future as the past to be directed on Christian principles towards the Christian ideal" (Grimley 2004, 195).

9. See Mitchell (1997, 329–51).

10. Eric Mascall (1905–93) was probably the most Thomistic of the Anglo-Catholics in the Metaphysicals, and his works, such as *He Who Is, Existence and Analogy, Via Media, Nature and Supernature,* and *Words and Images,* are often the clearest statements of Thomist positions from an English writer. This made Mascall a bridge between the Neo-Scholasticism of thinkers such as Etienne Gilson and Jacques Maritain, and the more general Anglicanism of Lewis, whom he also cited with approval.

11. Lewis attended meetings between Eastern Orthodox and Western Christians, as well as at least one Eastern Orthodox service (Walker 1992, 65–66).

12. In the 1950s, Neill offered a similar analysis, including their being unable to see the positive side of the Industrial Revolution (1977, 242–43).

13. Humphrey Carpenter notes that Lewis and his brother could refer to Irish Catholics as "bog-trotters" and "bog-rats," and at times he made Tolkien feel ashamed for his devotion to the saints (1981, 51–52).

14. A good study of Lewis's reception in various circles and across the decades is Samuel Joeckel's *The C. S. Lewis Phenomenon* (2013).

2. MYTH

1. The best general overviews of modern myth theory include Csapo (2005) and Von Hendy (2002). Dundes (1984) offers a collection of classic readings. More recently, Sterenberg (2013) conducts a cultural narrative of the use of myth in twentieth-century Britain.

2. Along with this were those who judged myth and religion as bad consciousness—Feuerbach, Marx, and Nietzsche—as alienation and the resentment of slaves and the proletariat. These later accounts gave to the new human sciences a more pessimistic understanding of human nature and culture; they also tended toward explanations of myth that stressed the primitive, the unconscious, and the irrational.

3. Scarborough also includes the structuralist approach of Claude Lévi-Strauss within this category, but his work comes after Lewis and Farrer (Scarborough 1994, 21–22).

4. Scarborough cites Lewis's position as one more example of what he is critiquing—a modernity phenomenologically divided against itself in holding science, history, and myth to be separate categories. Scarborough draws from Michael Polanyi's notion of tacit knowledge and Maurice Merleau-Ponty's body-subject (Scarborough 1994, 66–69, 80–84) to argue for a body-based postcritical reading of mythic experience. Yet, as I hope to show, Lewis's own understanding was somewhat more fluid than Scarborough's discussion might lead readers to believe.

5. The subject of Lewis and myth, as well as Lewis and *Sehnsucht,* is one of the most discussed aspects of his thought in the critical literature. See Carnell (1999, chapters 1, 6, 7); Sellars (2011, chapter 9); and McGrath (2014, chapter 5) for Lewis's inferential argument from desire or longing. McGrath (2014, chapter 3) has an up-to-date discussion of Lewis and myth, while Sterenberg (2013, chapter 4) discusses Lewis and Tolkien's views together.

6. Lewis would also employ myths as philosophical allegories in his pre-Christian, antitheistic play, *Loki Bound,* treating Odin as the voice of corrupt theism and Loki as the rebel liberator (*SBJ*, 15). It is perhaps not surprising that his tutor, William Kirkpatrick, was shaped not only by Arthur Schopenhauer's pessimism, but also by Frazer's comparative mythology (*SBJ*, 139).

7. Farrer's analysis, when he notes the cultural tension between the divine king and the prophetic shaman, also parallels Christopher Dawson's 1946–47 Gifford lectures, and Robert Slocum thinks that Farrer would be comfortable with Jung's insight into ancestral images as playing a strong role in human creativity (Slocum 2007, 51).

8. Brown's own comparisons are revealing. Brown reviews the approaches of Mary Douglas, Mircea Eliade, Carl Jung, and Paul Ricoeur, among others, as a way to offset this limitation. Each seeks to hold together the natural and supernatural elements of symbols. Douglas, in arguing that symbols arise in social contexts, nonetheless looks to them as evidence of the transcendent. Eliade looks to nature as manifesting sacred time, while Jung locates this creativity in the unconscious. Ricoeur brings these together, seeing the collective symbols as fecund and able to bring forth "new signs of the sacred" (Brown 2013, 139–46).

9. Lewis, after all, held that the so-called primitive society distinguished neither the subjective and objective, nor the noumenal and phenomenal worlds (Carnell 1999, 73).

10. Aulén (1970, 125–30); Jaspers and Bultmann (2005, 35–43).

3. ANALOGY

1. Lewis's concerns with Barth and the Barthians extended beyond the question of reason and faith. See Dyer and Watson (2016, 48–52).

2. Compare with Morgan (2010).

3. Darren M. Kennedy has compared and contrasted Farrer and Barth's views of free will and providence (2011, chapter 5). David W. Williams has explored the devotional practice of Lewis in some detail as over against Barth's views in order to show that they do converge in view of the transcendent greatness of God (2014, 22–23). P. H. Brazier has also explored these similarities and differences in their thought, though, to my judgment, he reads Lewis too often through the lens of Barthian neoorthodoxy (2012, 65–102).

4. For a discussion of Barth's changing views of the analogy of being and his own analogy of faith, see McCormack (2011, 88–144).

5. See John R. Betz's introduction to the English translation of Przywara's *Analogia Entis* (2014, 63–65). Betz's essay, "After Barth," also provides a further explication (2010, 58–64).

6. See Nielsen (1953) for a period view of this debate.

7. Farrer actually passed up the chance to study with Maritain and Gilson, preferring to study under Brunner and Barth (Curtis 1985, 96; MacSwain 2013b, 99–100).

8. *Fideism* itself as a term could be slippery, depending upon what species of reason or rationalism one had in view. Middle positions could be labeled "semi-fideism" or "soft rationalism" given the party in question (MacSwain 2013b, 56–69). Farrer cited fellow Anglican Eric Mascall's *Existence and Analogy* as an example of neo-Thomist defenses of the analogy of being. Farrer and Mascall, as members of the Metaphysicals, described themselves as opponents of logical positivism (B. Mitchell 1983, 1–8).

9. Farrer was obviously drawn to this aspect of Przywara's thought enough to commend a parallel form of it in a review of a volume by Melville Chaning-Pearce on the "Christian Co-ordination of Contraries." Farrer critiques Chaning-Pearce's theological modernism, yet could still praise a system that could "admit contraries in our present state, the polarity whose ultimate form is flesh and spirit, that world and this: and find them dominated, balance and transcended in the unity of Christ" (1937, 330).

10. Rodger Forsman, in working through Farrer's claims in *Finite and Infinite*, defines apprehension as "non-inferential awareness" involving four matters: (1) that God exists; (2) that the human self is a substance; (3) that there are real entities other than the self; and (4) that these substances have value (1983, 111–13).

11. Mascall pointed out that he and Farrer do not hold that one can make finite existence and God in any way *"logically identical"* (which had been Barth's charge against Przywara). At the same time, the cosmological approach that Farrer took was based on the *"contuition* of God in the apprehension of finite beings," that is, a sense of the perceived cause in the effect, not in-and-of-itself in any way (1956, 30).

12. Mascall, for example, employed a version of Aristotle's famous example: the symptomatic "health" of Mr. Jones's skin and the healthy environment of his town are both meaningful expressions of well-being only if there is a third category—the health of human beings—by which to judge them (1949, 101).

13. Here, too, Farrer shared much with Przywara. Without God's absolute transcendence, the analogy of creation is reduced to pantheism (as in constituent and substance), to idealism (as in interior effect and agency), or to a truncated theism in which God is only the demiurge (as in exterior operation and affect) (*FI*, 23–24).

14. In his last book, *Faith and Speculation*, Farrer seemed to have taken a far more fideist position. Basil Mitchell, one of the Metaphysicals, would recall the book as such and as a position he had not been expecting (1983, 176–77). Not all agree, however, that this was what happened. Edward Henderson has argued that between the more fideist position of *Faith and Speculation* and the clearly rationalist position of the early *Finite and Infinite*, Farrer was making transitions that can be seen in both *The Glass of Vision* and *Freedom of the Will*. Farrer had two ways of pursuing the question: intellectual apprehension and volitionalist knowledge (1985, 165–68). Others such as John Hick (1972, xiii–xiv) or Diogenes Allen (2004, 61) reach similar conclusions. Yet even this time line can be questioned, or at least complicated. Robert MacSwain has traced elements of fideism in Farrer's early academic study, as well as showing that more rationalist arguments are in Farrer's 1966 *Science of God?* (published in the United States as *God Is Not Dead*), a book falling in the late period privileging faith over reason (MacSwain 2013b, 183–94). MacSwain has proposed that the dialogue

between the philosopher and believer within *Faith and Speculation* may be there in part because Farrer could not quite make up his mind and saw the virtues of each position (2013b, 194). Perhaps this oscillation was what made the suspended middle of Przywara attractive to Farrer.

15. David Brown, too, has noted that even if Farrer moved from a strong Thomist stress on ontology and substance to a more voluntarist stress on epistemology and agency, he never abandoned his basic stress on analogy (2006, 100); indeed, given his growing linguistic awareness, he hardly could have.

16. Lewis would use R. G. Collingwood's observation on this point from *The Idea of Nature* to open his chapter on nature and supernature in *Miracles*: "Nature, though it is a thing that really exists, is not a thing that exists in itself or in its own right, but a thing which depends for its existence upon something else" (1960b, 25).

17. In the 1920s before his conversion, Lewis moved from Oxford Realism to for a season something more like the Idealism of T. H. Green. Alister McGrath discusses this period in chapter 2 of *The Intellectual World of C. S. Lewis*. James Patrick also examines it in more detail in both "C. S. Lewis and Idealism" and *The Magdalen Metaphysicals*. In the later book, Patrick argues that the young Lewis was never a modernist, and his transitional Idealism was never a full solipsism. Lewis always acknowledged some aspect of the body in human perception (1985, xxix, 117–19).

18. Lewis recommended Bevan's lectures to more than one reader (*Letters*, 3.1012, 1065, 1264).

19. Bevan, unfortunately, did not really understand the *analogia entis*, especially as an analogy of proportionality. If his Gifford Lectures are anything like his larger cast of mind, this is because Bevan was unable to see that reasoning by analogy is a form of critical realism, rather than a sacrifice of the correspondence theory of truth or a form of Idealism (Bevan 1938, 297–317).

20. *Oughtness* (aka the Muse) is a difficult notion to pin down philosophically, and Farrer suspected this is true too of the need to pin down things within a theological system, and yet he was careful to stress that we cannot quite force the poetry of the prophets into the same kind of subjectivity of post-Renaissance verse (*GV*, 100–103).

21. Jung, on the other hand, falsely equated the ludic with the gnostic—a kind of myth Lewis was willing to enjoy as fiction only (*SLE*, 297–300).

22. John D. Cox suggests that *The Silver Chair* is structured around layered worlds: England, Aslan's Country, Narnia, Underland, Bism (i.e., the Really Deep Land), and the whole novel is one of descending into the lower land only to arise in the end. As he points out, there is the paradox here that in many places, the smaller world is not inside the larger one, but the reverse (1977, 16468).

23. Alasdair MacIntyre's response during the period to *Finite and Infinite* is revealing because already he realized that the analogical nature of science caused problems for positivism's univocal claims, that behind the univocal was always some kind of conceptual analogy (1950–51, 48–50).

24. Useful comparisons can be made here to Janet Soskice's interanimative theory of metaphor—the various connotations of the metaphor interact in ways that cannot be said in proper propositions (1985, 31).

25. Henderson discusses how Farrer's approach to images must be treated analogically. By them, we draw near yet we cannot equate them with God, and it is this

movement that helps us avoid idolatry (2004, 69–71). Robert MacSwain, too, points out that in Farrer's own practice, "we overcome the impossibility of prayer by praying" (2009, 420).

4. VIRTUE

1. The Oxford conference had three hundred delegates in attendance, a somewhat disappointing number, and more so, since the majority were from Britain and the United States, even though fifty-one nations were in attendance. Yet many were public figures of note in the Western world, including Bishop George Bell, Reinhold Niebuhr, T. S. Eliot, Emil Brunner, and Walter Hamilton Moberly. The two largest gaps in representation were that of the Roman Catholics and the Evangelical German Churches, the latter who were denied travel by Adolf Hitler.

2. It is important to keep in mind that Brunner's "natural theology" was hardly that of a strong trust in "natural light of reason" such as that advocated by the 1910 Catholic Oath against Modernism. He was not promoting a version of Aquinas's Five Arguments. Instead, he was simply insisting that some natural capacity for hearing and receiving the word of revelation did remain (Grenz and Olson 1992, 84–85).

3. See Brunner and Barth ([1946] 2002).

4. I have reviewed this influence on Catholic writers David Jones, Christopher Dawson, and J. R. R. Tolkien. See P. I. Mitchell (2012, 2013).

5. For example, Boersma (2009); Duffy (1992); McCool (1989); and Mettepenningen (2010).

6. Mascall, in *Via Media*, also suggests that *theosis* is simply the extension of the incompleteness of human finitude that is nonetheless oriented to becoming more (1956, 153–57).

7. He was also responding to criticism from S. L. Bethell and E. F. Carritt. Carritt's critique, in particular, annoyed Lewis because the man was not a Christian and Lewis thought it odd not only that Caritt would take the time to write, but also that the journal would take him seriously, considering its theological forum (*Letters*, 2.401).

8. Eric Mascall could quite naturally draw together Farrer and Lewis's thought from *Finite and Infinite* and *Miracles* as examples of alternatives to Barth (1956, 30–31, 38–42).

9. Thomas Hurka has called the overarching assumption of these British moral philosophers "underivative duty," that is, moral assumptions are properly basic in a way no other judgment of a scientific or religious nature is allowed to be (2011, 24–25).

10. Alasdair MacIntyre, in his *A Short History of Ethics*, pointed out that the British intuitionalist can neither explain how a property such as the "good" can be present in various cases nor, in any case, why one would want to act on the good in question (1998, 244–45).

11. It was only with Elizabeth Anscombe's 1958 essay "Modern Moral Philosophy" that the possibilities of virtue ethics entered again into mainstream philosophical discussion.

12. Even today, a typical introductory ethics course often begins with the interplay of Kantian deontology, utilitarian consequentialism, and virtue ethics, and with good

reason: they represent three of the chief structural options of human understanding and living, and, thus, they shift between principles and circumstances, as well as motivations and practices, and they are constantly reorganizing themselves about matters of goodness or law or individual pleasure or societal balance.

13. Willed action is further complicated because strong desire in practice, as Farrer pointed out, equates with "incipient fulfillment" and "incipient prevalence in this moment" (*FI*, 112–13).

14. If Farrer bracketed out the objection from psychoanalysis that we are driven by unconscious instincts, he also rejected the scholastic claim that a universal object of desire a priori is always present in our choosing. Rather than our soliciting our desired good, it solicits us; the event arrives (so to speak) before the cause. "It might be too much to say that the lion was looking for stags or stag-like things, but it is far truer to say that the stag was out to attract lions or lion-like things" (*FI*, 137). The difference between the will to action and desire is often tacit at best. In a perfect utopia, perhaps the deliberative umpire would always precede lesser desires, but this is not the way of most action (*FI*, 140–43). Functional human experience is more complicated.

15. When Farrer specifically addressed the categorical imperative, he called Kant's universals thin "ghosts of thought" (*RF*, 128).

16. Farrer held, then, that there were three modes of freedom: (1) that which objectively motivates, which calls forth a need for honesty in our moral judgments; (2) those conditions that offer real alternatives of consequence, and which thusly demand a consistency on our follow-through; and (3) the particular situation, which ideally should ask of us imagination and inventiveness (*FI*, 160–63).

17. That the senior devil could quote with approval a theologian need not imply that Lewis thought Niebuhr's ideas were demonic in origin, but surely his distaste for them was all too present. Two years earlier, Lewis had written to his brother Warnie that Niebuhr's *Interpretation* was his "Sunday book," which he described as "very disagreeable but not unprofitable" (*Letters*, 2.324). Lewis, in particular, distrusted Niebuhr's desire to exalt the political over the personal.

18. Rowland, influenced by Alasdair MacIntyre, notes the four factors: (1) "conceptions of truth that are tradition dependent"; (2) "traditions [that] can be tested for rational coherence"; (3) "a transcultural standard of human flourishing"; and (4) a tradition that is "rationally coherent and able to yield an account of the principles of the natural moral law" (2003, 118).

19. Admittedly, Lewis's standard for incorrigible moral intuitions is rather high, and has been the subject of criticism. He argues that too many claims for intuitions are just the applications or outcomes of other actions. "Nothing is to be treated as an intuition unless it is such that no good man has ever dreamed of doubting" (*WG*, 70). Theologian Stanley Hauerwas, a pacifist, has argued that Lewis's position on just war denies the right for pacifists to have a moral intuition that rejects killing; and it also denies pacifists the move of appealing to their own list of authorities (2010, 194–95). Hauerwas has a case to make here; nevertheless, Lewis's claim in a softer form is not incoherent; namely, that uncontested intuitions make sense only within shared practices. As soon as those at odds find themselves in differing traditions of moral inquiry, then perhaps Hauerwas's objections apply. See also Cole (2003).

20. However, it is also a world where one can be flogged for insubordination, though Caspian elects to show Eustace a measure of clemency. It is a not a world of slavery, yet such a penal standard may seem at odds with the ethos of a free Narnia.

21. In this, he accepted some version of the Thomist understanding that the soul-body is a composite. (Farrer denied that this was an example of Ryle's category mistake.) We inevitably have to use analogical language to describe what action patterns actually signify (FOW, 60–63, 100). Farrer was concerned with showing that our intentions bring a higher free order to lower impulses and that these are chosen. At the same time, we cannot choose (i.e., control) others' actions toward us, so we are not autonomous as some might want to define freedom.

22. Farrer did accept that freedom makes sense only against a background of some natural nonpersonal forces (FOW, 173), and again, analogous narrative accounts for this: "A predictable regularity in nature is the condition of our imposing effective decisions; and so it is not alien from the picture of a free man's world, but intrinsic to it" (FOW, 178). Psychoanalysis and social psychology assume some pretense to freedom by which they can measure their determinist compulsions and statistical predictions, but these hardly help with practical decision-making. Occasions are not causes but rationales or reasons: "Personal understanding neither foresees, nor predicts from causes; it predicts from standing decisions, or policies of choice, which we do not expect the agent concerned to revoke," even though at times the agent does just that (FOW, 323).

23. In Farrer's essay "A Starting-Point for the Philosophical Examination of Theological Belief," written the same year as his Gifford Lectures and published in the collection Faith and Logic, he argued that nothing can be established beyond question or doubt, so the style of argument he proposed to set forth was one of coherence and suggestion rather than foundational proposition building. He asserted that every theological sentence (every sentence?) is a "parable" and that believers learn early "the art of balancing parables" (RF, 115). Here, he conceded that establishing to the nonbeliever's satisfaction the evidence of divine action was difficult (if not impossible), yet one could "read off" of general experience some basic moral observations, such as the real-world priorities people give to various "moral 'options,'" in particular those that are judged to have some impact on "desirable features in human life" (RF, 118–20). In arguing this, Farrer was again appealing to the Aristotelian/Thomist shape of virtue ethics.

24. Marcel lectured for the Oxford Socratic Club in 1948. Lewis was there and his opinion of him was mixed—positive as to character ("to see him is to love him" and "a perfect old dear") yet not terribly impressed as to personalist philosophy or existentialism in general (Letters, 3.24, 3.1238).

25. MacIntyre, for example, in making such a claim, is not suggesting that we are constant self-dramatizers or even that we are always experiencing our lives as continual narratives, but that such narratives play a role in self-assessment at various times (1998, 241).

26. For a discussion of Farrer and Lister's friendship, see Hein (2004, 128–35).

27. Farrer preaches three similar sermons about John Keble: one preached on a pilgrimage; another a reflection on his life, and a third one on Keble and the founding of the college. He stresses the virtue of Keble's life being able to avoid "the egoism of private choice" and the gift of a life spent "in holy self-forgetfulness" (BM, 149).

Farrer held up the unassuming nature of Keble, who found sanctity in simply seeking God with focused simplicity. "He looked at conscience within, at the situation
without, at history and scripture lying behind, with selfless candour, and opened his
mind to the teaching of God: for he loved him" (*EM,* 156).

5. HISTORY

1. See Philip Irving Mitchell (2018, 13–40) for an example of how Lewis's views
of ethics and history worked themselves out in *Studies in Words.*

2. It might seem strange that Lewis could praise medieval historiography when it
lacked "the sense of period," holding that the past is not that different than the writer's own times, yet here Lewis's concern with ethics comes to the forefront, for the
best readings of the past were moral expressions of the Tao: "Hector was like any
other knight, only braver." The saints and kings, lovers and warriors of the past were
"friends, ancestors, patrons in every age" (*DI,* 174–85).

3. This critique has been extended to Lewis's histories. Robert Boenig has pointed
out that Lewis's portrait of the medieval world assumes too uniform a picture, as if
all persons across a thousand years and dozens of regions believed the same things
(2012, 29). David Lyle Jeffrey describes how many medievalists now see *The Allegory
of Love* as mistaken in its basic premises, ones more post-Enlightenment than truly
medieval (2000, 77–80). Doris T. Myers locates similar shortcomings in Lewis's non-
political reading of Spenser and Chaucer (2000, 95–97).

4. Lewis has often been criticized for this: David Lyle Jeffrey, for example, while
praising Lewis's coverage of the texts of Late Antiquity, holds that Lewis often projects
nineteenth-century medievalist notions back on to the actual Middle Ages (2000, 79–
83). Michael Price has a similar critique to make of Lewis's coverage of John Donne
(2000, 142–43), as does Doris Myers of his treatment of Spenser (2000, 95–97).

5. Donald T. Williams assesses the changes in scholarly responses to Lewis's picture here. Most would agree that Lewis draws a one-sided portrait in need of balance,
yet some have begun to understand what Lewis's extreme as a corrective of an earlier
one (2007, 152–54).

6. That same year, the abbot of Downside Abbey, Dom B. C. Butler, published his
defense of Matthean priority, *The Originality of St. Matthew,* arguing that Mark could
have abridged Matthew, with Luke borrowing from Mark (Neill and Wright 1988, 127).
(Butler and Farrer were undergraduate friends, when Butler was still Anglican.)

7. The Farrer Hypothesis continues today as a minority argument worth investigating. See Poirier and Peterson (2015).

8. Sean P. Kealy's *Mark's Gospel: A History of Its Interpretation* (1982, chapter 4),
provides a fairly thorough survey of twentieth-century approaches to the gospel, including the foundational soucritical approaches, as well as the form critical texts and
early redaction critics that preceded Farrer's studies (1982, 90–151).

9. That Farrer held such, some have argued, led to his own too-assured reading
of the Gospels and often resulted in a lack of caution, yet perhaps for such critics it is
just as irksome that he would read the Gospels authoritatively to begin with (Titley
2010, 112).

10. Farrer understood that corporate names, such as "the Western democratic tradition," "the English Monarchy," or "the American people," were "diagrammatic fictions" in the sense that they anthropomorphize collectives, be they social imaginaries or period cultures (*FS,* 93).

11. This is a debatable claim, and Robert Titley is correct to complain that Farrer was not as nuanced as he could have been. Too often, Farrer assumed that the gospel of Mark was a poetic puzzle that could be unraveled in a purely typological fashion (Titley 2010, 142). While Farrer's suggestions could be intriguing, even inspired, at times they could be forced and fail to take serious account of the culture surrounding the Gospels.

12. It didn't bother Farrer, then, to acknowledge different ways of describing that past. Farrer allowed that Mark's account of a hiddenness, then gradual revealing (such as made famous by William Wrede's *The Messianic Secret*) did not have to reproduce a "literal transcription of what Christ said" to do justice to the events themselves. In AD 70, Mark would have addressed Christians in Rome different than Galileans in AD 29–30 (*SSM,* 246).

13. It was Karl Popper's *The Open Society* (1945) that first made this usage of *historicism* well known, yet the word was clearly a point of contention, and in 1950, Lewis's definition would have been stipulative. That it could be easily misunderstood says much about its contested ground. In 1954, *historicism* had at least five possible meanings: (1) "explanation or evaluation by means of history"; (2) "the historicization of life"; (3) "the historicization of philosophy"; (4) "historical relationism and relativism"; and (5) "historical prediction" (Lee and Beck 1954, 568). By 1964, Alan Richardson could cite eight different meanings for the term: (1) "as the disinterested search for facts"; (2) that "theological or philosophical truths can be established by 'objective' historical research"; (3) "the philosophy of history"; (4) "the establishment of general laws about human behavior or social development"; (5) "that historical prediction is the principle objective of the social sciences"; (6) "an adequate account of [the origin of] the nature of an idea or an institution"; (7) "historical relativism"; or (8) "simply the study of history as such" (Richardson 1964, 104n3).

14. Lewis spells his name "Henri," but the 1952 English translation spells it "Henry." I am following this spelling for reference purposes.

15. Even before his conversion to Christianity, Lewis trusted Marxist models "in effect, to dehumanize man" (Starr 2014, 38).

16. As early as his 1946 piece, "Modern Man and His Categories of Thought," Lewis had asserted that developmentalism, in which "the very standard of good is itself in a state of flux," is an explicit denial of the biblical notion of creation and fall (1986, 64).

17. See Rust (1963); Rottenberg (1964); Connolly (1965); Wilburn (1966).

18. Butterfield had famously debunked the Whig view of history, the claim that divine wisdom and British political progress were of a piece. Yet Butterfield, following World War II, had in turn risked the claim that God's judgment might be discerned against Fascism. English compromise, Butterfield contended, saw itself as "co-operating with history" because one treated one's opponent with civility instead of trying to master them (1950, 89, 97).

19. See Yolton (1955, 477) for a period overview of the term.

6. THEODICY

1. "Praises of the Creator" and "In His Image" (*BM,* 44, 45–47). The latter is reprinted in Como (2005, 383–86).

2. A comprehensive picture of Lewis's theodician development would also pay closer attention to his preconversion works, *Spirits in Bondage* and *Dymer,* and his World War I experiences (King 2001, chapters 3–4; McInnis 2012, 22–31; Krokstrom 2015, 131–43).

3. The bodily element of this connection is explored by Farrer in good detail in "The Body of Christ" (*CY,* 63–72).

4. The early John Hick's distinction between Augustinian free-will theodicy and Ireanean soul-improvement theodicies had Farrer's *Love Almighty* in mind for the latter (1966, 273–76). Sadly, Hick omitted this discussion of Farrer in the second edition.

5. Farrer thought that Leibniz's argument that God's perfect choices entirely predetermine our free actions overlooked another kind of reasoning: that of the artist. Leibniz argued that our thoughts must be inclined in a singular direction or only be capricious, but Farrer argued that artists can have a form in mind and yet adapt this as they go along. Farrer thought the idea that "the transcendent glory of divine freedom to be able to work infallibly through free instruments" was one closed off to early modern theodicy (1996, 32–33).

6. Nicola Hoggard Creegan has explored ways in which Lewis's concerns could be expanded in a more comprehensive manner to include animal pain and redemption (2014, 95–99). Stephen H. Webb does something similar, looking at those who criticize Lewis's distinction between domestic animals and wild ones. Webb argues that Lewis's distinction, while problematic, is the right place to begin since the world of animals we know is the one pets share with us (1998, 176–77).

7. This distinction does not render projects like Matthew Flanagan's or Michael Peterson's suspect, but it does at least raise the question as to whether Lewis's theodicy should be judged by analytic philosophical criteria. For examples of this latter approach, see Flanagan (2014) and Peterson (2008).

8. Lewis also thought it mistaken to argue that it was better for humans not to exist. "How should I, if I did not exist, profit by not existing?" (*PP,* 36).

9. Andrew Linzey argues that Lewis's conjectural theology is comparable to his views on literature—both suggestively open to us a large frame of possibilities (para. 18).

10. Don King, in his edition of Lewis's collected poems, speculates these were written in the 1960s, but Ward notes that Lewis referenced them in correspondence in the 1950s as having been written in the 1940s (Ward 2010, 218n45; *Letters,* 3.616–17).

11. See Hick ([1977] 2010, 6–10).

12. Farrer did hold, as Lewis did, that purgatory is temporary refinement (and, therefore, part of *theosis*). See Farrer (*SB,* 154) and Lewis (*LM,* 107–9).

13. Myk Habets discusses briefly the growing popularity of Eastern Orthodox soteriology, especially *theosis,* in English circles during this time (2014, 111–12).

14. Lewis additionally deals with the topic in *Mere Christianity* (*MX,* 156, 172) as well as in the short essay, "Man or Rabbit?" describing redeemed destiny as "an ageless god, a son of God, radiant, wise, beautiful, and drenched in joy" (*GD,* 112).

7. APOCALYPSE

1. Farrer took seriously this warning to be clearly understood, going so far as to craft a new translation of the *Dies Irae*, "The Dies Irae. A New Translation" (1957a, 157–59), later included in the collection *Said or Sung* as "The Great Assize" (1960b, 9–10).

2. See McGinn (1979, 7–10) for several models, including those of D. S. Russell, Gerhard von Rad, Klaus Koch, Paul Hanson, John Collins, and Bernard McGinn's own list.

3. Judith Kovacs and Christopher Rowland describe this distinction as between *decoding* (seeking a timetable) and *repeated actualization* (applicable to new circumstances) (2004, 8). For a general introduction to the genre, see Michaels (1992).

4. Here I agree with Erik Tonning that models which seek to unpack the transcultural impulses of the apocalyptic and the millennial have their place, yet they should not be used to avoid the specific historical debt Western modernism owes to the Jewish and Christian versions (Tonning 2015, 3–5).

5. For a brief discussion of such positions, see S. Connolly (2007, 92–96).

6. James Como identifies the notions of "authority, hierarchy, and ceremony" along with membership and transposition as some of the chief topoi of Lewis's speaking and writing, and traces how these belong in a pattern of thinking in which the ordinary and material draw us toward the good goal of our existence (1998, 168–71).

7. Michael Goulder summarizes these, though he argues that Farrer's work was breaking new ground and that even in patterns that Farrer came to disregard, there are some worth amending and reexamining. In particular, Farrer switched from a six-week scheme to a four-week one and kept only one cycle of Jewish festivals reinforced by symbols from the zodiac. Goulder thinks that the zodiacal symbols are forced, even absurd, yet the Jewish festival calendar as a structuring device carries great weight (Curtis 1985, 199–202). More than once in *Rebirth of Images*, Farrer admitted he was not sure whether John actually had the pattern in mind, even though he also imagined him as working around the patterns as a creative impetus (*RI*, 85). The 1964 volume, on the other hand, while highlighting the patterns of the Jewish year and the zodiac far less, still assumed them at times (*RJD*, 117, 169–70). Farrer continued to accept the difficulty with some of the patterns and wondered if John would have intentionally identified these (*RJD*, 20). Farrer admitted something similar after exploring connections with Purim and Esther, conceding that these could be better explained by other connections (*RJD*, 117).

8. Strictly speaking, Farrer's general approach was a preterist one, that is, one in which most of the prophetic materials of Revelation have already happened, and so he held only the very last events were still to come, though all the symbols had application to the present (*RI*, 294–98). As a point of comparison, H. H. Rowley's *The Relevance of Apocalyptic* (1944) was a late World War II book, and his book showed the importance of apocalyptic thinking to the war and postwar periods. His work stressed how the future enters the present and emphasized, not only an anticipation of eternal life and a Last Judgment, but also an assurance that there is the divine purpose for history and that in the face of twentieth-century evil, there was still hope for the Christian society (Koch 1970, 51–52). In this way, Rowley and Farrer had similar concerns, if not approaches.

9. Lewis admitted that once he found allegorical readings of Song of Solomon frigid and not a little absurd, but he had now come to a place where, provided we do not reject the literal reading of the texts, typological and allegorical readings do not worry him, as long as they remain anchored in the Church's tradition. Lewis treated the allegorical interpretations of patristic and medieval hermeneutics in much the same way as he did the mythic elements of scripture: "I think we can be sure that some of them really are [ridiculous]; we ought to be much less sure that we know which" (*RP*, 121).

10. Such a notion was one that Farrer looked to fairly early in his education. In 1931, Farrer recalled to his father a theological debate he had had with H. A. Hodges about Emil Brunner's dialectical theology. Hodges wondered if Brunner's strong either-or position left any room for the mystical. Hodges stressed that a revelation of the end of history was a necessary part of the human journey, which is "on the Way and not at the End." This helped clarify the issue of revelation and atonement for Farrer, as well as the need to heal the brokenness between God and his creatures (Curtis 1985, 80).

CODA

1. Yet this pluralism with its cognitive dissonance is hardly restricted to the West. Anthony Giddens argues that "modernity is inherently globalizing" since transnational economic, political, military, and technological systems separate ways of living from their local environments (2005, 285). In similar fashion, Arjun Appadurai notices that the twin elements of mass media and migration have created a global modernity in which people are deeply aware of others' lives, with results ranging from resentment to the paradoxical to a profound awareness of their own difference and what it implies (2005, 278).

2. This is essentially the case that Taylor makes in *A Secular Age*. For a briefer consideration of this, see Milbank (2010, 54–82).

3. Admittedly, the Western term *religion* has a number of shortcomings, though I am at something of a loss to employ another one with ease. For discussions of this question, see Nongbri (2015, 16–22) and Masuzawa (2005).

4. Certainly, they are not alone in reaching such conclusions. Indian Christians have concluded that the sacred texts of India prepared the way for Christ in much the same way as Lewis and Farrer argued for Christ the True Myth, so much so that it has led to a debate as to whether some passages from Hindu scriptures can be used in Christian worship (Tennent 2007, 68–69). Kwame Bediako, in similar fashion, has observed that the supreme creator deity of African traditional religion was waiting to be discovered as the "God of the Bible" (Tennent 2007, 207).

5. See Asad (2003).

6. See Rose (2017).

7. One might argue that Frank Kermode's treatment of pleroma, kairos, and *aevum* in *A Sense of an Ending* assumes something like this. At the least, they all are treated as human imaginative needs for ordering experience (2000, 52, 62–63, 70–72).

WORKS CITED

Adams, Marilyn McCord. 1990. *Horrendous Evils and the Goodness of God.* Ithaca, NY: Cornell Univ. Press.

Allen, Diogenes. 2004. "Farrer's Spirituality." In *Captured by the Crucified: The Practical Theology of Austin Farrer,* edited by David Hein and Edward Hugh Henderson, 47–65. New York: T&T Clark.

Ammerman, Nancy T. 2014. "Modern Altars in Everyday Life." In *The Many Altars of Modernity: Toward a Paradigm for Religion in a Pluralist Age,* 94–110. Boston: Walter de Gruyter.

Anscombe, G. E. M. 1958. "Modern Moral Philosophy." *Philosophy* 33, no. 124: 1–19.

Appadurai, Arjun. 2005. "Cultural Dimensions of Globalization." In *The Global History Reader,* edited by Bruce Mazlish and Akira Iriye, 276–91. New York: Routledge.

Archer, Ian W. 2020. "Austin Farrer as Warden of Keble (1960–1968)." In *Austin Farrer: Oxford Warden, Scholar, Preacher,* edited by Markus Bockmuehl and Stephen Platten with Nevsky Everett, 17–37. London: SCM Press.

Asad, Talal. 2003. *Formations of the Secular: Christianity, Islam, Modernity.* Stanford, CA: Stanford Univ. Press.

Aulén, Gustaf. 1970. *The Drama and the Symbols.* Translated by Sydney Linton. Philadelphia: Fortress.

Baillie, John. 1945. *What Is Christian Civilization?* New York: Charles Scribner's.

Balsdon, Dacre. 1957. *Oxford Life.* London: Eyre & Spottiswoode.

Barfield, Owen. 1973. *Poetic Diction: A Study in Meaning.* Middleton, CT: Wesleyan Univ. Press.

Barth, Karl. (1932) 1968. *The Epistle to the Romans.* 6th ed. Translated by Edwyn C. Hoskyns. Reprint, Oxford: Oxford Univ. Press.

———. (1936) 1963. *Church Dogmatics* I/1: *The Doctrine of the Word of God.* Translated by G. T. Thomson. Reprint, Edinburgh: T&T Clark.

Bartsch, Hans Werner. 1961. *Kerygma and Myth: A Theological Debate.* New York: Harper & Row.

Bebbington, David. 1990. *Patterns in History: A Christian Perspective on Historical Thought.* Vancouver, BC: Regent College Press.

Berger, Peter. 1969. *The Sacred Canopy: Elements of a Sociological Theory of Religion.* New York: Anchor Books.

———. 1970. *A Rumor of Angels: Modern Society and the Rediscovery of the Supernatural.* New York: Anchor.

———. 2014. *The Many Altars of Modernity: Toward a Paradigm for Religion in a Pluralist Age.* Boston: Walter de Gruyter.

Betjeman, John. 1938. *An Oxford University Chest.* London: John Mills.

Betz, John R. 2010. "After Barth: A New Introduction to Erich Przywara's *Analogia Entis.*" In *The Analogy of Being: Invention of the Antichrist or Wisdom of God?*, edited by Thomas Joseph White, 35–85. Grand Rapids, MI: Eerdmans.

———. 2014. "Introduction." In *Analogia Entis: Metaphysics, Original Structure and Universal Rhythm,* by Erich.Przywara. Translated by John R. Betz and David Bentley Hart, 1–116. Grand Rapids, MI: Eerdmans.

Bevan, Edwyn Robert. 1938. *Symbolism and Belief.* London: George Allen and Unwin.

Bilgrami, Akeel. 2010. "What Is Enchantment?" In *Varieties of Secularism in a Secular Age,* edited by Michael Warner, Jonathan VanAntwerpen, and Craig Calhoun, 145–65. Cambridge, MA: Yale Univ. Press.

Boenig, Robert. 2012. *C. S. Lewis and the Middle Ages.* Kent, OH: Kent State Univ. Press.

Boersma, Hans. 2009. *Nouvelle Théologie and Sacramental Ontology; A Return to Mystery.* Oxford: Oxford Univ. Press.

Bouquet, A. C. 1934. "A German Catholic Philosophy of Religion." *Theology* 20: 327–48.

Brague, Rémi. 2002. *Eccentric Culture: A Theory of Western Civilization.* Translated by Samuel Lester. South Bend, IN: St. Augustine's Press.

———. 2003. *The Wisdom of the World: The Human Experience of the Universe in Western Thought.* Translated by Teresa Lavender Fagan. Chicago: Univ. of Chicago Press.

———. 2018. *The Kingdom of Man: Genesis and Failure of the Modern Project.* Translated by Paul Seaton. Notre Dame, IN: Univ. of Notre Dame Press.

Brazier, P. H. 2012. *C. S. Lewis—The Work of Christ Revealed.* Eugene, OR: Pickwick.

Brewer, Derek. 2005. "The Tutor: A Portrait." In *Remembering C. S. Lewis: Recollections of Those Who Knew Him.* 3rd ed. Edited by James T. Como, 115–51. San Francisco: Ignatius.

Brown, David. 2006. "The Role of Images in Theological Reflection." In *The Human Person in God's World: Studies to Commemorate the Austin Farrer Centenary,* edited by Brian Heddlethwaite and Douglas Hedley, 85–105. London: SCM Press.

———. 2013. "God and Symbolic Action." In *Scripture, Metaphysics, and Poetry: Austin Farrer's* The Glass of Vision *with Critical Commentary,* edited by Robert MacSwain, 133–48. Dorset, UK: Ashgate.

Brunner, Emil. 1938. "The Christian Understanding of Man." In *The Christian Understanding of Man.* Vol. 2 of *The Oxford Conference on Church, State, and Society,* edited by J. H. Oldham, 141–78. New York: Willett, Clark, and Company.

———. 1949. *Christianity and Civilisation.* New York: Charles Scribner's.

Brunner, Emil, and Karl Barth. (1946) 2002. *Natural Theology.* Translated by Peter Fraenkel. Reprint, Eugene, OR: Wipf and Stock.

Bultmann, Rudolf. 1961. "New Testament and Mythology." In *Kergyma and Myth: By Rudolf Bultmann and Five Critics,* edited by Hans Werner Bartsch, 1–44. New York: Harper and Row.

Burke, Peter. 1969. *The Renaissance Sense of the Past.* London: Edward Arnold.

Bury, J. B. 1973. "Inaugural Address: *The Science of History.*" In *The Varieties of History: From Voltaire to the Present,* edited by Fritz Stern, 209–26. New York: Vintage.

Butler, Perry. 2004. "From the Early Eighteenth Century to the Present Day." In *The Study of Anglicanism,* rev. ed., edited by Stephen Sykes, John Booty, and Jonathan Knight, 30–54. Minneapolis: Fortress Press.

Butterfield, Herbert. 1950. *Christianity and History.* New York: Charles Scribner's.

Calhoun, Craig. 2012. "Time, World, and Secularism." In *The Post-Secular in Question: Religion in Contemporary Society,* edited by Philip S. Gorski, David Kyuman Kim, John Torpey, and Jonathan VanAntwerpen, 335–64. New York: New York Univ. Press.

Calhoun, Craig J., Mark Juergensmeye, and Jonathan VanAntwerpen, eds. 2011. *Rethinking Secularism.* Oxford: Oxford Univ. Press.

Calinescu, Matei. 2006. *Five Faces of Modernism: Modernism, Avant-Garde, Decadence, Kitsch, Postmodernism.* Durham, NC: Duke Univ. Press.

Carnell, Corbin Scott. 1999. *Bright Shadow of Reality: Spiritual Longing in C. S. Lewis.* Grand Rapids, MI: Eerdmans.

Carpenter, Humphrey. 1981. *The Inklings: C. S. Lewis, J. R. R. Tolkien, Charles Williams, and Their Friends.* New York: Ballantine.

Cassirer, Ernst. 1946. *Language and Myth.* New York: Harper.

Childs, Brevard S. 1962. *Myth and Reality in the Old Testament.* Eugene, OR: Wipf and Stock.

Clements, Keith W. 1998. *Lovers of Discord: Twentieth-Century Theological Controversies in England.* London: SPCK.

Cole, Darrell. 2003. "The Problem of War: C. S. Lewis on Pacifism, War & the Christian Warrior." *Touchstone 16, no. 3 (Apr.).* http://touchstonemag.com/archives/article.php?id=16-03-045-f.

Collingwood, R. G. 1995. *Essays in Political Philosophy.* Edited by David Boucher. Oxford: Clarendon Press.

———. 2005a. *The Idea of History.* Rev. ed. Edited by Jan van der Dussen. Oxford: Oxford Univ. Press.

———. 2005b. *The Philosophy of Enchantment: Studies in Folklore, Cultural Criticism, and Anthropology.* Edited by David Boucher, Wendy James, and Philip Smallwood. Oxford: Clarendon Press.

———. 2013. *An Autobiography and Other Writings.* Edited by David Boucher and Teresa Smith. New York: Oxford Univ. Press.

Como, James. 1998. *Branches to Heaven: The Geniuses of C. S. Lewis.* Dallas: Spence Press.

Como, James, ed. 2005. *Remembering C. S. Lewis: Recollections of Those Who Knew Him.* 3rd ed. San Francisco: Ignatius.

Connolly, James M. 1965. *Human History and the Word of God: The Christian Meaning of History in Contemporary Thought.* New York: MacMillan.

Connolly, Sean. 2007. *Inklings of Heaven: C. S. Lewis and Eschatology.* Herefordshire, UK: Gracewing Press.

Connolly, William E. 1999. *Why I Am Not a Secularist.* Minneapolis: Minnesota Univ. Press.

———. 2010. "Belief, Spirituality, and Time." In *Varieties of Secularism in a Secular Age,* edited by Michael Warner, Jonathan VanAntwerpen, and Craig Calhoun, 126–44. Cambridge, MA: Yale Univ. Press.

Cox, John D. 1977. "Epistemological Release in *The Silver Chair.*" In *The Longing for a Form,* edited by Peter Schakel, 159–68. Kent, OH: Kent State Univ. Press.

Creegan, Nicola Hoggard. 2014. "C. S. Lewis, Animals, and Nature Red in Tooth and Claw." In *A Myth Retold: Re-encountering C. S. Lewis as Theologian,* edited by Martin Sutherland, 93–109. Eugene, OR: Wipf and Stock.

Csapo, Eric. 2005. *Theories of Mythology.* Oxford: Blackwell.

Cullmann, Oscar. 1964. *Christ and Time: The Primitive Christian Conception of Time and History.* Philadelphia: Westminster Press.

Curtis, Philip. 1985. *A Hawk among Sparrows: A Biography of Austin Farrer.* London: SPCK.

Dalferth, Ingolf. 2013. "The Stuff of Revelation." In *Scripture, Metaphysics, and Poetry: Austin Farrer's* The Glass of Vision *with Critical Commentary,* edited by Robert MacSwain, 149–66. Dorset, UK: Ashgate.

Danielson, Dennis. 2010. "Intellectual Historian." In *The Cambridge Companion to C. S. Lewis,* edited by Robert MacSwain and Michael Ward, 43–57. Cambridge: Cambridge Univ. Press.

D'Arcy, Martin. (1930) 1964. "The Philosophy of St. Augustine." In *St. Augustine: His Life, Age, and Thought,* compiled by T. F. B., 153–96. Cleveland, OH: Meridan. Originally published as *A Monument to Saint Augustine.* London: Sheed and Ward.

Darwin, Charles. 1993. *The Correspondence of Charles Darwin 8 (1860).* Cambridge: Cambridge Univ. Press.

———. 2003. *The Origin of Species.* New York: Signet Classics.

Dawson, Christopher. 1939. *Beyond Politics.* London: Sheed and Ward.

———. 2002. *Dynamics of World History.* Edited by John J. Mulloy. Lexington, KY: ISI Books.

———. 2009. *Enquiries into Religion and Culture.* Washington, DC: Catholic Univ. of America Press.

———. 2013. *Religion and Culture.* Washington, DC: Catholic Univ. of America Press.

Dodd, C. H. 1938. *History and the Gospel.* New York: Charles Scribner's Sons.

Dlfert, IIngalf. 2013. "The Stuff of Revelation: Austin Farrer's Doctrine of Inspired Images." In *Scripture, Metaphysics, and Poetry,* edited by Robert MacSwain, 149–66. Dorset, UK: Ashgate.

Domestico, Anthony. 2017. *Poetry and Theology in the Modernist Period.* Baltimore: Johns Hopkins Univ. Press.

Dorrien, Gary J. 1997. *The Word as True Myth: Interpreting Modern Theology.* Louisville, KY: WJK.

Duffy, Stephen J. 1992. *The Graced Horizon: Nature and Grace in Modern Catholic Thought.* Collegeville, MN: Liturgical Press.

Dundes, Alan. 1984. *Sacred Narrative: Readings in the Theory of Myth.* Berkeley: Univ. of California Press.

Dupré, Louis. 1993. *Passage to Modernity: An Essay in the Hermeneutics of Nature and Culture.* New Haven, CT: Yale Univ. Press.

During, Simon. 2010. "Competing Secularism: The Mundane in the Neoliberal Era." In *Varieties of Secularism in a Secular Age,* edited by Michael Warner, Jonathan VanAntwerpen, and Craig Calhoun, 105–25. Cambridge, MA: Yale Univ. Press.

Dyer, Justin Buckley, and Micah Joel Watson. 2016. *C. S. Lewis on Politics and Natural Law.* Cambridge: Cambridge Univ. Press.

Eaton, Jeffrey C. 1980. *The Logic of Theism: An Analysis of the Thought of Austin Farrer.* Lanham, MD: Univ. Press of America.

Ebeling, Gerhard. 1967. *The Problem of Historicity in the Church and its Proclamation.* Philadelphia: Fortress.

Eliade, Mircea. 1957. *The Sacred and Profane: The Nature of Religion.* New York: Harcourt Brace Jovanovich.

Eliot, T. S. 1967. *Christianity and Culture.* San Diego, CA: Harcourt, Inc.

Farrer, Austin. 1935. Review of *Polarity,* by P. Erich Przywara. Translated by A. C. Bouquet, DD. *Theology* 31 (Dec.): 361–63.

———. 1936. Review of *The Doctrine of the Word of God,* translated by G. T. Thomson, and *God in Action,* translated by E. G. Homrighausen and K. J. Ernst, by Karl Barth. *Theology* 32–33: 370–73.

———. 1937. Review of *Religion and Reality: An Essay in the Christian Co-ordination of Contraries,* by Melville Chaning-Pearce. *The Church Quarterly Review* 123–24: 328–30.

———. 1947. "Thought as the Basis of History: Dr. Austin Farrer on R. G. Collingwood." *The Listener* 37 (Mar. 20): 424–25.

———. 1951. *A Study in St Mark.* Westminster, UK: Dacre Press.

———. 1952. *The Crown of the Year: Weekly Paragraphs for the Holy Sacrament.* Westminster, UK: Dacre Press.

———. 1955. "On Dispensing with Q." In *Studies in the Gospels: Essays in Memory of R. H. Lightfoot,* edited by D. E. Nineham, 55–88. Oxford: Blackwell.

———. 1957a. "The Dies Irae. A New Translation." *Theology* 59: 157–59.

———. 1957b. "Introduction." In *The Core of the Bible,* arranged by Austin Farrer, 7–15. New York: Harper and Brothers.

———. 1958a. *The Freedom of the Will.* New York: Charles Scribner's.

———. 1958b. "Revelation." In *Faith and Logic: Oxford Essays in Philosophical Theology,* edited by Basil Mitchell, 84–107. London: Allen and Unwin.

———. 1960a. *A Faith of Our Own.* Cleveland: World Press.

———. 1960b. *Said or Sung: An Arrangement of Homily and Verse.* London: The Faith Press.

———. 1961a. "An English Appreciation." In *Kergyma and Myth: By Rudolf Bultmann and Five Critics,* edited by Hans Werner Bartsch, 212–23. New York: Harper and Row.

———. 1961b. "Messianic Prophecy and Preparation for Christ." In *The Communication of the Gospel in New Testament Times,* 1–9. London: SPCK.

———. 1962a. *Lord I Believe.* 2nd ed. London: SPCK.

———. 1962b. *Love Almighty and Ills Unlimited.* London: Collins.

———. 1963. *A Rebirth of Images: The Making of St. John's Apocalypse.* Eugene, OR: Wipf and Stock.

———. 1964a. *The Revelation of St John the Divine: Commentary on the English Text.* Eugene, OR: Wipf and Stock.

———. 1964b. *Saving Belief.* London: Hodder and Stoughton.

———. 1965a. "The Christian Apologist." In *Light on C. S. Lewis,* edited by Jocelyn Gibb, 23–43. New York: Harcourt Brace Jovanovich.

———. 1965b. *The Triple Victory.* London: Faith Press.

———. 1966a. *God Is Not Dead.* New York: Morehouse-Barlow, 1966. Published in England as *A Science of God?* London: Geoffrey Bliss.

———. 1966b. *St Mathew and St Mark.* 2nd ed. Westminster: Dacre Press.

———. 1967. *Faith and Speculation.* New York: New York Univ. Press.

———. 1970. *A Celebration of Faith.* London: Hodder and Stoughton.

———. 1972. *Reflective Faith.* London: SPCK.

———. 1973. *The End of Man.* London: Camelot Press.

———. 1976a. *The Brink of Mystery.* London: Camelot Press.

———. 1976b. *Interpretation and Belief.* London: Camelot.

———. 1979a. *Finite and Infinite: A Philosophical Essay.* 1943. Reprint, New York: Seabury Press.

———. 1979b. "In His Image." In *Remembering C. S. Lewis: Recollections of Those Who Knew Him,* edited by James T. Como, 383–86. San Francisco: Ignatius Press. Previously titled *C. S. Lewis at the Breakfast Table.* New York: MacMillan.

———. 1993. *Words of Life: Forty Meditations Previously Unpublished.* Edited by Charles Conti and Leslie Houlden. London: SPCK.

———. 1996. "Introduction." In *Theodicy: Essays on the Goodness of God, the Freedom of Man and the Origin of Evil,* by Gottfried Wilhelm Leibniz. 7–48. Translated by E. M. Huggard, La Salle, IL: Open Court.

———. 2013. *The Glass of Vision.* In *Scripture, Metaphysics, and Poetry,* edited by Robert MacSwain, 12–119. Dorset, UK: Ashgate.

———. 2020. *Farrer in America: Four Unpublished Lectures (1966).* In *Austin Farrer: Oxford Warden, Scholar, Preacher,* edited by Markus Bockmuehl and Stephen Platten with Nevsky Everett, 101–67. London: SCM Press.

Fiddes, Paul. 1992. "C. S. Lewis the Mythmaker." In *A Christian for All Christians: Essays in Honor of C. S. Lewis,* edited by Andrew Walker and James Patrick, 132–55. Washington, DC: Regnery Gateway.

Flanagan, Matthew. 2014. "God and the Moral Law in C. S. Lewis." In *A Myth Retold: Re-encountering C. S. Lewis as Theologian,* edited by Martin Sutherland, 69–92. Eugene, OR: Wipf and Stock.

Forsman, Rodger. 1983. "'Apprehension' in *Finite and Infinite.*" In *For God and Clarity: New Essays in Honor of Austin Farrer,* edited by Jeffrey C. Eaton and Ann Loades, 111–30. Allison Park, PA: Pickwick.

Fourth Lateran Council. *Constitutions.* https://www.papalencyclicals.net/councils/ecum12-2.htm.

Frazer, James George. 2009. *The Golden Bough.* Oxford: Oxford Univ. Press.

Garvie, A. E. 1938. Review of *The Christian Doctrine of Man,* edited by J. H. Oldham. *Philosophy* 13, no. 51 (July): 359–60.

Gay, Craig M. 1998. *The Way of the (Modern) World: or, Why It's Tempting to Live as If God Doesn't Exist.* Grand Rapids, MI: Eerdmans.

Gay, Peter. 2008. *Modernism: The Lure of Heresy, From Baudelaire to Beckett and Beyond.* New York: Norton.

Gehring, Michael J. 2017. *The Oxbridge Evangelist: Motivations, Practices, and Legacy of C. S. Lewis.* Eugene, OR: Cascade.

Giddens, Anthony. 2005. "The Globalizing of Modernity." In *The Global History Reader,* edited by Bruce Mazlish and Akira Iriye, 285–91. New York: Routledge.

Green, S. J. D. 2011. *The Passing of Protestant England: Secularisation and Social Change, c. 1920–1960.* Cambridge: Cambridge Univ. Press.

Green, V. H. H. 1964. *Religion at Oxford and Cambridge.* London: SCM Press.

Grenz, Stanley J., and Roger E. Olson. 1992. *Twentieth-Century Theology: God and the World in a Transitional Age.* Downers Grove, IL: InterVarsity Press.

Griffin, Roger. 2007. *Modernism and Fascism: The Sense of a Beginning under Mussolini and Hitler.* London: Palgrave MacMillan.

Griffin, William. 1986. *Clive Staples Lewis: A Dramatic Life.* San Francisco: Harper and Row.

Griffiths, Paul J. 2009. *Intellectual Appetite: A Theological Grammar.* Washington, DC: Catholic Univ. of America Press.

Grimley, Matthew. 2004. *Citizenship, Community, and the Church of England: Liberal Anglican Theories of the State between the Wars.* Oxford: Clarendon Press.

Guarino, Thomas G. 2005. *Foundations of Systematic Theology.* New York: T&T Clark.

Habermas, Jürgen. 2008. "Notes on Post-Secular Society." *New Perspectives Quarterly* 25, no. 4: 17–29.

Habets, Myk. 2014. "Mere Christianity for Mere Gods: Lewis on Theosis." In *A Myth Re-told: Re-encountering C. S. Lewis as Theologian,* edited by Martin Sutherland, 110–29. Eugene, OR: Wipf and Stiock.

Harbison, E. Harris. 1964. *Christianity and History: Essays.* Princeton, NJ: Princeton Univ. Press.

Hartt, Julian. 1983. "Austin Farrer as Philosophical Theologian: A Retrospective and Appreciation." In *For God and Clarity: New Essays in Honor of Austin Farrer,* edited by Jeffrey C. Eaton and Ann Loades, 1–22. Allison Park, PA: Pickwick.

Hastings, Adrian. 1987. *A History of English Christianity, 1920–1985.* London: Collins.

Hauerwas, Stanley. 2010. "On Violence." In *The Cambridge Companion to C. S. Lewis,* edited by Robert MacSwain and Michael Ward, 189–202. Cambridge: Cambridge Univ. Press.

Hebblethwaite, Brian. 2007. *The Philosophical Theology of Austin Farrer.* Leuven, Belgium: Peetres.

Heck, Joel D. 2014. "'Modern Theology and Biblical Criticism' in Context." Supplement to *Seven* 31:1–17.

Hefling, Charles C., Jr. 1979. *Jacob's Ladder: Theology and Spirituality in the Thought of Austin Farrer.* Cambridge: Cowley.

Hein, David. 2004. "Farrer on Friendship, Sainthood, and the Will of God." In *Captured by the Crucified: The Practical Theology of Austin Farrer,* edited by David Hein and Edward Hugh Henderson, 119–48. New York: T&T Clark.

Henderson, Edward Hugh. 1982. "Knowing Persons and Knowing God." *The Thomist* 46: 394–422.

———. 1985. "Valuing in Knowing God: An Interpretation of Austin Farrer's Religious Epistemology." *Modern Theology* 1, no. 3: 165–82.

WORKS CITED

————. 2004. "The God Who Undertakes Us." In *Captured by the Crucified: The Practical Theology of Austin Farrer,* edited by David Hein and Edward Hugh Henderson, 66–99. New York: T&T Clark.

Henry, Paul. 1952. "The Christian Philosophy of History." *Theological Studies* 13, no. 3: 419–32.

Hick, John. 1966. *Evil and the God of Love.* London: Macmillan.

————. 1972. Foreword to *Reflective Faith,* by Austin Farrer, xiii–xv. London: SPCK.

————. (1977) 2010. *Evil and the God of Love.* 2nd ed. Reprint, New York: Palgrave MacMillan.

Hooper, Walter. 1996. *C. S. Lewis: A Complete Guide to His Life and Works.* San Francisco: HarperSanFrancisco.

Horan, David. 2000. *Oxford: A Cultural and Literary Companion.* New York: Interlink.

Hurka, Thomas. 2011. "Common Themes from Sidgwick to Ewing." In *Underivative Duty: British Moral Philosophers from Sidgwick to Ewing,* edited by Thomas Hurka, 6–25. Oxford: Oxford Univ. Press.

Jacobs, Alan. 2005. *The Narnian: The Life and Imagination of C. S. Lewis.* San Francisco: HarperSanFrancisco.

Jager, Colin. 2018. "The Secular and the Literary." *Christianity and Literature* 67, no. 3: 411–18.

Jaspers, Karl, and Rudolf Bultmann. 2005. *Myth and Christianity: An Inquiry into the Possibility of Religion without Myth.* Amherst, NY: Prometheus Books.

Jebb, Sharon. 2011. *Writing God and the Self: Samuel Beckett and C. S. Lewis.* Eugene, OR: Wipf and Stock.

Jeffrey, David Lyle. 2000. "Medieval Literature." In *Reading the Classics with C. S. Lewis,* edited by Thomas L. Martin, 72–86. Grand Rapids, MI: Baker.

Joeckel, Samuel. 2013. *The C. S. Lewis Phenomenon: Christianity and the Public Sphere.* Macon, GA: Mercer Univ. Press.

Kealy, Sean P. 1982. *Mark's Gospel: A History of Its Interpretation.* New York: Paulist Press.

Kelly, Joseph F. 2002. *The Problem of Evil in the Western Tradition: From the Book of Job to Modern Genetics.* Collegeville, MN: The Liturgical Press.

Kennedy, Darren M. 2011. *Providence and Personalism: Kart Barth in Conversation with Austin Farrer, John Macmurray and Vincent Brümmer.* Oxford: Peter Lang.

Kermode, Frank. 2000. *The Sense of an Ending: Studies in the Theory of Fiction with a New Epilogue.* New York: Oxford Univ. Press.

Kerr, Fergus. 2002. *After Aquinas: Versions of Thomism.* Oxford: Blackwell.

Kilby, Clyde S. 1964. *The Christian World of C. S. Lewis.* Grand Rapids, MI: Eerdmans.

King, Don W. 2001. *C. S. Lewis, Poet: The Legacy of His Poetic Impulse.* Kent, OH: Kent State Univ. Press.

Koch, Klaus. 1970. *Rediscovery of Apocalypse. Studies in Biblical Theology* 22. Napierville, IL: Allenson Press.

Kort, Wesley A. 2016. *Reading C. S. Lewis: A Commentary.* New York: Oxford Univ. Press.

Kovacs, Judith, and Christopher Rowland. 2004. *Revelation: The Apocalypse of Jesus Christ.* Oxford: Blackwell.

Krokstrom, Andrew. 2015. "Silent Wounds." In *Baptism of Fire: The Birth of the Modern British Fantastic in World War I*, edited by Janet Brennan Croft, 131–43. Altadena, CA: Mythopoeic Press.

Larrimore, Mark. 2001. "Introduction." In *The Problem of Evil: A Reader*, edited by Mark Larrimore, xiv–xxx. Oxford: Blackwell.

Lee, Dwight E., and Robert N. Beck. 1954. "The Meaning of 'Historicism.'" *The American Historical Review* 59, no. 3 (Apr.): 568–77.

Levenson, Michael. 2011. *Modernism*. New Haven, CT: Yale Univ. Press.

Lewis, C. S. 1938. *Out of the Silent Planet*. New York: Scribner.

———. 1940. *The Problem of Pain*. New York: Macmillan.

———. 1942. *The Screwtape Letters*. San Francisco: HarperCollins.

———. 1944. *Perelandra*. New York: Scribner.

———. 1945. *That Hideous Strength*. New York: Scribner.

———. 1945. *The Great Divorce*. New York: Macmillan.

———. 1950. *The Lion, the Witch, and the Wardrobe*. New York: Macmillan.

———. 1951. *Prince Caspian*. New York: Harper Collins.

———. 1952a. *Mere Christianity*. New York: MacMillan.

———. 1952b. *The Voyage of the Dawn Treader*. New York: Macmillan.

———. 1953. *The Silver Chair*. New York: Macmillan.

———. 1954a. *English Literature in the Sixteenth Century, Excluding Drama*. Oxford: Clarendon Press.

———. 1954b. *The Horse and His Boy*. New York: Macmillan.

———. 1955a. *The Magician's Nephew*. New York: Harper Collins.

———. 1955b. *Surprised by Joy: The Shape of My Early Life*. New York: Harcourt Brace.

———. 1955c. *The World's Last Night, and Other Essays*. San Diego, CA: Harcourt.

———. 1956. *The Last Battle*. New York: HarperCollins.

———. 1958. *Reflections on the Psalms*. Orlando, FL: Harcourt Brace.

———. 1960a. *The Four Loves*. New York: HBJ.

———. 1960b. *Miracles*. 2nd ed. New York: Macmillan.

———. 1961a. *An Experiment in Criticism*. Cambridge: Cambridge Univ. Press.

———. 1961b. *A Grief Observed*. San Francisco: HarperOne.

———. 1961c. *A Preface to Paradise Lost*. London: Oxford Univ. Press.

———. 1964a. *The Discarded Image: An Introduction to Medieval and Renaissance Literature*. Cambridge: Cambridge Univ. Press.

———. 1964b. *Letters to Malcolm (Chiefly on Prayer): Reflections on the Intimate Dialogue between Man and God*. New York: Mariner.

———. 1966a. *On Stories and Other Essays on Literature*. New York: Harcourt Brace.

———. 1966b. *Studies in Medieval and Renaissance Literature*. Edited by Walter Hooper. Cambridge: Cambridge Univ. Press.

———. 1967a. *Christian Reflections*. Edited by Walter Hooper. Grand Rapids, MI: Eerdmans.

———. 1967b. *Studies in Words*. 2nd ed. Cambridge: Cambridge Univ. Press.

———. 1969. *Selected Literary Essays*. Edited by Walter Hooper. Cambridge: Cambridge Univ. Press.

———. 1970. *God in the Dock: Essays on Theology and Ethics*. Grand Rapids, MI: Eerdmans.

———. 1972. *The Allegory of Love: A Study in Medieval Tradition.* New York: Oxford Univ. Press.

———. 1976. *The Weight of Glory.* New York: Harper Collins.

———. 1986. *Present Concerns.* San Diego: HBJ.

———. 1990. *Christian Reunion and Other Essays.* Edited by Walter Hooper. London: Collins.

———. 1996. *The Abolition of Man.* New York: Simon & Schuster.

———. 2005. *Collected Letters.* 3 vols. Edited by Walter Hooper. San Francisco: HarperSanFrancisco.

———. 2012. *Till We Have Faces: A Myth Retold.* Boston: Mariner Books.

———. 2014a. "On Bolshevism." In *Two Pieces from C. S. Lewis's 'Moral Good' Manuscript: A First Publication,* edited by Charles Starr. *Seven* 31: 31–62.

———. 2014b. *The Pilgrim's Regress.* Wade Annotated ed. Edited by David C. Downing. Grand Rapids, MI: Eerdmans.

———. 2015. *The Collected Poems of C. S. Lewis: A Critical Edition.* Edited by Don W. King. Kent, OH: Kent State Univ. Press.

Lewis, C. S., and E. M. W. Tillyard. 2008. *The Personal Heresy: A Controversy.* Edited by Joel D. Heck. Austin, TX: Concordia Univ. Press.

Lewis, John Underwood. 1983. "Austin Farrer's Notion of 'Conscience as an Appetite for Moral Truth': Its Metaphysical Foundation and Importance to Contemporary Moral Philosophy." In *For God and Clarity: New Essays in Honor of Austin Farrer,* edited by Jeffrey C. Eaton and Ann Loades, 111–30. Allison Park, PA: Pickwick.

Linzey, Andrew. 1998. "C. S. Lewis's Theology of Animals." *Anglican Theological Review* 80, no. 1: 60–82. http://search.ebscohost.com/login.aspx?direct=true&db=a9h&AN=304770&site=ehost-live.

Loades, Ann. 2004. "The Vitality of Tradition: Austin Farrer and Friends." In *Captured by the Crucified: The Practical Theology of Austin Farrer,* edited by David Hein and Edward Hugh Henderson, 15–46. London: T&T Clark.

Lundin, Roger. 1999. "Interpreting Orphans: Hermeneutics in the Cartesian Tradition." In *The Promise of Hermeneutics,* by Roger Lundin, Clarence Walhout, and Anthony C. Thiselton, 6–64. Grand Rapids, MI: Eerdmans.

MacIntyre, Alasdair. 1950. "Analogy in Metaphysics." *Downside Review* 69: 45–61.

———. 1998. *A Short History of Ethics.* London: Routledge.

———. 2007. *After Virtue.* 3rd ed. Notre Dame, IN: Univ. of Notre Dame Press.

MacMurray, John. 1939. *The Clue to History.* New York: Harper & Brothers.

MacSwain, Robert. 2008. "A Fertile Friendship: C. S. Lewis and Austin Farrer." *The Chronicle of the Oxford University C. S. Lewis Society* 5, no. 2: 22–45.

———. 2009. "Learning to Pray with Austin Farrer: A Meditation." *Sewanee Theological Review* 52, no. 4 (Michaelmas): 409–21.

———. 2012. "Correspondence and Documentation Related to Austin Farrer's Baptism in the Church of England on 14 May 1924." *Anglican and Episcopal History* 81, no. 3 (Sept.): 241–76.

———. 2013a. *Scripture, Metaphysics, and Poetry: Austin Farrer's* The Glass of Vision *with Critical Commentary.* Dorset, UK: Ashgate.

———. 2013b. *Solved by Sacrifice: Austin Farrer, Fideism, and the Evidence of Faith.* Leuven, Belgium: Peeters.

Manlove, Colin. 1991. "'Caught Up into the Larger Pattern': Images and Narrative Structures in C. S. Lewis' Fiction." In *Word and Story in C. S. Lewis,* edited by Peter J. Schakel and Charles A. Huttar, 256–76. Columbia: Univ. of Missouri Press.

Marcel, Gabriel. 2001. *The Mystery of Being.* 2 vols. Translated by G. S. Fraser. South Bend, IN: St. Augustine's Press.

Marsden, George M. 2016. *C. S. Lewis's* Mere Christianity*: A Biography.* Princeton, NJ: Princeton Univ. Press.

Martindale, C. C. 1936. "The Supernatural." In *God and the Supernatural,* edited by Fr. Cuthbert, 1–22. London: Sheed and Ward.

Mascall, Eric L. 1943. *He Who Is: A Study in Traditional Theism.* London: Longmans, Green and Co.

———. 1949. *Existence and Analogy. A Sequel to "He Who Is."* London: Longmans, Green and Co.

———. 1956. *Via Media: An Essay in Theological Synthesis.* London: Longman, Green, and Co.

Masuzawa, Tomoko. 2005. *The Invention of World Religions: Or, How European Universalism Was Preserved in the Language of Pluralism.* Chicago: Univ. of Chicago Press.

McCool, Gerald A. 1989. *From Unity to Pluralism: The Internal Evolution of Thomism.* New York: Fordham Univ. Press.

McCormack, Bruce L. 2011. "Karl Barth's Version of an 'Analogy of Being': A Dialectical No and Yes to Roman Catholicism." In *The Analogy of Being: Invention of the Antichrist or the Wisdom of God?,* edited by Thomas Joseph White, 88–144. Grand Rapids, MI: Eerdmans.

McGinn, Bernard. 1979. *Visions of the End: Apocalyptic Traditions in the Middle Ages.* New York: Columbia Univ. Press.

McGrath, Alister E. 2013. *C. S. Lewis—A Life: Eccentric Genius. Reluctant Prophet.* Carol Stream, IL: Tyndale House.

———. 2014. *The Intellectual World of C. S Lewis.* Chichester, UK: Wiley-Blackwell.

McInnis, Jeff. 2012. *Shadows and Chivalry: C. S. Lewis and George MacDonald on Suffering, Evil, and Goodness.* Hamden, CT: Winged Lion Press.

McIntire, C. T. 2004. *Herbert Butterfield: Historian as Dissenter.* New Haven, CT: Yale Univ. Press.

McLennan, Gregor. 2010. "The Postsecular Turn." *Theory, Culture, and Society* 27, no. 4: 3–20.

Meilaender, Gilbert. 1998. *The Taste for the Other: The Social and Ethical Thought of C. S. Lewis.* Grand Rapids, MI: Eerdmans.

———. 2010. "On Moral Knowledge." In *The Cambridge Guide to C. S. Lewis,* edited by Robert MacSwain and Michael Ward, 119–31. New York: Cambridge Univ. Press.

Menuge, Angus J. L., ed. 1997. *C. S. Lewis, Lightbearer in the Shadowlands: The Evangelistic Vision of C. S. Lewis.* Wheaton, IL: Crossway Books.

Mettepenningen, Jürgen. 2010. *Nouvelle Théologie New Theology: Inheritor of Modernism, Precursor of Vatican II.* London: T&T Clark.

Milbank, John. 2010. "A Closer Walk on the Wild Side." In *Varieties of Secularism in a Secular Age,* edited by Michael Warner, Jonathan VanAntwerpen, and Craig Calhoun, 54–82. Cambridge, MA: Yale Univ. Press.

Mills, David, ed. 1998. *The Pilgrim's Guide: C. S. Lewis and the Art of Witness*. Grand Rapids, MI: Eerdmans.

Milota, Megan. 2018. "Some Thoughts on the State of Secularity in the Lowlands." *Christianity and Literature* 67, no. 3: 531–47.

Milward, Peter. 1995. *A Challenge to C. S. Lewis*. Madison, NJ: Fairleigh Dickinson Univ. Press.

Mitchell, Basil. 1957. Introduction to *Faith and Logic: Oxford Essays in Philosophical Theology*, edited by Basil Mitchell, 1–8. London: George Allen and Unwin.

———. 1983. "Two Approaches to the Philosophy of Religion." In *For God and Clarity: New Essays in Honor of Austin Farrer*, edited by Jeffrey C. Eaton and Ann Loades, 177–90. Allison Park, PA: Pickwick.

Mitchell, Christopher. 1997. "University Battles: C. S. Lewis and the Oxford University Socratic Club." In *C. S. Lewis, Lightbearer in the Shadowlands: The Evangelistic Vision of C. S. Lewis*, edited by Angus J. L. Menuge, 329–51. Wheaton, IL: Crossway.

Mitchell, Philip Irving. 2012. "'Recession and Thickness Through': The Debate over Nature and Grace in David Jones's Roman Poetry and Painting." *Logos* 15 (Summer): 60–89.

———. 2013. "'But Grace Is Not Infinite': Tolkien's Explorations of Nature and Grace in His Catholic Context." *Mythlore* 31, no. 3/4 (Spring/Summer): 61–82.

———. 2018. "'Raised by Implication': C. S. Lewis's *Studies in Words* and Historical and Moral Judgment." *Sehnsucht* 12:13–40.

Morgan, D. Densil. 2010. *Barth Reception in Britain*. London: T&T Clark International.

Morris, J. N. 1994. "Religious Experience in the Philosophical Theology of Austin Farrer." *The Journal of Theological Studies* 45, no. 2 (Oct.): 569–92.

Myers, Doris T. 1994. *C. S. Lewis in Context*. Kent, OH: Kent State Univ. Press.

———. 2000. "Spenser." In *Reading the Classics with C. S. Lewis*, edited by Thomas L. Martin, 87–104. Grand Rapids, MI: Baker.

———. 2018. *Bareface: A Guide to C. S. Lewis's Last Novel*. Columbia: Univ. of Missouri Press.

Navone, John J. 1966. *History and Faith in the Thought of Alan Richardson*. London: SCM Press.

Neill, Stephen. 1977. *Anglicanism*. 4th ed. New York: Oxford Univ. Press.

Neill, Stephen, and Tom Wright. 1988. *The Interpretation of the New Testament, 1861–1986*. 2nd ed. Oxford: Oxford Univ. Press.

Neiman, Susan. 2002. *Evil in Modern Thought: An Alternative History of Philosophy*. Princeton, NJ: Princeton Univ. Press.

Nichols, Aidan, OP. 1993. *The Panther and the Hind: A Theological History of Anglicanism*. Edinburgh: T&T Clark.

Nicoli, Armand. 2003. *The Question of God: C. S. Lewis and Sigmund Freud Debate God, Love, Sex, and the Meaning of Life*. New York: The Free Press.

Niebuhr, H. Richard. 1975. *Christ and Culture*. New York: Harper and Row.

Niebuhr, Reinhold. 1949. *Faith and History: A Comparison of Christian and Modern Views of History*. New York: Charles Scribner's.

Nielsen, Niels C. 1953. "The Debate between Karl Barth and Erich Przywara: A New Evaluation of Protestant and Roman Catholic Differences." *Rice Institute Pamphlet, Rice University Studies* 40, no. 1: 24–46.

Nongbri, Brent. 2015. *Before Religion: A History of a Modern Concept.* New Haven, CT: Yale Univ. Press.

Oldham, J. H. 1937. *The Oxford Conference: Official Report.* New York: Willett, Clark, and Company.

Oliver, Simon. 1988. "The Theodicy of Austin Farrer." *The Heythrop Journal* 39: 280–97.

O'Regan, Cyril. 2009. *Theology and the Spaces of Apocalyptic.* Milwaukee, WI: Marquette Univ. Press.

Otto, Rudolf. 1958. *The Idea of the Holy.* Oxford: Oxford Univ. Press.

Overy, Richard. 2010. *The Morbid Age: Britain and the Crisis of Civilization, 1919–1939.* London: Penguin.

Packer, J. I. 1988. "Farrer, Austin Marsden." In *New Dictionary of Theology,* edited by Sinclair B. Ferguson and David F. Wright, 253. Downers Grove, IL: InterVarsity Press.

Patrick, James. 1985. *The Magdalen Metaphysicals: Idealism and Orthodoxy at Oxford, 1901–1945.* Macon, GA: Mercer Univ. Press.

———. 1998. "C. S. Lewis and Idealism." In *Rumors of Heaven: Essays in Celebration of C. S. Lewis,* edited by Andrew Walker and James Patrick, 156–73. Guildford, Surrey, UK: Eagle Press.

Pearce, Joseph. 2003. *C. S. Lewis and the Catholic Church.* San Francisco: Ignatius.

Pelser, Adam C. 2017. "Philosophy in *The Abolition of Man.*" In *Contemporary Perspectives on C. S. Lewis' 'The Abolition of Man': History, Philosophy, Education, and Science,* edited by Timothy M. Mosteller and Gayne John Anacker, 5–24. London: Bloomsbury.

Perrin, Norman. 1971. *What Is Redaction Criticism?* Philadelphia: Fortress Press.

Peterson, Michael. L. 2008. "C. S. Lewis on the Necessity of Gratuitous Evil." In *C. S. Lewis as Philosopher: Truth, Goodness and Beauty,* edited by David Baggett, Gary R. Habermas, and Jerry L. Walls, 175–94. Downers Grove, IL: InterVarsity Press.

Pickering, W. S. F. 1989. *Anglo-Catholicism: A Study in Religious Ambiguity.* London: PCK.

Poirier, John C., and Jeffrey Peterson, eds. 2015. *Marcan Priority without Q: Explorations in the Farrer Hypothesis.* London: Bloomsbury T&T Clark.

Popper, Karl R. 1961. *The Poverty of Historicism.* New York: Harper Torchbooks.

Price, Michael W. 2000. "Seventeenth Century." In *Reading the Classics with C. S. Lewis,* edited by Thomas L. Martin, 140–60. Grand Rapids, MI: Baker.

Przywara, Erich. 1935. *Polarity: A German Catholic's Interpretation of Religion* [*Religionsphilosophie kathlischer Theologie*]. Translated by A. C. Bouquet. London: Oxford Univ. Press.

———. 2014. *Analogia Entis: Metaphysics, Original Structure and Universal Rhythm.* Translated by John R. Betz and David Bentley Hart. Grand Rapids, MI: Eerdmans.

Ramsey, Arthur Michael. 1960. *An Era in Anglican Theology: From Gore to Temple, the Development of Anglican Theology between* Lux Mundi *and the Second World War, 1889–1939.* New York: Charles Scribner's.

Ramsey, J. Michaels. 1992. *Interpreting the Book of Revelation.* Grand Rapids, MI: Baker.

Reilly, R. J. 1971. *Romantic Religion: A Study of Barfield, Lewis, Williams, and Tolkien.* Athens: Univ. of Georgia Press.

Richardson, Alan. 1964. *History Sacred and Profane.* Philadelphia: Westminster.

Ricoeur, Paul. 1974. *The Conflict of Interpretations: Essays in Hermeneutics.* Edited by Don Ihde. Evanston, IL: Northwestern Univ. Press.

———. 1984. *Time and Narrative.* Vol. 1. Translated by Kathleen McLaughlin and David Pellauer. Chicago: Univ. of Chicago Press.

Ritter, Harry. 1986. *Dictionary of Concepts in History.* New York: Greenwood Press.

Roger, Jacques. 1986. "The Mechanistic Conception of Life." In *God and Nature: Historical Essays on the Encounter between Christianity and Science,* edited by David C. Lindberg and Ronald L. Numbers, 277–95. Berkeley: Univ. of California Press.

Rose, Matthew. 2017. "Our Secular Theodicy." *First Things* (Dec.). https://www.firstthings.com/article/2017/12/our-secular-theodicy.

Rottenberg, Isaac. 1964. *Redemption and Historical Reality.* Philadelphia: Westminster.

Rowland, Tracey. 2003. *Culture and the Thomist Tradition: After Vatican II.* New York: Routledge.

Rust, Eric C. 1963. *Towards a Theological Understanding of History.* New York: Oxford Univ. Press.

Ryle, Gilbert, 2000. *The Concept of Mind.* Chicago: Univ. of Chicago Press.

Sayer, George. 1994. *Jack: A Life of C. S. Lewis.* 2nd ed. Wheaton, IL: Crossway.

Scarborough, Milton. 1994. *Myth and Modernity: Postcritical Reflections.* Albany: Univ. of New York Press.

Schwartz, Sanford. 2009. *C. S. Lewis on the Final Frontier: Science and the Supernatural in the Space Trilogy.* Oxford: Oxford Univ. Press.

Seidel, Kevin. 2018. "A Secular for Literary Studies." *Christianity and Literature* 67, no. 3: 472–92.

Sellars, J. T. 2011. *Reasoning beyond Reason: Imagination as a Theological Source in the Work of C. S. Lewis.* Eugene, OR: Pickwick.

Slocum, Robert Boak. 2007. *Light in a Burning-Glass: A Systematic Presentation of Austin Farrer's Theology.* Columbia: Univ. of South Carolina Press.

Smith, Lyle H., Jr. 1991. "C. S. Lewis and the Making of Metaphor." In *Word and Story in C. S. Lewis,* edited by Peter J. Schakel and Charles A. Huttar, 11–28. Columbia: Univ. of Missouri Press.

Soskice, Janet Martin. 1985. *Metaphor and Religious Language.* Oxford: Clarendon Press.

Spengler, Oswald. 1991. *The Decline of the West.* Translated by Charles Francis Atkinson. Oxford: Oxford Univ. Press.

Stahl, John T. 1975. "Austin Farrer on C. S. Lewis as 'The Christian Apologist'." *Christian Scholars Review* 4: 231–37.

Starr, Charles W., ed. 2014. "Two Pieces from C. S. Lewis's 'Moral Good' Manuscript: A First Publication." *Seven* 31: 30–62.

Stephen, Neil, and Tom Wright. 1989. *The Interpretation of the New Testament: 1861–1986.* 2nd ed. Oxford: Oxford Univ. Press.

Sterenberg, Matthew. 2013. *Mythic Thinking in Twentieth-Century Britain.* New York: Palgrave Macmillan.

Stump, Eleonore. 2010. *Wandering in Darkness: Narrative and the Problem of Suffering.* Oxford: Clarendon Press.

Sutherland, Martin. 2014. "A Narnian Way to Heaven: Judgment, Universalism, and Hell in Lewis's Vision." In *A Myth Retold: Re-encountering C. S. Lewis as Theologian,* edited by Martin Sutherland, 130–44. Eugene, OR: Wipf and Stock.

Tallon, Philip. 2008. "Evil and the Cosmic Dance: C. S. Lewis and Beauty's Place in Theodicy." In *C. S. Lewis as Philosopher: Truth, Goodness and Beauty,* edited by

David Baggett, Gary R. Habermas, and Jerry L. Walls, 195–210. Downers Grove, IL: InterVarsity Press.

Tandy, Gary I. 2009. *The Rhetoric of Certitude: C. S. Lewis's Nonfiction Prose*. Kent, OH: Kent State Univ. Press.

Taylor, Charles. 2007. *A Secular Age*. Cambridge, MA: Harvard Univ. Press.

———. 2010. "Apologia pro Libro suo." In *Varieties of Secularism in a Secular Age*, edited by Michael Warner, Jonathan VanAntwerpen, and Craig Calhoun, 300–321. Cambridge, MA: Yale Univ. Press.

Tennent, Timothy C. 2007. *Theology in the Context of World Christianity*. Grand Rapids, MI: Zondervan.

Thompson, Michael G. 2015. *For God and Globe: Christian Internationalism in the United States between the Great War and the Cold War*. Ithaca, NY: Cornell Univ. Press.

Tillich, Paul. 1949. "The Present Theological Situation in Light of the Continental European Development." *Theology Today* 6, no. 3 (Oct.): 299–310.

Titley, Robert. 2010. *A Poetic Discontent: Austin Farrer and the Gospel of Mark*. London: T&T Clark International.

Tonning, Erik. 2014. *Modernism and Christianity*. New York: Palgrave Macmillan.

———. 2015. "Introduction." In *Modernism, Christianity, and Apocalypse*, edited by Erik Tonning, Matthew Feldman, and David Addyma, 1–25. Leiden, Belgium: Koninklijke Brill.

Toynbee, Arnold J. 1947. *Christianity and Civilisation*. Wallingford, PA: Pendle Hill.

Trevelyan, George Macaulay. 1945. *History and the Reader*. London: Cambridge Univ. Press.

———. 1973. "Clio Rediscovered." In *The Varieties of History: From Voltaire to the Present*, edited by Fritz Stern, 227–45. New York: Vintage.

Turner, Frank M. 1995. "Religion." In *The History of the University of Oxford, The Twentieth Century*, vol. 8, edited by Brian Harrison, 293–316. Oxford: Clarendon Press.

Tyrell, George. 1909. *Christianity at the Cross-Roads*. London: Longmans and Green.

Vanhoozer, Kevin J. 2010. "On Scripture." In *The Cambridge Companion to C. S. Lewis*, edited by Robert Macswain and Michael Ward, 75–88. Cambridge: Cambridge Univ. Press.

Vidler, Alec. 1971. *The Church in an Age of Revolution: 1789 to the Present Day*. Rev. ed. London: Penguin.

Von Balthasar, Hans Urs. 1994. *Theo-Drama: Theological Dramatic Theory IV. The Action*. Translated by Graham Harrison. San Francisco: Ignatius.

Von Hendy, Andrew. 2002. *The Modern Construction of Myth*. Bloomington: Indiana Univ. Press.

Walker, Andrew. 1992. "Under the Russian Cross: A Research Note on C. S. Lewis and the Eastern Orthodox Church." In *A Christian for All Christians: Essays in Honor of C. S. Lewis*, edited by Andrew Walker and James Patrick, 63–67. Washington, DC: Regnery Gateway.

Ward, Michael. 2010. "On Suffering." In *The Cambridge Companion to C. S. Lewis*, edited by Robert MacSwain and Michael Ward, 203–22. Cambridge: Cambridge Univ. Press.

————. 2014. "The Next C. S. Lewis? A Note on Austin Farrer." *Transpositions*, Institute for Theology, Imagination and the Arts blog, University of St Andrews (Feb.). http://www.transpositions.co.uk/austinfarrer/.

Warner, Francis. 2011. "Lewis' Involvement in the Revision of the Psalter." In *C. S. Lewis and the Church*, edited by Judith Wolfe and Brendan N. Wolfe, 52–64. London: Bloomsbury T&T Clark.

Webb, Stephen H. 1998. *On God and Dogs: A Christian Theology of Compassion for Animals*. Oxford: Oxford Univ. Press.

White, R. J. 1960. *Cambridge Life*. London: Eyre & Spottiswoode.

Wilburn, Ralph. 1966. *The Historical Shape of Faith*. Philadelphia: Westminster.

Williams, David W. 2014. "Convergence in Joy: A Comparison of the Devotional Practices of C. S. Lewis and That 'Dreadful Man Karl Barth.'" In *A Myth Re-told: Re-encountering C. S. Lewis as Theologian*, edited by Martin Sutherland, 1–23. Eugene, OR: Wipf and Stock.

Williams, Donald T. 2007. "English Literature in the Sixteenth Century: C. S. Lewis as a Literary Historian." In *C. S. Lewis: Life, Works, and Legacy: Scholar, Teacher, and Public Intellectual*, vol. 4, edited by Bruce L. Edwards, 52–64. Westport, CT: Praeger.

Wilson, William McFetridge, and Julian N. Hartt. 2004. "Farrer's Theodicy." In *Captured by the Crucified: The Practical Theology of Austin Farrer*, edited by David Hein and Edward Hugh Henderson, 100–118. New York: T&T Clark.

Woelfel, Craig Bradshaw. 2018. *Varieties of Aesthetic Experience: Literary Modernism and the Dissociation of Belief*. Columbia: Univ. of South Carolina Press.

Wolf, William J. 1979. "Anglicanism and Its Spirit" In *The Spirit of Anglicanism*, edited by William J. Wolf, 137–88. Wilton, CT: Morehouse-Barlow.

Wolfe, Judith. 2012. "C. S. Lewis and the Eschatological Church." In *C. S. Lewis and the Church: Essays in Honour of Walter Hooper*, edited by Judith Wolfe and Brendan N. Wolfe, 103–16. London: Bloomsbury.

————. 2018. "Theology in *The Abolition of Man*." In *Contemporary Perspectives on C. S. Lewis' 'The Abolition of Man': History, Philosophy, Education, and Science*, edited by Timothy M. Mosteller and Gayne John Anacker, 97–110. London: Bloomsbury.

————. 2020. "Austin Farrer and C. S. Lewis." In *Austin Farrer: Oxford Warden, Scholar, Preacher*, edited by Markus Bockmuehl and Stephen Platten with Nevsky Everett, 70–85. London: SCM Press.

Yolton, John W. 1955. "History and Meta-History." *Philosophy and Phenomenological Research* 15, no. 4: 477–92.

INDEX

Adam and Eve, xviii, 44, 54, 171, 176, 178, 180–86, 206; perfect natural Adam, 99

Addison, Joseph, 137–39

Alexander, Samuel, 46–48, 52–53, 251n1

Allen, Diogenes, 254n14

Ammerman, Nancy T., 244

analogy (*analogia entis*), xvi–xvii, 67–69, 100; analogy of attribution versus proportionality, 77–78; analogy in history, 140–42, 160, 163; in apocalypse, 208, 218, 228, 238; debate over *analogia entis*, 69–73; Farrer's position, 73–79, 84; in language, 87–90; Lewis's position, 79–83, 85–86; mysticism and prayer, 90–93; in theodicy, 175, 184–85, 189

Anglicanism, xvi, 5, 51, 56, 115; Anglo-Catholicism, 17–19, 25, 51, 146–47; Anglo-Evangelicalism, 17–18; divisions, 17–24, 161; ecumenism, 73, 96–97, 240; ignorance of, 12; liturgy, 18, 20, 231–32; numerical decline, 11; *via media*, 18–19. *See also* Modernism (Theological)

anonymous Christians, 202–3

Anscombe, Elizabeth, 7, 256n11

anthropology, xvi, 37, 42–45, 48–49, 61, 71; in ethics, 94–95, 100–101, 104, 119; in history, 134; in theodicy, 176

apocalypse, xviii, 246–47; characteristics, 208–10, 212, 217–21, 250; divine judgment, 210–11, 215, 225, 231–32; in ethics, 208, 210, 219; future, sense of, 212, 217; hierarchy in, 209–18, 230; in history, 208–10, 215, 225, 227; as liturgy, 209, 213–16, 226–29, 231–32; Millennium, 209, 221, 236; parody, 222–23; symbolism, 216–19,

228; in theodicy, 210; twentieth-century attitudes, 208–9, 225; violence and abuse, 218–26, 229–30, 234

Appadurai, Arjun, 263n1

Aquinas, Thomas, 70, 77, 100, 107, 140, 256n2

argument from desire, 41–42, 50, 102, 248

Aristotle, 99, 109, 120–21, 254n12

Arnold, Matthew, 102–3, 139

Asad, Talal, 243

Augustine, 158–59, 180, 182, 232

Aulén, Gustaf, 62

Ayer, A. J., 88, 107, 119–20

Baillie, John, 12–13, 67

Balsdon, Dacre, 14

Balthasar, Hans Urs von, 215, 219

Barfield, Owen, 6, 45, 53–54, 80, 220

Barth, Karl, 6, 21, 59, 142–43, 158, 256n1, 256n8; on analogy, 69–73, 254n11; debate with Brunner, 97, 256n2; Farrer's view of, 73–75, 96, 161, 253n3, 254n7; Lewis's view of, 66–67, 182

Baxter, Richard, 19

Beatific Vision, 91, 124, 211, 229–30, 232, 238, 250; of Caspian, 205; in ethics, 95, 98–99; in theodicy, 183, 197

Bediako, Kwame, 263n4

Bell, George, 256n1

Berger, Peter, 2–4, 191–92, 241, 244

Bergson, Henri, 13, 25

Bethell, S. L., 256n7

Betjeman, John, 13–14, 23

Bevan, Edwyn, *Symbolism and Belief*, 82, 255nn18–19

Bilgrami, Akeel, 247

Birmingham Conference on Politics, Economics, and Citizenship, 11
Bloch, Ernst, 246
Boenig, Robert, 259n3
Bonhoeffer, Dietrich, 24
Bornkamm, Günter, 145
Bouillard, Henri, 99
Bouquet, A. C., 73
Brague, Rémi, 4, 25, 29, 35
Brown, David, 49, 253n8, 255n15
Browne, Sir Thomas, 17
Brunner, Emil, 6, 12–13, 21, 59, 67, 143, 158, 254n7, 256nn1–2, 263n10; debate with Barth, 96–97
Bultmann, Rudolf, xvii, 8, 24, 31, 57–63, 143, 145, 161
Burke, Peter, 133
Bury, J. B., 134
Butler, B. C., 259n6
Butterfield, Herbert, 11, 162, 165, 167, 260n18

Calhoun, Craig, 243–45
Calinescu, Matei, 3
Cambridge University, xii, 16, 21; Farrer's address at Great St. Mary's, 151–55; Lewis's publications for, 9; Modernism (Theological), 23, 57; religious presence at, 13–14, 57–58; Zoological Laboratory, 139–41
Carpenter, Humphrey, 252n13
Carritt, E. F., 256n7
Cartwright, Thomas, 136
Cassirer, Ernst, 30–31, 33, 36
Chaning-Pearce, Melville, 254n9
Chapman, George, 136
Charles, R. H., 216
Chesterton, G. K., 28, 54, 182
Childs, Brevard, 57
Christ, 17–18, 24–25, 120, 238; apocalyptic imagery, 212–17, 226–30; the Crucifixion, 172, 193, 201, 204; the Incarnation, 12, 51, 64–65, 82–83, 155, 157–58, 163, 173, 183, 216, 239; master images, 48–51, 53–54, 64, 86–97; renewal in, 94, 96, 100–101; the Resurrection, 12, 56, 58, 161, 192, 202–4, 222; sacrifice for, 124–29; true myth, 31, 40–41, 46, 49–54, 108, 250, 263n4. See also historical Jesus, the
Christian civilization, debate over, 12–13
Coghill, Neville, 137
Collingwood, R. G., xv, 7, 26–28, 160–63, 255n16; historical reenactment, 147–50, 154–55, 215; view of myth, 36

Como, James, 262n6
Connolly, Sean, 179
Connolly, William, 244, 247
Cowling, Maurice, 251n7
Cox, John D., 255n22
Creegan, Nicola Hoggard, 261n6
Cullmann, Oscar, Christ and Time, 158

Danielson, Daniel, 134
Dante (Alighieri), 104, 140, 157, 232
D'Arcy, Martin, 14, 99
Darwin, Charles, 35, 177–78. See also evolution
Darwin, Erasmus, 35
Davidman, Joy, xiii, 8, 83, 191–96
Dawson, Christopher, xv, 11–13, 28, 54, 96, 142, 253n7; admiration by Lewis, 132, 156–57; on metahistory, 158–60; single-end for nature and supernature/grace, 158–59, 256n4
dialectical theology, xvii, 66–70, 96–98, 143. See also Barth, Karl; Brunner, Emil
Dibelius, Martin, 144–45
Dickens, Charles, 13
Dilthey, Wilhelm, 134
Dodd, C. H., 14, 151–52
double agency of God and humans, 29, 87, 99, 149, 163, 168–69, 201–2, 204
Douglas, Gawin, 136
Douglas, Mary, 253n8
Dowell, Joseph, 20
Dupré, Louis, 27
During, Simon, 247
Durkheim, Émile, 37
Dyson, Hugo, 6

Eaton, Jeffrey C., 78
Ebeling, Gerhard, 143
Einstein, Albert, 235
Eisenstadt, Shmuel, 240
Eliade, Mircea, 37, 253n8
Eliot, T. S., 11–13, 20, 28, 256n1
Empiricus, Sextus, 177
Enlightenment, the, 5, 25, 34, 114, 157, 167, 177–79, 184
Epstein, Jacob, 14–15
eschatology, 5, 157, 167, 198–208, 237–38, 242, 246; for animals, 187–88; meaning, 217. See also hope
ethics, xvii; analogy in, 119; of apocalypse, 218–24; archetypal virtues, 233; British ethics, 106–7, 119; cardinal and theological virtues, 103; Farrer's position, 119–22,

ethics (*cont.*)
257nn13–16; free will and character, 109–
12, 119–29, 135, 224; historical periods as
moral judgments, 141–42; Lewis's position, 111–19, 257n19; moral judgment,
114–15, 120–22; narrative and agency,
107–8, 165, 167, 183; natural ethics and
grace, 98–102, 113; natural law, 110–13;
telos and ethics, 234
evangelicalism, xvi, 5, 17–18, 20–21, 51
Every, George, 102–3
evolution, xviii, 5, 25, 35, 72, 84, 115, 139–40;
animal predation, 186; in ethics, 111; and
glorification, 200–202; in history, 154,
156; in postsecularity, 243; in theodicy,
171, 176–89, 206, 244
existentialism, xvi, 59–63, 101, 110, 121–23,
174, 258n24; demythologization, 51–52,
54, 59–65; in myth, 31, 34, 36–38, 47, 50;
in problem of evil, 190, 194, 212

Farrer, Austin: "Analogy," 8; Bampton Lectures, xiii–xiv, 8, 28–29, 44–45, 67–68,
73, 151–52, 161; "Can Myth Be Fact?,"
30, 51–57; "Causes," 26–27; "Christian
Apologist, The," xi, 10, 170–71; "Christian Doctrine of Man, The," 96–97; *Core
of the Bible*, 8, 152–53; "Creed and History," 161, 168; *Crown of the Year, The*, 8;
Deems Lectures, 9, 64, 154, 161–63, 168,
254n14, 260n10; "Does God Exist?," 76;
End of Man, The, 1, 15–16, 19, 23, 124, 207,
213, 236; "English Appreciation, An,"
60–62; "Epstein's Lazarus," 14–15; *Faith
of Our Own, A*, xi, 9–10, 123, 126–27, 172,
193, 249; *Faith and Speculation*, 9, 64,
154, 161–63, 168, 254n14, 260n10; "Fathers' Sons," 39–40; *Finite and Infinite*,
6, 8, 66, 76–79, 108, 119, 254n10, 254n14;
Freedom of the Will, 9, 39, 101, 119–22,
258nn21–22; *Glass of Vision, The*, xiii–xiv,
8, 28–29, 44–45, 67–68, 73, 151–52, 161;
God Is Not Dead, 9, 190, 201–2, 254n14;
"History and the Gospel," 151–53; "Immortal Hope," 2; "In the Conscience
of Man," 101; "Infallibility and Historical Revelation," 146–47; *Interpretation
and Belief*, 30, 33, 49, 53–54, 95, 100–102,
145–47, 165, 211; "Keble and His College," 1, 16; *Lord I Believe*, 8, 20, 92, 171,
187, 204; *Love Almighty and Ills Unlimited*, 9–10, 170–72, 174–76, 179, 183–89,

191–93, 202–4; "Mary, Scripture, and
Tradition," 164–65; "Messianic Prophecy and Preparation for Christ," 164;
"Nice and Worldly," 249; "On Dispensing with Q," 8, 144; "Radical Piety," 125;
Rebirth of Images, The, 8, 55, 63, 208, 210,
212–16, 219–20, 223, 227–29, 262n7; *Reflective Faith*, 26–28, 68–69, 75–77, 88–93,
100–101, 107–8, 123, 211; "Religion and
Philosophy" (BBC), 8; "Remembrance
Day: On Hugh Lister," 128; "Revelation," 64; "Revelation and History,"
161–63; *Revelation of St John the Divine,
The*, 9, 219, 225–30, 262nn7–8; *Said or
Sung*, xi, 262n1; *Saving Belief*, 9, 28, 65, 90,
127, 130–31, 150, 154, 161–64, 168, 199, 201,
216, 233; *Science of God?, A*, 9, 190, 201–2,
254n14; *Short Bible, A*, 8, 152–53; "Starting-Point for the Philosophical Examination of Theological Belief," 258n23; *St
Matthew and St Mark*, 8, 131, 154; *Study in
St Mark, A*, 8, 144–47, 150–55; "Thought
as the Basis of History," 147–48; "Transcendence and 'Radical Theology,'" 9;
Triple Victory, The, 9, 94, 126–27, 131, 201;
"Ultimate Hope, The," 9
Farrer, Katherine, xiii, 7, 56, 191, 251n2 (intro.)
Fascism, 5, 25, 97, 111, 155, 159, 169, 260n18; in
apocalypse, 207–8, 210, 224
Fenn, Eric, 20
Frazer, James, 35, 39–40, 253n6
freedom, xv, xviii, 64, 71–72, 97, 106–12, 124,
257n16, 258nn21–22; and causation, 135,
149, 155, 160, 163, 257n16, 258nn21–22;
and the future, 167–69; and God, 99, 149,
185, 201–4, 261n5; and grace, 127–29; and
hell, 199–200; in obedience, 224; political freedom, 132, 205, 225. *See also* slavery
in Narnia
Freudian psychoanalysis, 25–26, 36, 38, 69;
Farrer's view of, 84–85, 258n22; Lewis's
view of, 42–43, 81, 83, 85–86, 111, 173–74
friendship, xi, xiii, 6, 8, 128, 249, 258n6;
as love, 105, 220; praise by Farrer and
Lewis, xi, 9–10

Garrigou-Lagrange, Réginald, 99
Gay, Craig M., 4
Gay, Peter, 3–4, 85
Giddens, Anthony, 263n1
Gilson, Étienne, 11, 252n10, 254n7
Gore, Charles, 18, 161

Gospels, 2, 39–41, 59, 207, 245, 259n8; Farrer's approach (critique of), 260n11; mind of the Evangelists, 62–63, 150–55; Synoptic problem, 144, 150–52; theories of criticism, 143–47

Goulder, Michael, 262n7

Goya, Francisco, *Saturn Devouring His Sons*, 34

Graham, Billy, 21

Green, T. H., 255n17

"Green Book, The" (King and Ketley, *Control of Language, The*), 115

Greene, Graham, 11

Griffin, Roger, 3

Griffiths, Dom Bede, 20, 207–8

Griffiths, Paul, 27

Habermas, Jürgen, 243, 245

Harbison, E. Harris, 155

Harnack, Adolf von, 59, 143

Hartt, Julian N., 73, 179, 191

Hastings, Adrian, 21, 98

Hauerwas, Stanley, 257n19

heaven and hell, 94, 123, 176, 198–206, 226–27, 235–38, 246. *See also* argument from desire; eschatology; teleology

Hebblethwaite, Brian, 64

Hegel, Georg Wilhelm Friedrich, 35

Henderson, Edward, 214, 254n14, 254–55n25

Henry (Henri), Paul, "Christian Philosophy of History, The," 157–58

Henson, Hensley, 252n8

Hick, John, 254n14, 261n4

hierarchical universe, 38–39, 44–45, 71–72, 154, 239; as apocalyptic, 209–18, 227, 230, 238

historical Jesus, the, xviii, 53–54, 58–59, 69, 143, 151–55, 164; personal encounter with, 62–65, 152–53

history, xiv–xv, xvii–xviii; in apocalypse, 208–10, 215, 225, 227; definitions of, 133; historical analogies, 140–42; historical causation, 149, 154; historical judgment, 26, 132–36, 148; historicism, 148, 156–60, 225, 260n13; history of ideas, method, xv, 149–50; individual characterization in, 137–39; Lewis's practice (critique of), 259n3–5; metahistory, 130–31, 155–65, 215; periodization, 135–43, 260n10; personal history, 165–69; sacred history, 51, 131, 149, 153, 155, 163–64, 239

Hodges, H. A., 6, 263n10

Hölderlin, Friedrich, 34

Homer, 136, 220

Hooper, Walter, 7

hope, 81, 95, 122–23, 125, 129, 153, 159, 179, 250; in apocalypse, 216, 226–33; in theodicy, 195, 198

Hume, David, 177

Hurka, Thomas, 256n9

Huxley, Aldous, 9

Idealism, xii, 25–26, 159, 251n1 (intro.), 255n17, 255n19

inspiration of scripture, 49–50, 146–47, 153–55, 164–65

Irenaeus, 172

Jager, Colin, 243

Jaspers, Karl, 62

Jebb, Sharon, 90–91

Jeffrey, David Lyle, 259nn3–4

Jones, David, 54

Jungian analysis, 36, 38, 85, 253nn7–8, 255n21; Lewis's view of, 42–43

kairos, 209, 217, 228, 247–48, 263n7

Kant, Immanuel, xvii, 106–7, 109, 111, 256n12, 257n15

Keble, John, 16–17, 258–59n27

Kennedy, John F., 9

Kermode, Frank, 209, 234, 237, 263n7

Kilby, Clyde, 56–57

Kirkpatrick, William, 253n6

Knox, Ronald, 14

Kort, Wesley, xiv

Koselleck, Reinhart, 3

Kozelmann, Hans, 145

lectio divina, 50

Leibniz, Gottfried Willhelm, 175, 178, 197, 261n5

Lévi-Strauss, Claude, 252n3

Lewis, C. S.: *Abolition of Man, The*, xi, 7, 107, 112–16, 118, 128; "Adam at Night," 181; "Addison," 137–39; *Allegory of Love, The*, 6, 131, 258n3; *Beyond Personality*, 7; *Case for Christianity, or Broadcast Talks, The*, 7; *Christian Behavior*, 7, 113; "Christianity and Culture," 102–4, 115; "Christian Reunion," 22; "De Descriptione Temporum," 130, 160, 167; "*De Futilate*," 111; *Discarded Image, The*, 9, 21, 24–25, 29, 131, 179, 259n2; "Dogma and the Universe," 25; *Dymer*, 6, 260n2; *English Literature in the*

Lewis, C. S. (cont.)
   Sixteenth Century, Excluding Drama, 8,
      130–31, 134, 136, 141–42, 167; Experiment
      in Criticism, An, 9, 31–32, 38, 46, 48; "Five
      Sonnets," 196–97; Four Loves, The, 9, 105–
      6; Great Divorce, The, 7, 94, 104–5, 122,
      187–88; Grief Observed, A, 9, 83, 190, 193–
      98, 205; "Historicism," 157–60, 165–66;
      Horse and His Boy, The, 80, 82, 91, 118–19;
      "Imagination and Thought in the Middle
      Ages," 139–41; "Is History Bunk?," 134;
      "Language of Religion, The," 88; Last
      Battle, The, 119, 190, 203, 210, 220–21, 223,
      234, 237–38; Letters to Malcolm, 9, 24, 79–
      80, 87, 91–92, 95; Lion, the Witch, and the
      Wardrobe, The, 116; Loki Bound, 253n6;
      "Man or Rabbit?," 261n14; "Meditation
      in a Toolshed," 64; Magician's Nephew,
      The, 180–83, 186, 188; Mere Christianity,
      xi, 7, 19, 85, 110–11, 113–14, 123–26, 173,
      200; Miracles, 7, 54, 254n16; "Modern
      Man and His Categories of Thought,"
      260n16; "Myth Became Fact," 30, 51–57;
      "On a Picture by Chirico," 187–88; "On
      Ethics," 110–11; Out of the Silent Planet,
      43–44, 117, 186, 210, 232; "Pan's Purge,"
      187–88; Perelandra, 44, 91, 168–69, 180–
      83, 186, 210, 232, 237; Personal Heresy, The,
      7; Pilgrim's Regress, The, 6, 22, 25–26, 42;
      "Poison of Subjectivism, The," 111; Pref-
      ace to Paradise Lost, The, 7, 44, 114–15,
      133; Prince Caspian, 82, 166–67, 181, 205,
      258n20; Problem of Pain, The, 7, 171–77,
      180, 185–87, 190–91, 195, 198–99, 204; Re-
      habilitations and Other Essays, 7; Reflec-
      tions on the Psalms, xiii, 9, 56, 231, 262n9;
      Screwtape Letters, The, xi, 7, 58–59, 110,
      122, 124–27, 156; Screwtape Proposes a
      Toast, 9; Silver Chair, The, 85, 116, 205,
      244n22; "Solomon," 181; Spirits in Bond-
      age, 6; Studies in Words, 9; "Such Natural
      Love Twixt Beast and Man," 187–88; Sur-
      prised by Joy, xiii, 8, 21, 41, 46, 252n6; That
      Hideous Strength, 135–36, 186–87, 207,
      210, 220–25, 230, 232–34, 246–47; They
      Asked for a Paper, 9; Till We Have Faces,
      6, 39, 41–43, 80, 83, 86, 89–90, 197–98,
      203, 251n2 (intro.); "Transposition," 8,
      66, 80–81, 214–15, 230–31; Voyage of the
      Dawn Treader, The, 46–48, 80–81, 117–18,
      128, 205, 258n20; "Weight of Glory, The,"
      1–2, 200; "What Christians Believe," 20;
   "Why I Am Not a Pacifist," 114; 257n19;
      World's Last Night, The, 9, 167, 211–12,
      232, 235
Lewis, John Underwood, 121
Lewis, Warren "Warnie," xiii, 66, 132, 252n13,
      257n17
Lightfoot, R. H., 145–46
Linnell, Charles, 128–29
Lister, Hugh, 128
liturgy, 20, 164, 213–14, 226–33, 249–50
Loades, Ann, 251n5
Locke, John, xv
logical positivism, 69, 73, 87–88, 107, 254n8,
      255n23; historical positivism, 134–34, 149
love, 50, 53, 64, 89–90, 104–6, 113–14, 122,
      153; caritas, 1–2, 98, 127, 226; as final
      telos, 98, 202–6, 214, 229, 236–38, 248,
      250; God's love and suffering, 174, 187,
      193, 196; metaphor and love, 89–90; in
      obedience, 124, 128, 224; in perfection,
      76; praise of beloved, 195–98; praise of
      God, 71, 81, 127–28
Lubac, Henri de, 99
luminous apex, xiii, 4, 28–29, 44–45, 76, 84,
      240, 244
Lux Mundi Catholicism, 17–18

Macaulay, Thomas, 134
MacDonald, George, 104, 166
MacIntyre, Alasdair, 5, 23–24, 128, 249,
      255n23, 256n10, 257n18, 258n25
MacMurray, John, 12
MacSwain, Robert, 172, 251n2 (chap. 1),
      254n14, 256n25
Malinowski, Bronislaw, 37
Manlove, Colin, 213
Marcel, Gabriel, 11, 122–23, 226, 258n24
Marcion, 177
Maréchall, Joseph, 99
Maritain, Jacques, 11, 13, 28, 73, 96, 99, 252n10,
      254n7
Marxism, 5, 25, 33, 58, 60, 66, 72, 142, 246,
      252n2; Lewis's concern with, 111, 155, 159,
      165, 169, 207–8, 210, 260n15
Mascall, Eric, xii, 19, 75, 252n10, 254n8,
      254nn11–12, 256n6, 256n8
Mauriac, François, 11
Maurice, F. D., 11
McGrath, Alister, 7, 47, 52
medievalism, 6, 29, 114, 136, 139–41, 157, 167–
      68, 259n2–4

Meilaender, Gilbert, 113
mere Christianity (concept), 18–23
Merleau-Ponty, Maurice, 252n4
Metaphysicals, the, xii, 8, 11, 19, 252n10, 254n8, 254n14
Mill, J. S., 106
Milward, Peter, 21–22
Mitchell, Basil, xii, 9, 88, 254n14
Moberly, Walter Hamilton, 256n1
Modernism (Theological), 17–18, 22–24, 69
modernity, 3–5, 225; as apocalypse, 210–12, 218–19, 224; contested nature, xvi, 2, 24–26, 241; loss of the supernatural, 27–29, 240–42; pluralism, 241–42; waning of faith, 11–17. *See also* secularization
Moltmann, Jürgen, 246
Moore, G. E., 107, 119–21
Moore, Janie, 6, 8
Moral Re-Armament, 14
More, Hannah, 17
Morris, J. N., 78–79
Müller, Max, 35, 39, 62
Murdoch, Iris, xii
Myers, Doris T., 259nn3–4
mysterium tremendum, 62, 173–74, 197. *See also* numinous
myth, xvi–xvii, 94–95, 239–40, 245–46, 253n6; and analogy, 86–87, 119, 199; in Christian scripture, 51–65, 144–46, 161, 209–13, 216, 238; debated meaning, 32–38; demythologization, 57–65; Farrer's answers to, 39–40, 44–45; in Genesis, 54–55, 171, 180–84; Lewis's answers to, 41–44, 231–32; natural imagery, 46–51; sacred centers, 37. *See also* under Christ

nature and supernature/grace, xvi, 4, 28–29, 66–67, 95–96, 127–28, 158, 215; in analogy, 75–76, 92; debated meaning, 97–102; Farrer's position, 99–102, 146; in myth, 32–33, 64–65; and postsecularity, 239–42, 248; single-end in Lewis, 103–6, 113, 254n16
Neill, Stephen, 18, 252n12
neoorthodoxy, xvii, 66–70, 96–98, 143. *See also* Barth, Karl; Brunner, Emil
Neo-Scholasticism, xvii, 17, 19, 73–74, 252n10. *See also* Maritain, Jacques
Newman, John Henry, 17
New Testament, 58–61, 131, 151–54, 215–16, 237; as history, 159, 162. *See also* Gospels
Nicholi, Armand, 249

Nichols, Aidan, 18–19
Niebuhr, H. Richard, 95
Niebuhr, Reinhold, 14, 21, 110, 180, 256n1, 257n17
numinous, xvi, 31–32, 34, 231, 234; in myth, 41, 46, 48, 50; in theodicy, 173–75, 197

Oldham, J. H., 12, 96–97
Old Testament, 215, 217, 222; historicity of, 55–57, 162–64; myth in, 32–33, 54–58, 64–65, 180–83; Psalms, 56, 164, 230–31; symbolism of, 49–57, 63, 65, 263n9
Oppenheimer, Helen, xii
O'Regan, Cyril, 218
Otto, Rudolf, 37, 173–74. *See also* numinous
Oxford Conference on Church, Community, and State (1937), 96–97, 256n1
Oxford Intercollegiate Christian Union, the, 14
Oxford Movement, the, 16. *See also* Anglicanism
Oxford Socratic Club, the, xii, 7–8, 15–16, 76, 241, 258n24
Oxford University, xii, 6–7; religious presence at, 13–17

Packer, J. I., xii
Paley, William, 177
Pannenberg, Wolfhart, 246
Pascal, Blaise, 177
Patrick, James, 255n17
Pelser, Adam, 118
Penelope, Sister (CSMV), 18, 23, 232
Pieper, Joseph, 234
Plowman, Max, 162
Polanyi, Michael, 252n4
Pope, Alexander, 137–39
Popper, Karl, 260n13
postsecularism, xvi, xix, 243–49
Powell, Anthony, 11
Pre-Raphaelite Brotherhood, 34
Price, Michael, 259n4
Prichard, H. A., 107
problem of evil. *See* theodicy
Pusey, Edward, 17
Przywara, Erich, xv, 79, 89–92, 108, 148, 160, 244, 254n9, 254n13, 255n14; versus Barth, 70–76. *See also* suspended middle

Ramsey, Michael, 17
Rank, Otto, 84
Reilly, R. J., 63

Renaissance, the, 27, 136, 139, 141–42

Renan, Ernest, 143

ressourcement theologians, 98–100

Revelation of St John. *See* Farrer, Austin: *Rebirth of Images, The;* Farrer, Austin: *Revelation of St John the Divine, The*

Richardson, Alan, *History Sacred and Profane,* 161–63, 260n13

Ricoeur, Paul, 61, 88–89, 137–38, 253n8

Ritschl, Albrecht, 59

Robinson, John A. T., 23–24

Roman Catholicism, xvi, 5, 11, 21–23, 98–100, 146–47, 252n13; Anglo-Catholicism compared with, 18–19; Barth's view of, 69–70; ecumenism, 96, 256n1; Fourth Lateran Council, 71; Lewis's view, 21–22; in universities, 13–14; Vatican I, 69–70

Romanticism, 5, 34, 140, 225

Rouselot, Pierre, 99

Rousseau, Jean-Jacques, xv, 132

Rowland, Tracey, 112, 257n18

Rowley, H. H., 262n8

Rowse, Alfred Leslie, "Lazarus," 15

Russell, Bertrand, 88

Ryle, Gilbert, 119–20, 258n21

sacrament, xii, 20, 23, 25, 63, 82, 127, 192, 215, 249; in eschatological hope, 227–29; as transposition, xviii, 214, 231

Sayer, George, 20

Sayers, Dorothy, 11

Scarborough, Milton, *Myth and Modernity,* 35–38, 46, 59, 252nn3–4

Schelling, Friedrich Wilhelm Joseph, 34

Schopenhauer, Arnold, 107, 253n6

Schwartz, Sanford, 220, 225

Schweitzer, Albert, 58, 143, 211–12, 217

science, models of, 36, 178–79

Scott, Sir Walter, 13, 134

secularization, 2–4, 30, 99, 131, 210, 218, 239–42; at Oxford and Cambridge Universities, 13–17; of poetry, 53–54, 248; views of history, 157–59, 160, 163. *See also* postsecularism

Sehnsucht, 41–42, 50, 102

Seidel, Kevin, 248

Shaw, George Bernard, 25

Sidgwick, Henry, 106–7

slavery in Narnia, 116–19, 258n20

Slocum, Robert Boak, 227, 229, 253n7

Smith, Alic, 15

Smith, Lyle H., Jr., 88

Snow, C. P., 11

Soskice, Janet, 255n24

Spengler, Oswald, 160, 169

Stahl, John T., 172

Steele, Richard, 138

Sterenberg, Matthew, 32, 46

Strauss, David Friedrich, 143

Streeter, B. H., 144

Stump, Eleonore, *Wandering in Darkness,* 197–98

suspended middle, 75, 79–80, 84, 86, 89–90, 254–55n14; in apocalypse, 228; in history 148–49; humans as analogies, 71, 73–74, 79, 94; in the postsecular, 244, 249; in virtue, 108, 124, 127. *See also* Przywara, Erich

Swift, Jonathan, 137–39

Tallon, Philip, 174

Tao, the, xvii, 112–14, 160, 259n2. *See also* ethics

Taylor, Charles, 3, 28–29, 35, 177, 210, 240–41, 245, 248–49

Taylor, Edward, 35, 39

teleology, xiv, xvii, xix, 92, 199–200, 234, 248; in ethics, 101, 108–9, 112, 115, 117–18, 122–29; of hope, 125–28, 176, 179–80, 183, 240; loss of, 2, 26–28, 94–97, 121; in theodicy, 201–6. *See also* eschatology

Temple, William, 11, 17–18, 21

Tennyson, Lord Alfred, 35

theodicy, xvi, xviii, 83, 239, 241, 248; Adamic fall, 171, 180–83; analogy in, 175, 184–85; animal pain, 171, 185–90, 224; evil and biological misfit, 184; evolution and, 176–85; free will argument, 171, 179; history of theodicy, 173, 175, 177–78, 261n5; last things and, 183, 198–206, 210–11, 249–50; loss of loved ones, 190–91, 194–96; narrative and theodicy, 197–98; nature of God, 174–76, 185, 189–90, 236; original sin and, 182, 184; pain and sanctification, 171–72, 234; phenomenology of suffering, 172–73, 193–98, 204; practical problem of, 191–93; privation, 175; satanic, 171, 183, 185–87

theosis, xviii, 95, 235–38, 243, 248, 250, 256n6, 261nn12–13; and apocalypse, 211, 214, 229; and theodicy, 199–206; and virtue ethics, 101–2, 108, 122–29

Tillich, Paul, 24, 36–37, 161

Tillyard, E. M. W., 7

Titley, Robert, 260n11

Tolkien, J. R. R., 6, 21–22, 53–54, 252n13

Tonning, Erik, 3, 262n4
Toynbee, Arnold, 160, 169
Trevelyan, G. M., 134–35, 137
typology, 8, 46, 49–52, 228–31, 260n11, 262n9; in the Gospel of Mark, 153–55; in historical understanding, 159, 163–65
Tyrell, George, 57, 143

Universal Christian Conference of Life and Work, Stockholm, the, 11
utopia, 2–5, 188, 210, 212, 221, 235, 246, 257n14

Vanhoozer, Kevin, 55–56
via negativa and *via positiva*, 90–91
Vidler, Alec, 23, 57
virtue. *See* ethics

Ward, Michael, 190–91, 235–36
Waugh, Evelyn, 11
Webb, Stephen H., 261n6
Wesley, Charles, 17
Wesley, John, 17
White, R. J., 14
Wilberforce, William, 17
Williams, Charles, 80
Williams, Donald T., 259n5
Wilson, William M., 179, 191
Woelfel, Craig Bradshaw, 244
Wolfe, Judith, 51, 114, 205
Wrede, William, *The Messianic Secret*, 260n12